THE ORIGINS OF THE CONSUMER REVOLUTION IN ENGLAND

CW00550666

The Origins of the Consumer Revolu..... ... England explores the rise of consumerism from the end of the medieval period through to the beginning of the nineteenth century.

The book takes a detailed look at when the 'consumer revolution' began, tracing its evolution from the years following the Black Death through to the nineteenth century. In doing so, it also considers which social classes were included, and how different areas of the country were affected at different times, examining the significant role that location played in the development of consumption. This new study is based upon the largest database of English probate records yet assembled, which has been used in conjunction with a range of other sources to offer a broad and detailed chronological approach. Filling in the gaps within previous research, it examines changing patterns in relation to food and drink, clothing, household furnishings and religion, focussing on the goods themselves to illuminate items in common ownership, rather than those owned only by the elite.

Using a combination of qualitative and quantitative evidence to explore the development of consumption, *The Origins of the Consumer Revolution in England* will be of great use and interest to scholars and students of late medieval and early modern economic and social history, with an interest in the development of consumerism in England.

Joanne Sear teaches a range of local history courses at the Institute of Continuing Education, University of Cambridge. Her research focusses on consumption and trade in the Middle Ages and she is currently working on a volume on the manorial records of late medieval Newmarket.

Ken Sneath lectures in early modern history at the University of Cambridge and was formerly Assistant Director of Studies for Economic History at Peterhouse College. Ken has published articles on consumption and is a contributor to the forthcoming volume on the Huntingdonshire Hearth Tax.

Themes in Medieval and Early Modern History

Series Editor: Natasha Hodgson, Nottingham
Trent University.

This is a brand new series which straddles both medieval and early modern worlds, encouraging readers to examine historical change over time as well as promoting understanding of the historical continuity between events in the past, and to challenge perceptions of periodisation. It aims to meet the demand for conceptual or thematic topics which cross a relatively wide chronological span (any period between c. 500-1750), including a broad geographical scope.

Available titles:

War in the Iberian Peninsula, 700–1600
Edited by Francisco García Fitz and João Gouveia Monteiro

Writing War in Britain and France, 1370-1854: A History of Emotions
Edited by Stephanie Downes, Andrew Lynch and Katrina O'Loughlin

Drama in Medieval and Early Modern Europe: Playmakers and their Strategies
Nadia Thérèse van Pelt

Florence in the Early Modern World
Nicholas Baker and Brian Maxson

Dynastic Change: Legitimacy and Gender in Medieval and Early Modern Monarchy
Edited by Ana Maria S. A. Rodrigues, Manuela Santos Silva and Jonathan W. Spangler

The Origins of the Consumer Revolution in England: From Brass Pots to Clocks
Joanne Sear and Ken Sneath

https://www.routledge.com/Themes-in-Medieval-and-Early-Modern-History/book-series/TMEMH

THE ORIGINS OF THE CONSUMER REVOLUTION IN ENGLAND

From Brass Pots to Clocks

Joanne Sear and Ken Sneath

Routledge
Taylor & Francis Group

LONDON AND NEW YORK

First published 2020
by Routledge
2 Park Square, Milton Park, Abingdon, Oxon OX14 4RN

and by Routledge
52 Vanderbilt Avenue, New York, NY 10017

Routledge is an imprint of the Taylor & Francis Group, an informa business

© 2020 Joanne Sear and Ken Sneath

British Library Cataloguing-in-Publication Data
A catalogue record for this book is available from the British Library

Library of Congress Cataloging-in-Publication Data
A catalog record has been requested for this book

ISBN: 978-0-367-34112-1 (hbk)
ISBN: 978-0-367-34111-4 (pbk)
ISBN: 978-0-429-32396-6 (ebk)

Typeset in Bembo
by Integra Software Services Pvt. Ltd.

MIX
Paper from
responsible sources
FSC® C013985

Printed in the United Kingdom
by Henry Ling Limited

CONTENTS

IMAGES

FIGURES

MAPS

TABLES

ACKNOWLEDGEMENTS

Many people and organisations have assisted us in producing this volume. First of all, thanks are due to Professors John Hatcher and Craig Muldrew who supervised our doctoral research at University of Cambridge. Participants at various seminars at University of Cambridge and the Institute of Historical Research have helped to shape and refine our thinking as have many of our colleagues and students who have listened to our theories and challenged some of our assumptions. The late Mary Carter, Pam Sneath, the late Peter Northeast and Kimbolton History Society transcribed some of the probate documents on which this analysis is based. We are grateful to those who commented on various drafts of the book including Nick Amor, James Davis, Nick Gray, Evelyn Lord, Roger Merritt, Dinah Reed and Tim Sneath. We would like to thank Morwenna Scott, Emily Boyd, Christopher Taylor and the team at Routledge for guiding us through the processes leading to publication.

We are indebted to those who have given permission to use illustrations contained in this book, the staff of the record offices for preparing and extracting documents and Graeme Fayers for drawing the maps. The Goodliff Fund of Huntingdonshire Local History Society supported this publication with a generous grant which was very gratefully received.

And, finally, to our families who have supported us throughout what has been a long and time-consuming process. Thank you for your forbearance and encouragement.

ABBREVIATIONS

ANF	Archdeaconry of Norfolk
ANW	Archdeaconry of Norwich
CA	Cambridgeshire Archives
CAMPOP	Cambridge Group for the History of Population and Social Structure
ERO	Essex Record Office
GDP	Gross Domestic Product
HA	Huntingdonshire Archives
MS	Manuscript
NCC	Norwich Consistory Court
NRO	Norfolk Record Office
PCC	Prerogative Court of Canterbury
SROB	Suffolk Records Office, Bury St Edmunds
TNA	The National Archives

INTRODUCTION

When Neil McKendrick argued that a consumer boom occurred in England during the eighteenth century, he recognised that insufficient quantitative work to support this judgement had yet been completed. McKendrick's book *The Birth of a Consumer Society* set off a wave of consumption studies which has continued to the present day.[1] Two major responses to McKendrick's challenge were provided by Lorna Weatherill in *Consumer Behaviour and Material Culture in Britain 1660–1760* and Mark Overton *et al.* in *Production and Consumption in English Households 1600–1750*.[2] Whilst both studies made major contributions to our knowledge of consumption, important gaps remain.

This latest study by Joanne Sear and Ken Sneath aims to fill some of these gaps and bring a wider perspective to the topic. First of all, it is unique in covering a continuous period from the end of the medieval period to the beginning of the nineteenth century. Lorna Weatherill focussed on just 50 years, 1675–1725. Mark Overton *et al.* extended Weatherill's chronological period, although not sufficiently forward to capture the second half of the eighteenth century which was key to McKendrick's thesis. The period prior to the seventeenth century is also important because the origins of the consumer revolution were in the period after the Black Death when economic and demographic changes led to higher wages, more employment opportunities and lower food prices. These in turn led to revised income patterns which gradually changed consumption patterns.

Secondly, the more than 9,000 probate records (wills, inventories, probate accounts) used in this study to provide evidence of the emergence of a consumer society in England represent both a larger collection, and a longer chronological span, than any previous study. The records cover both the period prior to 1600 in which the beginnings of consumer change can be seen and the crucial years after 1750 when McKendrick's consumer boom is alleged to have occurred. For the fifteenth- and sixteenth-century period, over 1,000 wills and more than 500 inventories have been analysed. In addition, purchasing records and household accounts have been used to provide evidence about unit costs and sources of supply for a range of consumption items, including foodstuffs as well as household and clothing items. Many historians have suggested that probate inventories survived in only very small numbers (if at all) after 1730. However, a more recent survey of surviving inventories by the present authors found that many thousands of probate inventories relating to individuals who died after 1750 were held in record offices across the country. The selected sample of inventories for the present study includes over 1,100 for the second half of the eighteenth century.

The third important reason for this volume is the **wider social spectrum** covered by the analysis. Both Weatherill's and Overton et al.'s sample contained very few labourers. Weatherill had only 26 labourers in her sample of 2,902 inventories and Overton et al. also had a very low percentage. Little can be done if records do not exist for the largest social group in society. However, the present authors have unearthed 351 labourers' inventories, mostly from the middling county of Huntingdonshire. Whilst these inventoried labourers represent the more affluent of their social group, this additional evidence takes us further down the social scale in understanding consumption. This is important if a requirement for a consumer revolution is that ownership of goods has spread throughout most of society. This new evidence shows that this had taken place by the second half of the eighteenth century, when clock ownership was recorded in 40 per cent of labourers' inventories.

This study also covers **more locations (15)** throughout the country, providing results for both urban and rural areas. McKendrick called for interregional comparisons on consumption patterns and the large dataset in this volume has made this possible. The main three study areas are Huntingdonshire, Yorkshire and Dorset. Large samples of published inventories from a sizeable urban settlement (Bristol) and a small urban settlement (Marlborough) together with two rural areas (Gloucestershire and Shropshire) have also been analysed. Using the same time periods as Overton et al. enabled the results to be compared with Kent and Cornwall, thus giving a comprehensive picture of England as a whole.

The present analysis is based on a **broader definition of consumption** than has previously been explored by economic historians. It places a greater emphasis on the essentials that households spent most of their income on, namely food and clothing, but also charts changes to domestic goods as well as expenditure on religion. From the end of the medieval period onwards, there were significant changes in food consumption and diets generally improved both in terms of their nutritional value and the variety of items that were eaten. At the same time, clothing not only became a means of displaying status, but clothing styles were increasingly subject to change as the concept of 'fashion' began to emerge. The expansion in domestic space led to changes in household goods as people progressively began to adopt individual living spaces which had an increased emphasis on comfort as well as practicality. Religious consumption is often neglected by economic historians; however, this not only attracted a considerable amount of expenditure during this period, but was subject to altered priorities as religious allegiance changed and different groups emerged.

Finally, visits were made to many **museums** throughout the country to view items and make comparisons with objects documented in probate records. Many consumer goods were made from different materials and were produced in different sizes and quality. Much more can be learned from greater engagement with the objects themselves as well as from their description in the records. Chapters 3, 4 and 5 evaluate the considerable changes in the items used for cooking, clothing and in the home environment for the period of this study.

Notes

1 N. McKendrick, J. Brewer and J. Plumb, *The Birth of a Consumer Society: The Commercialization of Eighteenth-Century England* (London: Hutchinson, 1983).
2 L. Weatherill, *Consumer Behaviour and Material Culture in Britain 1660–1760* (Abingdon: Routledge, 1996); M. Overton, J. Whittle, D. Dean and A. Hann, *Production and Consumption in English Households 1600–1750* (Abingdon: Routledge, 2004).

1

THE CONSUMER REVOLUTION

In 1785, John Goodes, a carpenter from Huntingdon, died. The value of possessions recorded in his inventory totalled £32 7s, considerably below the median
value of inventories for craftsmen in the second half of the eighteenth century.
His tools and various sorts of wood in his workshop represented about a quarter
of the valuation. In his parlour was a tea table, china dishes, tea cups and saucers,
a teapot, teaspoons. silver spoons and prints. In the kitchen were knives and forks,
a warming pan and a 30-hour clock. In the bed chamber was a four-post bed-
stead, a featherbed, a looking glass and a chest of drawers. There were nine pictures in the bed chamber and two window curtains and rod.[1] Just over a century
earlier in 1677, another carpenter, William Robotham, had died in Huntingdon.
Like John Goodes he did not own any animals or crops and his inventory was
valued at just £9 18s 4d.[2] Robotham also slept on a featherbed but this was
the only item which also appeared in the list of goods owned by John Goodes.
These two examples suggest a transformation in the living standards of craftsmen in
a small market town and might be used to support the suggestion that a 'consumer
revolution' had taken place. However, how representative are these anecdotes and
to what extent is there evidence of a consumer revolution? If it occurred, when
did it take place? Was it confined to certain areas of the country or did it spread
throughout the nation? And who were the beneficiaries?

The present study seeks to answer some of these questions by exploring the
changing ownership of goods from the late Middle Ages through to the beginning
of the industrial revolution. A range of different sources have been used to provide a quantitative and qualitative approach to this investigation. This chapter considers the historiography of consumption as it relates to the key questions to be
addressed. However, it is important to note that recent writing on the subject has
explored new approaches and sources, particularly with regard to material culture
and the impact of the built environment upon consumption.

When did consumer change take place?

In 1982, Neil McKendrick argued that a consumer revolution occurred in the eighteenth century and that the pre-industrial world was characterised by poverty, poor diet and 'few comforts … to sustain them'.[3] McKendrick's pioneering work marked the beginning of a range of studies which considered various points in history and dated the expansion of consumerism earlier, or later. Whilst all of these authors, and others, have made valuable contributions to the debate, the present study suggests that it is inappropriate to try and specify a date for a 'consumer revolution', or to claim that a specific aspect caused such an event. We argue that what was actually occurring was a long, drawn out evolution of consumption which started around 1350 and subsequently affected various groups within society differently, both in terms of the timing and nature of changes to consumption patterns. Not only did this process impact variously on different societal groups, but the pattern of adoption of new goods varied by region. The cumulative effect of these changes was such that by the dawn of the industrial revolution, most people in England were actively enjoying a wide range of consumer goods. This development was not instigated by one event or outcome but fuelled by a complex interaction of factors which affected both the supply and demand of consumption goods.

Whilst no single element can be cited as the cause of the 'consumer revolution', the social and economic consequences of the Black Death were a key instigator. In the period after 1350, increased access to cheap land and food, combined with rising wages, promoted wider consumption, particularly amongst the peasantry. Other factors were also coming into play; for example, at the same time as these poorer groups were accessing a wider range of basic goods and services, an increasingly diverse range of luxury goods were being imported from the Far, South and Middle East into southern Europe, and then into England, which encouraged consumption by the wealthier members of society. An ongoing range of new and exciting imports continued to attract the attention of 'middle-class' consumers throughout the early modern period. As the goods which they had found desirable were imported in increasing numbers and unit costs fell, they in turn became the goods of choice for poorer groups. What emerged was increased consumption of an expanding range of goods which was characterised by a cascading effect: new goods were initially introduced in small numbers and at a high cost and adopted by the social elite, but as volumes increased and prices fell, the wider availability of these items would cascade downwards through the various tiers of English society. Whilst this general process was occurring throughout the period in question, certain factors stimulated, or restricted, demand or supply at various times. Some of these will be considered in greater detail throughout this study.

Revolution or evolution?

Regardless of speed, revolutions are profound in their effect so that for a 'consumer revolution' to have taken place, a change needed to have occurred whereby most members of society had moved from being passive consumers of a limited range of predominantly sustenance goods, to one where they were active participants in the consumption of a much wider range of goods and services. A 'consumer society' must have emerged in which members of all social groups were consumers and consumption was not just associated with the elite. Although many commentators consider that a consumer society had emerged by the end of our period, there is far less consensus on when this process began.

Christopher Dyer and Maryanne Kowaleski both asserted that the 'consumer revolution' began in the Middle Ages although for Dyer it continued for half a millennium between the period 1250–1750. Dyer pinpointed the 'later Middle Ages' as the time when consumption changed significantly with new patterns in the acquisition and use of material goods which had a wide impact on the whole economy.[4] Kowaleski claimed that the devastating fall in the population caused by the Black Death stimulated higher *per capita* expenditure and encouraged spending on a growing diversity of goods and services. She maintained that many features of the early modern consumer boom – new consumer goods, the attraction of novelties, changes in attitudes towards spending, increases in the amount and diversity of possessions and the penetration of consumer demand further down the social hierarchy – can all be seen in the Middle Ages.[5]

More recently, Tara Hamling and Catherine Richardson's *A Day at Home in Early Modern England* endorsed Craig Muldrew's '*birthplace*' of consumption' at around 1550 and argued that the divide between the sixteenth and seventeenth centuries was key to understanding the broader shifts in materiality that impacted most strongly on domestic life and consumption.[6] Sara Pennell highlights archaeological evidence that the age of transition for material change in England was 1400–1600, noting that it was more profitable to seek out continuities than to focus on the periodisation of the birth of consumption changes.[7] Pennell further supported Joan Thirsk in emphasising the importance of changes in consumption in the seventeenth century.[8] For Pennell, change was expressed in three ways: in new hearth goods, smoking (and thus tobacco) and mundane goods such as drinking glasses and brass thimbles.[9] Pennell also identified an important paradigm shift in consumption with a change in focus from durable goods, which involved repair and maintenance, to novelty.[10]

By contrast, Mark Overton argued that there was an absence of consumer goods in the sixteenth century and little that any extra income could be spent on, so that there was 'much voluntary underemployment' as once basic needs were satisfied, people preferred greater leisure time to earning more money.[11] This view was widely held by contemporaries and was encapsulated by Bernard Mandeville who asserted in 1714 that 'everybody knows that there is a vast number of journey-men ... who if by four days labour in a week they can maintain themselves will hardly be persuaded to work the fifth'. Thus, for Mandeville, high wages bred laziness, disorderliness and debauchery and other 'injurious practices' such as tea-drinking which he considered to be wasteful of time and destructive of industry.[12]

Based on his work on Dutch rural inventories, Jan de Vries argued for an 'industrious revolution' which began in the second half of the seventeenth century and marked a change when people became motivated by new consumer aspirations and began to prefer working longer hours for more money rather than greater leisure time. Within households, leisure time was reallocated as husbands worked longer hours and wives and children took on paid work so that greater *household* earnings allowed more consumer goods to be bought.[13] Although de Vries dated his 'industrious revolution' to before the classic years of the industrial revolution, Julian Hoppit suggested that this event was also accompanied by a significant change in behaviour and that consumers reacted to changes on the supply side of the economy by consuming more goods and services rather than spending more time at leisure.[14] Carole Shammas also highlighted this period as being significant and showed that it was marked by a significant rise in the consumption of groceries (in the form of tobacco, sugar products and caffeine drinks), and semi-durables (including textiles, pottery and glass). Shammas argued that the most surprising aspect of this spread of new consumer commodities was that it occurred among 'a broad spectrum of people'. This included people who could be identified as being malnourished and poorly housed which suggested that this increased consumption had embraced those who were some way down the social scale.[15] David Eversley also argued that low food prices in the period 1730–50 allowed 'large sections of the working population' to eat well and still retain sufficient surplus income to purchase consumer goods.[16]

In *The Birth of a Consumer Society* referred to earlier, McKendrick argued that a consumer boom which reached revolutionary proportions occurred in England in the third quarter of the eighteenth century (although he also highlighted the break in trend between Stuart and Georgian England). He was in the forefront of a revisionist school which drew attention to the demand side of the economy and he claimed that a greater proportion of the population than in any previous society in human history was able to enjoy the pleasures of buying consumer goods which included not only necessities, but 'decencies' and even luxuries.[17] Maxine Berg also explored this increase in consumer demand and argued that desire for new consumer goods during the eighteenth century was a prime mover of economic change and a spur to industrialisation.[18] Berg wrote of a 'product revolution' of new consumer goods made with new materials, fabricated with novel production methods and deploying division of labour. Markets for these new commodities evolved as a response to luxury goods imported by the East India companies during the seventeenth and eighteenth centuries.[19] Colin Campbell also placed the beginning of the consumer revolution towards the end of the eighteenth century. For Campbell, consumers were hedonists of the mind who reproduced their 'day dreams' through material objects so that consumerism was about self-improvement and aesthetic enjoyment.[20]

For other historians, the move to a consumer society was not a 'revolution' but a gradual evolution which only reached maturation in more recent years. Frank Trentmann suggested that although all human societies have been engaged in consumption, 'it has only been in specific context in *the nineteenth and twentieth centuries* that some practices of consumption have been connected to a sense of being a consumer'.[21] Other historians also dated the emergence of an all-encompassing consumer market to this period. Peter Gurney suggested that the market did not expand to encompass the majority fully until the nineteenth century. This was when consumption expanded beyond the elite and middling orders to the working class and Britain became the world's leading shopping nation.[22] For Thomas Richards, the consumer economy did not reach the working class until the end of the nineteenth century.[23] Peter Mathias and William Hamish Fraser both argued that the second half of the nineteenth century saw the emergence of a mass consumer market; and John Benson suggested that the late nineteenth and twentieth centuries were important periods in the development of consumer society.[24] For Benson, consumer societies were ones in which choice and credit were readily available, social value was determined in terms of purchasing power and material possessions and there was a desire for that which was new and fashionable.[25] Nancy Cox agreed that most scholars of modern economic and social history believed that the only true consumer revolution occurred in the late nineteenth and early twentieth centuries when urbanisation and industrialisation produced a working class with opportunities which had not been available to their forbears. For Cox, the consumer revolution was synonymous with mass production, mass marketing and mass consumption.[26]

Derek Aldcroft placed consumer change in the inter-war period between 1919 and 1939 when over four million new houses were built.[27] Although Peter Stearns adopted a gradualist model and suggested that the consumer revolution began in the seventeenth and eighteenth centuries and reached maturity in the nineteenth, he also argued for another consumerist phase after the Second World War.[28] This position was also adopted by both George Goodwin and Paul Addison, with Goodwin highlighting the importance of 1956, the year of the Suez Crisis, as a time when austerity and cultural deference were being replaced by American-style mass consumer culture.[29] Addison suggested that the ever-expanding consumer culture of the British was to a great extent imported from the United States after the Second World War as households acquired washing machines, vacuum cleaners and televisions in ever increasing numbers.[30] Dominic Sandbrook pointed out that ownership of these consumer goods extended to the poorest areas and even in Nottingham's deprived St Ann's district, by the late 1960s four out of five people owned a television and two out of five had a washing machine.[31] In the Thatcher years of the 1980s, new consumer goods such as the deep freezer, tumble drier, microwave oven, video recorder and CD player became widely owned and this decade also saw the launch of those icons of modern consumerism, the home computer and the mobile phone.[32]

One reason why historians have claimed that the consumer revolution occurred during defined timespans is that they have focussed their work on specific periods and period-specific goods; for example, despite the title of her book, Lorna Weatherill focussed on just 50 years (1675–1725) which she considered to be significant in the expansion of consumption, whilst Overton *et al.* extended Weatherill's chronological period and suggested that the key period of changes in consumption was between 1550 and 1750.[33] However, as what was actually taking place was a drawn out process of evolutionary change, all of these periods are likely to have shown evidence of increasing consumption. Indeed, the previous analysis of the claims of various historians goes some way towards supporting Brian Cowan's argument that 'every era' had a consumer revolution and suggests that pinpointing a precise date is a futile exercise.[34] This present study will draw these arguments together and show that the emergence of consumer society was largely an evolutionary process which began in the post-Black Death period of the fourteenth century, rather than in the sixteenth or subsequent centuries, and which took over four hundred years to complete. The process had largely been completed by the beginning of the industrial revolution although has been subject to change and refinement since this time.

Where did consumer change occur?

Location is key to studying changes in consumption. Consumption change had its roots in urban centres, particularly London, which was not only the commercial capital of England, but developed as a focus of consumption, a place to which people travelled to spend money that they had acquired elsewhere on the range of goods and services that it could offer.[35]

In the medieval period, Kowaleski argued that consumer demand was strongest in towns, whilst Dyer also recognised the importance of the urban environment and particularly highlighted the role of London.[36] Jeremy Goldberg also demonstrated that there was a contrast between the material culture exhibited by peasant households and that found in urban 'bourgeois' households.[37] In the early modern period, both Weatherill and Overton *et al.* demonstrated the importance of considering location in consumption studies. Goods were far less frequently recorded in probate records in areas distant from London, such as Cumbria and Cornwall.[38] Urbanisation was also important, and Carl Estabrook found that urban areas were associated with higher levels of consumption.[39] The importance of London for consumption also continued beyond our period. For Peter Gurney, the metropolis was in the vanguard of a burgeoning consumer culture that took off following the end of the Napoleonic Wars.[40]

This study continues to explore the role of location in changing patterns of consumer behaviour by expanding the chronological and geographical basis of this investigation. It charts how the first stirrings of consumer change in the late medieval period focussed on London and the south-east and gradually spread outwards to other areas of England and considers the role of towns as a focus of both demand and supply. It also expands on the locations chosen by both Overton *et al.* and Weatherill by filling in the picture for Middle England in rural districts including the counties of Huntingdonshire and Dorset and some areas of Yorkshire such as Rydal and Holderness; as well as rapidly industrialising areas, particularly West Yorkshire.

International dimension

It is important to place consumer change in context for it did not begin in England. Renaissance scholars have traced the beginnings of the consumer revolution to Florence and Venice, cities which were gateways for trade in goods such as spices, Turkish carpets and oriental silks between Europe and the Orient.[41] Evelyn Welch, drawing on a wide range of primary sources, explored how people from the middling sort to the elite in Milan, Venice, Florence and Rome engaged in consumption in the transition from the medieval to the early modern period. Welch sees much evidence of continuities rather than revolution.[42] The early use of forks was seen in medieval Italy.[43] Books were also owned by Italian bakers, carpenters and metalmakers in the sixteenth century and not confined to the elite.[44] Lisa Jardine asserted that Venice was the location of mass-produced printed volumes, many of which were exported to London. They included Pliny's *Natural History* and Plutarch's *Lives*. The trade stimulated the establishment of English printing presses to supply the growing demand.[45]

The rise of the Atlantic trade resulted in the centre of commercial life shifting to Amsterdam and London.[46] After the Dutch Republic secured its independence from Spain in 1581, its economy developed rapidly and its urbanising society enjoyed consumer goods such as linen from Haarlem, ceramics from Delft and cloth from Leiden. The Dutch East India Company (Vereenigde Oost-Indische Compagnie, founded in 1602) imported Chinese porcelain, spices, silk, textiles and coffee. By the late seventeenth century, clocks, carpets, curtains, silver, paintings and books were increasingly to be found in the homes of Dutch farmers. Mirrors became ubiquitous by 1700.[47]

The American colonies soon followed. Shammas painted a picture of increasing consumption of goods in the Thirteen Colonies.[48] Among them were significant amounts of tea, a trigger for the Revolutionary War, which was imported mostly illegally, by the mid-eighteenth century.[49] Textiles were also important, and the price of woollens and linens fell sharply during the eighteenth century, facilitating their purchase.[50] Consumption patterns in early Virginia were captured by Ann Smart Martin who examined the account books of John Hook, a country merchant in the Upper Shenandoah Valley in the latter eighteenth century. Hook sold not just textiles, clothing and sewing items but groceries (including tea, coffee, sugar and chocolate), household items (coffee pots, skillets, porringers, knives and forks) and books (including Bibles, sermons and Bunyan's *The Pilgrim's Progress*).[51]

Who was affected by the 'consumer revolution'?

As has been explored earlier, for a consumer revolution to have occurred, society must have moved from a position where most members had only a passive engagement with the act of consumption, to one in which the majority of the population were eager and active participants in the consumption of a wide range of goods and services. This study will demonstrate that comprehensive change did occur in the period between 1350 and 1800, but that this universal process consisted of a series of stages which affected different groups within society at various times and in diverse ways.

This study will show that for the late medieval period, the most significant consumption change related to diet so that all societal groups ate more wheaten bread and meat and drank more ale. This brought the greatest benefit to the poorer classes, although those further up the social scale enjoyed a wider range of foodstuffs and also engaged in the consumption of more and varied material goods. For these groups, clothing was increasingly important as a means of displaying status and wealth, and dress became subject to changes in taste; and the expansion of domestic space and increased adoption of individual living spaces led to a wider ownership of items with which to furnish the household environment.

By contrast, the key beneficiaries of changes in the early modern period were the 'middling sort'. Both class and status were important so that professional people, the gentry, substantial yeoman and tradesmen were the most innovative and active consumers.[52] This was particularly the case for the beginning of the seventeenth century but, towards its end, ownership of material goods was becoming more widespread and mainly associated with these higher-status groups.

Gender

Consumption was also influenced by the gender of the consumer. Gender not only directed the actual goods that were consumed, it could also affect who made the consumption decisions within a household and, where this involved the purchase of goods, who physically shopped for these consumption items. It might also impact on the emotions so that the behaviours exhibited by the different sexes in relation to consumption might vary quite widely.

In considering the impact of gender on goods consumed, it is evident that much of the clothing worn by men and women was gender specific so that, for example, testamentary evidence shows that men often possessed doublets, jackets and jerkins, whilst women owned kerchers and kirtles. Household items could also be associated with gender; Janet Loengard noted that at the time of marriage, women often brought to the household beds and bedding, brass pots and pans, tablecloths and other kitchen and bedroom equipment, and that although married women lacked possessions, these might remain to her so that she would receive them back if she survived her husband.[53] Amanda Vickery identified items such as a gentleman's shaving table and a backgammon table which had been purchased by men; and noted that furniture design manuals could be a source of explicitly gendered language by offering such items as 'Lady's dressing stools', 'Lady's Desk' and 'Lady's Bookcase'.[54]

Goldberg suggested that bourgeois wives were actively engaged in deciding priorities within the household budget as they were more involved in the market economy than their rural counterparts.[55] Nevertheless, decisions about expenditure on the more public areas of the house were probably shared, with the wife's priority being the chamber or, more specifically, the bed.[56] In *Consuming Splendor*, Linda Levy Peck argued that for all social levels, consumption decisions for the household were made by women.[57] In their study *Consumption and Gender in the Early Seventeenth-Century Household: The World of Alice Le Strange*, which focussed on an upper gentry household in the first half of the seventeenth century, Jane Whittle and Elizabeth Griffiths suggested that whilst decisions on everyday shopping were made by females, they were acting under the overall control of men as the heads of the household.[58] For women of the social elite, the act of shopping might be a pleasurable experience, with Helen Berry suggesting that going shopping was a familiar part of the rhythm of the lady's day. Nonetheless, Whittle and Griffiths observed that for most women shopping was associated with food and was not necessarily pleasurable.[59] Margot Finn drew attention to the role of men who she argued were active both as participants and as initiating agents in a range of consumer activities which historians have frequently associated with women.[60] For Finn, the diaries of James Woodforde, William Holland and Robert Sharp exemplify male acquisitive impulses unleashed by the consumer revolution.

The interplay between consumption and the emotions has also been explored. Women's consumption practices were often derided by contemporaries who considered that whilst men were rational and sociable, women were less so and more likely to be swayed by their emotions. In her study of the developing ideas of rational masculinity, however, Amanda Vickery found that, in practice, male acquisitions tended to be occasional, impulsive or expensive and dynastic.[61] In addition, Vickery explored items such as wallpaper and ribbons, which might be considered to be the preserve of female consumers, and found that men more frequently ordered wallpaper than women, although it was often unclear as to whether the items had been chosen by the husband or wife.[62] Nevertheless, she noted that advertisements by linen drapers, mercers and other dealers in clothing were often specifically addressed 'to the ladies', while furniture sellers were more sparing in gendered language.[63]

Consumption goods and consumers

In discussing consumption, it is apparent that the act of consuming did not simply involve material goods, but could also include items such as food, drink, fuel, religion, leisure, travel and other services. In the context of this study, food and drink are covered in some detail (in Chapters 3 and 4) as these were subject to significant changes over the period in question, whilst religion is also explored in Chapter 6 as substantial amounts of money were often spent on commodities and services associated with religion in both the late medieval and early modern periods. Other non-material consumption items are referred to, but not explored in depth. Some of these have been considered by other commentators, for example, Peter Borsay has explored leisure in England since 1500.[64]

At the most basic level, 'consumers' included the considerable number of people who eked out a very basic existence at a sustenance level and who had few options about, for example, what they ate or how they clothed themselves. Despite this, most people would argue that consumption incorporates some element of choice: not simply in terms of whether or not to consume in the first place; but, more importantly, in the amount and type of resources that will be consumed. Such implied choices go beyond the simple use of goods at a sustenance level. This is clearly understood in the modern context and there is a ready acceptance that we choose to consume the goods that we purchase and deliberately select those items which reflect our values and lifestyle. It is harder to relate this concept of 'choice' to 'consumers' who existed at a basic sustenance level in the late medieval and early modern periods and who exercised little or no choice in their consumption decisions.

For those people who could make choices about goods and services, consumption could happen for a range of reasons. Many of the material goods that first appeared within households in the late medieval period were chosen because they offered enhanced comfort so that sheets and pillows were added to beds, which increasingly had flock or feather mattresses rather than simply straw-filled sacks. Other consumption items were taken for a range of social reasons: social emulation became increasingly prevalent throughout the period so that people chose to purchase goods which were already in the possession of their social superiors. Related to this was the perception that ownership of certain goods conveyed an image of respectability which brought enhanced social acceptance. Other consumer decisions were motivated by novelty so that people were attracted to new and unusual goods which they chose to purchase over more traditional and less exciting items. Whilst most consumers 'chose' to participate in consumption, such actions could also incorporate an element of desire which drove consumption and limited rational choice.

Religious consumption

The present investigation seeks to expand the definition of consumption items beyond that used in other studies. In particular, it explores consumption associated with religion. A number of studies have considered the various ways in which money could be spent on aspects associated with religion, particularly in the late medieval period; for example, John S. Lee surveyed the 'myriad of different commemorative enterprises' available to the religious consumer in late medieval Cambridge.[65] Despite the existence of studies such as these, expenditure on religion has invariably been neglected in studies of consumption despite the fact that it was a vital element in people's lives and could absorb a significant proportion of household expenditure. Prior to the Reformation, evidence shows a large aggregate expenditure on items such as prayers, masses, pilgrimages and gild membership, as well as on the maintenance of the parish church, its furnishings and the clothing and accoutrements of its priests. Whilst the abolition of purgatory during the

Reformation led to a decline in the expenditure on rituals and beliefs associated with this doctrine, in the early modern period funerals became increasingly significant and the focus of often considerable outlay.

Secondhand goods

When considering consumption during the late medieval and early modern periods, it is important to note that many goods were not purchased 'new', but were acquired 'secondhand' which led Giorgio Riello to state that 'recycling' was commonplace in a world of material dearth.[66] Various sources confirm that the secondhand economy was both widespread and flourishing and was an important aspect of consumption, particularly since for many people it may have been the main way, or, possibly the only way, in which they could acquire material goods.[67] Although it is difficult to quantify, the trade in secondhand goods has been considered by a number of historians including James Davis in his exploration of secondhand marketing activities in late medieval England, and Beverley Lemire, who has considered a number of themes connected to the secondhand trade in early modern England.[68]

Secondhand items were obtained from a range of different sources. Many were inherited or passed down as part of a gift economy. In the context of this work, wills contain abundant evidence of bequests of a range of household items as well as clothing and jewellery which were frequently given to family members, but also to friends, business acquaintances and even to servants. Many were bestowed as a form of 'remembrances' or were evidently heirloom items, particularly rings, silver spoons and mazers, thereby constructing a social memory which went far beyond the economic value of the item. Gifts might also be given for other reasons; in his diary John Carrington records a silver cup given by the Marquess of Salisbury to Mr Whittenbury as a reward for his valour in intervening in a robbery.[69]

Other bequests had a more practical purpose and were given with the expectation that the recipient would wear or use the object rather than it be a keepsake item. Other 'heirloom' bequests included items of furniture which were passed down through families, but were clearly intended for use, such as the 'little featherbed which her grandmother Wilson had', which Thomas Wilson of Boreham gave in turn to his daughter.[70]

Bequests of clothing to servants were clearly made on the understanding that the items were serviceable and probably better than what was already owned. Similarly, many clothing bequests were charitable gifts to those in need. Other articles were both sentimental and practical. Goods which were passed on in this manner retained a personal element, so that the recipient would have had a connection with the previous owner.

Goods could also be acquired through secondhand marketing, either directly from a previous household, or via more formal trading arrangements such as markets or shops. These goods were integrated into the commercial economy and the personal connection with the previous owner was less important, or even negligible.

Clothing in particular was frequently traded secondhand and Lemire noted that 'the secondhand clothes trade was a vital reflection of consumer demand in preindustrial and early industrial England'.[71] The importance of this trade was such that it is explored in more detail in the relevant sections.

Involuntary consumption

Many consumption decisions were not made by the consumer but were forced upon them by another party. This involuntary consumption could take various forms. Servants were often required to wear livery provided by their employers and, in some cases, were expected to pay for this themselves. In 1532/3, Thetford Priory spent £9 18s on 11 pieces of cloth for liveries which was subsequently made up into gowns for their servants.[72] Charitable gifts were also given by the priory including the shilling spent in 1516/17 on 'a cote making pro ydiot'.[73] Although donations such as these were almost certainly gratefully received, the involvement of the recipients in the consumption choice was negligible. John Styles showed that rented accommodation often included furnishings which were provided by landlords but that the tenants had no input into what this was.[74]

Other consumption decisions were taken in which the individual *knowingly* acted against his best interests. Examples can be found in diaries; Thomas Turner was aware that excessive consumption of alcohol was not beneficial and regularly resolved to reform his behaviour:

> People make themselves slaves to that poison gin (8 January 1757).
> I am prodigiously silly and apish when I am in liquor. I will renew my former resolution ... not to get drunk again if I can avoid it (27 January 1756).

Two days later (29 January 1756), he complained that there was not enough beer at a funeral he attended.[75] Turner regularly visited the house of Jeremiah French, a substantial yeoman farmer in East Hoathly, mostly for evenings playing cards and heavy drinking. Turner played in order to avoid being sneered at by the company (24 January 1760) but resolved not to play cards again 'if I can possibly help it' (8 February 1760).[76] He invariably returned home inebriated from these evenings and regretted losing money:

> It grieves me to lose so much money ... especially when I think it wrong.[77]

Social pressures weakened Turner's resolve to avoid gambling and he frequently returned to social evenings that involved drinking and gambling.

Consumption: positive or negative?

Throughout our period, commentators were divided as to whether consumption was a positive or negative force. In the late medieval period, consumption was generally viewed unfavourably, especially when it was by the lower orders of society, and often regarded as the antipathy to spiritual well-being. In Piers Plowman, William Langland identified sinful consumers from all degrees of the social hierarchy from tramps and beggars who went to bed 'glutted with food and drink', through to lawyers in silk gowns 'pleading their cases for as much money as they could get' and clearly regarded consumption as an unhealthy devouring of material resources.[78] In the early modern period, such negativity about consumption was often attached to specific goods so that tobacco, alcohol and sugar were all singled out for contemporaneous criticism with Puritans in particular railing against the excessive consumption of alcohol. The shift in cultural belief after the Restoration of the Monarchy in 1660 led to a move away from the notion that accumulation of wealth and material goods was sinful and vain and that only poverty and an ascetic lifestyle was virtuous, towards the belief that economic progress was desirable.[79] For McKendrick, the eighteenth-century 'consumer revolution' was the overcoming of the Puritan ethic against consumption.

Changes in consumption were not simply driven by economics; cultural changes could be equally relevant. Woodruff Smith drew attention to the importance of genteel behaviour which was significant since those claiming genteel status increased in number at the same time as the nature of gentility broadened to encompass notions of respectability as well as birth and family.[80] The notion of 'respectability' emphasised education, curiosity about the physical world and refinement of tastes, and behaviours associated with these were expressed in material ways, including the sensual experience of commodities.[81] Virtue could also embrace materialism; for example, John Wesley, the leader of the new Methodism, encouraged his followers to wear respectable and clean clothing that would command respect since he held that Christian families should not eschew the small comforts that 'God provided' and flaunt apparent poverty as a source of pride.[82]

New approaches

Material culture

Several historians have written on material culture. David Hinton used both physical and documentary evidence to examine the significance of material culture to people from the Anglo-Saxon to the late medieval period, whilst Roberta Gilchrist's study of the materiality of the life course, c. 1050–1540 drew heavily on the field of social archaeology as well as using other sources to explore the goods that people owned.[83] The theme of the wider purpose of various objects in both the late medieval and early modern periods was explored in a volume edited by Hamling and Richardson.[84] In their introduction, the editors noted:

> Knowing about people's possessions is crucial to understanding their experience of daily life, the way they saw themselves in relation to their

peers and their responses to and interactions with the social, cultural and economic structures and processes which made up the societies in which they lived.[85]

Writers from a wide range of disciplines considered different aspects of a common theme, namely, the objects experienced by people in their everyday lives.[86] Many of these writers made the point that the value and meaning attached to similar objects changed over time.

Beverly Lemire argued that students of history attained a clearer vision of the past through critical interpretation of common goods and that information gleaned from artefacts complemented that obtained from written records.[87] Sara Pennell suggested a need to go beyond museum artefacts which predominantly represented exclusive items made for the social elite. The material goods used by the poorer classes have rarely survived since they were roughly made from course materials and used until they wore out, yet Pennell claimed that it was these objects which can speak of those who have left little documentary evidence.[88] She further warned against the quantitative approach to inventory data which does not take sufficient account of the variety and range of objects, for example, aggregating data on 'saucepans' obscures the important differences between them.[89]

Some material culture studies also include consideration of the materials from which artefacts were manufactured. The nature of clothing is indicative of gender and the fabric from which clothing was made can signify social status.[90] Style and the age of garments also provide important insights into the evolution of personal clothing.

Karen Harvey has also explored how material culture can illuminate the historical study of consumption; she argued that history is impoverished without reference to the study of material culture which goes beyond the physical attributes of the objects and recognises that they have agency.[91] Objects are embedded in a social world and help to create and shape relationships.[92] In the same volume, Giorgio Riello concurred with the notion that material objects are themselves important primary sources.[93]

A second new approach considered the impact of the environment upon the material life of households. Chris Briggs, Alice Forward, Ben Jervis and Matthew Tompkins used the location of forfeited possessions, as revealed by escheators' inquests and accounts, to explore the use of space in the houses and outbuildings of lower-status people in the fourteenth and fifteenth centuries.[94] In *A Day at Home in Early Modern England*, Hamling and Richardson investigated the complex relationship between households of the 'middling sort' and their domestic space.[95] They focussed on the West Country, Kent and the Midlands to produce an account of history 'from the middle' using qualitative evidence from a range of sources. Most relevant to the present study is the changing function of rooms so that, for example, the parlour ceased to be a room for sleeping and became a room for sitting and dining. Householders experienced both increasing comfort and privacy in their sleeping arrangements facilitated by the creation of upstairs chambers for sleeping. Chambers became increasingly comfortable and furnished with cushions and window curtains.[96]

Unreal wages

Some of the studies that have been referred to in this chapter have made the reasonable assumption that living standards are inexorably linked to wages, and that, therefore, periods of high wages coincide with observable increases in consumption. For example, Kowaleski stated that:

> the early modern 'consumer revolution' actually began in the late middle ages, when the unusual economic conditions following the demographic devastation of the Black Death stimulated higher per capita expenditure and fostered spending on a growing diversity of goods and services.[97]

McKendrick also related the growing democratisation of consumption to substantial increases in income.[98]

Many of these studies were based on the real wages indices compiled by a number of historians and most notably those of Henry Phelps-Brown and Sheila Hopkins which indicated that the purchasing power of the daily wages of urban building craftsmen doubled between the first half of the fourteenth and the third quarter of the fifteenth centuries; and more recently that of Gregory Clark, which showed that the real wages of agricultural labourers at least doubled and occasionally almost trebled during the same time period.[99] Interpretation of these indices has led to the perception that the fifteenth and early sixteenth centuries were 'a golden age' for the masses and a general belief that living standards were almost universally heightened to an extent that was not subsequently achieved until after the advent of the industrial revolution.[100]

More recently, the methodology used to estimate real wages has been challenged. John Hatcher noted that the work done on wage rates by Phelps-Brown and Hopkins was based on a wage rate for full-time working, i.e. a full week's work, and on evidence of daily and weekly wage rates paid to building craftsmen as one of the few groups that have left evidence of money paid for time-work.[101] Hatcher identified that it was inappropriate to apply these real wage indices to the population as a whole as 'the conventional measures used to compute them are ill-suited to their task' since agricultural labourers, for example, were likely either to be employed on annual contracts at relatively low rates of pay, or to depend on casual labouring, the demand for which varied according to the season.[102] In his most recent work, Hatcher concluded that the wage and income data which has for so long supported measurements of living standards are 'unreliable and beset by weaknesses, biases, inaccuracies and misapprehensions'.[103]

The scepticism expressed by Hatcher has been endorsed by Jane Humphries and Jacob Weisdorf who also highlighted other difficulties with existing real wages indices. In particular, they were especially critical of the reliance placed by previous researchers on the supposition that 'workers always and everywhere worked for 250 (or sometimes 260) days per year' and stated their belief that: 'existing estimates of annual incomes in England are badly off target, because they overestimate the medieval working year but underestimate the working year during the industrial revolution'.[104]

Humphries and Weisdorf further noted that wage rates based on this assumption did not concur with trends in GDP such that the discrepancy brought into serious doubt theories which provide explanations of when and how Western Europe grew rich.[105]

In response to this problem, Humphries and Weisdorf devised a new income series based on male workers employed on annual contracts. This work not only produced a real annual income series which mirrored trends in GDP *per capita*, but also indicated that the working year changed considerably over time so that whereas the post–Black Death working year was possibly as short as 100 days, the industrial working year could be as long as 325 days.[106] These income estimates suggest that a range of revisions need to be applied to some of the assumptions that have been made about the rise of consumption in late medieval and early modern England, including some which have been outlined in this chapter, which used real wage data to support theories of changing consumption patterns. Instead, these revised income estimates suggest that the so-called 'golden age' of the fifteenth and early sixteenth centuries 'glittered much less brightly' as the real-wage peak was much lower than previously suggested.[107] In addition, although living standards did improve in the aftermath of the Black Death, this was not maintained so that real earnings did not grow continuously until after *c.* 1580. This, in turn, suggests that although the late medieval period saw some level of increased consumption, it was not until 1580 that this pattern became firmly established. Furthermore, the rise in the number of days in the working year, from 100 in the post–Black Death period to 325 in the industrial working year suggested by the revised income estimates gives credence to the view of de Vries that the period saw an 'Industrious Revolution'. Finally, and most importantly in relation to this present study, the work shows that real earnings did not show a marked 'jump' in the late fourteenth and early fifteenth centuries, as suggested by the studies made by Phelps-Brown and Hopkins and Clark, but rose gradually and over a longer period of time. This gives some level of support to the claim of this study that a 'consumer revolution' did not occur at any stage during the late medieval and early modern periods, but that what actually occurred was a longer evolution of consumption which started in the late fourteenth century and developed in the following four centuries.

Approach to sources

Much historical research on the development of consumption has relied heavily on a qualitative approach. This is particularly the case for the late medieval period as, for various reasons, medievalists have traditionally been reluctant to use quantitative methods of historical research. Qualitative research of this nature has a long and valued tradition and has resulted in differing perspectives and healthy debates and this study recognises its continued significance. However, in relation to the development of consumption, whilst a qualitative approach can provide valuable evidence of aspects such as the availability of various goods and services and individual ownership of goods, it cannot be used to explore, for example, whether the ownership of a particular item was typical and how general it was across a particular group of people. Consequently, whilst this study continues to use qualitative material, this is combined with the use of quantitative data, as outlined later, in an attempt to discern variations in the possession of material items over the period in question. This data will be used to explore chronological changes, but with particular emphasis on how social and geographical differences impacted on ownership. This use of both qualitative and quantitative data has reinforced suppositions and allowed for firmer conclusions than might be obtained from one methodology alone.

A number of historians have placed a greater emphasis on the use of quantitative methods and their techniques and approaches have heavily influenced the present study. Weatherill analysed 2,902 probate inventories for eight regions, but her sample sizes for each region were not large, the highest being 390 inventories.[108] Mark Overton led a team of people which produced the much larger sample of around 8,100 inventories for just two counties: Kent and Cornwall. Their sample was therefore around ten times larger than Weatherill's for each of their locations.[109] This study uses a range of probate records (wills, inventories and probate accounts) which represent both the largest collection and the longest chronological span of these records and which cover both the period prior to 1600, in which the beginnings of consumer change can be seen, and the crucial years after 1750 which McKendrick claimed as a period of consumer boom. For the pre-1600 period, an analysis of over 1,000 wills and more than 500 inventories has been used in conjunction with purchasing records in the form of household accounts to provide evidence about unit costs and sources of supply. Although it has been claimed that probate inventories survive in only very small numbers (if at all) for the period after 1730, a survey of surviving inventories by the present authors found that many thousands of post-1750 probate inventories are held in record offices across the country. The selected sample of inventories for the present study includes over 1,100 for the second half of the eighteenth century.

Scope of the study

Despite the extensive literature on the development of consumption and consumerism in England, much remains unknown or subject to ongoing debate. This study focusses on specific areas to explore the chronology, the pattern of increased ownership by different social groups, the importance of location and the scope of religious consumption. In this, consumption will be considered over a longer timescale than earlier studies and will be explored using a larger database of evidence than that previously developed. Chapter 2 now considers that evidence and the many problems of its interpretation.

Notes

1 HA AH18/7/274.
2 HA AH18/18/105.
3 N. McKendrick, J. Brewer and J. Plumb, *The Birth of a Consumer Society: The Commercialization of Eighteenth-Century England* (London: Hutchinson, 1982), pp.5, 9, 30–31. Whilst McKendrick specifically argued for the third quarter of the eighteenth century in *The Birth of a Consumer Society* (p.9), he also pinpoints the sharp break in trend between Stuart and Georgian England (p.5).
4 C. Dyer, *An Age of Transition; Economy and Society in England in the later Middle Ages* (Oxford: Oxford University Press, 2005), pp.42, 128, 147–48.
5 M. Kowaleski, 'A consumer economy', in R. Horrox and W. M. Ormrod (eds), *A Social History of England 1200–1500* (Cambridge: Cambridge University Press, 2006), p.239.
6 C. Muldrew, *The Economy of Obligation: The Culture of Credit and Social Relations in Early Modern England* (Basingstoke: Palgrave Macmillan, 1998), pp.3–4, 20–21; T. Hamling and C. Richardson, *A Day at Home in Early Modern England: Material Culture and Domestic Life, 1500–1700* (New Haven: Yale UP, 2017), p.12.
7 S. Pennell, 'Material culture in seventeenth-century Britain: the matter of domestic consumption', in F. Trentmann (ed.), *The Oxford Handbook of the History of Consumption* (Oxford: Oxford University Press, 2012), p.70.
8 *Ibid.*, p.70.
9 *Ibid.*, pp.76–78.
10 *Ibid.*, pp.78ff.
11 M. Overton, *Agricultural Revolution in England* (Cambridge: Cambridge University Press, 1996), p.38.
12 J. Hatcher, 'Labour, leisure and economic thought before the nineteenth century', *Past and Present*, 160 (1998), p.64; S. Hindle, 'Representing rural society: labor, leisure, and the landscape in an eighteenth-century conversation piece', *Critical Inquiry*, 41 (2015), p.636.
13 J. de Vries, 'The industrial revolution and the industrious revolution', *Journal of Economic History*, 54 (1994), pp.249–70; J. de Vries, *The Industrious Revolution: Consumer Behaviour and the Household Economy, 1650 to the Present* (Cambridge: Cambridge University Press, 2008), p.122.
14 J. Hoppit and E. Wrigley, *The Industrial Revolution in Britain* (Oxford: Oxford University Press, 1994), p.xxvii.
15 C. Shammas, *The Pre-Industrial Consumer in England and America* (Oxford: Clarendon, 1990), p.361.
16 D. Eversley, 'The home market and economic growth in England, 1750–80', in E.L. Jones, J.D. Chambers and G.E. Mingay (eds) *Land, Labour and Population in the Industrial Revolution* (London: Hambledon Press, 1967), pp.208, 240.
17 McKendrick, 'The consumer revolution', in McKendrick *et al.*, *The Birth of a Consumer Society*, p.9.
18 M. Berg, *Luxury and Pleasure in Eighteenth-Century Britain* (Oxford: Oxford University Press, 2005), pp.22–23.
19 *Ibid.*, pp.4–20.
20 C. Campbell, *The Romantic Ethic and the Spirit of Consumerism* (Basingstoke: Palgrave Macmillan, 2018).

21 F. Trentmann, 'Introduction', in Trentmann, *Oxford Handbook of the History of Consumption*, pp.1–2; F. Trentmann; *The Making of the Consumer* (Oxford: Oxford University Press, 2006), p.2.
22 P. Gurney, *The Making of Consumer Culture* (London: Bloomsbury, 2017), pp.13, 19.
23 T. Richards, *The Commodity Culture of Victorian England* (Stanford: Stanford University Press, 1990), pp.7–8.
24 P. Mathias, *Retailing Revolution* (London: Longmans, 1967); W. Hamish Fraser, *The Coming of the Mass Market 1850–1914* (Basingstoke: Palgrave Macmillan, 1982); J. Benson, *The Rise of Consumer Society in Britain, 1880–1980* (London: Longman, 1994).
25 Benson, *The Rise of Consumer Society in Britain*.
26 N. Cox, *The Complete Tradesman; a Study of Retailing 1550–1820* (Aldershot: Ashgate, 2000), p.2.
27 D. Aldcroft, *The Inter-War Economy, 1919–1939* (New York: Columbia University Press, 1971), pp.41, 367–69.
28 P. Stearns, 'Stages of consumerism: recent work on the issues of periodization', *Journal of Modern History*, 69 (1997), pp.102–103, 115.
29 G. Goodwin, 'What was history's most dramatic year?', *BBC History Magazine*, Christmas (2016), p.35.
30 D. Sandbrook, *Never Had It So Good: A History of Britain from Suez to the Beatles* (London: Abacus, 2005), p.103ff; P. Addison, *No Turning Back: The Peacetime Revolutions of Post-War Britain* (Oxford: Oxford University Press, 2010), p.56.
31 D. Sandbrook, *State of Emergency: The Way We Were, Britain 1970–1974* (London: Allen Lane, 2010), p.19.
32 Addison, *No Turning Back*, pp.319 and 364.
33 L. Weatherill, *Consumer Behaviour and Material Culture in Britain 1660–1760* (London: Routledge, 1996); M. Overton, J. Whittle, D. Dean and A. Hann, *Production and Consumption in English Households 1600–1750* (London: Routledge, 2004).
34 B. Cowan, *The Social Life of Coffee: The Emergence of the British Coffeehouse* (New Haven: Yale University Press, 2005), p.257.
35 F. Fisher, 'The development of London as a centre of conspicuous consumption in the sixteenth and seventeenth centuries', *Transactions of the Royal Historical Society*, 30 (1948), p.38.
36 Kowaleski, 'A consumer economy', pp.239, 242, 247–49, 252–53; C. Dyer, *Making a Living in the Middle Ages: The People of Britain 85–1520* (New Haven: Yale University Press, 2002), pp.305, 307, 322–24, 356–57.
37 P.J.P. Goldberg, 'The fashioning of bourgeois domesticity in later medieval England: a material culture perspective', in M. Kowaleski and P.J.P. Goldberg (eds), *Medieval Domesticity: Home, Housing and Household in Medieval England* (Cambridge: Cambridge University Press, 2011), pp.124–44.
38 Weatherill, *Consumer Behaviour*, pp.60 and 70ff; Overton *et al.*, *Production and Consumption*, p.171.
39 C. Estabrook, *Urbane and Rustic England: Cultural Ties and Social Spheres in the Provinces, 1660–1780* (Stanford: Stanford University Press, 1998), p.154.
40 Gurney, *The Making of Consumer Culture*, pp.22–23.
41 F. Trentmann, *Empire of Things: How We Became a World of Consumers, from the Fifteenth Century to the Twenty-First* (London: Allen Lane, 2016), pp.22, 28.
42 E. Welch, *Shopping in the Renaissance: Consumer Cultures in Italy, 1400–1600* (New Haven: Yale University Press, 2009).
43 In 1475, the silk merchant Jacopo di Giannozzo Pandolfini bought a set of 12 silver forks and spoons and Domenico Capello left 12 decorated and gilded spoons and forks and 42 plainer forks; Trentmann, *Empire of Things*, p.29.
44 Trentmann, *Empire of Things*, p.32.
45 L. Jardine, *Wordly Goods, New History of the Renaissance* (London: Macmillan, 1996), pp.143–44.

46 Trentmann, *Empire of Things*, p.32.
47 S. Schama, *The Embarrassment of Riches: An Interpretation of Dutch Culture in the Golden Age* (Oakland: University of California Press, 1988), pp.129–88, 289–343; J. de Vries, *The Dutch Rural Economy in the Golden Age 1500–1700* (New Haven: Yale University Press, 1974), pp.219–21; Trentmann, *Empire of Things*, pp.54–55.
48 Shammas, *The Pre-Industrial Consumer*; C. Shammas, 'Changes in English and Anglo-American consumption from 1550 to 1800', in J. Brewer and R. Porter (eds) *Consumption and the World of Goods* (London: Routledge, 1993), pp.177–205.
49 Shammas, *Pre-Industrial Consumer*, p.103.
50 *Ibid.*, p.120.
51 A. Smart Martin, *Buying into the World of Goods: Early Consumers in Back Country Virginia* (Baltimore: John Hopkins University Press, 2008), pp.76–85.
52 Weatherill, *Consumer Behaviour*, p.166ff.
53 J.S. Loengard, '"Which may be said to be her own": widows and goods in late-medieval England', in Kowaleski and Goldberg (eds), *Medieval Domesticity*, pp.162–64, 172.
54 A. Vickery, *Behind Closed Doors: At Home in Georgian England* (New Haven: Yale University Press, 2009), pp.279, 284–85.
55 Goldberg, 'The fashioning of bourgeois domesticity', pp.124–38.
56 *Ibid.*, pp.137–38.
57 L. Levy Peck, *Consuming Splendor: Society and Culture in Seventeenth-Century England* (Cambridge: Cambridge University Press, 2005), p.68–69.
58 J. Whittle and E. Griffiths, *Consumption and Gender in the Early Seventeenth-Century Household: The World of Alice Le Strange* (Oxford: Oxford University Press, 2012), pp.9–10.
59 H. Berry, 'Polite consumption: shopping in eighteenth-century England', *Transactions of the Royal Historical Society*, 12 (2002), pp.380–81; Whittle and Griffiths, *Consumption and Gender*, pp.10–11.
60 M. Finn, 'Men's things: masculine possession in the consumer revolution', *Social History*, 25 (2000), p.142.
61 A. Vickery, 'Golden age to separate spheres: a review of the categories and chronology of English women's history', *Historical Journal*, 36 (2) (1993), pp.383–414; Vickery, *Behind Closed Doors*, p.278.
62 Vickery, *Behind Closed Doors*, pp.169–71.
63 *Ibid.*, p.286.
64 P. Borsay, *A History of Leisure: The British Experience since 1500* (Basingstoke: Palgrave, 2006).
65 J.S. Lee, 'Monument and memory: a university town in late medieval England', in J.S. Lee and C. Slater (eds), *The History of the University of Cambridge: Texts and Studies, Volume 9, Commemoration in Medieval Cambridge* (Woodbridge: Boydell, 2018), pp.10–33.
66 G. Riello 'Material culture and historical narratives', in K. Harvey (ed.), *History and Material Culture: A Student's Guide to Approaching Alternative Sources* (Abingdon: Routledge, 2018), p.35.
67 S. Horrell, J. Humphries and K. Sneath 'Cupidity and crime', in M. Casson and N. Hashimzade (eds), *Large Databases in Economic History* (London: Routledge, 2013), p.253.
68 J. Davis, 'Marketing secondhand goods in late medieval England', *Journal of Historical Research in Marketing*, 2 (3) (2010), pp.270–86; B. Lemire, 'Consumerism in preindustrial and early industrial England: the trade in secondhand clothes', *Journal of British Studies*, 27 (1) (1988), pp.1–24; B. Lemire, 'Peddling fashion: salesmen, pawnbrokers, taylors, thieves and the second-hand clothes trade in England, 1700–1800', *Textile History*, 22 (1) (1991), pp.67–82; B. Lemire, 'The theft of clothes and popular consumerism in early modern England', *Journal of Social History*, 24 (2) (1990), pp. 255–76.

69 S. Flood (ed.), *John Carrington, Farmer of Bramfield, His Diary, Volume 1, 1798–1810: Hertfordshire Record Publications Vol.26* (Hertford: Hertfordshire Record Society, 2011), p.105.

70 F. Emmison, *Wills of the County of Essex (England): Vol. 1, 1558–1565* (Washington: National Genealogical Society, 1982), p.30.

71 Lemire, 'Consumerism in preindustrial and early industrial England', p.1.

72 D. Dymond (ed.), *The Register of Thetford Priory, Part II: 1518–1540: Norfolk Record Society Vol.LX* (Oxford: Oxford University Press, 1995 and 1996), p.602.

73 *Ibid.*, p.341.

74 J. Styles, 'Lodging at the Old Bailey: lodgings and their furnishings in eighteenth-century London', in J. Styles and A. Vickery (eds), *Gender, Taste and Material Culture in Britain and North America: 1700–1830* (New Haven: Yale University Press, 2006), p.61.

75 D. Vaisey (ed.), *The Diary of a Village Shopkeeper: 1754–1765* (London: Folio Society, 1998), pp.32–33, 104.

76 *Ibid.*, pp.258, 261.

77 *Ibid.*, p.258.

78 J. Goodridge (trans. and ed.), *Piers the Ploughman: William Langland* (Harmondsworth: Penguin, 1971), pp.26, 31; M. Kim, 'The politics of consuming worldly goods: negotiating Christian discipline and feudal power in "Piers Plowman"', *Traditio* 59 (2004), pp.339–68.

79 J. Mokyr, 'An age of progress' in R. Floud, J. Humphries and P. Johnson (eds), *The Cambridge Economic History of Modern Britain* (Cambridge: Cambridge University Press, 2014) p.267; A. Ryrie, *Being Protestant in Reformation Britain* (Oxford: Oxford University Press, 2013) p.40; T. Watson, *The Beatitudes* (London: Banner of Truth, 2014) p.16.

80 W. Smith, *Consumption and the Making of Respectability, 1600–1800* (Abingdon: Routledge, 2002), p.224.

81 *Ibid.*, pp.76, 225.

82 *Ibid.*, pp.136 and 232–33.

83 D. Hinton, *Gold and Gilt, Pots and Pins: Possessions and People in Medieval Britain* (Oxford: Oxford University Press, 2005); R. Gilchrist, *Medieval Life: Archaeology and the Life Course* (Woodbridge: Boydell, 2014).

84 T. Hamling and C. Richardson (eds), *Everyday Objects: Medieval and Early Modern Material Culture and its Meanings* (Farnham: Ashgate, 2010).

85 T. Hamling and C. Richardson, 'Introduction', in Hamling and Richardson (eds), *Everyday Objects*, p.1.

86 *Ibid.*, p.1.

87 B. Lemire, 'Draping the body and dressing the home' in Harvey (ed.), *History and Material Culture*, pp.89–90.

88 See also H. Berry 'Regional identity and material culture' in Harvey (ed.), *History and Material Culture*, p.192.

89 S. Pennell, 'Mundane materiality or should small things still be forgotten?', in Harvey (ed.), *History and Material Culture*, pp.224, 229.

90 D. Miller, *Stuff* (Cambridge: Cambridge University Press, 2010) p.12; Berry 'Regional identity and material culture', p.190.

91 K. Harvey, 'Introduction: historians, material culture and materiality', in Harvey (ed.), *History and Material Culture*.

92 *Ibid.*, pp.2–6.

93 G. Riello, 'Things that shape history: material culture and historical narratives', in Harvey (ed.), *History and Material Culture*, pp.27–50.

94 C. Briggs, A. Forward, B. Jervis and M. Tompkins, 'People, possessions and domestic space in the late medieval escheators' records', *Journal of Medieval History*, 45 (2) (2019), pp.145–61.

95 Hamling and Richardson, *Day at Home*.
96 *Ibid.*, pp.51, 187 and 239ff.
97 Kowaleski, 'A consumer economy', p.239.
98 McKendrick *et al.*, *The Birth of a Consumer Society*, p.23.
99 E. Phelps-Brown and S. Hopkins, 'Seven centuries of building wages', *Economica*, 22 (1955), pp.195–206; G. Clark, 'The long march of history: farm wages, population and economic growth, England, 1209–1869', *Economic History Review*, 60 (2007), pp.97–135.
100 J. Rogers, *Six Centuries of Work and Wages: The History of English Labour* (London: Allen Unwin, 1949), p.326 cited in J. Hatcher, 'Unreal wages: long-run living standards and the "Golden Age" of the fifteenth century', in B. Dodds and C. Liddy (eds), *Commercial Activity, Markets and Entrepreneurs in the Middle Ages: Essays in Honour of Richard Britnell* (Woodbridge: Boydell, 2011), p.3.
101 Hatcher, 'Unreal wages', pp.1–24.
102 *Ibid.*, p.7.
103 J. Hatcher, 'Introduction', in J. Hatcher and J.Z. Stephenson (eds), *Seven Centuries of Unreal Wages: The Unreliable Data, Sources and Methods that have been used for Measuring Standards of Living in the Past* (London: Palgrave Macmillan, 2019), p.2.
104 J. Humphries and J. Weisdorf, 'Unreal wages? Real income and economic growth in England, 1260–1850', *Centre for Economic Policy Research*, Discussion Paper Series, Discussion Paper DP119999 (London, 2017), pp.1, 4.
105 *Ibid.*, p.2.
106 *Ibid.*, p.6.
107 *Ibid.*, p.5.
108 Weatherill, *Consumer Behaviour*, p.46.
109 Overton *et al.*, *Production and Consumption*, p.9.

2

SOURCES AND THEIR INTERPRETATION

Probate evidence

The main source used for this study of consumption patterns is probate records. Although these were created for a very different purpose, they contain evidence of the ownership of goods and take the form of wills (for the period from 1430 to 1579), probate inventories (from 1551 to 1800) and probate accounts (from 1605 to 1789). Around 5,500 selected probate records were transcribed for this study and these were supplemented by data from a number of published wills and inventories. The resulting data was recorded and analysed using the SPSS statistical analysis software.[1]

The probate process

Church courts (also referred to as ecclesiastical courts) were established separately from secular courts during the eleventh century. These operated under canon law and their responsibilities ranged from church administration to the most intimate aspects of personal life.[2] Church courts were also responsible for testamentary business and oversaw the distribution of 'moveable goods' including credits and leasehold property, but not real estate which comprised freehold and copyhold land and buildings and which was initially the responsibility of manorial courts and subject to common law.[3]

Prior to 1858, when ecclesiastical probate was superseded by civil district registries, there were three levels of church court.[4] At the highest level were the prerogative courts of the two ecclesiastical provinces of Canterbury and York which together had overriding jurisdiction over the whole of England and Wales. Below this level were the courts of the bishops (also known as consistory or commissary courts) which had jurisdiction over the various dioceses. At the lowest level of ecclesiastical jurisdiction were the archdeaconry and peculiar courts.

Probate records were usually proved in the lowest court which had jurisdiction over the whole of the area in which the relevant individual had property so in the relevant archdeacon's court if all of the holdings lay within the jurisdiction of that court, in a bishop's court if property was held in more than one archdeaconry and in the relevant prerogative court if it was spread over two or more dioceses.[5] If property was held in both provinces, the probate record was proved in the Prerogative Court of Canterbury as the more senior of the prerogative courts.[6] As wealthier people often had property in two or more bishoprics and so used one of the prerogative courts, in time it became the standard practice for well-off individuals to use the prerogative courts regardless of whether they strictly met the criteria so that, broadly speaking, probate records proved at the prerogative courts tended to be those of the most affluent members of society, those proved at the bishops' courts were broadly related to people who held lower levels of wealth and status, whilst those proved at the archdeacons' courts were generally those of individuals who had smaller holdings although there was some level of flexibility with these arrangements particularly with regard to the prerogative courts. Regardless of this apparent hierarchy of wealth, it is important to stress that the majority of the population of England during the late medieval and early modern periods did not make a will or have an inventory made of their goods so that all of the people that made these documents can be regarded as being well-off by the standards of the time, regardless of the level at which their probate was proved.

The church court arrangements were further complicated by the existence of peculiar courts which were, broadly speaking, extra territorial jurisdictions although the reasons for their existence were various. A bishop might have a jurisdiction over a parish outside his diocese, or a nobleman or landowner, or the crown, might have ownership of a parish or an estate which then had a special jurisdiction outside the diocese.[7] Some clergy also had the right to hold their own courts and these were exempt from the authority of the archdeacon and sometimes that of the bishop. In almost all cases, wills were proved in one or other of these various church courts, however, between the thirteenth and sixteenth centuries a very few wills were registered in the borough courts which operated within some of the boroughs of late medieval England. Although surviving examples are rare, two of the wills from Thetford used in this study were registered in the borough court of the town rather than the relevant church court.[8]

An illustration of how the hierarchy of church courts related to each other in Huntingdonshire is given in Figure 2.1.

Wills

In England, the practice of making a will dates back over a thousand years with a very few documents described as wills surviving from as far back as the ninth century. However, for various reasons, relatively few wills from before the mid-fifteenth

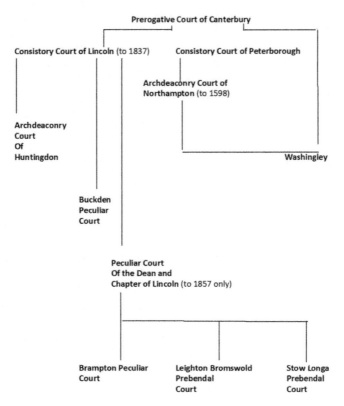

FIGURE 2.1 Probate arrangements in Huntingdonshire

Source: Image by courtesy of Alan Akeroyd, Huntingdonshire Archives

century are still in existence. From this date, courts began to register wills and this formal process led to an increased survival rate so that Nigel Goose and Nesta Evans calculated that whereas just under 36,000 indexed wills remained in existence for the fifteenth century, there were over 463,000 for the seventeenth century.[9] Exact figures have yet to be calculated; however, Amy Erickson estimated that as many as two million wills date from between the mid-sixteenth and mid-eighteenth centuries.[10] Even these may only represent a small percentage of the wills actually made since not all wills were registered and proved, whilst many probate records have not survived.[11] In addition, despite evidence showing that will-making became increasingly popular from the fifteenth century onwards, it must be remembered that it remained a minority activity.

Wills were generally made when the testator was close to death and were dictated to a scribe in the presence of witnesses.[12] Once written, a will needed to be approved by an appropriate court in order to become valid. If approved, and on payment of a fee, the will was then copied into the relevant court register and a standard written statement was added to confirm that the will had been approved by the court. The last will and testament established formally and legally how the will-maker wanted his (or less frequently her) affairs to be settled after death.

The making of a will has been described as 'the last pious act of a Christian usually near death'.[13] Nevertheless, despite this assertion of religiosity, the reasons for making a will were various. Although the original purpose had undoubtedly been spiritual, with Catholic influences encouraging gifts to the church and other acts of piety, by the early modern period will-making was less concerned with the care of the soul and more with the need to ensure that holdings of land, property and personal goods were passed on effectively to descendants. Within this broad framework, the document gave the opportunity for the will-maker to address four general areas: to take stock of possessions and to determine how and to whom they should be bequeathed (including future provision for dependents); to settle outstanding matters, both business and personal; to determine the administrative details necessary for these arrangements to be effectively undertaken; and (for the late medieval period) to make appropriate provision for the progress of the soul through purgatory.[14] Wills can therefore be used to provide evidence relating to a number of areas including wealth, possessions and holdings, occupation and occupational practices, the locality of the testator, business and social acquaintances, religion and religious practices, the family and the role of women and servants and attitudes towards charity and charitable donations.

The will of Alice West, a widow from Godmanchester, is dated 1532 (Figure 2.2). She bequeathed her soul to God, the Virgin Mary and all the holy company of heaven and asked that her body be buried in the parish church. Her religious bequests began with tithes negligently forgotten and a payment to the mother church of Lincoln. Her other bequests included clothing, plates, candlesticks, tablecloths and silver.

If the deceased did not leave a will or nominate an executor, or the will proved to be invalid, the church court could appoint an administrator by granting letters of administration. Administrators were chosen according to rules of consanguinity and next of kin. Administrators were usually required to enter into an administration bond together with at least two guarantors to indemnify the church court against liability for any maladministration. Values of administration bonds would be of a greater amount than the value of the estate and could be as much as double, therefore on their own, bonds could only suggest a very rough approximation of the worth of an estate. Administrators were required to compile an inventory within six months of the date of the grant of administration and an account within 12 months from the grant of administration.[16]

Probate inventories

The purpose of a probate inventory was to avoid disputes over estates. Inventories also helped to safeguard executors or administrators against excessive claims on the estate and provided evidence for the determination of fees due to the

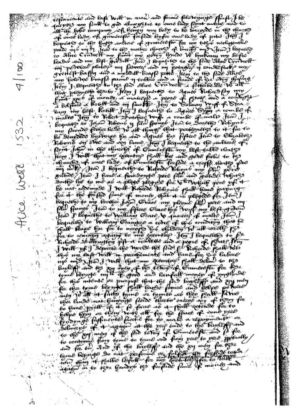

FIGURE 2.2   Extract from the will of Alice West, 1532[15]

probate court.[17] Production of an inventory as part of the process of probate and administration was required by ecclesiastical law from 1342 although some inventories were produced before this date.[18] The requirement to produce an indented inventory of the deceased's estate as a 'true and just account' was laid down in statute in 1529.[19] In 1653, the Court for the Probate of Wills and the Granting of Administrations was established in London but the court ceased to function in 1659. In theory, all probate records of persons dying in this period should be amongst the records of this civil court which are held at the National Archives, however, it appears that some executors and administrators avoided this new court because of the expense and inconvenience involved. Some wills seem to have been implemented without formal probate and others were proved retrospectively after restoration of ecclesiastical courts in 1660.[20] During the eighteenth century, the practice of exhibiting probate inventories diminished although the rate of reduction varied significantly across England reflecting local diocesan decisions rather than a central ruling.[21] For example, Winchester inventories almost disappeared from diocesan records by 1720. Keith Wrightson and David Levine also found that at Whickham in north-east England, survival of inventories was rare after the second decade of the eighteenth century.[22] John Styles asserted that in most parts of England, probate inventories survived in only very small numbers (if at all) after 1730.[23] However, a more recent survey of inventories by Ken Sneath found that even after 1750 many thousands of probate inventories were held in record offices across the country. The selected sample of inventories for the present study includes over 1,100 for the second half of the eighteenth century. The study ends in 1800 after which very few probate inventories remain.

An example of an extract from the probate inventory from 1686 relating to Marc Descow, a gentleman who lived at Bodsey House, Ramsey, Huntingdonshire is given in Figure 2.3 and his house is shown in Photo 2.1.[24]

It was the custom of the ecclesiastical courts to insist that local men make the inventory of the personal estate of the deceased. Clause 4 of the 1529 Act set

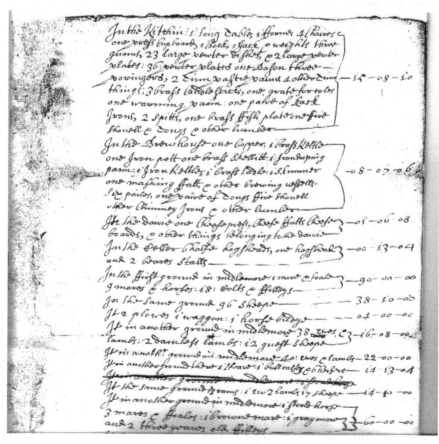

FIGURE 2.3 Extract from the probate inventory of Marc Descow, 1686[25]

PHOTO 2.1 Bodsey House, Ramsey, owned by Marc Descow in 1686

out how the inventory should be made by the executor or administrator including the qualifications of appraisers.[26] At least two appraisers were required who should have been 'honest and skilful'.[27] Carl Estabrook suggested that appraisers were ordinary people who were usually familiar with the deceased and possibly of the same status or occupation.[28] Donald Spaeth estimated that one in four men served as appraisers in Thame, Oxfordshire and suggested that appraisers had little formal training and developed a variety of classificatory procedures in recording and valuing movables, for example, goods could be recorded spatially by room, by function or by type of material such as pewter or linen.[29]

Appraisers were required to produce 'a true and perfect inventory' and were bound to value items according to the price they would fetch at auction.[30] The items to be appraised and recorded in the inventory were movable goods including livestock and crops, furnishings, cash and debts due to the deceased. Probate accounts provide insights into how goods were sold to facilitate payment of the deceased's outstanding debts, for example, accounts from Huntingdonshire recorded payments for crying the sale and for selling and looking after goods. Some accounts also include references to remuneration for appraisers and to the provision of bread and beer for them. Payments for appraising goods appeared to relate to total valuations of the deceased's goods.

Karen Grannum and Nigel Taylor stated that the appraisal was carried out usually within a few days after the death.[31] However, this was not always the case; as Wrightson pointed out, there was no time limit in law for making an inventory.[32] Thomas Turner, a Sussex shopkeeper, recorded in his diary how the appraisal of his mother's inventory, which included a considerable amount of shop goods, was not completed until over a month after death, with Turner (a beneficiary of the will) doing much of the work himself.[33] The case of Mr Piper was also reported in the diary which gave the timetable of events following his death:

> April 22 1761 Death of Mr Piper.
>
> May 20 1761 Mr Porter [vicar] and myself went to the dwelling house of the late Mr Piper and took a rough kind of inventory of the stock on the ground, household furniture and husbandry.

On 9 June Mr Porter and Turner balanced the accounts of Piper's debtors and creditors and on 11 June Turner rode to Lewes to prove Piper's will.[34] It is impossible to know how typical these two cases were but the evidence shows that appraisals could take place weeks, rather than days, after the death.

Some historians have cast doubt on the accuracy of the appraisal process. It has been argued that many appraisers were, at best, semi-literate and that their knowledge of the value of goods was inadequate so that valuations were often 'ridiculously low' and reflected what ordinary people thought possessions were worth rather than the actual value of goods.[35] Lena Orlin went further and argued that goods could be fraudulently undervalued in order to deceive creditors and protect an estate for the benefit of others. By contrast, other commentators had a higher estimate of appraisers' abilities. Jeff and Nancy Cox contended that appraisers generally valued goods realistically in terms of their sale potential so that, for example, values of cattle showed a close correspondence with market prices.[36] Mark Overton carried out a study of inventory valuations from three counties for the period 1550–1750 and found that inventory prices were robust and followed changes in market prices.[37] Probate accounts also shed light on the valuation process. If sale prices of assets fell short of their valuations, the differences could be shown as an expense in the account and where assets were sold at prices greater than valuations the 'charge' amount for which the accountant had to account to the court would be increased.

The question also arises as to whether estates of deceased persons were deliberately misrepresented to avoid payment of duty. During the eighteenth century, the state became increasingly interested in the possibility of taxing wealth at death. This culminated in the introduction of legacy duty but not until 1796. Legacy duty was, with certain exemptions, payable on estates, legacies and personal effects passed on by wills or letters of administration.[38] Prior to the introduction of legacy duty, estates were subject to probate duty.[39] When this was introduced in 1694 it was a uniform charge of 5 shillings on estates of more than £20 but the charge was doubled four years later and continued until 1779, when three scales of duty were introduced. The only estates where there was an incentive to misrepresent their value were those which were worth around the £20 threshold.

Probate accounts

Probate accounts, which set out how estates were settled, were presented to church courts by 'accountants'. Probate accounts revealed how assets were disbursed (known as the discharge) and recorded payment of funeral costs, debts owed by the deceased, wages due to employees, court fees, medical expenses, rents and payments for the care of surviving children. Probate accounts recorded payments over what could sometimes be a considerable period following the death of the deceased person. Unlike probate inventories, they were not a 'snapshot in time'. Farms continued to function and children had to be cared for.

The accountants required to submit probate accounts were either the executors of estates where there was a will, or administrators in cases of intestacy. Accountants were predominantly female; in the sample of probate accounts covered by this study, 64 per cent of accountants in Yorkshire and 58 per cent in Huntingdonshire were women. Accountants were 'charged' with the value of the estate as set out in the probate inventory. The purpose of the account was to acquit the executor of further responsibility for debts of the deceased and to ensure that the residue of the estate was distributed according to the will or, in cases of intestacy, according to law.[40]

Erickson calculated that about 43,000 accounts for England and Wales are extant which represents less than 5 per cent of the number of surviving inventories.[41] However, the total included over 10,000 accounts (24 per cent) from the Prerogative Court of Canterbury and a further 19,590 accounts (46 per cent) that relate to just two counties, Kent and Lincolnshire. Huntingdonshire, with 310 surviving usable accounts, had the seventh highest survival rate of probate accounts in England. The number of surviving accounts for Yorkshire was unknown as no index of probate accounts had been compiled but Peter Spufford recorded a figure of 536 surviving probate accounts for Yorkshire relating to the period 1606–1855.[42] By contrast, Philippa Hoskin, Archivist at the Borthwick Institute, estimated that a rather lower figure of 'about 400 accounts' survive for Yorkshire.[43] All of the Huntingdonshire surviving accounts and a random sample of 100 Yorkshire accounts were used in the present study.

An Act of Parliament in 1685 removed the powers of church courts to call for accounts. After 1685 accounts were only to be created at the instigation of legatees, relatives or creditors of the deceased.[44] The number of probate accounts was therefore strongly biased by time period. Ian Mortimer studied probate accounts in four of the five counties with the highest survival rates of probate accounts, i.e. East Kent, West Sussex, Berkshire and Wiltshire.[45] In all four counties approximately two thirds of surviving probate accounts related to the first half of the seventeenth century. All four counties had substantially fewer accounts after 1685 when the power of the church courts to call for accounts was removed. Huntingdonshire had 93 accounts for the period 1680–84 but only 24 for the years 1685–89 (Table 2.1).

TABLE 2.1 Surviving probate accounts from five counties

	Huntingdonshire		East Kent		West Sussex		Berkshire		Wiltshire	
	No.	%	No.	%	No.	%	No.	%	No.	%
1600–1629	3	1	4,808	43	400	36	696	45	459	35
1630–1649	6	2	2,319	21	307	28	382	25	418	32
1650–1659	1	0	6	0	22	2	9	0	6	0
1660–1669	1	0	993	9	53	5	125	7	39	3
1670–1679	122	39	1,413	13	183	17	181	12	231	18
1680–1684	93	30	754	7	121	11	103	7	73	6
1685–1689	24	7	258	2	9	1	32	2	37	3
1690–1719	36	12	538	5	4	0	28	2	40	3
1720–1749	14	5	0	0	0	0	0	0	0	0
1750–1799	10	3	0	0	0	0	0	0	0	0
Total	310	100	11,089	100	1,099	100	1,556	100	1,303	100

Very few accounts survived for the first half of the seventeenth century in both Huntingdonshire and Yorkshire and two thirds of extant accounts in Huntingdonshire related to the period 1670–84.

Other sources

Wills and probate inventories were used in this study to provide both quantitative and qualitative evidence. Their use is supported by a range of other evidence, particularly from qualitative sources, in an attempt to construct a more robust picture of consumption patterns during this period.

For the late medieval period, a range of manorial records were used. As with probate records, those used included both manuscript sources and printed manorial records. Manorial court rolls often included details about marketing within the manor and, in particular, information about the nature of goods being traded. Whilst manorial accounts primarily detailed the annual income and expenditure of the manor, those from more urbanised manors often included information relating to marketing such as receipts from shops and stalls. Manorial records of rural manors generally contained limited information about trade and commerce but often included, for example, details of household items given by poorer peasants as heriot payments such as the brass pot worth 16d received by the manorial lord of Norton in Hertfordshire following the death of John Healder in 1413.[46]

Purchasing records in the form of a range of household accounts were used for both the late medieval and early modern periods which contained details about various aspects of the lives of households. Particular use was made of one of the three extant Registers of accounts for Thetford Priory, spanning the period 1482 to 1540.[47] Other qualitative material was used including diaries.

Seven are used in this study, those of Ralph Josselin, John Evelyn, James Wood-forde, Thomas Turner, Samuel Pepys, Thomas Marchant and Sarah Hurst.

Problems with sources

General problems with sources

The use of primary sources present a number of problems which can be summarised as: difficulties associated with using evidence from documents created for very different purposes to that for which they are being used; concerns about the incomplete survival of records; bias, particularly since most of the sources used predominantly related to more affluent members of society; and issues relating to reliability and the fact that statistics collected during this period were for immediate administrative and fiscal purposes and were often at best vague estimates.[48] Although these issues are general and relate to most primary sources from this period, a number of other issues relate specifically to wills and inventories.

Problems with wills

Some historians have been critical of the use of wills as a source and this has led to an ongoing debate about the validity of testamentary evidence.[49] Late medieval wills in particular have been viewed as being solely an expression of faith and a means of ordering an estate after death to meet religious obligations and endeavour to secure a safe passage through purgatory, so that their value as evidence for any other purpose has been disputed.[50] Such criticisms should not be ignored; however, wills do contain valuable evidence and have been used by a number of historians to very good effect in exploring and enhancing our understanding of a wide range of religious and social themes.[51]

Whilst the original purpose of wills had undoubtedly been religious, there were changes to both their structure and purpose during the late medieval period which reflected social changes of the time.[52] A testator making his or her will until the end of the fourteenth century would probably have created two separate documents: a testament, which stipulated the intended disposal of movable goods in the form of personal property, chattels, money and debts; and a will which dealt with real estate. During the fifteenth century, the two documents increasingly merged into one which became the 'testament and last will' although some testators continued to make two separate documents well into this period, particularly if they had a large amount of real estate to dispose of such as, for example, the gentleman Robert Rokewoode of Thetford, who made his testament and will in 1487.[53] Prior to 1450, wills were almost always written in Latin but in the following half century, they were increasingly written in English so that only a few wills made after 1500 were in Latin. In very few cases, wills were written in a combination of English and Latin, particularly if a distinction was made between the testament and the will. In the case of Robert Rokewoode referred to previously, the testament was written in Latin and the will in English despite the two documents having the same date and other indications that they were created at the same time and were written by the same scribe. By the end of the fifteenth century, not only were most wills written in English, but they almost always took the form of one document which dealt with the disposal of both lands and goods, usually in an order which reflected the earlier distinction between the two types of property. From the early fifteenth century, wills also increasingly included personal and business-related aspects such as provisions for maintaining dependents, instructions for the disposal of business assets and directives for the collection of outstanding debts.

Wills can be used to provide evidence of consumption since they often refer, to some extent, to the belongings of the testator, and may also include quite detailed descriptions of these items. Goods which might be referred to included personal items in the form of clothing and jewellery, household items such as cooking utensils, linen and furniture, and tools and utensils associated with the trade of the testator. Bequests of such items generally followed a standard pattern so that a recipient was identified and then the goods they were to be given were listed. The goods bequeathed to each recipient were usually grouped by type so that, for example, bedding items were listed together, as were items of kitchenware, clothing, jewellery, etc. Further information about the item was often given such as the colour or material from which it was made (particularly clothing), its size, where in the house it was sited, what ranking it had amongst similar objects, or how much it cost. So, for example, Nicholas Edwardes of Thetford gave 'a fetherbedde somtyme Sir Thomas Wynnynghame', 'my duble Cowntre standinge in the parlor' and 'my best velvett dublett'.[54]

Wills do, therefore, provide some evidence of the ownership of material goods, however, their use in this context presents problems. Clive Burgess drew attention to the fact that it cannot be assumed that the absence of a reference to something in a will confirmed that it had not existed and that other arrangements ensured that the main beneficiaries understood their dues without items being specifically named and identified in the will.[55] In the case of material items, many were probably simply given away, either before or after death, as there was no requirement that such items be included in a will. In addition, wills often include frustrating cover-all terms such as 'all my goods of household' or 'goods moveable and immoveable' so that it is impossible to identify exactly what goods a testator was gifting. In the context of this study, it is accepted without question that wills do not provide the same level of affirmation of the ownership — or non-ownership — of goods as is given by probate inventories; however, what is beyond question is that wills do contain a substantial amount of evidence about the different domestic possessions that will-makers owned and can be used to shed light on consumption during this period.

In this connection, it is worth making a few observations about the recording of key luxury items which suggests that they were often included in a will if they were owned by the testator. By the end of the Middle Ages, a petty form of conspicuous consumption appears to have emerged amongst some will-makers so that certain high-end items were specifically identified if they were owned by a testator; in particular silver goods and featherbeds appear to have been items which testators were keen to refer to in their wills. This practice was identified by Karine Dauteuille in her study of Norwich wills, whilst in his work on early modern inventories Ken Sneath noted that possession of certain items was considered by testators and their contemporaries to be an indicator of wealth, taste and status.[56] It was these items which were the most likely to be identified with descriptive phrases such as those referred to earlier in the case of Nicholas Edwardes which, again, suggests that testators took the most care to ensure that these goods were bequeathed in accordance with their wishes. Dauteuille also noted that the more valuable an item, the more complete was the description given of it.[57]

In relation to the use of all-inclusive phrases such as 'all my goods of household' referred to earlier, some testators include such cover-all phrases, but then proceed to specify what goods these vague definitions included so that Isabella Sprot bequeathed 'all the ymplementes of my howshold' to her sister Joan Sare in 1487 and listed these as being:

> my beddyng with coverlytes, blankettes, shetes with all the hooll, the secund braspot and braspan, spetes, awnderns, pewter vessell with all the hole tabyll, formes, tressell & bordes with all the holl ymplementes with hempe & flex & with all the holw howsold.[58]

Examples such as this show that these terms were used to refer to a range of basic household goods, but not exceptional or unusual items. It therefore seems reasonable to suggest that in most cases if a testator owned luxury or untypical goods, he or she was likely to identify them within the will. As will be considered in more detail within this study, the one important exception to this was the gentry who appear to have been much less inclined to identify personal and household possessions and placed a far greater emphasis on recording bequests of property.

Whilst wills were generally expressed in the first person singular, they were not written by the testator in person.[59] The identity of the writer is very rarely revealed; however, the standard approach and phraseology suggests that wills were written by scribes who had some expertise in dealing with legal documents and, in the case of pre-1500 wills, were Latin-literate. In the late Middle Ages, these were usually clerics and this has led to the claim that the church had a significant say in the disposal of assets and testators were not free to make their own choices; for example, Virginia Bainbridge suggested that wills were 'snapshots' taken by those in authority.[60] Although clerics undoubtedly had a major influence on the process of will-making and on the destination of many bequests, many wills contain statements which are so personal that they could only have been specified by the testator. Whilst many of these are expressions of faith which may have been directed by the will writer, others include declarations of affection, detailed instructions on how the testator wished to be remembered after death and specific instructions to executors and others which could only be made with knowledge of their characters and abilities, such as the stipulation made by Robert Wade of Coggeshall in 1561 that his sister-in-law 'shall not meddle within my house at no time nor with nothing in no wise'.[61] Such statements suggest that testators did play a role in the making of their wills and expected them to incorporate some level of individuality. In the context of this study, it is also worth making the point that even if it was exerted, clerical influence could not affect the material goods owned by testator, only the eventual destination of these goods.

A final, but significant, problem associated with the use of testamentary evidence is the fact that wills were only ever made by a limited proportion of the population, so that will-making was always a minority activity generally undertaken by three broad and often mutually inclusive groups – the wealthier classes, men and older members of society. Although the use of wills to devise land was encouraged by the Statute of Wills of 1540 (which enabled landowners to leave land to whoever they wished rather than as determined by rules of descent such as primogeniture) and subsequent legislation, it could still be passed on by common law or manorial custom, whilst personal goods were often distributed prior to death without any need for a formal will.[62] Consequently, a large proportion of the population relied on these methods to pass on their goods and property and never made a will. Inevitably, given that it was the wealthiest classes that held the largest amounts of property and were most concerned to ensure that it was effectively bequeathed, these were the groups that were most likely to respond to the Statute of Wills and, as a consequence, the lower tiers of society were severely underrepresented amongst will-makers. Not only were wills largely (but not exclusively) the preserve of the upper tiers of society but, in addition, there was a strong gender bias so that women made wills far less frequently than their male counterparts. Very few wills were made for married women prior to the Married Women's Property Act of 1882 because married women's possessions were treated as the property of their husband. Married women could only write a will with their husband's approval so that most of the limited number of female will-makers were widows and wills from married women or women who can be identified as never married are especially infrequent. Finally, as wills were usually made at the very end of life, they were generally made by older people who, again, were not representative of wider society.

Whilst acknowledging that there are problems associated with the use of wills, the fact remains that they can be used to provide important evidence about the consumption of material goods and how patterns of ownership changed over time. Particular care has been taken in this study to ensure that testamentary material is used carefully and in an appropriate manner: firstly, as has been noted earlier, it has been used in conjunction with evidence from other sources; secondly, it has been aggregated to identify common themes and practices; and finally, it has been used as both a qualitative and a quantitative source and, in those instances where quantitative testamentary evidence is given, it is presented as tentative. This careful approach has enabled reasonable suppositions to be made and explored and ideas to be developed even if it is difficult to establish firm conclusions.

Problems with probate inventories

Discussions of probate inventories often begin with their deficiencies as historical sources. These problems were set out by Margaret Spufford in 'The limitations of the probate inventory' and more recently by Lena Cowen Orlin, in 'Fictions of the early modern English probate inventory'.[63] It is important therefore to acknowledge the limitations of probate inventories at the outset.

Firstly, it is not possible to measure an individual's wealth using only probate inventories as a source. Inventories recorded moveable assets including leases of property but not real estate as this was outside the jurisdiction of the ecclesiastical courts.[64] Thus it was possible for a person to bequeath far greater amounts in their will than they possessed in moveable assets according to their probate inventory. Items bequeathed in wills were sometimes omitted from inventories.[65] One purpose of inventories was to help executors wind up an estate by paying off creditors through the sale of goods.[66] Items already bequeathed were not available to executors for potential sale. The more serious omission from probate inventories is debts of the deceased person due to other people. Probate inventories usually recorded gross moveable wealth rather than net wealth after debts owing by the deceased had been taken into account. Debts of the deceased due to others appeared in probate accounts but these accounts survive in much smaller numbers than probate inventories.

Inventories only recorded goods owned at death and were therefore only a snapshot at a moment in time. Goods may have been recent acquisitions or owned for several years. They may not have been purchased as new goods but inherited or acquired from the secondhand market. Overton argued that consumption activities of individuals varied considerably throughout their lifetime.[67] The age distribution of probate inventory samples will therefore influence patterns of consumption calculated from that source. Inventoried wealth may also be related to age at death. Overton *et al.* matched inventories from Milton, Kent to accounts, wills and parish registers to reveal ages of the deceased and their offspring. They found that for the period 1580–1711, the age distribution of 351 inventoried persons was close to that for England as a whole. This suggests that if the parish of Milton was at all typical, inventories were more representative of the age and household structure of the population than is popularly assumed.[68] By contrast, Lyn Boothman found that the age distribution of inventoried persons was biased. She completed a family reconstitution of Long Melford and calculated age at death for 81 people from a sample of 94 Long Melford probate inventories.[69] Whilst this is not a large sample, it produced a mean age of death of 58 and a median of 59.

One benefit of qualitative material is that it might include records of economic activity over time. A model is Alan Macfarlane's analysis of Ralph Josselin's diary even though the diary is a strongly biased source as Josselin was a very affluent clergyman. Josselin's diary reveals a problem of using records that are a snapshot in time. Resources do not pass between generations only at death; for example, the diary records that only a month before he died, Josselin gave his daughter Rebecka a dowry of £500 but in his will, he left her only 10s.[70] He was not alone in this practice. John Wallington senior, a London turner in the seventeenth century, had given away most of his 'fortune' by the time he made his will in 1635.[71]

A distinction between high- and lower-quality goods was often not made in inventories. One indicator of quality is valuation, but consumer items recorded in probate inventories were not often individually priced in sufficient numbers to draw meaningful conclusions. The one exception was clocks. However, results from Amsterdam inventories suggested that differences in the value of goods were greater than the differences in the number of items analysed by social rank.[72]

Probate inventories were sometimes incomplete or lacking in their description of goods. Certain goods, particularly low value items, were not valued or included within catch-all phrases such as 'other lumber' or 'hustlement'. Patterns of recording items could change over time, particularly when there was a significant change in the value of those goods. In 15 locations, recorded book ownership declined from 28 per cent in 1630–59 to only 11 per cent after 1750. In view of the substantial increase in books published, this is extremely unlikely to reflect ownership levels and is much more the result of recording practice. David Vaisey wrote that statements based on inventory evidence often suggested that most households possessed a Bible and only a small percentage possessed anything else. He contended that appraisers might be relied on to recognise Bibles, but they were likely to have had neither the time, inclination or education to note down any others.[73]

Farmers' inventories sometimes only recorded details of animals and crops together with their values. It is possible to omit these obviously truncated inventories from the population of cases available for selection. Overton et al. discussed this issue at some length and also demonstrated how the use of logistic regression could be used to predict the likelihood of a particular item being recorded in an inventory.[74] Whilst some cases gave clear indications of truncation, other cases were not so clear cut and this is an area for further research. There was also evidence that inventories were less fully recorded in the eighteenth century, so increases in ownership of goods in this period were probably even higher than the data suggests.

Certain items were sometimes grouped together with other goods and at other times listed separately. For example, sheets were commonly included amongst linen but at other times separately identified. Crops such as wheat and barley were usually separately identified but, in some inventories, were listed only as 'crops in the field'.

Even spelling and punctuation can present problems of interpretation. Careful transcription of inventories is important if data analysis of inventories is to be robust. Clocks could easily be confused with crocks (pans or pots). The 'clocke' in Thomas Coll's inventory (probably 1606) and again in Margaret Pyd's inventory (1559) were clearly cloaks.[75] Chairs could be confused with chains. An inventory for Thomas Ward (1765) listed a 'horse bridle and saddle'.[76] This could be interpreted as just a bridle and a saddle or the phrase may have meant that there was a horse present as well. Valuations can often assist in the correct interpretation of such cases.

Finally, the issue of bias must be addressed. Bias in historical documents occurs for various reasons. Most were written by the literate for a particular purpose and frequently excluded significant sections of the community. Wills and probate inventories were socially biased documents, as they were almost exclusively produced by people at the upper end of the social spectrum. Females were underrepresented in the records as property of women became the possession of their husbands upon marriage. As they were likely to be produced towards the end of life (wills), or after death (inventories), they were also generally representative of older members of society. In addition, Sebastian Keibek and Leigh Shaw-Taylor recently found that the by-employed were also more likely to be probated than those with only one source of income.[77]

Based on the probability of being inventoried, Keibek has also produced a new methodology aimed at neutralising the wealth bias of probate inventories.[78] He argued that this methodology enabled the researcher to extend results from just the inventoried population to all households. Using data from Cheshire and Lancashire, Keibek showed that ownership levels of consumer goods of the inventoried population were considerably higher than the whole population, particularly in the case of inventoried labourers.[79] Whilst Craig Muldrew's work and this book have provided much more evidence for acquisition of goods by labourers, it is not contested that they represent only a small, relatively wealthy proportion of all labourers.[80] Keibek's methodology will no doubt be tested more widely but offers a promising approach for future research.

There is therefore a debate about what precisely is being measured by using data recorded in probate inventories. Like Overton et al., this book does not attempt to consider consumption patterns beyond the inventoried population. It is fully recognised that there is an inherent bias in using probate inventories, for they largely relate to the 'middling sort'. Whilst the term has been much debated, it does have meaning. Henry French concluded that it represented those situated between the landed gentry and the dependent poor.[81] The overwhelming majority of those who were probated fell into French's group.

Historians should be aware of the problems in interpreting historical sources, including probate records. Orlin was correct to warn of the dangers of using inventories with faith rather than scepticism. Probate inventories should not be used without reference to other documents including wills, probate accounts, tax records and parish registers to aid interpretation.[82] Despite all the difficulties, inventories still represent 'a most remarkable window into the daily life of the early modern household'.[83]

Problems with qualitative sources

The qualitative sources used for this study present other challenges; for example, the household accounts are those of high-status families and their consumption patterns are far from typical of the wider population. Nonetheless, many of the purchases made by these households were also made by members of other social groups so the household accounts do provide useful details about the costs and provenance of certain consumer items. Although the diaries are those of people with a less elevated social status, it is equally difficult to argue that they record typical lifestyles; each diary relates to only a single individual and, with the exception of that of Sarah Hurst, they are written by men. Once again, however, the diaries still provide valuable information about many of the goods selected for study in this volume such as tea-drinking, silver goods and clothing.

Numbers of wills

The wills used for this study date from 1430 to 1579 and were the probate records of testators who lived in a range of locations including both rural and urban settlements. Wills were made before the fifteenth century; however, as most courts only began to register wills from this date, the survival of pre-fifteenth-century wills is poor and patchy. For this study, it was only possible to find a very few wills for the period prior to 1430, but from this date onwards, wills were available in increasingly large numbers so that this was chosen as a suitable point at which aggregated testamentary evidence could be considered to have some validity for the exploration of consumption. Although a few inventories were also often made during this period, survival is very limited, particularly when compared to wills. However, from the 1529 Act (see p.31 and Note 36), extant probate inventories increased in numbers so that by the middle of the sixteenth century they become a viable source for the study of consumption. For an overlapping period in the second half of the sixteenth century, both wills and inventories have been included in the study. After 1600, probate inventories have been used in preference to wills, although related wills still provided some supporting details.

In order to study changes in consumption patterns over time, the wills were analysed chronologically using 30-year periods (Table 2.2). Broadly speaking, the number of surviving wills increased on an almost yearly basis from the early fifteenth century, although there were fluctuations which probably reflected periods of epidemic disease and an increase in the number of people making wills. The years 1479–80 and 1499–1500 witnessed very high levels of will-making and can almost certainly be associated with recurrences of the plague.[84]

The numbers and locations of the testators are indicated in Table 2.2.

TABLE 2.2 Will sample by county

	1430–59	1460–89	1490–1519	1520–49	1550–79	Totals
Cambs	17	26	24	1	N/A	68
Essex	40	4	2	1	79	126
Herts	N/A	206	105	20	61	392
Hunts	N/A	15	16	11	19	61
Norfolk	17	62	82	79	15	255
Northants	N/A	43	4	13	17	77
Suffolk	75	131	128	131	72	537
Totals	149	487	361	256	263	1,516
Percentage	9.9	32.1	23.8	16.9	17.3	100

Will sample

The will sample consists of a total of 1,516 wills (Table 2.2). Many wills were initially used as one of the sources for the thesis undertaken by Joanne Sear on trade and consumption in certain East Anglian market towns during the late medieval period.[85] As part of this doctoral study, all the extant wills of people who resided in the towns of Thetford (Norfolk), Newmarket and Mildenhall (Suffolk) during this period were analysed together with a number of wills made by individuals who could be identified as having been associated with these towns. This latter group included people who resided in east Cambridgeshire, just across the county boundary from Suffolk.

For the purposes of the present study, other wills were also used. In the first instance, the wills from the three initial study towns were supplemented with other wills from people who resided in the three counties of Cambridgeshire, Norfolk and Suffolk to make the will sample more representative of these three East Anglian counties. This included wills of people who lived in larger urban settlements, such as Bury St Edmunds, Norwich and Cambridge, and rural areas which did not have such easy access to the marketing facilities provided by towns. The Cambridgeshire wills were also supplemented by wills from Huntingdonshire. A number of these wills were from published collections, but the majority were from extant will registers held by the National Archives and local record offices.

All four counties were predominantly agricultural during the late Middle Ages; however, East Anglia encompasses a wide range of soil types and landscape characteristics which resulted in different patterns of production during this period. Much of East Anglia falls into one of a number of regions of good-quality soil including the wet Fenlands, the South Norfolk and High Suffolk Claylands, the 'Good Sands' of north-west Norfolk and the Bedfordshire and Cambridgeshire Claylands.[86] Although these regions practiced varying levels of mixed farming, the emphasis was very much on arable and the production of a range of grains including wheat, barley, rye and oats (and mixes of these grains). By contrast, the Breckland region, in which the two original study towns of Mildenhall and Thetford lie, is an area of poor, sandy soil with under-lying chalk which combine to make the region dry and almost lacking in any form of natural drainage networks. Consequently, although arable farming was important in the Middle Ages, pastoral farming predominated with large areas of the region given over to sheep flocks and rabbit warrens.[87] Newmarket and Cambridge both lie in the region known as East Anglian chalk which, whilst not as poor as the Breckland region, is also characterised by low-quality soil.[88] During this period this region was mainly used for sheep farming although arable crops were also grown, including barley and the high value *crocus sativis* (saffron crocus).

Each of these counties contained a range of urban settlements. Charter or custom evidence showed that sizeable, although varying, numbers of markets were founded in each of these four East Anglian counties prior to the Black Death and that commerce and urban development was strong.[89] Although many markets did not survive the economic turmoil after 1350, by the end of the medieval period three of these four counties contained at least one significant urban settlement (Cambridge and Ely in Cambridgeshire; Lynn and Norwich in Norfolk; and Ipswich and Bury St Edmunds in Suffolk), whilst all of them also incorporated a number of smaller but significant towns. Markets were regularly held at all of these places and at a range of less urbanised settlements. East Anglia lies in relatively close proximity to London, which was as much a dominant capital in the late Middle Ages as today, and there were strong trade links between the metropolis and the main urban settlements of the region. In add-ition, the growing importance of the woollen cloth trade centred on south Suf-folk and north Essex led to particularly strong links between these areas and London which Mark Bailey noted were not only based on commerce but were also social, political and legal.[90]

The second stage of this process included adding wills from a range of other counties. Essex and Hertfordshire were chosen partly because many wills from these counties were available in a published form, but also because this enabled the study to explore whether the proximity of these two counties to London, with its greater range of goods and services, resulted in different patterns of ownership of goods.[91] Both of these counties contained a number of urban settlements and regions which prospered in the later Middle Ages, for example the areas of north Essex associated with the cloth trade, and areas which declined during the period, especially north-east Hertfordshire which experienced severe agrarian recession and a high level of deserted medieval villages.[92] Wills from Northamptonshire were also included – once again, a number of these published or available online – but the county also provided a useful contrast in that it was comparatively rural, particularly in the north of the county.[93] Most urban settlements were located towards the south such as the borough town of Northampton which had been a significant trading centre in the twelfth century with good transport connections, but which was in a period of decline from the late thirteenth century to the end of the Middle Ages.[94]

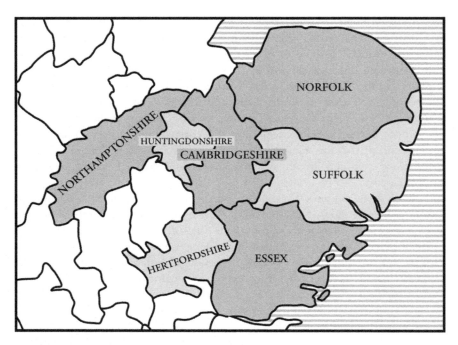

MAP 2.1 Eastern counties, by courtesy of Graeme Fayers

In summary, these counties were chosen because they exhibited various characteristics which suggested that people living within them were likely to show some propensity to consume such as evidence of urbanisation and market towns. In his work on urban density in the late medieval period, Stephen Rigby estimated this for three of the counties chosen for this study.[95] Cambridgeshire was just below both the average of 15.6 per cent for his study counties for 1377 and the average of 13.7 per cent for 1524, and Northamptonshire was also slightly below the average in 1377, but just above it in 1524. By contrast, late medieval Suffolk was the most urbanised county of England with 41 per cent of taxpayers in 1377 residing in settlements which could be regarded as urban and 36.7 per cent in 1524.[96] Although the urban density of the other counties is harder to identify, all contained towns which were ranked highly in terms of taxable wealth. Indeed, Norfolk included three towns which ranked in the top 20 in 1524/25 (Norwich ranked first, Lynn sixth and Great Yarmouth 18th).[97] Whilst Hertfordshire only included one town which ranked in the top 50 (St Albans at 31st), the very high number of small towns within the county was such that as much as 20 per cent of the population may have lived in an urban settlement.[98]

The probate inventory sample

The inventory sample consists of two groups. The first comprises three counties: Huntingdonshire, Yorkshire and Dorset. These inventories were selected samples and analysed chronologically using the same 30-year periods employed by Overton *et al.* The three counties were mainly selected because of the number of surviving inventories from these counties after 1750, crucial for evaluating Neil McKendrick's thesis of a consumer revolution in the third quarter of the eighteenth century. Huntingdonshire also had large numbers of labourers' inventories providing an insight into those towards the lower end of the social spectrum.

The results of the study of Cornwall and Kent by Overton *et al.* were included for comparison. This immense study included 4,119 inventories from Cornwall and 3,979 from Kent. However, the study concluded in 1750 and there were relatively few inventories from Kent from the 1730s (84) and 1740s (27) included in the sample. Despite Overton *et al.*'s reference to 'few inventories surviving after 1750' in Kent, in fact more than 600 survive for the second half of the eighteenth century and data from a sample of over 250 post-1750 Kent inventories are included in this volume.[99] The analysis of the post-1750 Kent inventories was carried out by Peter Thompson for his undergraduate dissertation under the supervision of one of the authors and his results have been incorporated into the present volume.[100]

Huntingdonshire has a rich legacy of surviving probate records with approximately 5,000 probate inventories for the years 1601–1800. The 1419 Huntingdonshire inventories selected for analysis (28 per cent of the total) represented all of the surviving and legible seventeenth- and eighteenth-century inventories from 20 selected parishes, together with all surviving inventories for labourers in the county. Parishes were chosen to reflect a balance of urban and rural settlements. Five parishes with market towns were included which were located in all of the three ecological regions of the county: Huntingdon, St Ives and Godmanchester in the Ouse Valley; Ramsey in the Fenlands; and Kimbolton in the clay uplands. Fifteen rural parishes also reflected a geographical spread of the county (Map 2.2).

Huntingdonshire had seven small towns in the 1670s but none had populations of more than 2,500 people.[101] The county town of Huntingdon had less than a thousand people in the first part of the seventeenth century and according to John Morrill was a 'small and unprosperous market town'.[102] Celia Fiennes agreed that Huntingdon was 'but a small Shire town' in 1697 and in 1771 George Culley thought it was 'a poor town to be the chief of the county'.[103] Nevertheless, it was the social, judicial and ecclesiastical centre of the county and its people left more valuable household goods than any other of Huntingdonshire's parishes. Huntingdon's location on the Old North Road and the development of turnpike roads gave it strategic importance and helped to revive its prosperity. St Ives, the largest market town in the county, had a very good market for fatted cattle, sheep and provisions.[104]

Ramsey had been economically dependent upon its abbey and potentially faced ruin with its closure.[105] However, its market which 'lies so convenient for the

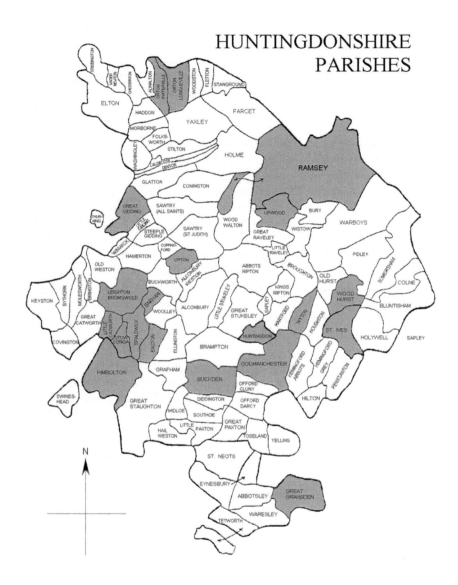

MAP 2.2 Huntingdonshire selected parishes, template by courtesy of Alan Akeroyd, Huntingdonshire Archives

sale of fat and lean cattle which must be brought thither since the draining of the Fens' prospered.[106] Godmanchester had a population of approximately 1,200 in 1674 based on hearth tax returns. There were many tradesmen and craftsmen living in this small town.[107] Even before the Black Death, Godmanchester had a number of tradesmen including carpenters, butchers, bakers, millers, tanners, weavers, candle makers, masons and fishermen.[108] Kimbolton was dominated by the castle owned by the earl of Manchester, one of the great landowners of the county. It was the smallest of the five market towns selected for study, but it had a weekly market and two annual fairs in July and August. The other two Huntingdonshire market towns were St Neots and Yaxley.

Huntingdonshire remained primarily an agricultural county during the period covered by this book. The shallow valleys of the Ouse and the Nene were predominantly used for arable with some dairying and rearing of livestock. On the clay uplands, soil was heavier and in places, especially in the west of the county, arable had often been converted to pasture. The middle of the seventeenth century brought great changes in the Fens. Between 1640 and 1650, the Adventurers led by the duke of Bedford drained the levels which proved a significant boost to the economy. Farming in seventeenth-century Huntingdonshire was also boosted by the growth of the London market.[109]

A major problem of selecting the sample of 1,522 inventories in Yorkshire was that unlike Huntingdonshire, the number of surviving records in Yorkshire was unknown and there was no catalogue. Yorkshire records were filed chronologically. There was at least one large box of inventories for each month of each year, so considerably more than a thousand boxes in total for the eighteenth century. The sampling strategy adopted in Yorkshire was therefore to take sample years and select all inventories that had not been significantly damaged for that year for three selected deaneries.

The selected inventories from Yorkshire came from three deaneries: Pontefract, Rydale (or Rydall) and Holderness, including the town and county of Kingston upon Hull. Pontefract Deanery (Map 2.3) in West Riding was the heartland of industrial change. The West Riding was the most populated and prosperous part of Yorkshire and about half of the county's population lived there in 1672. By the end of the eighteenth century, two out of every three Yorkshiremen lived in West Riding.[110] The growing importance of the rapidly industrialising parts of West Riding, such as Halifax, Bradford, Huddersfield and Wakefield, was reflected in the probate inventory evidence. These four textile towns represented a third of the inventory sample from Yorkshire. Rydale Deanery in North Riding comprised of high moors and dales and its economy was dominated by agriculture. Rydale was a mainly rural area with several market towns including Malton and Helmsley. Holderness Deanery covered most of the claylands on the plain in the south-east part of East Riding.[111] Holderness was almost an island during the Middle Ages and experienced drainage problems and coastal erosion but subsequent drainage schemes enabled it to develop both arable and pastoral farming.[112] The town and county of Kingston upon Hull, adjacent to Holderness Deanery, had two parishes. The port of Hull was important because of its links with West Yorkshire and its role in the export of textiles. As a result of this trade it became the fourth largest port after London, Liverpool and Bristol.[113] The Yorkshire inventory sample included 100 inventories from Hull.

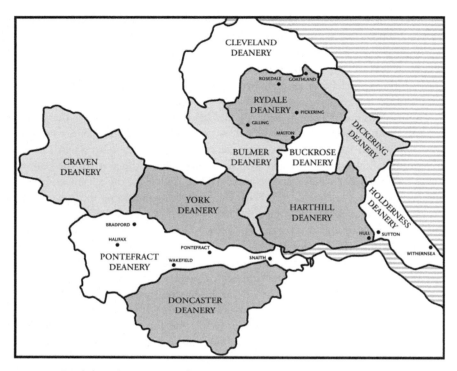

MAP 2.3 Yorkshire, by courtesy of Graeme Fayers

Dorset is a large county from Cranborne in the east to Lyme Regis on the border with Devon (Map 2.4). When John Speed produced his map of 'Dorset-shyre' in 1610 he was impressed by the agricultural potential of the county for both arable farming in the central zone and pastoral farming in both the north and south.[114] Dorset had 18 market towns including Dorchester, Wimborne, Sherborne and Shaftesbury and some small ports such as Bridport, Weymouth, Poole and Lyme Regis. Daniel Defoe described Dorchester as 'populous, tho' not large, the streets broad, but the buildings old'.[115] It had markets and fairs and a charter. It was the county town, a parliamentary borough and where the assize met but had a population of only about 2,000 at the beginning of the seventeenth century.[116] Dorset has large numbers of surviving inventories from the eighteenth century, including the second largest number of post-1750 inventories in the present sample. Over 1,000 inventories, which may represent around two thirds of the total, have been sampled from parishes across the county.[117]

Published inventories

The collection of probate inventories from Huntingdonshire, Yorkshire and Dorset has been supplemented by data from published inventories.

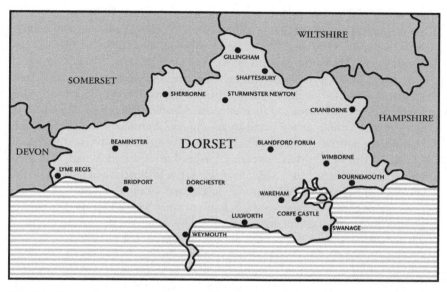

MAP 2.4 Dorset, by courtesy of Graeme Fayers

Urban inventories

As a port which engaged in international trade, particularly the import of spices and wines and dealing in English wool and woollens, Southampton had been 'one of the great trading centres of England'.[118] However, it was already in serious decline by 1524 when it was counted among the 30 largest provincial towns in England, and this continued throughout the sixteenth century as international trade shifted to London.[119] According to Colin Platt, the population of the town was around 4,200 by the end of the century.[120]

The Southampton inventories came mainly from the ancient parishes located within the walls of the city.[121] A fifth of the published inventories were for merchants and shopkeepers which reflected the importance of trade in the settlement. The median inventory value of the whole sample was £28 which was much higher than that for the Surrey sixteenth-century inventories (£20). The median value of the 15 sixteenth-century merchant inventories in Southampton was £100.

Bristol was a trading centre with a mint in the eleventh century and by 1334 was the second wealthiest town after London.[122] Following decline in the fourteenth and fifteenth centuries, Bristol developed trade with the New World and the Iberian Peninsula at the beginning of the early modern period. It was a hub of a trading triangle which took goods to Africa and slaves to the American colonies. The gild of Merchant Adventurers stood at the heart of the city's mercantile community.[123] At the beginning of the seventeenth century, Bristol had a population of around 12,000 and, despite great loss of life by plague, this grew to about 20,000 at the end of the century.[124] At this time it was a significant provincial centre and the third largest city in England after London and Norwich.[125] Bristol approximately doubled in size between 1700 and 1750 and overtook Norwich to become the country's second city with a population of over 58,000 by 1801.[126]

The 321 selected Bristol inventories were transcribed by Edwin and Stella George and published in three volumes by the Bristol Record Society.[127] They represent the city of Bristol and its immediate suburbs. They were chosen 'to be a representative sample of the occupations and social groups to be found within the Bristol inventories' and covered about 9 per cent of extant inventories from the City of Bristol.[128] Most inventories related to tradesmen and craftsmen, including six from merchants, and very few related to agricultural ranks.

Lincoln had been the third largest city in England during the thirteenth century and was the seventh wealthiest 'town' in England when assessed for the Lay Subsidy in 1334. This period of prosperity was followed by significant downturn: the Black Death and repeated epidemics of the fourteenth century led to long-term decline; and during the sixteenth and seventeenth centuries the city suffered as a result of the dissolution of the monasteries, the diminution of its textile trade and the impact of the Civil War.[129] In 1584, William Lambarde commented that the decayed city was 'little better than ... a common market town' and in 1661 its population was estimated to have fallen to around 3,500 although its economy revived in the eighteenth century.[130] The 60 Lincoln probate inventories were selected from 590 that survived for 13 parishes between 1661 and 1714.[131] They were urban parishes and the profile of occupations was similar to those for Bristol.

By 1603, the population of Ipswich exceeded that of Lincoln and was approaching 5,000, despite a severe outbreak of plague in 1597–98.[132] By the late seventeenth century, Ipswich's population had grown to around 10,000 and it was the ninth largest town in England. By this time, it was a commercially active port town involved in the export of cloth and in the Newcastle to London coal trade, whilst its wide range of goods and services were not simply marketed within the town itself, but were also traded with its hinterland. The collection of inventories published for the Suffolk Records Society was the earliest surviving collection for the inhabitants of Ipswich found in the archives of the Archdeaconry of Suffolk and the Consistory Court of the Diocese of Norwich. The inventories covered the years from 1583 to 1631 and related mainly to tradesmen and craftsmen.[133]

Marlborough in Wiltshire was important as a coaching town in the second half of the seventeenth century when it was the second largest settlement in the county after Salisbury.[134] In 1676, it had a population of a little over 3,000 which placed it among the largest 100 towns in Britain.[135] The two Marlborough parishes fell within the peculiar jurisdiction of the Bishop of Sarum. The collection of 421 probate inventories cover the period 1591–1775 and were published by Wiltshire Record Society.[136]

Inventories from Stockport covered the period 1578–1619 when it was a modest market town within a pastoral region. The inventories related to the market town and not to the much larger Ancient Parish. All known surviving probate inventories for the Stockport township in the period were included in the analysis except for very few which were clearly truncated. Most were from the seventeenth century and only 11 inventories related to the previous century. Just over one in five were for females. Projecting backwards from the Hearth Tax returns of 1664, the town probably had a population of about 1,000 at the turn of the seventeenth century.[137]

The mainly rural inventories

The Surrey probate inventories were from the archdeaconry courts which were part of the ancient Diocese of Winchester until the nineteenth century and came from parishes across the county.[138] In the sixteenth century, Surrey was an agricultural county with some market towns although it included parts of London such as Southwark. Cloth manufacturing had been an important industry within the county with 'cloths of Guildford' being held in particularly high regard. By the sixteenth century the cloth industry was in decline in the county and whilst the probate inventories used for the study included a large number from yeoman and husbandmen, only three were of men whose occupation was recorded as 'clothier'.

Gloucestershire inventories represented the largest collection of published probate records analysed in the present study. They comprised two volumes, both edited by John Moore of the University of Bristol. The first volume contained inventories from Frampton Cotterell and its district and represented five parishes: Stoke Gifford, Frampton Cotterell, Iron Acton, Westerleigh and Winterbourne.[139] The importance of agriculture to these parishes was reflected in the occupations attached to the probate inventories: when widows and spinsters were excluded, more than half were those of yeomen and husbandmen. This was particularly pronounced in Stoke Gifford where 40 (85 per cent) out of 47 male inventories were for yeomen or husbandmen and was broadly consistent with the Muster Roll for 1608 which indicated that nearly three quarters of the population of the parish were engaged in agriculture.[140] Although the other four parishes were categorised by Moore as mainly industrial, the 1608 Muster Roll showed that around 40 per cent of the population were engaged in farming and nearly a quarter were employed in textile industries. Nevertheless, at this time there was no sharp division between agrarian and non-agrarian and most people were engaged in some level of agricultural activity.[141]

The second volume edited by Moore covered the area around Clifton and Westbury and included inventories from Clifton, Westbury, Redland, Southmead, Shirehampton and Lawrence Weston for the years 1609–1761.[142] Just over half of these inventories were those of people who held agricultural occupations, whilst a significant number (16 per cent) were of men employed in the shipping trades. Clifton had a population of around 450 in 1712 but grew rapidly in the second half of the eighteenth century so that by the end of the century this figure had been increased almost tenfold.

There was a dearth of surviving inventories for Essex and those used for this study related only to the parish of Writtle and the adjoining chapelry of Roxwell which are situated to the west of Chelmsford in mid-Essex. Writtle and Roxwell were a peculiar jurisdiction under the responsibility of the Warden and Fellows of New College, Oxford. The collection was published by Essex Record Office and contained 248 inventories from the years 1635–1749.[143] Where the inventories recorded an occupation, 60 per cent of the men to which they relate were yeomen or husbandmen.

The inventories from Cheshire were from Wrenbury including Wrenbury Frith, Chorley, Newhall, Smeatonwood, Sound and Broomhall (a township within Wrenbury parish). Wrenbury lies to the south-west of Nantwich, four miles from the county border with Shropshire and in 1801 had a population of 404. The Wrenbury inventories were held in Cheshire Record Office and covered an early period from 1542 to 1661.[144] The area was overwhelmingly rural, as indicated by the recorded occupations in the inventories, so that almost all of the men were either gentry (25 per cent), yeomen (49 per cent) or husbandmen (17 per cent).

The smallest collection of inventories came from the parishes of Stoneleigh and Ashow in Warwickshire.[145] These agricultural communities are located close to the city of Coventry. Almost all the inventories related to gentry, yeomen, husbandmen and labourers. Only four of the inventories were those of tradesmen.

The Shropshire inventories were published in two collections: those from north Telford came from the parishes of Dawley, Lilleshall, Wellington and Wrockwardine; whilst those from south Telford represented the parishes of Benthall, Broseley, Little Wenlock and Madeley.[146] These communities were predominantly agricultural in the period under investigation as industrial expansion largely took place in the nineteenth century.[147] Coalbrookdale fell within the parish of Madeley. There were about 480 households in the northern parishes in 1672 and a further 223 in the four southern parishes. Barrie Trinder and Nancy Cox claimed that the selection of inventories provided a consistent sample of occupations, levels of wealth and places of residence.[148]

The probate inventories from Sussex came from the parish of Angmering which is located between Littlehampton and Worthing in West Sussex. From the late sixteenth to the early eighteenth centuries, Angmering's population was around 300–400.[149] The 130 inventories were held at West Sussex Record Office and have been published online. Where the occupation of the deceased was recorded, over two thirds of the men were noted as being yeomen or husbandmen.

Buckinghamshire inventories were included for comparison only as they were from the Prerogative Court of Canterbury and therefore likely to represent only the wealthiest members of society.[150] They have been analysed separately since any comparison with inventories from a lower court would be inappropriate and invalid. The sample came from across the county, but mainly from villages and small towns, the largest of which was High Wycombe. No towns in Buckinghamshire had more than 2,000 inhabitants at the end of the seventeenth century.

These published inventories have been used in this study to complement the main body of evidence. The very early inventories from Surrey and Southampton were important because they bridge the chronological gap between will evidence and probate inventory evidence. Buckinghamshire inventories from the Prerogative Court of Canterbury provided insight into the scale of differences between inventories from prerogative and archdeaconry courts. The remainder included a selection of urban and mainly rural inventories from various parts of the country. The selection is inevitably limited by the extent to which published volumes have been produced.

Inventory analysis

The sample of inventories covered by the present study ranges from the beginning of the second half of the sixteenth century to the end of the eighteenth century, a period of 250 years. Surviving probate inventories relating to non-elite individuals were very rare before about 1530. One exception was the collection from York edited by Philip Stell but Christopher Dyer, who has critically examined transcriptions in this collection, identified a significant number of important errors which made their use problematic.[151]

Results from over 15,500 probate inventories were considered in this volume. They represent more than 7,000 inventories from 16 counties analysed specifically for this study, together with around 8,000 from the study of Kent and Cornwall by Overton *et al.* A further 257 inventories for Kent covering the vital period 1750–1800 were added to the sample produced by Overton *et al.* (Table 2.3).[152] The total number of inventories sampled represents about 1.5 per cent of the 'one million or so' total extant probate inventories.[153]

The probate records included in this volume represent both the largest collection and the longest chronological span of these records that has been assembled to provide evidence of the emergence of a consumer society in England. As with all historical records, they are not without problems and should not be used mechanistically. The following four chapters use the data together with the historiography to outline and examine consumption patterns relating to food and drink, clothing, household goods and religious consumption, both before and after death! The final chapters seek to address the central questions of this study: when did the 'consumer revolution' begin; and who were the first people to own new consumer goods. Chapter 7 uses evidence from probate records to explore the role that location played in the ownership of goods. In Chapters 8 and 9 the data is used to investigate the relationship between social status and the ownership of selected goods and how this changed over time. The results provide clear trends in the changing ownership patterns of consumer goods, their spread across the country and the extent of their diffusion across society.

TABLE 2.3 Inventory sample by location

	1551– 1600	1601– 1629	1630– 1659	1660– 1689	1690– 1719	1720– 1749	1750– 1800	Totals
Huntingdonshire	N/A	144	160	384	308	280	143	1,419
Yorkshire	N/A	N/A	N/A	N/A	474	572	476	1,522
Dorset	N/A	74	48	124	280	340	159	1,025
URBAN (Published)								
Bristol	N/A	46	62	107	58	31	15	319
Southampton	110	N/A	N/A	N/A	N/A	N/A	N/A	110
Lincoln	N/A	N/A	N/A	41	19	N/A	N/A	60
Ipswich	31	36	2	N/A	N/A	N/A	N/A	69
Marlborough	18	54	57	134	128	27	3	421
RURAL (Published)								
Gloucs	N/A	80	71	174	183	85	22	615
Essex	N/A	N/A	26	132	50	31	N/A	239
Cheshire	17	104	44	N/A	N/A	N/A	N/A	165
Surrey	397	46	N/A	N/A	N/A	N/A	N/A	443
Warwickshire	12	9	6	6	10	10	1	54
Shropshire	N/A	N/A	N/A	138	142	145	23	448
Sussex	1	17	31	43	16	20	2	130
Bucks	N/A	N/A	N/A	113	31	N/A	N/A	144
Sub Totals	**586**	**610**	**507**	**1,396**	**1,699**	**1,541**	**844**	**7,183**
Percentage (%)	**8**	**9**	**7**	**19**	**24**	**21**	**12**	**100**
Cornwall	N/A	845	529	1,133	973	639	0	4,119
Kent	N/A	1,160	753	1,149	665	252	257	4,236
Totals	**586**	**2,615**	**1,789**	**3,678**	**3,337**	**2,432**	**1,101**	**15,538**
Percentage (%)	**4**	**17**	**11**	**24**	**21**	**16**	**7**	**100**

Notes

1 Most of the transcribing was carried out by the authors. We wish to record our thanks to the late Peter Northeast for the loan of his transcriptions of some of the wills used for this study, and to Pamela Sneath, Mary Carter and a Kimbolton Local History Society working group for transcribing other selected inventories.
2 M. Ingram, *Church Courts, Sex and Marriage in England, 1570–1640* (Cambridge: Cambridge University Press, 1987), p.1.
3 T. Arkell, 'The probate process' in T. Arkell, N. Evans and N. Goose, (eds), *When Death Do Us Part* (Oxford: Leopard's Head Press, 2000), p.7.
4 A.L. Erickson, *Women and Property in Early Modern England* (London: Routledge, 1993), pp.32–33.
5 K. Grannum and N. Taylor, *Wills and Other Probate Records: A Practical Guide to Researching your Ancestors' Last Documents* (Kew: The National Archives, 2004), p.15.
6 Prerogative Court of Canterbury (PCC) wills from 1384 to 1858 are held by the National Archives in series PROB 11 and available online, http://discovery.nationa larchives.gov.uk/browse/r/h/C12122 [last accessed 20 June 2019].

7 M. Pearsall, *The Parish Administration and Records* Podcast, the National Archives, http://media.nationalarchives.gov.uk/index.php/the-parish-administration-and-records/[last accessed 22 September 2016].

8 NRO T/C1/N11 (Carman), (Laurence).

9 N. Goose and N. Evans, 'Wills as an historical source', in Arkell *et al.* (eds), *When Death Do Us Part*, p.39.

10 Erickson, *Women and Property*, p.204 cited in Goose and Evans, 'Wills as an historical source', p.3.

11 Goose and Evans, 'Wills as an historical source', p.9.

12 Some wills were nuncupative, made by word of mouth before witnesses, and subsequently written out by a scribe. A handful of nuncupative wills have been included in this study.

13 K. Lewis, 'Women, testamentary discourse and life-writing in later medieval England', in N. Menuge (ed.), *Medieval Women and the Law* (Woodbridge: Boydell, 2000), p.60.

14 J. Kermode, *Medieval Merchants: York, Beverley and Hull in the Later Middle Ages* (Cambridge: Cambridge University Press, 1998), p.71.

15 HA AH15-1–4 Wills 1530–1534 Vol. 4/100.

16 Grannum and Taylor, *Wills and Other Probate Records*, pp.46–53.

17 M. Overton, J. Whittle, D. Dean and A. Hann, *Production and Consumption in English Households 1600–1750* (Abingdon: Routledge, 2004), p.13.

18 Grannum and Taylor, *Wills and Other Probate Records*, p.71.

19 An Act concerning Fines and sums of Money to be taken by the Ministers of Bishops and other Ordinaries of the Holy Church for the Probate of Testaments, 21 Henry VIII, c.5; Grannum and Taylor, *Wills and Other Probate Records*, pp.91–92.

20 Grannum and Taylor, *Wills and Other Probate Records*, p.17.

21 Executors and administrators were charged with exhibiting the inventory of the testator's or intestate's personal estate in court within six months of the grant of probate or administration; Grannum and Taylor, *Wills and Other Probate Records*, p.93; J. Cox and N. Cox, 'Probate 1500–1800', in Arkell *et al.* (eds), *When Death Do Us Part*, p.27; A. Tarver, *Church Court Records* (Chichester: Phillimore, 1995), p.66.

22 K. Wrightson and D. Levine, *The Making of an Industrial Society: Whickham 1560–1765* (Oxford: Oxford University Press, 1991), p.239.

23 J. Styles, 'Clothing the North: the supply of non-elite clothing in the eighteenth-century North of England', *Textile History*, 25 (2) (1994), p.142; J. Styles, *The Dress of the People: Everyday Fashion in Eighteenth-Century England* (New Haven: Yale University Press, 2007), p.137.

24 Marc Descow was the third child of Peter Descow and his wife Marie. He was baptised on 16 May 1658 in Thorney, Cambridgeshire; L. Scadding, *The Descow Family History* (self-published, 2012), p.70.

25 HA AH18/4/143.

26 An Act concerning Executors of last Wills and Testaments, 21 Henry VIII, c.4, 5; 21 Henry VIII, c.5.; the reason for the production of an inventory was to identify the value of the deceased's personal estate and make it public and to facilitate payment of the deceased's outstanding debts, Grannum and Taylor, *Wills and Other Probate Records*, p.93.

27 Grannum and Taylor, *Wills and Other Probate Records*, p.93.

28 C. Estabrook, *Urbane and Rustic England: Cultural Ties and Social Spheres in the Provinces 1660–1780* (Stanford: Stanford University Press, 1998), p.130.

29 D. Spaeth, 'Constructing order in a world of goods: appraisers and appraisal in seventeenth-century England', seminar in early modern social and economic history, University of Cambridge, 26 January 2006.

30 M. Overton, 'Prices from probate inventories', in Arkell *et al.* (eds), *When Death Do Us Part*, p.124.

31 Grannum and Taylor, *Wills and Other Probate Records*, p.93.

32 K. Wrightson, *Ralph Tailor's Summer: A Scrivener, his City and the Plague* (New Haven: Yale University Press, 2011), p.114.

33 D. Vaisey (ed.), *The Diary of a Village Shopkeeper, 1754–1765* (London: Folio Society, 1998) pp.233–37.

34 *Ibid.*, pp.295–96.

35 N.J.G. Pounds, *The Culture of the English People* (Cambridge: Cambridge University Press, 1994), p.171; F. Steer, *Farm and Cottage Inventories of Mid-Essex 1635–1749* (Chichester: Phillimore, 1969), p.5; Estabrook, *Urbane and Rustic England*, p.130.

36 J. and N. Cox, 'Valuations in probate inventories, part I', *The Local Historian*, 2 (1985), pp.467–78; J. and N. Cox, 'Valuations in probate inventories, part II', *The Local Historian*, 8 (1986), pp.85–100.

37 Overton, 'Prices from probate inventories', p.127.

38 G.Z. Fijalkowski-Bereday, 'The equalizing effects of the death duties', *Oxford Economic Papers* New Series, Vol. 2, No. 2 (Oxford: Oxford University Press, 1950), pp.176–96.

39 A. Owens, D.R. Green, C. Bailey and A.C. Kay, 'A measure of worth: probate valuations, personal wealth and indebtedness in England, 1810–40', *Historical Research*, 79 (2006), p.386.

40 A.L. Erickson, 'Using probate accounts', in Arkell *et al.* (eds), *When Death Do Us Part*, p.103.

41 *Ibid.*, p.104.

42 *Ibid.*, p.104.

43 Philippa Hoskin, Archivist at the Borthwick Institute, University of York, 8 March 2006, pers. comm.

44 An Act for reviving and Continuance of several Acts of Parliament therein mentioned, I James II, c.17; Tarver, *Church Court Records*, p.72.

45 I. Mortimer, 'Why were probate accounts made? Methodological issues concerning the historical use of administrators' and executors' accounts', *Archives*, 31 (2006), pp.2–17.

46 P. Foden (trans.) and Norton Community Archaeology Group (ed.), *Records of the Manor of Norton in the Liberty of St. Albans, 1244–1539: Hertfordshire Record Publications Vol. XXIX* (Hertford: Hertfordshire Record Society, 2014), p.231.

47 These have been transcribed by David Dymond and published by the Norfolk Record Society, D. Dymond (ed.), *The Register of Thetford Priory: Part 1 1482–1517: Norfolk Record Society Vol. LIX* (Oxford: Oxford University Press, 1994); D. Dymond (ed.), *The Register of Thetford Priory, Part II: 1518–1540: Norfolk Record Society Vol. LX* (Oxford: Oxford University Press, 1995 and 1996).

48 S. Rigby, 'Urban decline in the later Middle Ages: some problems in interpreting statistical data', *Urban History*, 6 (1979), p.46.

49 See, for example, C. Burgess, 'Late medieval wills and pious convention: testamentary evidence reconsidered', in M. Hicks (ed.), *Profit, Piety and the Professions in Later Medieval England* (Gloucester: Sutton, 1990), pp.14–33; R. Swanson, *Church and Society in Late Medieval England* (Oxford: Oxford University Press, 1989), pp.265–68; Goose and Evans 'Wills as an historical source', pp.50–54.

50 For further discussion, see Burgess, 'Late medieval wills', pp.14–33.

51 See, for examples, C. Barron and A. Sutton (eds), *Medieval London Widows: 1300–1500* (London: Bloomsbury, 1994); A. Betterton and D. Dymond, *Lavenham: Industrial Town* (Lavenham: Dalton, 1989); J. Kermode, *Medieval Merchants: York, Beverley and Hull in the Later Middle Ages* (Cambridge: Cambridge University Press, 1998); S. Sweetinburgh, 'Clothing the naked in late medieval East Kent', in C. Richardson (ed.), *Clothing Culture: 1350–1650* (Aldershot: Ashgate, 2004), pp.109–21.

52 J. Middleton-Stewart, *Inward Purity and Outward Splendour: Death and Remembrance in the Deanery of Dunwich, Suffolk, 1370–1547* (Woodbridge: Boydell, 2001), pp.41–42.

53 NRO NCC Caston 342 (Rokewoode).

54 NRO ANW Aleyn 271 (Edwardes).

55 In this instance, Burgess refers to a chantry service set up for a testator's late wives which is only mentioned within a will because payment is owing and makes the point that if this had not been the case, we would not have known that the chantry had been established, Burgess, 'Late medieval wills', pp.19–20.

56 K. Dauteuille, 'Household materials and social networks in Norwich 1371–1500: a study of testamentary evidence' (unpublished PhD thesis, University of Cambridge, 2003), p.24; K. Sneath, 'Consumption, wealth, indebtedness and social structure in early modern England' (unpublished PhD thesis, University of Cambridge, 2008), pp.235, 254, 274–75, 302, 313.

57 Dauteuille, 'Household materials', p.24; Sneath, 'Consumption, wealth, indebtedness', p.22.

58 S. Flood (ed.), *St Albans Wills, 1471–1500: Hertfordshire Record Publications Vol. IX* (Hertford: Hertfordshire Record Society, 1993), p.88.

59 A handful of the wills are nuncupative, i.e. oral wills that were written down after the death of the testator on the basis of the testimony of at least two witnesses, and are written in the third person plural; R. Houlbrooke, *Death, Religion and the Family in England: 1480–1750* (Oxford: Oxford University Press, 2000), p.89.

60 V. Bainbridge, *Gilds in the Medieval Countryside: Social and Religious Change in Cambridgeshire, c.1350–1558* (Woodbridge: Boydell, 1996), p.59.

61 F. Emmison (ed.), *Wills of the County of Essex (England): Vol.1 1558–1565* (Washington: National Genealogical Society, 1982), p.58.

62 An Act how Lands may be willed by Testament, 32 Hen.VIII, c.1.; Goose and Evans, 'Wills as an historical source', p.44.

63 M. Spufford, 'The limitations of the probate inventory', in J.A. Chartres and D. Hey (eds), *English Rural Society, 1500–1800* (Cambridge: Cambridge University Press, 1990), pp.140–74; L.C. Orlin, 'Fictions of the early modern English probate inventory', in H.S. Turner (ed.), *The Culture of Capital: Property, Cities and Knowledge in Early Modern England* (London: Routledge, 2002), pp.51–83.

64 Grannum and Taylor, *Wills and Other Probate Records*, p.93.

65 Overton et al., *Production and Consumption*, p.15; Spufford, 'The limitations of the probate inventory', p.144.

66 Overton et al., *Production and Consumption*, p.15; M. Reed (ed.), *The Ipswich Probate Inventories, 1583–1631: Suffolk Record Society, Vol. 22* (Woodbridge: Boydell, 1981), p.1.

67 M. Overton, *Wealth, lifecycle and consumption*, unpublished paper, p.1.

68 For example, see M. Reed (ed.), *Buckinghamshire Probate Inventories, 1661–1714: Buckinghamshire Record Society, Vol. XXIV* (Aylesbury: Buckinghamshire Record Society, 1998), p.x.; Overton et al., *Production and Consumption*, pp.27–28, 208.

69 L. Boothman, 19 March 2008, pers. comm.

70 A. Macfarlane, *The Family Life of Ralph Josselin, a Seventeenth-Century Clergyman: An Essay in Historical Anthropology* (New York: Norton, 1976), p.64.

71 P. Seaver, *Wallington's World: A Puritan Artisan in Seventeenth-Century London* (Stanford: Stanford University Press, 1985), p.118.

72 A. Schuurman, 'Probate inventories: research issues, problems and results', in A. Van Der Woude and A. Schuurman (eds), *Probate Inventories: A New Source for the Historical Study of Wealth, Material Culture and Agricultural Development* (Wageningen: Hes & De Graff Publishing, 1980), pp.27–28.

73 D.G. Vaisey, 'Probate inventories and provincial retailers in the seventeenth century', in P. Riden (ed.), *Probate Records and the Local Community* (Gloucester: Sutton, 1985), p.101.

74 Overton et al., *Production and Consumption*, pp.14–18.

75 M. Reed, *Ipswich Probate Inventories 1583–1631* (Woodbridge: Boydell, 1981), p.63; E. Roberts and K. Parker, *Southampton Probate Inventories 1447–1575 Volume 1* (Southampton: Southampton University Press, 1992).

76 Probate inventories 1645–1800 (no accession number) York, Borthwick Institute of Historical Research, University of York.
77 S.A.J. Keibek and L. Shaw-Taylor, 'Early modern rural by-employments: a re-examination of the probate inventory evidence', *Agricultural History Review*, 61(2) (2013), pp.244–81.
78 S.A.J. Keibek, 'Correcting the probate inventory record for wealth bias', Cambridge Working Papers in Economic and Social History Working Paper no. 28, March 2017. www.econsoc.hist.cam.ac.uk/docs/CWPESH_number_28_March_2017. pdf [last accessed 16 July 2018].
79 Keibek, 'Correcting the probate inventory record', p.22.
80 C. Muldrew, *Food, Energy and the Creation of Industriousness* (Cambridge: Cambridge University Press, 2011).
81 H. French, *The Middle Sort of People in Provincial England, 1600–1750* (Oxford: Oxford University Press, 2007), p.266.
82 Orlin, 'Fictions of the early modern English probate inventory', pp.74–76.
83 A. McCants, 'Poor consumers as global consumers', *Feeding the Masses, Economic History Review* (S1) (2008), p.178.
84 P. Slack, *The Impact of Plague in Tudor and Stuart England* (London: Routledge, 1985), pp.69–78.
85 J. Sear, 'Consumption and trade in East Anglian market towns and their hinterlands in the late Middle Ages' (unpublished PhD thesis, University of Cambridge, 2014).
86 The Countryside Agency, *Countryside Character Volume 6: East of England* (Cheltenham: Countryside Agency, 1999), pp.6–7, 16; only relatively small areas of The Fens had been drained by this date, more substantial draining did not happen until the seventeenth century.
87 M. Bailey, *A Marginal Economy? East Anglian Breckland in the Later Middle Ages* (Cambridge: Cambridge University Press, 1989), pp.135, 137.
88 The Countryside Agency, *Countryside Character Volume 6*, pp.81–85.
89 Evidence exists for 140 pre-Black Death markets in Norfolk, 58 in Suffolk and 38 in Cambridgeshire; D. Dymond, 'Medieval and later markets' in P. Wade-Martins (ed.), *An Historical Atlas of Norfolk* (Norwich: Norfolk Museums Service, 1993), p.76; N. Scarfe, 'Medieval and later markets' in D. Dymond and E. Martin (eds), *An Historical Atlas of Suffolk* (Ipswich: Suffolk Books, 1999), p.76; www.history.ac. uk/cmh/gaz/gazweb2.html - Gazetteer of Markets and Fairs in England and Wales to 1516 [last accessed 30 June 2016].
90 M. Bailey, *Medieval Suffolk: An Economic and Social History* (Woodbridge: Boydell, 2007), p.173.
91 Flood (ed.), *St Albans Wills*; F. Emmison, *Elizabethan Wills of South-West Essex* (Waddesdon: Kylin Press, 1983); F.G. Emmison, *Wills of the County of Essex (England): Vol. 1, 1558–1565* (Washington: National Genealogical Society, 1982); F.G. Emmison, *Wills of the County of Essex (England): Vol. 2, 1565–1571* (Boston: New England Historic Genealogical Society, 1983); F.G. Emmison, *Wills of the County of Essex (England): Vol. 3, 1571–1577* (Boston: New England Historic Genealogical Society, 1986); F. Emmison, *Elizabethan Life: Wills of Essex Gentry and Yeoman* (Chelmsford: Essex Record Office, 1980); F. Emmison, *Elizabethan Life: Wills of Essex Gentry and Merchants* (Chelmsford: Essex Record Office, 1978).
92 Charter or custom evidence exists for 86 pre-Black Death markets in Essex although only 26 appear to have survived to the end of the medieval period; and 38 pre-Black Death markets in Hertfordshire of which only 21 of these appear to have survived; www.history.ac.uk/cmh/gaz/gazweb2.html – Gazetteer of Markets and Fairs in England and Wales to 1516 [last accessed 4 July 2016]; M. Bailey, 'A tale of two towns: Buntingford and Standon in the later Middle Ages', *Journal of Medieval History*, 19 (1993), p.360.

93   D. Edwards, M. Forrest, J. Minchinton, M. Shaw, B. Tyndall and P. Wallis (eds), *Early Northampton Wills Preserved in Northamptonshire Record Office* (Northampton: Northamptonshire Record Society, 2005); www.northamptonshirewills.solutions. on-rev.com – Northamptonshire Wills [last accessed 5 August 2019].

94   Evidence exists for 48 pre-Black Death markets in Northamptonshire but only 14 seem to have been in operation by the end of the Middle Ages – www.history.ac. uk/cmh/gaz/gazweb2.html – Gazetteer of Markets and Fairs in England and Wales to 1516 [last accessed 4 July 2016].

95   S. Rigby, 'Urban population in late medieval England: the evidence of the lay subsidies', *Economic History Review*, 63 (2) (2010), pp.393–417.

96   *Ibid.*, p.405.

97   A. Dyer, *Decline and Growth in English Towns: 1400–1640* (Cambridge: Cambridge University Press, 1991), pp.62–63.

98   T. Slater and N. Goose (eds), *A County of Small Towns: The Development of Hertfordshire's Urban Landscape* (Hertford: Hertfordshire Record Society, 2008), p.5.

99   Overton *et al.*, *Production and Consumption*, p.29.

100 P. Thompson, 'A consumer revolution in the eighteenth century: Kent reconsidered' (unpublished undergraduate dissertation, University of Cambridge, 2015).

101 P. Corfield, 'East Anglia', in P. Clark (ed.), *The Cambridge Urban History of Britain: Vol. 2 1540–1840* (Cambridge: Cambridge University Press, 2000), p.36.

102 J. Morrill, 'The making of Oliver Cromwell', in J. Morrill (ed.), *Oliver Cromwell and the English Revolution* (Harlow: Longman, 1990), p.22.

103 J. Hillaby (ed.), *The Journeys of Celia Fiennes* (London: MacDonald, 1983), p.88; A. Orde (ed.), *Matthew and George Culley: Travel Journals and Letters, 1765–1798* (Oxford, Oxford University Press, 2002), p.79.

104 M. Wickes, *The History of Huntingdonshire* (Chichester: Phillimore, 1985), p.80.

105 S. Doran and C. Durston, *Princes, Pastors and People: the Church and Religion in England, 1500–1700* (London: Routledge, 2003), p.154.

106 Wickes, *The History of Huntingdonshire*, p.80.

107 K. Sneath and P. Sneath, *Godmanchester A Celebration of 800 Years* (Cambridge: EAH Press, 2011), p.53ff.

108 J.A. Raftis, *A Small Town in Late Medieval England* (Toronto: Pontifical Institute of Medieval Studies, 1982), p.135.

109 M.P. Carter, 'An urban society and its hinterland: St Ives in the seventeenth and early eighteenth centuries' (unpublished Ph.D. thesis, University of Leicester, 1988), p.79.

110 D. Hey, *A History of Yorkshire: County of the Broad Acres* (Lancaster: Carnegie, 2005), pp.282–84.

111 M.F. Pickles, 'Labour migration: Yorkshire 1670–1743', *Local Population Studies*, 57 (1996), pp.45–46.

112 Hey, *A History of Yorkshire*, pp.4, 249; M. Overton, *Agricultural Revolution in England: The Transformation of the Agrarian Economy, 1500–1850* (Cambridge: Cambridge University Press, 1996), pp.89–90.

113 Hey, *A History of Yorkshire*, p.292.

114 A. Hawkyard and N. Nicolson (eds), *The Counties of Britain: A Tudor Atlas by John Speed* (London: British Library, 1988), p.69.

115 J. Chandler, *Wessex Images* (Gloucester: Sutton, 1990), p.72.

116 D. Underdown, *Fire from Heaven: Life of an English Town in the Seventeenth Century* (New Haven: Yale University Press, 1992), pp.2, 227.

117 The card index for inventories at Dorset History Centre record 'approximately and probably in excess of 1500 named individuals', S. Morgan, Senior History Centre Assistant, Dorset History Centre, 2 December 2016, pers. comm.

118 D.H. Sacks and M. Lynch, 'Ports 1540–1700', in Clark, *Cambridge Urban History: Vol. 2*, p.399.

119 P. Slack, 'Great and good towns 1540–1700', in Clark, *Cambridge Urban History: Vol. 2*, p.352.

120 Hawkyard and Nicolson (eds), *Counties of Britain*, p.88; C. Platt, *Medieval Southampton. The Port and Trading Community, A.D. 1000–1600* (London: Law Book Co of Australasia, 1973), p.184.

121 Roberts and Parker (eds), *Southampton Probate Inventories 1447–1575*.

122 R. Britnell, *Britain and Ireland 1050–1530: Economy and Society* (Oxford: Oxford University Press, 2004), p.120.

123 D.H. Sacks, *The Widening Gate: Bristol and the Atlantic Economy 1450–1700* (Los Angeles: University of California Press, 1993), p.87.

124 *Ibid.*, p.353.

125 J.M. Ellis, *The Georgian Town, 1680–1840* (Basingstoke: Palgrave, 2001), pp.14, 149.

126 S.J. Thompson, 'Population growth and corporations of the poor, 1660–1841', in C. Briggs, P. Kitson and S. Thomson (eds), *Population, Welfare and Economic Change in Britain 1290–1834* (Woodbridge: Boydell, 2014), p.205; J. Barry, 'South-West' in Clark (ed.) *Cambridge Urban History: Vol. 2*, p.73.

127 E. and S. George (eds), *Bristol Probate Inventories, Part 1 1542–1650: Bristol Record Society's Publication Vol. 54* (Bristol: Bristol Record Society, 2002); E. and S. George (eds), *Bristol Probate Inventories, Part 2 1657–1689 Bristol Record Society's Publication Vol. 57* (Bristol: Bristol Record Society, 2005); E. and S. George (eds), *Bristol Probate Inventories, Part 3 1690–1804: Bristol Record Society's Publication Vol. 60* (Bristol: Bristol Record Society, 2008).

128 George and George, *Bristol Probate Inventories, Part 1*, p.xi.

129 Britnell, *Britain and Ireland*, pp.120, 350.

130 P. Clark and P. Slack, *English Towns in Transition, 1500–1700* (Oxford: Oxford University Press, 1976), pp.2, 101; J.A. Johnston (ed.), *Probate Inventories of Lincoln Citizens, 1661–1714: Lincoln Record Society Vol. 80* (Woodbridge: Boydell, 1991), p.xx.

131 Johnston, *Probate Inventories of Lincoln Citizens*, p.xv.

132 Reed (ed.), *Ipswich Probate Inventories*, p.1.

133 *Ibid.*, pp.2, 8.

134 D. Gerhold, *Bristol's Stage Coaches* (Salisbury: HobNob Press, 2012), pp.15, 25–26.

135 Ellis, *Georgian Town*, p.12.

136 L. Williams and S. Thomson (eds), *Marlborough Probate Inventories, 1591–1775: Wiltshire Record Society Vol. 59* (Chippenham: Wiltshire Record Society, 2007).

137 C.B. Phillips and J.H. Smith (eds), *Stockport Probate Records, 1578–1619: Publications of the Record Society of Lancashire and Cheshire Vol. CXXIV* (Liverpool: Record Society of Lancashire and Cheshire, 1985), pp.ix–xvi.

138 D.M. Herridge (trans.), *Surrey Probate Inventories, 1558–1603: Surrey Record Society Vol. 39* (Woking: Surrey Record Society, 2005).

139 J.S. Moore, *The Goods and Chattels of our Forefathers: Frampton Cotterell and District Probate Inventories: 1539–1804* (Chichester: Phillimore, 1976).

140 *Ibid.*, p.12.

141 *Ibid.*, p.26.

142 J. Moore (ed.), *Clifton and Westbury Probate Inventories, 1609–1761* (Bristol: Avon Local History Association, 1981).

143 Steer, *Farm and Cottage Inventories*.

144 P. Pixton (ed.), *Wrenbury Wills and Inventories, 1542–1661: Record Society of Lancashire and Cheshire Vol. 144* (Liverpool: Record Society of Lancashire and Cheshire, 2009).

145 N.W. Alcock, *People at Home: Living in a Warwickshire Village, 1500–1800* (Chichester: Phillimore, 1993).

146 B. Trinder and J. Cox, *Yeomen and Colliers in Telford: Probate Inventories for Dawley, Lilleshall, Wellington and Wrockwardine:1660–1750* (Chichester: Phillimore, 1980); B. Trinder

and J. Cox, *Miners and Mariners of the Severn Gorge: Probate Inventories for Benthall, Broseley, Little Wenlock and Madeley, 1660–1764* (Chichester: Phillimore, 2000).

147 Trinder and Cox, *Yeomen and Colliers*, pp.10, 113.

148 *Ibid.*, p.6; Trinder and Cox, *Miners and Mariners*, p.7.

149 www.angmeringvillage.co.uk/history/inventories1.htm [last accessed 28 January 2016].

150 Reed (ed.), *Buckinghamshire Probate Inventories*, p.x.

151 C. Dyer, 'Living in peasant houses in late medieval England', *Vernacular Architecture*, 44 (2013), p.20; P. Stell (ed.), *Probate Inventories of the York Diocese, 1350–1500* (York: York Archaeological Trust, 2006).

152 Transcribed and analysed by P. Thompson, undergraduate student at Sidney Sussex College, University of Cambridge, for his unpublished dissertation 'A consumer revolution in the eighteenth century: Kent reconsidered'.

153 Arkell *et al.* (eds), *When Death Do Us Part*, p.72.

3

FOOD AND DRINK

For almost everyone during the late medieval and early modern periods, consumption goods predominantly related to food and drink rather than more material items such as household equipment or clothing. Basic sustenance needs, such as those for food and drink, could be met in three main ways: either through the household's own production of items subsequently retained for its own use; by barter and exchange whereby items produced by one household could be exchanged for those produced by another; or through using earned income to purchase goods in the marketplace or from other sources. Although most households met much of their own nutritional needs through domestic production, expenditure on food and drink still consistently formed the largest component of a household's budget throughout the period covered by this study. This chapter considers the range of products that were eaten and drunk during the late medieval and early modern periods, and the material items that were acquired to enable and supplement the acts of eating and dining, many of which were integral to the development of consumption in England.

Food

The main dietary component for everyone in the Middle Ages was grain which was consumed in the form of bread, ale and the thick soup known as pottage. The importance of bread and ale to the medieval diet was reflected in the assize of bread and ale which entered into statute law sometime in the thirteenth century and which regulated the price, weight and quality of bread and ale.[1] Despite the emphasis on subsistence living, these basic commodities were often purchased from markets and other retail outlets, particularly in the urban economy, so that it was essential to maintain an open and constant supply through careful regulation rather than leave people vulnerable to market forces.[2] Bread in particular was eaten in large quantities by all social classes although there was a very wide variety in quality and types of bread. Inevitably, bread production was heavily influenced by the types of grain which were grown locally, whilst cost and fashion ensured that the bread consumed by the nobility and gentry was very different from that consumed by poorer sections of society.[3] The most valued bread grain was wheat which produced a desirable white bread known as wastel.[4] Wheat, rye, maslin, barley and oats were all used in various proportions and combinations to make coarser, lower-quality breads, whilst peas and beans provided the cheapest, poorest and roughest bread, often referred to as 'horse bread'.[5] The proportion of wheat in bread broadly declined in direct relationship to the social status of the consumer so that the bread consumed by the nobility and gentry was predominantly of wheat, whilst that consumed by other classes contained lower amounts of wheat and increasingly higher ratios of other grains, or contained no wheat at all.[6] This had particularly been the case prior to the Black Death when wheaten bread was only consumed on a regular basis by those of high social status and most people generally ate bread made from other grains and even legumes. The pressure on land at this time encouraged landholders to grow grain crops such as rye and barley which were more reliable and higher yielding than wheat.[7] After the Black Death, falling grain prices, rising wages and a reduction in the need to maximise yields all led to an increased demand for wheaten bread at the expense of bread made from cheaper grains.[8] Whilst this demand was widespread, it did not extend to the poorest social groups so that even by 1587, William Harrison noted that:

> the gentility commonly provide themselves sufficiently of wheat for their own tables, whilst their household and poor neighbors in some shires are enforced to content themselves with rye or barley, yea, and in time of dearth, many with bread made either of beans, peason, or oats, or of all together and some acorns among, of which scourge the poorest do soonest taste.[9]

Whilst bread was bought in by most households, the thick soup–stew known as pottage (the basic dish of the Middle Ages) was mostly cooked within the domestic environment. The grain most commonly used for pottage was oats (in the form of oatmeal) although a wide range of other grains were used depending on what was available, together with peas and beans.[10] This main component was supplemented by other foodstuffs according to household taste, availability and affluence; for example, the range of recipes from extant medieval English culinary manuscripts collected together and published by Constance Hieatt showed that pottages could be based on a range of grains, vegetables, fruit, nuts, eggs and flowers as well as meat and fish.[11] For most peasants, however, pottage was usually a basic, vegetarian dish as the consumption of meat remained limited. The third use of grains was for ale which was also an important source of calories in the late medieval period and was clearly regarded as a further important form of sustenance. This will be considered in greater detail later in this chapter.

By the early modern period, bread and beer or ale were still the principal sources of calories for the average adult male in England.[12] These were still supplemented by meat, milk, butter and cheese, as well as sugar and vegetables and herbs, although the relative proportions of the English diet varied by region, sex and social rank.[13] Optimistic interpretations of labourers' diets were given by several historians. Craig Muldrew argued that substantial amounts of meat were eaten by labourers whilst Joan Thirsk asserted that everybody ate vegetables and herbs.[14] Greenstuff was a basic ingredient in pottage and common folk ate it so regularly that it rarely attracted comment.[15] Sara Horrell accepted that even labouring households eventually shared in the expansion of consumption and were able to enjoy wheaten bread, tea, sugar and imported spirits.[16] Robert Allen's 'respectability' basket included some expensive sources of calories: 26kg of meat per person per year as well as 5.2kg of cheese and 52 eggs.[17] This diet provided 2,500 calories per person per day and was enjoyed by 'respectable labourers in Britain'. According to Allen, this was affordable because of relatively high wages in the British economy which were more than three times subsistence in London during most of the seventeenth and eighteenth centuries.[18] Jane Humphries did not share Allen's optimism, particularly his argument that British women and children enjoyed one of the highest standards of living in the world during the eighteenth century. Humphries argued that Allen had focussed on male wages and had not taken full account of the caloric needs of women and children. For Humphries, poverty was widespread amongst the working class during the industrial revolution and men got the lion's share of resources at the expense of women and children.[19] David Meredith and Deborah Oxley argued that the rapidly rising population began to put pressure on food resources towards the end of the eighteenth century and this situation continued throughout much of the nineteenth century.[20]

Meat and fish

Throughout our period, the foodstuffs which supplemented grain products included legumes, vegetables, fruit, nuts, flavourings, meat, fish, dairy products and eggs. The range and variety of these varied according to status so that most people of low status were limited to legumes, vegetables and, occasionally, low-quality meat and fish, whilst those further up the social scale ate increasingly smaller amounts of grain products, legumes and vegetables, together with larger amounts of meat, fish and dairy products.

The pre-Black Death land shortage was such that almost all available land was used for arable farming and the consequent produce consumed directly rather than fed to meat animals. Providing grass (for summer grazing) and hay, straw and pulses (as winter fodder) was an inefficient use of land resources when compared to the amount of grain, pulses or legumes for human consumption that could be produced from the same amount of land. Consequently, the meat of the small number of animals raised solely for consumption was expensive and largely the preserve of the nobility and gentry, although meat from old or diseased animals which had primarily been used for wool or dairy production was consumed by people outside these social groups when it was available. The demographic decline of the later Middle Ages, which resulted in the shortage and high cost of labour and a long-term decline in the price of grain, made arable farming less profitable. This was at a time when rising living standards led to increased demand for meat and dairy produce amongst all strata of medieval society, including the lower social orders who were keen to emulate the diets that they perceived their peers to have. For example, Christopher Dyer noted that harvest workers in the thirteenth century were predominantly given bread, supplemented by small amounts of cheese and even smaller quantities of ale, fish and meat, but that by the fifteenth century the proportion of meat being given had risen from a tenth of the food budget in the earlier period to between a quarter and a third.[21] Although evidence is patchy, Britnell considered that it was sufficient to suggest a rise in pastoral farming in the early fifteenth century in many areas of England so that the late Middle Ages saw a much wider availability of a range of meats which became cheaper and easier to acquire in both fresh and preserved forms, particularly beef as cattle farming expanded.[22] This expansion in cattle farming also ensured that dairy produce became an increasingly important source of protein in the late Middle Ages. This was produced both as milk for immediate consumption and in the preserved forms of butter and cheese which added protein to the diet at those times of the year when fresh sources were difficult to obtain.[23]

The consumption of fish also increased in the late medieval period, particularly since it could be eaten on fast days when the flesh of most four-legged animals was prohibited. As with meat and dairy products, the quantity and quality of the fish consumed varied significantly according to affluence.[24] A very wide variety of freshwater, marine and shellfish was eaten, although availability was limited both by the fact that fresh fish was difficult to transport and decayed quickly, and by the careful manorial control of fishing rights for freshwater fish within their rivers. Consequently, most consumption was of marine fish, usually in a preserved form after having been salted, smoked or dried. Cod, herring and ling were all caught along the English coast and, increasingly, through deep sea fishing. Much of this fish was preserved, often at the ports where it was landed, whilst large amounts of dried cod, known as stockfish, were imported into England from Norway and Iceland. Fresh shellfish, particularly oysters, were also consumed as it was easier to transport to inland markets from the various coastal locations where it was caught.[25]

Flavourings and spices

From the late medieval period, there was a rise in the consumption of products which added flavour or interest to basic foodstuffs. These were commonly known as 'spicery goods' but can be divided into two main groups: grocery items which included such items as dried fruits, nuts, rice, honey, mustard seed and salt; and spices such as cinnamon, cloves, ginger, mace, pepper, sugar and saffron. The different statuses of these two groups of flavourings is demonstrated by Table 3.1 which shows the varying prices paid for these items as recorded in the accounts of Thetford Priory.[26]

Table 3.1 suggests that the cost of grocery items was such that they could be bought by many households on at least an occasional basis. The one exception was mustard which was widely grown and, when purchased, was inexpensive so that it was commonly used by most households both as a means of providing piquancy to sauces and as a preservative.[27]

TABLE 3.1 Prices of grocery items and spices purchased by Thetford Priory between 1482 and 1540

Item specified in the accounts	Price paid per unit
GROCERY ITEMS	
Almonds	2.5d–3.5d per pound
Currants (raisins of Corinth)	1.75d–4.5d per pound
Dates	3d–10d per pound
Figs (including figs de orte and figs marchant)	2s–7s per frayle (figs marchant)
	2s 4d per topnet (figs de orte)
	0.5d–4d. per pound
Isinglass	1s 11d–2s per pound
Honey	16s 8d–£1 16s per barrel (26.25 gallons)
	6s 8d–10s 6d per firkin (9 gallons)
	10d–1s 4d per gallon
	4d per pint
Licorice	2d–3d per pound
Mustard seed	10d–2s 8d per bushel
	1s per measure
	4s–8s per coomb
	5d per peck
Prunes	1d–4d per pound
Raisins (including great raisins)	5s–11s per hundredweight
	7s 3.5d per peck
	4s 6d–8s per frayle
	1d–2d per pound
Rice	1.5d–3d per pound
Salt (type unspecified)	18s–£1 6s 8d per wey
	1s 8.5d–3s 3d per coomb
	6.5d–8.5d per bushel
Salt (bay salt)	£1 3s 4d–£1 9s 3d per wey
	2s 8d–6s 8d per coomb

(Continued)

TABLE 3.1 (Cont.)

Item specified in the accounts	Price paid per unit
	9.5d–2s per bushel
Salt (white salt)	2s 8d–3s 8d per coomb
Salt (grey salt)	4d per coomb
Small raisins	4d per pound
Vinegar	1d–8d per gallon
SPICES	
Cinnamon	4s–6s 8d per pound
Cloves	4s 4d–6s 8d per pound
Ginger (including ginger, bottom ginger, ginger case, small ginger and uncoloured ginger)	1s 4d–3s 4d per pound
Grains of paradise	8.5d–1s 11d per pound
Mace	5s 4d–15s 4d per pound
Nutmeg	10s 8d per pound
Pepper	1s 3.5d–3s 8d per pound
Long pepper	5s 4d per pound
Saffron	8s 10d–18s 8d per pound
Sandalwood	1s 2d–3s per pound
Sugar	5d–8.5d per pound
	10d–5s per sugar loaf of varying weights
Turnsole	1s 2d–1s 4d per pound

By contrast, spices remained exclusive, luxury goods throughout the late medieval period and into the early modern period. Most of these spices were grown in southern China, the Moluccas, Malaya and India, shipped to Italy by Genoese or Venetian merchants and subsequently distributed throughout north-west Europe including to England. Other spices, such as saffron and licorice, came from Spain (although saffron was widely cultivated in England, particularly in Cambridgeshire and Essex).[28] By this period sugar was grown as sugar cane in a range of Mediterranean islands, including Cyprus, Rhodes and Crete, and refined with the resultant syrup usually hardened into sugarloaves before being exported.[29] Most of these spices were imported into London and came under the control of the Grocers' Company (formerly known as the Pepperers' Fraternity of St Antonin) who organised the domestic trade and distribution.[30] Imported spices were bought up by members of the company and sold on to agents and traders who then marketed them around the country.[31] Regional fairs played an important role in this distribution network, although London remained the main source for rarer spices and for more regular supplies than could be obtained from the annual fairs.[32] The exclusivity of London was enhanced by various measures taken by the Grocers' Company to concentrate the spice trade in the capital which included forbidding members from visiting regional fairs.[33]

The transport and import costs associated with spices ensured that their costs remained high throughout the late medieval period and beyond the means of most households. Saffron in particular was prohibitively expensive for all but the very wealthy as its cost reflected not only transport costs (when it was imported), but also the high levels of labour required to gather the tiny stigmas from individual flowers.[34]

Salt

The grocery item most widely consumed, and in the largest quantities, was salt. In the form known as 'bay salt' its use was essential as a means of preserving various foodstuffs, but it was also increasingly used as 'white salt' by the social elite to add flavouring to foods.[35] The term 'bay salt' had originated as a reference to the Bay of Bourgneuf in France where much salt was produced, but was commonly used to describe all of the salt produced along the Atlantic coast of France, northern Spain and Portugal.[36] Seawater was evaporated using the heat of the sun to leave salt crystals in a process which resulted in a coarse, dark salt which worked well in the preserving process.[37] Related products included holland salt (bay salt bought and refined by the Dutch) and grey salt (a moist salt produced in the same way and regions as bay salt), although these do not appear to have been as popular as preserving salts.[38] White salt was produced domestically by boiling and evaporating brine (obtained through various different processes) to produce a fine, white salt used as a table salt.[39] These various salts were moderately expensive commodities throughout the late Middle Ages and into the early modern period which reflects the fact that they were either the result of a labour intensive process (white salt) or were imported (bay salt), whilst salt production was also subject to the vagaries of the weather which could raise its price, particularly following wet summers.[40] It is worth making the point that even bay salt was only purchased by households who could also afford to acquire the meat and fish which it was commonly used to preserve. Nevertheless, the most commonly documented type of meat in probate inventories was bacon; for example, in Surrey bacon was recorded in a quarter (111) of the inventories in the second half of the sixteenth century. The salting process was also evidenced by troughs and powdering tubs which were variously described as bacon, brine, powdering, salting and silting troughs and powdering or salt tubs. Salt itself was recorded only twice in the Surrey sample.

The white salt purchased by Thetford Priory in the early sixteenth century ranged from 2s 8d to 3s 8d per coomb but the priory could afford to buy in bulk quantities so that its price was much below that which would have been paid by domestic households for smaller quantities. Its relatively high cost was such that it remained a fashionable, elite commodity and was not commonly adopted by lower social groups. This use by the wealthier members of society is reflected in testamentary bequests of pewter or silver 'salts' or salt cellars, which were a means of serving it at meals. Although the earliest reference in the wills used for this study was the 'j couple of silver saltes with j covere' given by Thomas Stotevile, esquire, of Dalham in 1466, there were very few other bequests of salts in the fifteenth century and it was not until the sixteenth century that these items began to appear with some frequency in wills.[41] Although most of the earlier references are in the wills of people of high social standing, increasingly, ownership spread down the social spectrum so that by the end of the century, they are recorded in the probate inventories of men from low-status trades, for example, shoemakers, sawyers and bakers. Pepper boxes were much less commonly recorded than salt cellars although pepper itself appeared in grocers' inventories. In 1693, William Spackman's stock of pepper was valued at around 1d per ounce. He also sold mace at 18s 8d per pound and cloves at 8s per pound (for price comparisons see Table 3.1).[42] John Burroughs, a mariner from Bristol, had a hogshead of pimento recorded in his inventory which was valued at £25.[43] The detailed inventory of John Brooke, a grocer in Wakefield in 1727, recorded pepper, sugar, cinnamon, ginger, caraway seeds and raisins. Grocers' inventories are an important source of information on food, drink and spices and a comprehensive study of their contents has been carried out by Jon Stobart.[44]

Food utensils

Households in the late medieval and early modern periods owned a range of vessels for cooking food together with various items for storing, preparing and eating including baskets, tubs and vats, cloths, cookware, flatware (for eating and serving food), drinking vessels and items of cutlery.

In the late Middle Ages most domestic cooking consisted of boiling food over an open hearth using earthenware or metal cooking pots suspended over the fire using a system of pothangers and hooks which allowed the height of the pot to be adjusted. The traditional open hearth became increasingly contained from the late medieval period onwards: in the first stage, the open hearth was replaced by a fireplace with a smoke bay; in the second, the fireplace was enclosed within a framed smoke hood; and finally, the fireplace was enclosed within a purpose-built brick or stone structure which contained the fire within a firebox or firepit, and which incorporated a chimney to vent smoke upwards and out of the house.[45] Whilst the need for smoke control had been the driving force behind these changes, these adaptations allowed for increased control and versatility in the cooking process which was also reflected in an increased range of equipment, whilst a rise in the use of coal led to more efficient fire furniture.[46] There was a decline in cauldrons hanging over a woodfire and more use of kettles, saucepans and stewpans.[47] Other cooking equipment which also reflected changed cooking practices became more widespread: the roasting of meat required the use of spits which rested on fire dogs or andirons; whilst dripping pans were placed underneath the roasting meat to collect the meat juices. The grilling of fish (and, to a lesser extent, meat) was done on a gridiron placed over the fire, which could also be used as a flat rack for pans to stand on.[48] In addition, the 'necessary ironware belonging to the use of the fireplace' expanded to include the grate and its cheeks, fire back, fender and associated implements such as fire shovel and andirons.[49]

Cooking vessels

The most basic cooking pot was of earthenware but, by the late Middle Ages, there was an increased use of cooking pots made of metal, particularly brass, rather than pottery (Photo 3.1). In his work on the peasantry of Worcestershire, R.K. Field identified that brass cooking pots or pans were almost always owned by the households used for his study, whilst Christopher Dyer suggested that these were being used by everyone with the main demand coming from peasants and artisans.[50] Testamentary evidence from this study suggested that from at least the mid-fifteenth century, basic metal cooking vessels were in common ownership by

PHOTO 3.1 Medieval cooking pot
Source: Image by courtesy of Athelstan Museum, Malmesbury

members of the middle and upper tiers of English society. Wills from this time onwards contained abundant references to pots and pans which could be heated over a fire and used to boil or stew food, not only brass pots, which were the household item most commonly referred to in the wills used for this study, but also kettles, 'stelyd' pans, cauldrons, leads and posnets.[51] The frequency with which brass pots were bequeathed probably reflected a perception that they were items of some worth and evidence from other sources shows that they could have some value. Three given as heriots on the Hertfordshire manor of Norton were valued at 2s (in 1358), 12d (in 1383) and 16d (in 1413), whilst two attached in debt cases in Newmarket were valued at 20d (in 1404) and 6s 8d (in 1408).[52] A number of testators state the capacity of the brass pots they were bequeathing: John Dey referred to his brass pot containing two and a half gallons in 1479 and Geoffrey Knyte bequeathed his brass pot of a gallon in 1527.[53] References such as these suggest that the pots were large enough to make a meal such as a basic pottage for an entire household, although they would also have been used for domestic brewing.

Christopher Green suggested that by 1600, the skillet had largely superseded the posnet (Photo 3.2), however, inventory evidence revealed that this suggestion might be somewhat premature.[54]

PHOTO 3.2   Skillet

Source: Image by courtesy of Ashmolean Museum, Oxford

Cauldrons were recorded in 29 per cent of Surrey inventories from the second half of the sixteenth century, a quarter recorded posnets but only 17 per cent recorded skillets. In the first half of the seventeenth century, 27 per cent of inventories from Marlborough recorded posnets and 22 per cent recorded skillets. As late as 1749, Richard Latham, a small-scale farmer from Lancashire, could still refer to having his posnet mended at a cost of 4d.[55]

Stephen Broadberry et al. referred to a number of consumption changes where new and more fashionable goods replaced more traditional goods and suggested that cauldrons were increasingly replaced by saucepans.[56] Cauldrons were recorded in 22 per cent of Kent inventories from 1600–29 but no saucepans were recorded. By the period from 1690–1719, however, cauldrons had ceased to appear in Kent inventories but 11 per cent of inventories recorded saucepans and for the subsequent period, from 1720–49, ownership of saucepans had jumped to a third of Kent inventories. Even in a county like Kent which was in the vanguard of social change, a significant increase in ownership of saucepans did not occur until well into the eighteenth century.

As with references to salts, the growing number of testamentary and inventory references to metal pans, spits and andirons from the late medieval period onwards illustrate an important dietary change which was particularly occurring amongst the higher groups of English society. As has been noted, the general consumption of meat rose after the Black Death; however, roasted meat remained a choice product which was not widely consumed by everyone. Meat for roasting needed to be of a better quality than that added to a pottage or stew and it was consequently more expensive. In addition, there was a higher cost associated with the process of roasting meat since roasting was both immoderate with fuel and required a higher labour input to turn the meat on the spit and watch it to ensure that it didn't overcook.[57] Consequently, the frying pan, dripping pans, spits and andirons associated with roasting meat were regarded as status items and tended to only be owned by elite households. Whilst testamentary evidence suggested a broad ownership from the mid-fifteenth century of the metal cooking pots associated with stewing and boiling foodstuffs, bequests of cooking utensils for roasting meat were much more limited. There were very few bequests of such items prior to the sixteenth century and although they increased from this date, almost all references to such items were made in the wills of people of high or intermediate social standing. As with brass pots, the cost of such items was not inconsequential; two dripping pans purchased on two separate occasions by Thetford Priory cost a total of 2s 9d and 3s 10d, whilst frying pans cost between 1s 1d and 1s 4d each.[58] The earliest reference to a spit was that made in the will of Thomas Stotevile esquire in 1466, whilst the only other fifteenth-century bequest was that of John Flecher, fishmonger and burgess of Thetford, in 1499.[59] By the second half of the sixteenth century, however, 43 per cent of the Surrey inventories referred to a spit and 29 per cent recorded andirons. Spits were originally powered by hand but other forms of power were subsequently introduced whereby spits were turned by hot air as it went up the chimney or by dogs.[60] Minwel Tibbott suggested that turnspit dogs were still in use in some parts of Britain in the nineteenth century.[61] A jack wheel owned by Daniel Snow in Marlborough in 1661 might have been a wheel turned by a dog.[62] Clockwork spit jacks were developed and the jack was usually worked by a weight suspended on a chain and a system of gears for keeping a steady rotation of the spit. Jacks were of considerable value; a jack owned by the yeoman John George in 1638 was a rare example of a jack separately valued and this was appraised at 10s.[63] References to jacks, jack chains and jack weights in probate inventories were frequent but often imprecise so that it was usually not possible to determine the exact nature of the jack. A further possible complication was that large jugs made of leather were also called jacks.[64]

Muldrew examined the presence of cooking equipment in labourers' probate inventories and this implied that meat was generally boiled and occasionally roasted. More than two thirds of labourers' inventories recorded pots and kettles but ownership of roasting equipment such as spits, jacks or roasting pans declined from almost half of the inventories to less than a quarter by the eighteenth century.[65]

Items for storing, preparing and eating food

Most of the food-related goods not used for cooking were made from wood, basketry and earthenware, although cloths of different types of linen were also used. Wooden goods were used for food preparation and eating, including bowls, spoons and trenchers, and were also used for storage: liquids in casks and tubs; and bread and grain in wooden arks and hutches. Basketry items were generally preferred for collecting and carrying and for the storage of some foodstuffs. Earthenware goods came in three principal forms: cooking pots; bowls, pans or dishes; and jugs or pitchers, and were used for cooking, but also for storage, fetching and carrying, and for dining and serving.[66]

Utensils for eating and drinking could include plates, knives, forks, spoons and drinking vessels. Plates originally took the form of a slice of bread known as a trencher upon which food was placed to eat. By the late medieval period the trencher had evolved into a flat piece of wood which could be either rectangular or round.[67] They were generally of low value and are rarely referred to in wills as specific items. Over time, the practice of serving food on wooden trenchers was gradually replaced by the use of platters made from pewter, wood or earthenware, and then by plates although probate inventory evidence suggested that the replacement of trenchers and platters by plates was slow. In the second half of the sixteenth century, 20 per cent of the Surrey inventories recorded trenchers and 57 per cent (251) recorded platters. Of the 251 recorded platters, 95 did not specify the material from which they were made, 124 specified that they were made from pewter, 31 from wood and one from earthenware. In Kent, Overton et al.'s data showed that 85 per cent of inventories recorded platters in 1600–29 and this fell gradually to only 33 per cent by 1720–49. Over the same period, the median number of plates increased from two to 13.[68] In Marl-borough, John Phillipps, a Blacksmith (died 1687), had a trencher rack and 12 trenchers as did William Spackman, a grocer who died in 1693. Trenchers were often grouped with other items, but it was clear that they were being valued at less than a penny each.[69] Edward Sweeper's inventory of 1683 revealed that they were literally two a penny. His four dozen trenchers and rack were valued at 2s.[70] In the middle of the eighteenth century, trenchers were still in use; Edward Thomas of Madeley Wood, a coalminer, had 18 trenchers valued at a total of 2s in 1754.[71] Stephen Willoughby in Marlborough had a trencher rack and 11 trenchers in 1746.[72]

During this period, it was essential that households could store foodstuffs safely and effectively. This required the use of appropriate containers for fresh ingredients and, perhaps more importantly, for preserved foodstuffs which needed to be stored longer term for use during the winter and early spring when fresh foodstuffs were in short supply. Many of these preserved foodstuffs were salted or smoked and packed into earthenware containers or hung up around walls, whilst dried goods were stored in wooden barrels or baskets (Photo 3.3). Thetford Priory bought a range of storage vessels over the period of the accounts including earthenware pots and basketry products. Basketry items ranged in price from 1½d for a maund to 5d for a large skep.[73]

PHOTO 3.3 Basketry

Source: Image by courtesy of Weald and Downland Museum

Cutlery

Implements for preparing, serving and eating food were in common use by the late medieval period. Knives have been used for cutting food since antiquity and in the medieval period, single knives were carried on the person for use at the table.[74] When solid food such as bread or meat was eaten it was cut with a knife and brought to the mouth with fingers.[75] Spoons were also widely available and made of various materials including tin, wood, latten, brass and pewter. These were used both for measuring quantities and mixing ingredients in cooking and also for eating, particularly consuming liquid foods.[76] By contrast, table forks were a much more recent phenomenon and their increased use throughout the early modern period reflected changing eating habits and, in particular, shows how the perception of what was considered to be appropriate dining behaviour was evolving.[77]

Religion has often been cited as the reason for the slow adoption of forks as they were perceived by Catholic clergy to be a symbol of Satan and their use considered sinful. In reality, their limited use was more likely that forks were not a practical commodity since much of the food consumed during the late Middle Ages and into the early modern period was relatively liquid in the form of pottages and either eaten using a spoon or consumed straight from the bowl.[78] Indeed, it has been argued that the earliest use of forks in England was not to convey food to the mouth but to serve food and, in particular, to carry it from the dish to the trencher.[79] Forks are only infrequently referred to in wills from this period and those that are recorded do seem to have been used to serve food such as the 'silvir forke for grene gyngour' bequeathed by the wealthy clothier John Baret of Bury St Edmunds in 1468.[80]

Fernand Braudel claimed that ordinary table forks originated in Venice and were luxury items found in elite homes from the sixteenth century.[81] In the early seventeenth century, the use of forks in Italy fascinated the traveller Thomas Coryat from Somerset who recorded that: 'The Italian, and also most strangers that are commorant in Italy, doe alwaies, at their meales use a little forke when they cut the meate.'[82]

Coryat gave the reason for the use of forks in Italy as hygienic and adopted the practice himself when he returned home. In England, James I used a fork but by the time of his death in 1625 'hardly anyone' had followed his lead.[83] Nicholas Breton similarly rejected the need for forks in 1618 stating that 'We need no little forks to make hay with our mouths'.[84] By the second half of the eighteenth century the use of forks was rising and reflected 'growing European taboos' against touching food with the hands.[85] Norbert Elias saw this as a civilising process in which people carried out their daily activities and for Stephen Mennell, this reflected the transition from an agricultural to an industrial society.[86]

Maxine Berg suggested that the use of tableware penetrated the 'middling classes' rapidly and deeply so that by the first quarter of the eighteenth century *most* of those aspiring to 'middling class' status and artisan respectability bought their knives, forks and spoons in sets.[87] Inventory evidence did not support Berg's dating of the adoption of forks since there were very few references to forks in the seventeenth century, the earliest being 1662. In 1639, Robert Birde, a cutler in Bristol, had over 20 dozen Sheffield knives and 17 dozen London knives in his inventory but there was no mention of any forks.[88] In 1662, Henry Cartwright, a cutler in Bristol, had very large stocks of knives and knife sets but again no forks.[89] With the exception of the gentry, it was not until the second half of the eighteenth century that a sharp rise in the ownership of forks took place. Only 3 per cent of inventories recorded forks in the period 1720–49 but in the second half of the eighteenth century this increased to 12 per cent. It was much higher in Kent and Bristol where more than a third of inventories recorded forks and intriguingly also in Dorset where 30 per cent of inventoried households owned forks. An eighteenth-century fork and seventeenth- or eighteenth-century knife found in a garden in Godmanchester, Huntingdonshire is shown in Photo 3.4. By 1748, Francis Gregory, a cutler from Marlborough, had several sets of knives and forks in his shop which were of various quality with handles made of buckshorn, ivory, staghorn, blackhorn buck ruffhorn and coco. Half a dozen knives and forks varied in price from 2s for the blackhorn to 10s for the ivory.[90]

Tablecloths and napkins

Household textiles associated with serving and eating food became increasingly important and included napkins, tablecloths and towels for wiping hands. These

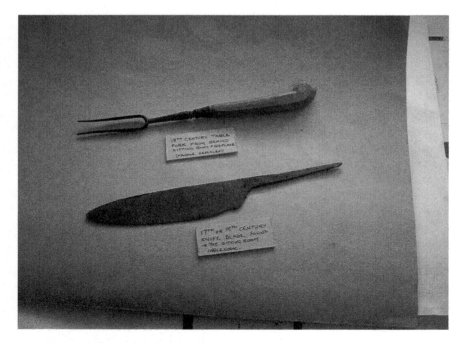

PHOTO 3.4   Knife and fork from Godmanchester

were made of linen although this could take a variety of forms ranging from very rough, domestically produced cloth made from hemp and flax, through to fine diaper cloth and linen damask imported from the continent. Dyer suggested that all but the poorest households owned a tablecloth; however, these were probably made from the coarsest domestic linen rather than finer fabrics.[91] Fine linen was always associated with status. Manufacture involved a higher level of labour input which was subsequently reflected in cost so that fine linen was as much as 13d per yard whereas domestic linen cost from as little as 1½d upwards. In addition, its ongoing maintenance required the input of servants skilled in the specialised task of washing and finishing so that the linen retained its whiteness.

The wills contained numerous bequests of linen goods associated with dining including napkins, tablecloths and towels. Such bequests can be found in some of the earliest wills used for this study which suggests that linen was commonly associated with dining by at least the mid-fifteenth century; for example, in her will of 1462 Agnes Kyng of Thetford gifted each of her four children a tablecloth (*mappa*).[92] Women frequently gifted such items which reflects the fact that these were goods which they often brought to a marriage and which returned to them on the death of the husband.[93] Most bequests of household linen were simply referred to as napkins, tablecloths or towels, so it is impossible to identify the quality of the items being given, although John Hole, fishmonger of St Albans, was careful to clarify that some of the towels and tablecloths which he left to his daughter were of 'diapre', whilst others were simply of 'playncloth'.[94] Nevertheless, it is evident that many bequests were of fine linen and most of these were given by people who held high social status within their communities; Margery Howton, widow of the Mildenhall draper Thomas Howton, left her diaper tablecloth in her will of 1515 and the Thetford surgeon John Hert gave a diaper towel in his will of 1520.[95]

Contrary to Dyer, Lorna Weatherill argued that table linen was already in use in 1675 but was uncommon.[96] Neither the evidence from wills referred to earlier or subsequent inventory evidence fully support Weatherill's contention. In Surrey, tablecloths were recorded in more than half of inventories (54 per cent) and napkins were recorded in 28 per cent of inventories in the second half of the sixteenth century. More of the inventoried population may have owned tablecloths and napkins but these items may have been recorded merely as linen. During the seventeenth and eighteenth centuries, ownership of table linen was more difficult to calculate accurately. Probate inventories increasingly recorded items such as tablecloths and napkins within the general category of linen or sometimes more specifically as table linen without specifying individual items. However, tablecloths and napkins continued to be recorded in many inventories. Napkins were often recorded by the dozen whereas numbers of tablecloths were not always specified. As has been noted, the ownership of forks even among the inventoried population was still rare until the second half of the eighteenth century so that the great majority of people continued to handle their food whilst eating and the need for napkins remained.

Drink

The main drink for all groups of society in the Middle Ages was ale, although the strength, quality and quantity drunk by the poorer classes was somewhat lower than that consumed by their social superiors.[97] Each brewing produced several worts and those drawn off first produced a finer and stronger ale than subsequent drawings.[98] In Piers Plowman, Rose the regrator sells her best ale at a gallon a groat (4d), whereas her 'peny-ale' and 'poddyng-ale' is for labourers and low folk.[99] The main grain used in ale production was barley (which was malted before brewing) although other grains could be used, particularly oats, wheat and dredge (a mixture of oats and barley). The lower calorific value of ale when compared to bread or pottage may have restricted consumption by the peasantry prior to the Black Death so that they tended to drink cheaper and weaker ales, or even milk and water.[100] Once again, this was a result of land pressure and the need to maximise the production and use of grain; however, from the late fourteenth century, the same factors that increased demand for wheaten bread also led to a *per capita* rise in the demand for ale amongst all social groups and to a rising consumption of better-quality ale by those who could afford to do so. This increase in ale drinking also led to the rising commercialisation of brewing during this period which was reflected in a growth in the popularity of alehouses where ale was brewed and sold for immediate consumption on the premises.[101] In addition, whereas ale-brewing had traditionally been the preserve of occasional and by-industrial brewers who were predominantly women, increasingly the trade became concentrated into the hands of a smaller number of professional male brewers, particularly within towns.[102]

Ale did not keep very long and quickly went sour, especially when the weather was hot. As a result, it had to be brewed frequently with monasteries and large households brewing up to six times a month to ensure that their ale was fresh. From the late Middle Ages, ale began to be replaced by hopped beer which was easier to transport and preserve than ale. Although there is possible evidence for the use of hops in late Anglo-Saxon England, beer imported from the Low Countries did not begin to appear in east and south coast towns until the 1370s and was not regularly brewed in England until the early fifteenth century.[103] It has been claimed that the late medieval period saw a dramatic rise in the consumption of beer; however, its adoption seems to have been limited to certain towns and regions so that in most areas of the country it was not regularly consumed until the sixteenth century or even later. Although beer was being imported into the east coast port of Ipswich in the fourteenth century and was being produced commercially in the town by the 1410s, there are no references to beer being available in the fifteenth century in inland Thetford (34 miles from Ipswich) despite frequent references to the sale of ale.[104] Early in the sixteenth century, however, Thetford Priory purchased two barrels of beer for 2s 8d and by 1528/29 the household was regularly brewing beer for its own use with four separate purchases of hops in this year and in subsequent years.[105] Whilst most of the hops purchased by Thetford Priory were bought from Lynn, on one occasion, the priory bought hops which had been imported into Ipswich.[106]

The supplanting of ale by beer was not universally welcomed. Many ale brewers resented what they regarded as the usurpation of their trade by beer brewers, many of whom had come to England as immigrants from the Low Countries. In 1436, a number of London beer breweries were attacked and the sheriffs of London issued a writ to the effect that beer-brewing should continue despite attempts to prevent this by claiming that it was a poisonous drink which caused drunkenness.[107] Such assertions continued to be made; for example, Andrew Boorde, the sixteenth-century English physician, protested 'Ale for an Englysshe man is a natural drynke' whereas beer was bad for health:

> And nowe of late dayes it [beer] is moche used in Englande to the detriment of many Englysshe men, specially it kylleth them the which be troubled with the colycke, and the stone and the strangulation.... it doth make a man fat and doth inflate the bely.[108]

The domestic production of ale was reflected in both testamentary and probate evidence. Within the wills, there were frequent references to brewing vessels, particularly by female testators, which illustrated the fact that brewing was largely performed by the women of the household. Margery Goch was regularly amerced in the Mildenhall courts for brewing against the assize and in her will of 1443 she left all her brewing vessels to her son John.[109]

The wealthiest classes also drank wine which remained an exclusive luxury commodity throughout this period.[110] Prior to the Black Death, the most highly regarded wine was that imported from Gascony, although wines from northern France and the Rhineland were also consumed.[111] In the post-Black Death period, the Gascon region was beset by a series of problems including wars and fluctuations in the weather which affected trade.[112] As a result, the period saw an overall decline in wine imports from the region and the increased popularity in England of strong sweet wines from the Mediterranean such as malmsey and rumney.[113] This reduced availability of Gascon wine affected its cost so that it rose from between 3d and 4d per gallon just prior to the Black Death, to an average of 6d to 8d a gallon in the fifteenth century, although in the years which saw the most constrained production, prices increased to as much as 1s 2d per gallon.[114] Sweet Mediterranean wines generally tended to be more expensive than those from Gascony so that James Thorold Rogers recorded sweet wine purchased in Oxford in 1425 as costing 1s 4d per gallon.[115]

In some areas of the country, agricultural workers also drank cider and their drinks were carried in a costrel, a leather drinking bottle. Costrels are rare examples of surviving consumer goods owned by labourers in the medieval period.[116] Although leather drinking vessels were commonly used in the late Middle Ages, most people drank from bowls or cups made from wood or earthenware. For the majority of the population, wooden drinking bowls were roughly made from whatever wood was available and unadorned, but amongst the social elite, wooden drinking bowls known as mazers became increasingly popular. These were fashioned by craftsmen from a variety of quality woods, and even coconut shell, with the use of maplewood being especially prized as this could be carefully worked by the turner to bring out the beauty of the speckled grain; indeed, Sheila Sweetinburgh noted that the word may derive from the Old High German *másá*, meaning 'a spot'.[117] The basic wooden bowl of the mazer was usually adorned with other features including an ornamental band (often inscribed), a mount (which turned the vessel into a standing mazer) and a cover (fashioned from wood and embellished with metal). These adornments could be of a variety of metals but silver and silver-gilt were particularly used and precious stones were also often added; for example, a mazer held in the Treasury of Canterbury Cathedral holds a crystal which was believed to have come from the shoe of Thomas Becket.[118] The popularity of mazers during the late medieval period was indicated by the regularity with which they were bequeathed in wills, particularly by people of status, and usually to close family members which suggested that they were given as a means of commemoration by providing an ongoing reminder to the recipient of the deceased through use of the item which reflected Sweetinburgh's observations about the purpose of the mazers used by the monks of Christ Church Priory, Canterbury (Photo 3.5).[119] In 1483, Agnes Dunston, widow, of Thetford, gave a mazer with cover referred

PHOTO 3.5 Sixteenth-century mazer with silver-gilt ornamental mount and a central boss bearing the sacred monogram IHC

Source: Image by courtesy of the Royal Cornwall Museum and reproduced by kind permission of The Royal Institution of Cornwall

to as being called 'le note' (suggesting that it was made from a mounted coconut shell) to her son Peter Coket, and in 1561, Thomas Rande of Coggeshall left a mazer bound with silversmith's work to his son Thomas.[120]

In the second half of the sixteenth century, the odd mazer appeared in probate inventories; for example, in 1564 John Hull, gentleman, of Hambledon, Surrey owned a little mazer banded with silver and gilt and in 1570, Robert Altham, yeoman, of Tooting Bec owned a mazer edged with silver valued at 3s 4d.

Hot drinks

In the Middle Ages, popular hot milk drinks such as caudles and possets were occasionally served either at the end of supper to close the stomach, or to those who were ill. These drinks were made with cow or almond milk, curdled with wine or ale and thickened with egg.[121] Lady Macbeth used poisoned possets to knock out the guards outside Duncan's quarters in Shakespeare's *Macbeth*:

> The doors are open, and the surfeited grooms
> Do mock their charge with snores. I have drugged their possets.[122]

Another drink consumed in the Middle Ages was made from aleberries, oatmeal, saffron and ale which was drunk warm rather than hot and appears to have been a drink for the gentry classes and above. Like possets and caudles, it was also a drink for those 'of a delicate disposition'.[123]

Coffee

In the seventeenth century, traditional patterns of drinking began to be transformed by new products of foreign origin in the form of coffee and tea which appeared in England at around the same time.[124] It has been suggested that coffee arrived with English Levant merchants from the Smyrna factory in the 1630s and 1640s and in 1637 John Evelyn recorded in his diary in 1637 that Nathaniel Conopius came to Oxford and was the first that he ever saw drink coffee.[125] Coffee was originally valued for its medicinal properties so that Thomas Willis, who began his medical practice in Oxford in the mid-seventeenth century, frequently sent his sick patients to the coffee house rather than to the apothecary.[126] In 1652, a handbill issued by Pasqua Rosée promoted the medicinal properties of coffee as a cure for headaches, consumption, coughs and other ailments.[127]

There is disagreement over which was the first coffee house to be established in England. Bryant Lillywhite, Frank Trentmann and Brian Cowan argued that the first was that opened in 1650 by a Jewish merchant named Jacob at the Angel, Oxford.[128] Markman Ellis and John Wills preferred the claims for Pasqua Rosée's London coffee house in Cornhill.[129] Samuel Pepys repeatedly referred to coffee houses in his diary and visited coffee houses in Exchange Alley and Cornhill in London.[130] During the entire period of his diary, from 1660 to

1669, he recorded 99 visits to a coffee house.[131] Coffee houses became centres of conviviality and were used not just for refreshment, but for business, discussing politics, auctions, medical treatment, news gathering, hiring servants or just conversation.[132] They were also fundamentally male and an expression of rational masculinity.[133]

Although coffee houses sold other drinks so that, for example, the 1682 inventory of William Peart, recorded as a gentleman and coffee house proprietor in Lincoln, listed 'ale, beare, meade and cyder' in the cellars with a valuation of £15 4s, drinking coffee was considered to be a more conducive drink for effectively doing business than beer.[134] Initially, the clientele of coffee houses was the 'leisured class', however, increasingly social barriers were lowered and tradesmen and gentlemen sat down together and discussed business. Many coffee houses adopted house rules:

The Rules and Orders of the Coffee-House

> Enter sirs freely, but first if you please,
> Peruse our Civil-orders, which are these:
> Firstly, Gentry, Tradesmen, all are welcome hither,
> And many without Affront sit down Together;
> Pre-eminence of Place, none should here Mind,
> But take the next fit seat he can find:
> Nor need say, if Finer Persons come,
> Rise up to assigne to them his Room;
> To limit men's expenc we think not fair,
> But let him forfeit Twelve-pence that shall Swear:[135]

Coffee houses spread rapidly but not all approved of this development.[136] Charles II was concerned that coffee houses were centres of 'speaking evil' against the government.[137] In 1674, *The Women's Petition Against Coffee* accused the beverage of leading men to trifle away their time and spend their money.[138] Cowan estimated that London had at least several hundred coffee houses by the end of the seventeenth century, although precise numbers are difficult to determine as many were unlicensed.[139] Coffee houses flourished as hospitable and informative gathering places and spread rapidly to the provinces. York had a coffee house by the end of the 1660s, Bristol had John Kimber's coffee house and Huntingdon subsequently had a licensed coffee house run by John Fisher.[140] John Kimber died in 1681 and his inventory recorded coffee berries valued at £10.[141]

Coffee consumption per head stagnated during the eighteenth century despite falls in its price.[142] Trentmann calculated that in 1724, 'all of England' had to make do with 660 tons of coffee which equated to each inhabitant enjoying a weak cup of coffee every three weeks.[143] Reasons advanced for the relative decline of coffee included a reduction in quality and the need for roasting and grinding, but whatever the cause, tea established itself as the nation's preferred beverage.[144]

Tea

The East India Company began importing Chinese tea and it became popular among higher ranks of society when the drink was adopted by Charles II's wife, Katherine of Braganza. Samuel Pepys noted the first time he took tea in his diary in 1660, describing it as 'a china drink of which I never had drunk before'.[145] Initially tea prices were very high, and tea was regarded as an expensive and exotic luxury; a pound of tea cost between £6 and £10 in London in 1650 at a time when £6 represented six months' wages for a labourer. In 1678, imports of less than 5,000lb of tea were said to have completely glutted the London market.[146] Although tea prices fell to 16s per pound by the turn of the century, coffee consumption *per capita* was still ten times as great as tea.[147] After trade was established with Canton in 1713, however, tea imports increased rapidly so that tea became the new 'wonder commodity' that powered trade with China.[148] By the 1720s, the value of tea imported into Britain was substantially higher than the value of imported coffee and between 1721 and 1760 the quantity of tea imported rose five-fold.[149] By the end of the eighteenth century, tea accounted for more than 60 per cent of the trade of the East India Company. Whereas in 1783 only three million pounds of tea were delivered out of the Company's warehouses for home consumption, by 1800/1 this had increased seven-fold to 21 million pounds.[150]

Tea consumption spread rapidly throughout England and throughout society in the eighteenth century. In London, Thomas Twining bought Tom's Coffee House on The Strand in 1706 and subsequently transformed it into a tea shop. In Norwich, advertisements in the *Norwich Gazette* from 1708 recorded that coffee and tea could be purchased from Jane Pyecrafts in the city. Overton *et al.* suggested that the 1720s was probably the first decade in which mass consumption of tea spread outside of London. Consumption of tea doubled in the 1730s and 1740s as prices fell and by the mid-eighteenth century tea-drinking had spread far beyond the elite and middling sorts.[151] One of the attractions of the reopened Vauxhall Tea Gardens in 1732 was taking tea.

For Giorgio Riello, cups, saucers and teapots were the necessary tools of polite sociability, but in *Consuming Splendor*, Linda Levy Peck goes beyond that and identified the *gendered* social rituals associated with the new tea goods.[152] This is not immediately evident from using probate inventories, but diaries add further insights to the probate material. With few exceptions, male diaries recorded taking tea with other males and female diaries recorded taking tea with females. In Sarah Hurst's diary, she regularly recorded drinking tea with female friends. In a sample month in 1760, Sarah recorded that she took tea nine times, mainly with female friends but also with Quakers of unknown sex and her uncle.[153] There were many more references to drinking tea than coffee in the years 1800–4 in John Carrington's diary. Carrington drank tea mainly with men (Mr Randall, a fellow farmer and overseer, Mr Ilott and Mr Cock), but in one case with a woman (Mrs Watson).[154]

Thomas Turner's diary revealed both the extent to which tea-drinking became widespread by the mid-eighteenth century but also his disapproval of the practice. On 15 July 1758, Turner wrote: 'The exorbitant practice of tea-drinking have in such a manner corrupted the morals of people of almost all ranks'.[155] Again, on 26 September 1763, Turner expressed his strong disapproval: 'Custom has brought tea and spirituous liquors so much in fashion…they prove our ruin … hurt our health'.[156]

The Commutation Act of 1784 reduced the tax on tea from 119 per cent to 12.5 per cent so that tea-drinking became affordable to all but the very poorest groups by the end of the eighteenth century and was regularly drunk by the 'working classes'.[157] Frederick Eden found that in the 1790s poor families in Middlesex and Surrey drank tea not only in the morning and evening but in large quantities even at dinner. James Walwin concluded that the luxuries of an earlier generation had become cheap basics even in the diet of the poor, although it still cost Allen's 'Ealing gardener' 4s per pound for tea.[158] Whilst this was a massive reduction from the mid-seventeenth century, it still represented more than a day's work working from 6.00 in the morning until 6.00 at night.[159] The cleric David Davies wrote in 1795 that the rural poor did not drink high-quality tea but spring water coloured with a few leaves of the lowest-priced tea and sweetened with the brownest sugar.[160] Davies calculated that tea with bread provided one meal for a whole family every day at no greater expense than approximately a shilling a week. Davies suggested that the rural poor would drink milk if they could afford to keep a cow but that this was beyond the means of most of them. The only thing remaining to moisten their bread was tea due to the high cost of both malt and procuring milk.[161]

Tea came in different types and qualities including Bohea (black tea), Hyson (green tea), Congou (black Chinese tea) and Souchong (a superior quality tea). Common Bohea tea tended to be much cheaper than the Hyson and Souchong varieties. Tea was recorded in a few retailers' inventories but the type and quantity was not always sufficiently specified. Daniel Bridges had green tea in his shop valued at 8s a pound and Bohea tea at 9s 10d a pound in 1725.[162] A Wakefield grocer, John Brook, had tea recorded in his probate inventory in 1727 and among the items in his shop were a canister of Bohea tea valued at £6 16s and a canister of green tea valued at £2 10s. Thomas Marchant recorded payments of 16s for a pound of tea in 1714 and 7s 6d for half a pound of Bohea tea in 1719, whilst Thomas Turner wrote that he paid 9s 3d for a pound of green tea on 1 August 1759.[163]

Thomas Turner was not alone in deploring the rapid expansion of tea-drinking. Many objections were for health reasons so that Samuel Johnson warned against drinking tea for it encouraged a lifestyle which weakened the constitution: 'Tea is one of the stated amusements of the idle and luxurious. The whole mode of life is changed, … every exercise that strengthened the nerves and the muscle is fallen into disuse'.[164]

Jonas Hanway also argued that tea-drinking was deleterious for the diet of wet nurses, since it caused them to produce inadequate milk and thus weak and sickly children.[165] Polly Honeycombe, a comedy play by George Colman written in the mid-eighteenth century, reveals contemporary health fears of tea-drinking.

Polly Honeycombe

> Mrs. HONEYCOMBE's Apartment; Mrs. HONEYCOMBE alone,
> I am not at all well to-day. [yawns, as if just waking]
> Such a quantity of tea in a morning, makes one quite Nervous and
>   Mr. Honeycombe
> does not chuse it qualified. 1 have such a dizziness in my head, it absolutely
>   turns round with me. I don't think neither that the Hysterick Water is
>   warm enough for my stomach.
> I must speak to Mr. Julep to order me something rather more comfortable.[166]

John Wesley also argued in the mid-eighteenth century that drinking tea was both deleterious to health and expensive, although he subsequently changed his mind:

> I was a little surprised at some symptoms of a paralytic disorder. I could not imagine what should occasion the shaking of my hand, till I observed it was always worst after breakfast, and that, if I intermitted drinking tea for two or three days, it did not shake at all. Upon inquiry, I found tea had the same effect upon others also of my acquaintance.[167]

Whilst these medical explanations of the ill effects of widespread tea-drinking might not fully persuade, an economic approach might carry more conviction. If poor families afforded tea by reducing their consumption of more nutritious protein-rich foodstuffs, then increased consumption of tea might indeed have been injurious to health.[168]

Chocolate

Chocolate, made from the cocoa pods which are the fruit of the cacao tree, was important to the Aztec, Inca and Mayan cultures where it was used in religious rituals as a food for the gods and as a currency.[169] Although cocoa was introduced to Europe at the beginning of the sixteenth century, when Christopher Columbus returned from Nicaragua with cocoa beans for Isabella and Ferdinand, it was originally of limited appeal to Europeans because of its bitter taste. Subsequently, the Spanish began to import the beans and improved its taste with the addition of sugar and by 1657, chocolate was being advertised as a drink in England and was being drunk in the coffee houses of London.[170] Samuel Pepys recorded visiting a coffee house to drink chocolate on 24 November 1664 and noted that it was 'very good'.[171] The drink was promoted for good health so that on 24 April 1661, Pepys was brought chocolate to settle his stomach after consuming excessive amounts of alcohol the previous evening, the day of the coronation of Charles II.[172] Chocolate was also believed to be an aphrodisiac by provoking blood flow which, according to Galen, stimulated sexual ardour, whilst it also began to appear at late seventeenth-century breakfasts in the form of a rich drink containing chocolate mixed with eggs and spices.[173]

As with tea and coffee, drinking chocolate required a range of cups, saucers and pots to enjoy the drink. Chocolate cups, saucers, chocolate mills and chocolate pots all appeared in the probate inventory collection although these references were much more limited than those associated with the drinking of tea and coffee. Clement Raynolds, a brazier who died in 1724, owned three chocolate mills, used for grinding the chocolate to a powder, and four chocolate pots. The four chocolate pots were valued at £1 1s 6d.[174] Silver chocolate pots could be of considerable value; Charles Goodale, of the parish of St Margaret, Westminster, was tried and found guilty at the Old Bailey for stealing a silver chocolate pot valued at £12 and a silver teapot valued at £7 in 1711.[175] Nevertheless, the limited references to chocolate in probate inventories confirmed Stobart's assertion that chocolate never really caught on in eighteenth-century Britain because of the alternatives of tea and coffee.[176]

Sugar

In the late medieval period, sugar was an imported good viewed as a luxury.[177] It remained prohibitively expensive for almost everyone except the nobility and gentry so that honey was commonly used as an alternative sweetener by all except the lowest social groups for whom even honey was an elusive product.[178] Sugar purchased by Thetford Priory in the late fifteenth and early sixteenth centuries cost between 5d and 8½d per pound with sugar loaves of various weights ranging from 10d to 5s per loaf.

Sugar cultivation was introduced into the Atlantic islands of Spain and Portugal in the fifteenth century, particularly the Madeira Islands but also the Cape Verde Islands and others. The techniques and methods used on these islands became the basis for the sugar plantations developed in the Americas which used slave labour. English settlers in the Americas were quick to follow the lead of the Spanish and Portuguese by establishing sugar plantations in Barbados in the early seventeenth century. At this time, domestic demand for sugar was increasingly rapidly as it was closely associated with the introduction and rising popularity of tea and coffee and, to a lesser extent, chocolate, as it was used as a sweetener for these hot drinks. Stanley Mintz referred to sweetened tea as 'a rarity in 1650, a luxury in 1750, and a virtual necessity in 1850'.[179] Sugar imports for home consumption rose twelvefold in a century and a half: from around 2lb *per capita* in the 1660s to 24lb by the end of the eighteenth century.[180] At the same time, rapidly rising production was such that the price fell from between 1s 6d to 2s per pound in the early seventeenth century, to 6d to 8d per pound a century later.[181] Stobart found that more than half (52.9 per cent) of grocery retailers stocked sugar in his sample covering the period 1660–1830.[182] In the 1740s, Richard Latham from Lancashire, whose social standing was equivalent to that of a well-off labouring family, was purchasing 50lb of sugar per annum.[183] By the end of the eighteenth century, consumption of sugar had extended to the 'Ealing gardener' who bought about two pounds of sugar a week, around 10 per cent of the household income.[184] After bread, sugar represented the second biggest item in the family budget, the same amount as rent.[185]

Before the introduction of granulated and cubed sugar, sugar continued to be supplied in hard loaves. Pieces of sugar were broken off with a small chopper or nippers and were then conveyed to the cup with sugar tongs. Both sugar and associated equipment were recorded in the probate inventories: Edmund Pruett of Bristol had the proceeds of 33 hogsheads of sugar valued at £343 7s in 1729; Joseph Clarke of Roxwell had 5 cwt of brown sugar valued at 34s per cwt in 1692; Daniel Bridges had two pounds of loaf sugar plus 12 pounds of rice in his grocer's shop which were valued together at 5s in 1725; and John Brook, a Wakefield grocer, had sugar valued at 19s a stone and his total stock of sugar was valued at over £23 in 1727.[186] Sugar tongs, often of silver, were also recorded. [187]

Tableware associated with hot drinks

The new luxury hot drinks created a demand for specialised tableware. The material of choice for such tableware was porcelain but this was not manufactured in England before the 1740s so that prior to this date it was an expensive import only owned by more affluent households. The East India Company imported large quantities of porcelain from China and Japan including teapots, cups and saucers and in 1730 alone the company brought in over 517,000 pieces. Shipwrecks often provide testimony to the scale of this trade since about 5 per cent of the East India Company's sailings between 1600 and 1833 ended in disaster. There were 231 ships lost and an additional 110 reported as wrecks.[188] Many of these wrecks have been located in recent years but they have not been excavated in a scientific way and much valuable information has been lost; for example, the *Geldermalsen*, a Dutch sailing ship which sank in 1751, was loaded with a cargo of tea, silk, gold and 160,000 pieces of porcelain – the largest cargo of Chinese export porcelain found to date. The *Geldermalsen* was looted for the commercial sale of its contents and without concern for its historical context, so that the wreck itself was destroyed.[189]

Until domestic manufacture lowered the cost of porcelain and made it more widely affordable, most people drank their tea from lower-quality, domestically produced goods such as earthenware and salt-glazed stoneware.[190] Domestic manufacture often imitated imported goods. In the seventeenth century, ceramic teapots were imported from China made from red Yixing stoneware, the dominant material for teapots in coastal areas of China where English traders obtained their goods.[191] English manufacturers such as Dwight at Fulham and the Elers brothers at Vauxhall manufactured domestic copies of the red Yixing stoneware teapots.[192] In 1698, Celia Fiennes went to Newcastle-under-Lyme, Staffordshire, home of the English pottery industry, 'to see them making the fine tea-potts cups and saucers of the fine red earth, in imitation and as curious as that which comes from China.'[193] Staffordshire potteries also created 'creamware', an imitation of oriental porcelain.[194]

The secret of making porcelain was allegedly conveyed to the west by the Jesuit missionary Père D'Entrecolles.[195] The first hard-paste porcelain produced in Europe was manufactured at Meissen in Saxony in 1709 and from the mideighteenth century, rising Chinese porcelain prices stimulated the production of goods in England.[196] Many manufacturers replaced other production with porcelain; for example, the tin-glazed earthenware known as majolica was made at Bow and Chelsea by 1745, but Daniel Defoe could later refer to Bow as 'where a large manufactory of porcelain is carried on. They have already made large quantities of tea-cups'.[197] In the 1750s, the Worcester potteries began to produce large quantities of blue and white soft-paste porcelain tea wares for the home market.[198] Based on Père D'Entrecolles descriptions, William Cookworthy patented his hard-paste porcelain formula in 1768 and built a factory to produce porcelain ware.[199]

Berg argued that during the eighteenth century, the equipment involved in drinking tea was a priority in the consumer expenditure of people of the respectable artisan and middling groups, as well as the elites. This equipment varied in quality according to wealth but included silver and china vessels for tea making, tea tables, japanned papier-mâché tea trays, tea caddies, tea sets and cutlery.[200] Berg considered that the role of imports such as those associated with tea was crucial in the debate about the growth of luxury consumer goods, although it has often been ignored.[201] Certain items that appear in greater numbers after 1750 in probate inventories, such as items associated with hot drinks, were more closely linked with imports than others including looking glasses and window curtains that appeared earlier. However, the pattern of imports and home production of goods was not straightforward. Probate inventory evidence did not measure the consumption of new drinks but the extent of ownership of the paraphernalia of goods associated with drinking them: teapots, teacups, tea trays, tea tables, tea caddies, coffee pots, coffee cups, etc. (Photo 3.6).[202]

This growth in ownership was surprisingly modest despite, for these purposes, ownership of just one of these items resulting in a count of ownership. Only 1 per cent of the inventory collection recorded any of these items prior to 1700 and it was only in the second half of the eighteenth century that ownership of these goods rapidly expanded, being recorded in 25 per cent of inventories overall and 73 per cent of those in Bristol with gentry and high-status professionals (HST) leading the way. By the fourth quarter of the eighteenth century, Peter King found a rapid expansion of tea-related items recorded even in pauper inventories which rose from 20 per cent in the period up to 1769 to 71 per cent after 1770, whilst the rise in coffee-related items was much more modest and rose from 5 per cent to just 14 per cent.[203] Joseph Harley found similar results in a much larger sample of 'pauper inventories' from Kent, Dorset and Norfolk where tea-related goods expanded rapidly in the 1770s but ownership of goods related to coffee-drinking remained low.[204]

a) b)

c) d)

PHOTO 3.6 Tea and coffee utensils: a) Creamware 1760–70 (Leeds); b) Creamware tea caddy (Staffordshire); c) Creamware 1763 (Staffordshire); d) Coffee pot 1769–70 (Cookworthy)

Source: Images by courtesy of the Royal Cornwall Museum and reproduced by kind permission of The Royal Institution of Cornwall

Conclusion

Expenditure on food and drink continued to comprise the largest proportion of the household budget throughout our period; however, subtle but important changes were taking place in the actual items being consumed. Prior to the Black Death, food was predominantly vegetarian with an emphasis on cheaper grains and legumes supplemented by vegetables and fruits. It was monotonous, particularly in the winter months when it consisted of grains and legumes which could be stored for lengthy periods. It also lacked essential minerals and vitamins: whilst it was high in fibre, it lacked adequate protein, calcium, folic acid and vitamins B12 and C and was likely to have led to an increased susceptibility to conditions such as beriberi, scurvy, anaemia and rickets, whilst malnutrition of this nature would also have reduced protection against infectious diseases including plague.[205] As land pressure was eased after the Black Death, food was more widely available and this, together with a rise in household incomes, ensured that the period saw an overall improvement to diets, both in terms of quantity and quality. Although the food consumed by most people continued to be predominantly grain-based, the proportions of different grains altered so that diets generally included a higher proportion of wheat (for bread) and barley (for ale).[206] In addition to grain, almost all consumers ate more animal protein in the form of milk, cheese, meat and fish which ensured that food was generally more varied, particularly in the winter when stored grain and legumes were increasingly supplemented by preserved meat, fish and cheese. While these dietary improvements were relatively small, they are likely to have had a significant impact on the lives of the lower classes. Further up the social scale, a rising consumption of grocery goods added a further level of variety and interest to the diets of the more affluent classes, whilst the higher classes ate food seasoned with the spices which were being imported into England in ever increasing amounts and varieties. From the seventeenth century, these dietary changes were supplemented by the arrival of the new hot drinks, coffee and tea sweetened with sugar. Although these were initially only consumed by the most affluent, as prices of the drinks fell dramatically, they became accessible to all classes and tea established itself as the hot drink of choice for the English.

The processes of cooking, eating and drinking necessitated the use of various household goods. By the end of the Middle Ages brass pots were possessed by almost all households whilst other metal cooking vessels were often owned. Dripping pans, spits and other items associated with roasting meat were increasingly acquired by more affluent households and reflected a rising consumption of roasted meat by these classes. Whilst the lower classes continued to eat from wooden trenchers and platters, those who could afford to do so were choosing to eat from pewter plates and dishes. The slow adoption of table forks led to new ways of eating. Tea- and coffee-drinking implied not just cups and saucers but tea kettles, coffee pots, tea trays and even tea tables. The extent of ownership of these consumer goods is explored in Chapters 7 and 9.

After food and drink, spending on clothing was the second largest item in the household budget. In terms of basic physiological human needs, clothing was also essential and is explored in the next chapter.

Notes

1 J. Davis, 'Baking for the common good: a reassessment of the assize of bread in Medieval England', *Economic History Review*, 57 (3) (2004), p.465.
2 *Ibid.*, p.467.
3 D. Stone, 'The consumption of field crops in late medieval England', in C. Woolger, D. Serjeantson and T. Waldron (eds), *Food in Medieval England: Diet and Nutrition* (Oxford: Oxford University Press, 2006), p.17.
4 The most highly regarded bread was simnel bread which was made from the very finest, top-quality sieved flour and which was twice-baked or boiled before being baked in a biscuit form. However, simnel bread was generally associated with

religious festivals and was not commonly consumed except by the very wealthiest members of society; Davis, 'Baking for the common good', p.471.

5 Maslin was the name given to a mixed crop of wheat and rye; Stone, 'The consumption of field crops', p.13; Davis, 'Baking for the common good', pp. 470–71.

6 Stone, 'The consumption of field crops', p.17.

7 D. Stone, *Decision-Making in Medieval Agriculture* (Oxford: Oxford University Press, 2005), p.270.

8 *Ibid.*, p.215.

9 G. Edelen (ed.), *The Description of England: The Classic Contemporary Account of Tudor Social Life by William Harrison* (Washington: Folger Shakespeare Library and New York: Dover Publications, 1994), p.133.

10 Stone, 'The consumption of field crops', p.13; C. Wilson, *Food and Drink in Britain from the Stone Age to Recent Times* (Harmondsworth: Penguin, 1984), p.181.

11 C. Hieatt, *The Culinary Recipes of Medieval England: An Epitome of Recipes from Extant Medieval English Culinary Manuscripts* (Totnes: Prospect Books, 2013).

12 C. Muldrew, *Food, Energy and the Creation of Industriousness: Work and Material Culture in Agrarian England, 1550–1780* (Cambridge: Cambridge University Press, 2011), p.156.

13 Muldrew, *Food, Energy and the Creation of Industriousness*; J. Thirsk, *Food in Early Modern England: Phases, Fads, Fashions, 1500–1760* (London: Continuum, 2007); S. Horrell 'Consumption, 1700–1870', in R. Floud, J. Humphries and P. Johnson (eds), *The Cambridge Economic History of Modern Britain* (Cambridge: Cambridge University Press, 2014); R. Allen, *The British Industrial Revolution in Global Perspective* (Cambridge: Cambridge University Press, 2009); J. Humphries, 'The lure of aggregates and the pitfalls of the patriarchal perspective: a critique of the high wage economy interpretation of the British Industrial Revolution', *Economic History Review*, 66 (3) (2013), pp.693–714; J. Humphries, *Childhood and Child Labour in the British Industrial Revolution* (Oxford: Oxford University Press, 2010); D. Meredith and D. Oxley, 'Nutrition and health 1700–1870', in Floud *et al.* (eds), *Cambridge Economic History of Modern Britain.*

14 Muldrew, *Food, Energy and the Creation of Industriousness*, p.85ff.

15 Thirsk, *Food in Early Modern England*, pp.284–85.

16 Horrell, 'Consumption', p.261.

17 Allen, *British Industrial Revolution*, pp.35–36.

18 *Ibid.*, pp.40, 105.

19 Humphries, 'The lure of aggregates', pp.693–714; Humphries, *Childhood and Child Labour*, pp.140–41.

20 Meredith and Oxley, 'Nutrition and health', p.145.

21 C. Dyer, 'Changes in diet in the late Middle Ages: the case of harvest workers', *Agricultural History Review*, 36 (1988), pp.21, 27.

22 R. Britnell, 'English agricultural output and prices, 1350–1450: national trends and regional divergences', in B. Dodds and R. Britnell (eds), *Agriculture and Rural Society after the Black Death: Common Themes and Regional Variations* (Hatfield: University of Hertfordshire Press, 2008), pp.30, 34.

23 C. Woolgar, 'Meat and dairy products in late medieval England', in C. Woolgar, D. Serjeantson and T. Waldron (eds), *Food in Medieval England: Diet and Nutrition* (Oxford: Oxford University Press, 2006), p.88.

24 D. Serjeantson and C. Woolgar, 'Fish consumption in medieval England', in Woolgar *et al.* (eds), *Food in Medieval England*, p.102.

25 A. Grant, 'Animal resources', in G. Astill and A. Grant (eds), *The Countryside of Medieval England* (Oxford: Oxford University Press, 1988), pp.172–73.

26 D. Dymond (ed.), *The Register of Thetford Priory: Part I: 1482–1517: Norfolk Record Society Vol. LIX* (Oxford: Oxford University Press, 1194); D. Dymond (ed.), *The Register of Thetford Priory: Part II: 1518–1540: Norfolk Record Society Vol. LX* (Oxford: Oxford University Press, 1995 and 1996).

27 C. Dyer, 'Gardens and garden produce', in Woolgar *et al.* (eds), *Food in Medieval England*, p.36.

28 Wilson, *Food and Drink in Britain*, p.252.

29 *Ibid.*, pp.252–53.

30 *Ibid.*, p.253.

31 *Ibid.*, p.254.

32 Thorold Rogers suggests that nutmeg was so rarely sold that he was unable to produce a price for a defined quantity, J. Thorold Rogers, *A History of Agriculture and Prices in England from the Year after the Oxford Parliament (1279) to the Commencement of the Continental War (1793): Vol. IV 1401–1582* (Oxford: Oxford University Press, 1882), pp.663, 680–88; Nutmeg was only bought by Thetford Priory on one occasion and the purchase was made in London. The context of the purchase within the accounts suggests that it may have been bought in connection with a visit to the priory by the duke of Norfolk, Dymond (ed), *Thetford Priory: Part II*, p.469.

33 P. Nightingale, *A Medieval Mercantile Community: The Grocers' Company and the Politics and Trade of London, 1000–1485* (New Haven: Yale University Press, 1995), pp.560–69.

34 C. Dyer, *Standards of Living in the Later Middle Ages: Social Change in England, c.1200–1520* (Cambridge: Cambridge University Press, 1989), p.63; Wilson, *Food and Drink in Britain*, p.255.

35 Nightingale, *Medieval Mercantile Community*, p.21.

36 *Ibid.*, p.38.

37 *Ibid.*, p.38.

38 *Ibid.*; http://en.wikipedia.org/wiki/Sel_gris [last accessed 14 January 2014].

39 Nightingale, *Medieval Mercantile Community*, pp.30, 39.

40 J. Thorold Rogers, *A History of Agriculture and Prices in England from the Year after the Oxford Parliament (1279) to the Commencement of the Continental War (1793): Vol. I - 1279–1400* (Oxford: Oxford University Press, 1866).

41 TNA PCC PROB 11/5/23 (Stotevile).

42 L. Williams and S. Thomson, *Marlborough Probate Inventories 1591–1775* (Chippenham: Wiltshire Record Society, 2007), p.207.

43 E. and S. George (eds), *Bristol Probate Inventories, Part 2 1657–1689 Bristol Record Society's Publication Vol. 57* (Bristol: Bristol Record Society, 2005), p.134.

44 J. Stobart, *Sugar and Spice: Grocers and Groceries in Provincial England 1650–1830* (Oxford: Oxford University Press, 2013).

45 J. Grenville, *Medieval Housing* (Leicester: Leicester University Press, 1999), p.135.

46 S. Pennell, 'Material culture in seventeenth-century "Britain": the matter of domestic consumption', in F. Trentmann (ed.), *The Oxford Handbook of the History of Consumption* (Oxford: Oxford University Press, 2012), p.72.

47 *Ibid.*

48 N.W. Alcock, *People at Home: Living in a Warwickshire Village, 1500–1800* (Chichester: Phillimore, 1993), pp.224–26.

49 B. Trinder and J. Cox, *Miners and Mariners of the Severn Gorge: Probate Inventories for Benthall, Broseley, Little Wenlock and Madeley, 1660–1764* (Chichester: Phillimore, 2000), p.56.

50 R. Field, 'Worcestershire peasant buildings, household goods and farming equipment in the later Middle Ages', *Medieval Archaeology*, 9 (1965), pp.137–45; C. Dyer, *Making a Living in the Middle Ages: The People of Britain, 850–1520* (New Haven: Yale University Press, 2003), p.297; C. Dyer, *An Age of Transition? Economy and Society in England in the Later Middle Ages* (Oxford: Oxford University Press, 2007), pp.140–41.

51 'Stelyd' refers to a vessel which has been fitted with a 'stele' or handle, P. Northeast (ed.), *Wills of the Archdeaconry of Sudbury, 1439–1474: Wills from the Register 'Baldwyne', Part I: 1439–1474* (Woodbridge, 2001), p.xxxiii; see, for examples, NRO NCC Attmere 74 (Ballys), NRO ANF Liber 3a (Bemond) 5 (Brightmer), NRO ANW Aleyn

115 (Manninge), SROB Baldwyne 298 (Ray); a cauldron was a three-legged container with handles that could either be suspended over the hearth or stood in the embers of the fire and which varied in size with the largest having a capacity of up to 60 gallons; a posnet was a small metal cooking pot like a cauldron with three legs which were designed to stand on the hearth among the embers; a skillet was either shaped like a small tripod cooking pot, or took the form of a frying pan, and was characterised by a long handle with which it could be placed onto or over a fire.

52 P. Foden (trans.) and Norton Community Archaeology Group (ed.), *Records of the Manor of Norton in the Liberty of St. Albans, 1244–1539: Hertfordshire Record Society Vol. XXIX* (Hertford: Hertfordshire Record Society, 2014), pp.161, 192, 231; SROB 1476/1/16, 20.

53 SROB Johnson 225 (Knyte); SROB Hervye 169 (Dey).

54 C. Green, 'Cast bronze cooking pots in England, 1500–1720' in J. Allan, N. Alcock and D. Dawson (eds) *West Country Households 1500–1700* (Woodbridge: Boydell, 2015), p.309.

55 L. Weatherill (ed.), *The Account Book of Richard Latham, 1724–1767* (Oxford: Oxford University Press, 1990), p.75.

56 S. Broadberry, B. Campbell, A. Klein, M. Overton and B. van Leeuwen, *British Economic Growth, 1270–1870* (Cambridge: Cambridge University Press, 2015), p.298.

57 N. Sykes, 'From cu and sceap to beffe and motton', in Woolgar *et al.* (eds), *Food in Medieval England*, p.71.

58 D. Dymond (ed.), *Thetford Priory: Part I*, pp.137, 259; Dymond (ed.), *Thetford Priory: Part II*, pp.409, 547, 549.

59 TNA PCC PROB 11/5/23 (Stotevile); NRO NCC Sayve 13 (Flecher).

60 http://pilgrim.ceredigion.gov.uk/index.cfm?articleid=3196 [last accessed 18 December 2016].

61 S. Minwel Tibbott, *Cooking on the Open Hearth* (Cardiff, 1982), p.11; A. Sim, *Food and Feast in Tudor England* (Stroud, 1997), p.22.

62 Williams and Thomson, *Marlborough Probate Inventories*, p.106.

63 F. Steer, *Farm and Cottage Inventories of Mid-Essex 1635–1749* (Chichester, 1969), p.82.

64 Williams and Thomson, *Marlborough Probate Inventories*, p.343.

65 Muldrew, *Food, Energy and the Creation of Industriousness*, p.100.

66 C. Woolgar, *The Culture of Food in England, 1200–1500* (New Haven: Yale University Press, 2016), p.32.

67 F. Braudel, *Civilization and Capitalism, 15th–18th Century: Volume 1, The Structures of Everyday Life, the Limits of the Possible* (London: Collins, 1981), p.205.

68 Broadberry *et al.*, *British Economic Growth*, p.299.

69 Williams and Thomson, *Marlborough Probate Inventories*, pp.31, 184, 206.

70 George and George, *Bristol Probate Inventories, Part 2*, p.133.

71 Trinder and Cox, *Miners and Mariners*, p.323.

72 Williams and Thomson, *Marlborough Probate Inventories*, p.296.

73 Dymond (ed.), *Thetford Priory: Part 1*, pp.93 and 117; a skep was a lidless basket predominantly used for storage and a maund was a small basket with handles which would have predominantly been used for carrying.

74 R. Gilchrist, *Medieval Life: Archaeology and the Life Course* (Woodbridge: Boydell, 2012), p.126.

75 N.J.G. Pounds, *Hearth and Home: A History of Material Culture* (Indiana: Bloomington, 1989), p.208.

76 Thirsk, *Food in Early Modern England*, p.186.

77 Forks for cutting meat and toasting should not be confused with table forks and have been excluded from this analysis.

78 S. Moore, *Table Knives and Forks* (Princes Risborough: Shire Publications, 2006), p.3.

79 C.T.P. Bailey, *Knives and Forks* (London: Medici Society, 1927), p.5.

80 S. Tymms (ed.), *Wills and Inventories from the Registers of the Commissary of Bury St Edmunds and the Archdeacon of Sudbury* (London: Camden Society, 1850), p.40.
81 Braudel, *Civilization and Capitalism*, pp.183, 206ff.
82 T. Coryat, *Coryat's Curdities Hastily Gobbled up in Five Months Travels in France, Savoy, Italy, &c.* (London: James MacLehose, 1611).
83 R. Sarti, *Europe at Home: Family and Material Culture 1500–1800* (New Haven: Yale University Press, 2002). pp.151–52.
84 L. Worsley, *If Walls Could Talk: An Intimate History of the Home* (London: Faber and Faber, 2011), p.301.
85 A.S. Martin, *Buying into the World of Goods: Early Consumers in Backcountry Virginia* (Baltimore: Johns Hopkins University Press, 2008), p.185.
86 P. Corrigan, *The Sociology of Consumption* (London: Sage Publications, 1997), p.115ff.
87 M. Berg, *Luxury and Pleasure in Eighteenth-Century Britain* (Oxford: Oxford University Press, 2005), p.162.
88 E. and S. George (eds), *Bristol Probate Inventories, Part 1 1542–1650: Bristol Record Society's Publication Vol. 54* (Bristol: Bristol Record Society, 2002), p.107.
89 George and George, *Bristol Probate Inventories Part 2*, p.14.
90 Williams and Thomson, *Marlborough Probate Inventories*, p.303.
91 Dyer, *Making a Living*, pp.311–22; Dyer, *Age of Transition?*, p.137.
92 NRO NCC Cobald 62 (Kyng).
93 J. Loengard, '"Which may be said to be her own": widows and goods in late-medieval England', in M. Kowaleski and P. Goldberg (eds), *Medieval Domesticity: Home, Housing and Household in Medieval England* (Cambridge: Cambridge University Press, 2008), p.172.
94 S. Flood (ed.), *St Albans Wills, 1471–1500: Hertfordshire Record Publications Vol.IX* (Hertford: Hertfordshire Record Society, 1993), p.157.
95 NRO NCC Briggs 28 (Howton); NRO NCC Briggs 83 (Hert).
96 L. Weatherill, *Consumer Behaviour and Material Culture in Britain 1660–1760* (London: Routledge, 1996), p.28.
97 Stone, 'The consumption of field crops', p.18.
98 J. Bennett, *Ale, Beer and Brewsters in England: Women's Work in a Changing World, 1300–1600* (Oxford: Oxford University Press, 1999), p.17.
99 D. Pearsall (ed.), *Piers Plowman by William Langland: An Edition of the C-text* (Berkeley: University of California Press, 1982), p.119.
100 Stone, 'The consumption of field crops', pp.18–19; B. Campbell, 'Matching supply to demand: crop production and disposal by English demesnes in the century of the Black Death', *Journal of Economic History*, 57 (1997), pp.834–85.
101 Bennett, *Ale, Beer and Brewsters*, p.45.
102 *Ibid.*, pp.47–48.
103 N. Amor, *Late Medieval Ipswich: Trade and Industry* (Woodbridge: Boydell, 2011) p.71; Bennett, *Ale, Beer and Brewsters*, pp.9, 79.
104 M. Kowaleski, 'A consumer economy', in R. Horrox and W.M. Ormrod (eds), *A Social History of England, 1200–1500* (Cambridge: Cambridge University Press, 2006), p.243; Bennett, *Ale, Beer and Brewsters*, p.43; Amor, *Late Medieval Ipswich*, pp.71, 154; Bennett, *Ale, Beer and Brewsters*, p.43.
105 Dymond (ed.), *Thetford Priory: Part II*, pp.547, 548.
106 *Ibid.*, p.485.
107 R. Unger, *Beer in the Middle Ages and the Renaissance* (Philadelphia: University of Pennsylvania Press, 2007), p.99.
108 A. Boorde, *A Compendyous Regyment* (London: Robert Wyer, 1562), p.256.
109 SROB E18/451/4; NRO NCC Doke 2 (Goch).
110 Dyer, *Making a Living*, p.322.
111 M. James, *Studies in the Medieval Wine Trade* (Oxford: Oxford University Press, 1971), p.6.

112 *Ibid.*, pp.15–31.
113 James, *Medieval Wine Trade*, pp.38, 39–40, 45–6; Dyer, *Standards of Living*, p.62.
114 James, *Medieval Wine Trade*, pp.50–4.
115 Rogers, *History of Agriculture and Prices in England: Vol. IV 1401–1582*, p.638.
116 See, for example, the late fourteenth-century costrel in the Museum of London: www.museumoflondonprints.com/image/59587/unknown-leather-costrel-late-14th-century [last accessed 8 January 2017].
117 W.H. St John Hope, 'On the English medieval drinking bowls called mazers', *Archaeologica*, 50 (1887), p.129; S. Sweetinburgh, 'Remembering the dead at dinner-time', in T. Hamling and C. Richardson (eds), *Everyday Objects: Medieval and Early Modern Material Culture and its Meanings* (Farnham: Ashgate, 2010).
118 Sweetinburgh, 'Remembering the dead', p.258.
119 *Ibid.*, p.264.
120 NRO ANW Fuller alias Roper 66 (Dunston); Will of Thomas Rande of Coggeshall 1561 in F. Emmison, *Wills of the County of Essex (England): Vol. 1, 1558–1565* (Washington: National Genealogical Society, 1982), p.224.
121 P. Brears, *Cooking and Dining in Medieval England* (Blackawton: Prospect Books, 2012), p.287.
122 A.R. Braunmuller, (ed.) *The New Cambridge Shakespeare: Macbeth* (Cambridge: Cambridge University Press, 1997), Act II, Scene ii.
123 Wilson, *Food and Drink in Britain*, p.335.
124 J. Burnett, *Liquid Pleasures: A Social History of Drinks* (London: Routledge, 1999), p.1.
125 W. Bray (ed.), *The Diary of John Evelyn* (London: W.W. Gibbings, 1890), p.21.
126 B. Cowan, *The Social Life of Coffee: The Emergence of the British Coffeehouse* (New Haven: Yale University Press, 2005), p.25.
127 *Ibid.*, p.49.
128 B. Lillywhite, *London Coffee Houses* (London: Allen and Unwin, 1963), p.17; Cowan, *Social Life of Coffee*, p.90. F. Trentmann, *The Empire of Things* (London: Allen Lane, 2016), p.86.
129 M. Ellis, *The Coffee-House: A Cultural History* (London: Weidenfeld and Nicolson, 2004), p.30; M. Ellis, 'Pasqua Rosée's Coffee House, 1652–1666', *London Journal*, 29 (2004), pp.1–24; J.E. Wills, 'European consumption and Asian production' in J. Brewer and R. Porter (eds), *Consumption and the World of Goods* (London: Routledge, 1993), p.141.
130 10 December 1660, 19 July 1663, 19 October 1663.
131 Ellis, *Coffee-House*, p.56.
132 A. Clayton, *London's Coffee Houses: A Stimulating Story* (London: Historical Publications, 2003).
133 W. Smith, *Consumption and the Making of Respectability, 1600–1800* (London: Routledge, 2002), p.236.
134 J.A. Johnston (ed.), *Probate Inventories of Lincoln Citizens, 1661–1714: Lincoln Record Society Vol. 80* (Woodbridge: Boydell, 1991), p.79.
135 Rules and Orders of the Coffee House printed on a London Broadsheet from 1674. Courtesy of The Bridewell Museum, Norwich.
136 R. Shoemaker, *The London Mob: Violence and Disorder in Eighteenth Century England* (London: Hambledon Continuum, 2004), p.8.
137 Ellis, *Coffee-House*, p.88.
138 *Ibid.*, pp.63–64, 138ff.
139 Cowan, *Social Life of Coffee*, p.154.
140 C. Estabrook, *Urbane and Rustic England: Cultural Ties and Social Spheres in the Provinces 1660–1780* (Stanford: Stanford University Press, 1998), p.76; A. Akeroyd and C. Clifford, *Huntingdon: Eight Centuries of History*, (Derby: Breedon Books, 2004), p.35.
141 George and George, *Bristol Probate Inventories Part 2*, p.120.

142 Broadberry *et al.*, *British Economic Growth*, p.287; J. de Vries, *The Industrious Revolution: Consumer Behaviour and the Household Economy, 1650 to the Present* (Cambridge: Cambridge University Press, 2008), p.183.
143 Trentmann, *Empire of Things*, p.81.
144 Ellis, *Coffee-House*, p.209.
145 R. Kennedy, 'Taking tea', in M. Snodin and J. Styles (eds), *Design and the Decorative Arts Britain, 1500–1900* (London: V & A Publications, 2001), p.252.
146 J.M. Ellis, 'Consumption and wealth', in L.K.J. Glassey (ed.), *The Reigns of Charles II and James VII and II* (Basingstoke: Macmillan Press, 1997), p.202.
147 J. de Vries, *The Economy of Europe in an Age of Crisis, 1600–1750* (Cambridge: Cambridge University Press, 1976), p.136; Thomas Marchant, a yeoman farmer from Hurstpierpoint, recorded in his diary that he paid 16s for a pound of tea in 1714, A. Bower (ed.), *A Fine Day in Hurstpierpoint – The Diary of Thomas Marchant 1714–1728* (Hurstpierpoint: Hurst History Study Group, 2005), p.2.
148 A. Farrington, *Trading Places: The East India Company and Asia, 1600–1834* (London: British Library Publishing, 2002), p.89.
149 Cowan, *Social Life of Coffee*, p.75; K.N. Chaudhuri, *The Trading World of Asia and the East India Company* (Cambridge: Cambridge University Press, 1978), p.388.
150 H.C. Mui and L.H. Mui, *Shops and Shopkeeping in Eighteenth-Century England* (London: Routledge, 1989), pp.250–51.
151 M. Overton, J. Whittle, D. Dean and A. Hann, *Production and Consumption in English Households 1600–1750* (Abingdon: Routledge, 2004), p.106; Stobart, *Sugar and Spice*, p.194.
152 G. Riello 'Things that shape history: material culture and historical narratives' in K. Harvey (ed.), *History and Material Culture: A Student's Guide to Approaching Alternative Sources* (London: Routledge, 2009), p.38; L. Levy Peck, *Consuming Splendor: Society and Culture in Seventeenth-Century England* (Cambridge: Cambridge University Press, 2005), p.116.
153 S. Djabri (ed.), *The Diaries of Sarah Hurst, 1759–1762: Life and Love in Eighteenth-Century Horsham* (Horsham: Horsham Museum Society, 2009), pp.87–92.
154 S. Flood (ed.), *John Carrington, Farmer of Bramfield, His Diary, 1798–1810, Part I, 1798–1804: Hertfordshire Record Publications Vol. XXVI* (Hertford: Hertfordshire Record Society, 2014), pp.51, 62, 70, 82, 85, 90, 95, 173.
155 T. Turner, *The Diary of a Village Shopkeeper, 1754–1765* (London: Folio Society, 1998), p.206.
156 *Ibid.*, p.364.
157 A. Vickery, *Behind Closed Doors: At Home in Georgian England* (New Haven: Yale University Press, 2009), p.272; Mui and Mui, *Shops and Shopkeeping*, p.249; Cowan, *Social Life of Coffee*, p.77.
158 J. Walwin, 'A taste of empire, 1600–1800', *History Today*, 47 (1997), p.12; R. Allen, 'The high wage economy and the industrial revolution: a restatement', *Economic History Review*, 68 (2015), p.3; according to his budget, the Ealing gardener purchased 2 oz. of tea a week at a cost of 6d; Humphries, 'The lure of aggregates', p.696.
159 *Ibid.*, p.696.
160 D. Davies, *The Case of Labourers in Husbandry* (London: C. G. and J. Robinson, 1795).
161 S.W. Mintz, *Sweetness and Power: The Place of Sugar in Modern History* (Harmondsworth: Viking, 1985), p.115.
162 Steer, *Farm and Cottage Inventories*, p.258.
163 Bower (ed.), *Fine Day in Hurstpierpoint*, pp.2, 198–99; Turner, *Diary of a Village Shopkeeper*, p.244.
164 S. Johnson, 'Review of Jonas Hanway, A Journal of Eight Days Journey', *The Literary Magazine*, 2, no. 13 (1757).
165 E. Kowaleski-Wallace, *Consuming Subjects: Women, Shopping and Business in the Eighteenth Century* (New York: Columbia University Press, 1996), p.32.

166 www.archive.org/details/pollyhoneycombed00colmuoft [last accessed 18 August 2018]

167 Letter 10 December 1748, http://wesley.nnu.edu/john-wesley/the-letters-of-john-wesley/wesleys-letters-1748, [last accessed 22 February 2015]; Smith, *Consumption and the Making of Respectability*, p.233.

168 B. A'Hearn, 'The British industrial revolution in a European mirror' in Floud *et al.*, *Cambridge Economic History of Modern Britain*, p.11; Davies, *Case of Labourers*, p.40.

169 L.E. Grivetti, *Chocolate: History, Culture, and Heritage* (Oxford: Oxford University Press, 2009), pp.5–6.

170 Thirsk, *Food in Early Modern England*, p.308.

171 G. Smith (ed.), *The Diary of Samuel Pepys* (London: Macmillan, 1929), p.290.

172 *Ibid.*, p.82.

173 Cowan, *Social Life of Coffee*, p.43; Worsley, *If Walls Could Talk*, p.285.

174 Williams and Thomson, *Marlborough Probate Inventories*, p.281.

175 The Proceedings of the Old Bailey, Reference Number: t17111205-29, www.old baileyonline.org/browse.jsp?id=t17111205-29&div=t17111205-29&terms=chocola te#highlight [last accessed 22 January 2016].

176 Stobart, *Sugar and Spice*, p.36.

177 H. van der Wee, 'Structural changes in European long-distance trade, and particularly in the re-export trade from south to north, 1350–1750', in J. Tracy (ed.), *The Rise of Merchant Empires: Long-Distance Trade in the Early Modern World, 1350–1750* (Cambridge: Cambridge University Press, 1990), p.25.

178 Wilson, *Food and Drink in Britain*, pp.251, 253, 256, 261–62.

179 Mintz, *Sweetness and Power*, p.148.

180 C. Shammas, 'Changes in English and Anglo-American consumption from 1550 to 1800' in Brewer and Porter (eds), *Consumption and the World of Goods*, p.182.

181 Muldrew, *Food, Energy and the Creation of Industriousness*, p.113.

182 Stobart, *Sugar and Spice*, p.26.

183 Muldrew, *Food, Energy and the Creation of Industriousness*, pp.51–56.

184 Chapter 1.

185 Allen, 'High wage economy', p.3.

186 E. and S. George (eds), *Bristol Probate Inventories, Part 3 1690–1804: Bristol Record Society's Publication Vol. 60* (Bristol: Bristol Record Society, 2008), p.127; Steer, *Farm and Cottage Inventories*, pp.213, 258.

187 An example of silver sugar tongs dated 1718 is on display at the Royal Albert Memorial Museum in Exeter. The tongs were made by Pentecost Symons, Plymouth, Exhibit 157, Royal Albert Memorial Museum, Exeter.

188 Farrington, *Trading Places*, p.29.

189 The UNESCO Convention on the Protection of the Underwater Cultural Heritage, http://unesdoc.unesco.org/images/0014/001430/143085E.pdf [last accessed 16 July 2007]; www.nma.gov.au/collections/collection_interactives/european_voyages/eur opean_voyages_to_the_australian_continent/trade/tea_and_china/the_geldermalsen_ wreck [last accessed 8 January 2017].

190 J. Poole, *English Pottery* (Cambridge: Cambridge University Press, 1995), p.4.

191 D. Barker and T. Majewski, 'Ceramic studies in historical archaeology', in D. Hicks and M. Beaudry (eds), *The Cambridge Companion to Historical Archaeology* (Cambridge: Cambridge University Press, 2006), p.214.

192 J. Styles, 'Product innovation in early modern London', *Past and Present*, 168 (2000), p.141.

193 J. Pettigrew, *A Social History of Tea* (London: National Trust, 2001), p.36.

194 Berg, *Luxury and Pleasure*, pp.82, 89.

195 R.H. Blumenfield, *Blanc De Chine: The Great Porcelain of Dehua* (Berkeley: Ten Speed Press, 2002), p.200.

196 Berg, *Luxury and Pleasure*, p.71.

197 *Ibid.*, p.81; Pettigrew, *Social History of Tea*, p.83.
198 K. Clark, 'The workshop of the world: the industrial revolution', in J. Hunter and I. Ralston (eds), *The Archaeology of Britain: An Introduction from the Upper Palaeolithic to the Industrial Revolution* (London: Routledge, 1999), p.294; Berg, *Luxury and Pleasure*, pp.80, 131.
199 Berg, *Luxury and Pleasure*, p.138; H. Fox, *The Story of William Cookworthy* (Kingsbridge: Goss Albion, 1972), p.15.
200 Berg, *Luxury and Pleasure*, pp. 86, 241, 250.
201 M. Berg, 'Consumption in Britain', in Floud *et al.* (eds), *Cambridge Economic History of Modern Britain*, p.364.
202 The caddies were lockable in order to safeguard the expensive tea leaves.
203 P. King, 'Pauper inventories and the material lives of the poor in the eighteenth and early nineteenth centuries' in T. Hitchcock, P. King and P. Sharpe (eds), *The Voices and Strategies of the English Poor, 1640–1840* (Basingstoke: Palgrave MacMillan, 1997), pp.178–79.
204 J. Harley, 'Material lives of the English poor: a regional perspective 1670–1834' (unpublished PhD thesis, University of Leicester, 2016), pp.68, 165, 171, 178.
205 T. Waldron, 'Nutrition and the skeleton', in Woolgar *et al.* (eds), *Food in Medieval England*, pp.258–62.
206 Stone, 'The consumption of field crops', pp.20–25.

4
CLOTHING

Regardless of social status, everyone wore clothing as a means of covering the body and providing protection against the elements. In her study of fashion in the years 1340 to 1365, Stella Newton charted the considerable changes in dress styles and cloth preferences adopted by the royal household and subsequently by the aristocracy in this period and noted that clothing increasingly became a means of adorning the body and displaying wealth and social status.[1] In the post-Black Death period, this interest in clothing spread down the social scale so that clothing progressively became a signifier for more and more people. It is no coincidence that Fernand Braudel observed that at this time European society moved away from a reliance on traditional, unchanging dress and dated the beginning of 'fashion' in Europe to around 1350. At this date, he noted that men largely dispensed with long robes in favour of shorter, tighter costumes, whilst women adopted close-fitting bodices cut with a large *décolleté*.[2]

This chapter will explore the changing role of clothing in the post-Black Death and subsequent periods and examine how dress and fashion became increasingly significant, particularly as a means of indicating status and substance. For a growing proportion of society, clothing was no longer simply a practical necessity which provided warmth and comfort, but an important consumption item which conveyed a wider message about the wearer.

Clothing from the late medieval period to the seventeenth century

The everyday outfit of a late medieval man or woman, regardless of social status, generally comprised the seven basic clothing items of undergarment, garment, overgarment, outergarment, hose, shoes or boots and headgear.[3] The main undergarment for both sexes was a shirt (or smock), whilst men also wore breeches or 'braies' and women often wore 'clouts' on the lower half of their bodies and 'breast-bands'.[4] A garment in the form of a tunic (referred to by both sexes as a tunic or, for women only, a kirtle) was worn over the undergarment by members of both sexes whilst men wore hose over their breeches and some women also wore knee-length hose.[5] Many men also wore the short, tight-fitting sleeved garment known as a doublet over their tunics. Overgarments were of a variety of forms including gowns, petticoats, waistcoats, coat-hardies, super-tunics and surcoats, although from the end of the fourteenth century, gowns were the most popular form of overgarment for both men and women.[6] There were also various types of outergarment but the most common were mantles and cloaks worn by both sexes, or the hooded cloak referred to as a 'hewk' or 'huke' which was only worn by women. Outfits were completed with shoes or low boots worn by both men and women and headgear in the form of hoods and hats worn out of doors by both sexes, whilst women also wore a kerchief, or 'kercher' over their hair when indoors.[7] Finally, the outfit was finished by a belt, usually termed a 'girdle', used both to keep clothing in place and as a means of hanging small valuables such as purses, rosaries and other items in such a manner as to be easily accessed by the wearer and observed both by the user and by others.[8]

Cloth

Most of the cloth used for late medieval and early modern clothing was made from wool. Woollen cloth had many advantages; it provided warmth, had some level of water resistance, held dyes effectively and was readily available.[9] In addition, it could be used to produce a wide variety of fabrics including frieze, fustian, kersey and russet so that woollen fabrics were used for all garments except undergarments (for which it was too irritating and uncomfortable). The most widely used woollen cloths identified by James Thorold Rogers for the period between 1447 and 1540 were the basest cloths (costing an average of just over 9¼d a yard), frieze (at an average of nearly 8d per yard), blanket (which varied widely in quality and price but averaged 1s 5¾d per yard), fustian (at an average price of 8d to 10d per yard) and worsted (which, again, varied widely in quality and price and cost between 5¼d and 6s per yard).[10] Woollen cloths such as these were commonly used for overgarments, particularly gowns, and outergarments, such as cloaks, coats and hats, as well as for bedcovers and blankets.[11] One woollen fabric valued as a luxury cloth was scarlet, which was distinguishable from other cheaper and less desirable fabrics by a shearing and finishing process which created smooth, felted cloth.[12] Scarlets were originally produced in a variety of colours but ultimately became associated with the bright red colour created using an expensive dye extracted from the Mediterranean kermes insect.[13] Kermes was also used to create other colours including 'sanguine', but its use was always associated with expensive luxury cloth.

Cloth was also made from plant fibres in the form of hemp (used to make hempen cloth) and flax (used to make linen). Hemp produced a very coarse, low-quality cloth from which the very roughest over- and outergarments and bedding were made, together with undergarments for the poorest members of society. Linen came in a variety of forms and was used for the undergarments of most members of society as well as for sheets, towels and tablecloths and the 'kerchiefs' worn over their hair by women. Flax was grown widely in England so that the cheapest linen cloth, known as 'hedlacke' or 'harden', cost only 1½d to 3d a yard. However, although better-quality linen was also produced domestically and was particularly associated with a thriving East Anglian linen industry centred on the north Norfolk towns of Cawston and Aylsham, the wealthiest classes did not use domestic linen for their undergarments. Instead they purchased fine-quality linen such as diaper and linen damask imported from the continent and particularly from the Brabant region of the Low Countries. Linen from Liège cost three times that of linen produced domestically in Aylsham.[14]

The clothing fabrics held in the highest regard during the late Middle Ages and into the early modern period were cloth of gold, velvet, damask, silk, satin, sarcenet and camlet.[15] With the exception of cloth of gold, which was predominantly a ceremonial textile associated with royal and aristocratic processions and religious vestments, these were used to make a variety of upper garments.[16] From the fourteenth century, Italian weavers also began to produce less expensive silk fabrics such as samite and taffeta which were lighter in weight and of plainer colours and which were used as a main fabric of garments, for lining woollen garments and for accessories such as girdles, ribbons and braid.[17] Despite a wider availability of silk and the introduction of cheaper silk fabrics, it remained an exclusive and luxury commodity which was only affordable by the wealthy, particularly since it was not produced domestically so was only available as an imported product.[18] It is no coincidence that the vast majority of these goods were imported directly into London with its high concentration of consumers who could afford such high-end luxuries.[19]

Use of dyes

To the wearer wishing to display status through clothing, not only was the quality of the cloth used to make garments important, but the colour of the cloth was equally significant. Different colours could be achieved by dying the textile fibre which could be done prior to it being spun into thread, once it had been spun into thread, but most frequently once the thread had been woven into cloth. Whichever process was used entailed the additional use of resources in terms of both the dye materials and the labour input and this increased the cost of the finished cloth product. Consequently, cheap cloth was either dyed using less expensive dyes, dyed using the 'exhaust dye' previously used to dye better-quality cloth or remained undyed.[20] These practices resulted in muted colours which were further diluted by washing and fading and were accentuated by the fact that most clothes continued to be used until they were worn out. The use of deep shades not only demonstrated that a garment was a relatively recent purchase, since colours faded with age and use, but that the wearer could afford more expensive cloth since the cost of stronger dyes remained high and was reflected in the cost of the finished cloth.

Tailors

Various sources suggested that most garments were made from cloth purchased in lengths and subsequently made into clothing either within the household, or externally through the services of a tailor or seamstress, although the cloth itself could also be produced domestically. Extant accounts showed that noble, gentry and monastic households generally purchased lengths of cloth in this manner and Christopher Dyer cited the example of the gentry family of the Eyres of Hassop (Derbyshire) who bought a wide range of cheap woollens, cottons, canvas and linens in lengths of around two to three yards at a time, but which totalled as much as 100 yards in one year. Silks were also bought, but in much smaller quantities.[21] Thetford Priory bought a large amount and a very wide range of cloth, from low-quality broadcloth (costing upwards of 1d a yard) and basic linen (costing from 1½d per yard), through to sarcenet (at a cost of 4s per yard) and satin (6s 8d per yard). The number of tailors operating in England confirms that many households employed the services of local people to make up purchased cloth into garments; however, the labour intensive nature of hand-stitching was such that the fees paid to a professional tailor could raise the cost of clothing quite considerably. The priory accounts included payments to local tailors for making up garments and some of these are substantial; for example, 16s 6d was paid in 1538/39 for 'le makyng of gownes & other garmentes', and three subsequent payments of 6s 8d and one of 6s were made to John Skynner, tailor, of Banham.[22] Consequently, it seems likely that the making up of more basic garments was undertaken either within the household itself, or on a casual basis by women. Again, the priory accounts included payments to local women for the making up of a range of simple clothing and household items such as those made in 1531/32 to the wife of a Thetford mercer who was paid 1s for making up six pillowcases, 3s for making up six albs and 7d for two pairs of sheets and a cupboard cloth.[23]

Ready-made and secondhand clothing

A few clothing items could be acquired 'ready-made', particularly undergarments and headwear. Together with other cheap manufactured goods, these were often sold by itinerant chapmen and pedlars who 'flourished on the edges of official markets and in the unregulated arenas of suburbs, villages, inns and private houses' and who sold goods such as 'pursys, knyvys, gyrdlys, glassys, hattes or odyr penyware'.[24] The itinerant nature of these traders was such that sources contained limited references to their activities, particularly those of pedlars.[25] References to the sale of these goods within the court rolls used for this study are limited to a few attachments in relation to debt cases against traders such as a kirtle, gloves, purses and cradlecloth which were all attached during the late fourteenth and early fifteenth centuries in Newmarket.[26] However, a wider availability was suggested by the ready-made goods purchased by Thetford Priory including head-kerchiefs, caps, girdles, linen hose and linen shirts. These came from a range of sources including from the town of Lynn and Ely Fair as well as through the services of a local mercer.[27] Again, Dyer noted that the Eyre family also bought some ready-made goods including hats which cost 10d and 1s 2d.[28]

Most clothes continued to be used until they were worn out with garments regularly being repaired, worn by a succession of users and ultimately cut up and used to patch and repair other garments.[29] It seems likely that there was a very buoyant market in used clothing although, as with ready-made clothing, the peripheral nature of this secondhand marketing has left few records in the sources and is impossible to quantify.[30] The 1472/73 account roll for Newmarket referred to three shops lying in 'le Shraggeryrowe', the name given to the trading row dedicated to the sale of old clothes, whilst Cambridge is also known to have had a row dedicated to the sale of 'shraggery'.[31] Testamentary evidence considered later confirmed that items of personal clothing were regularly passed on to be used by others, whilst the market for secondhand clothes is also shown by references such as that in the will of Elizabeth Mancer made in 1520 in which she asked that 'all my clothes to besold & the mony comyng theroff to go to the Reparacons off the chirch most necessary'.[32]

Use of fur and leather in clothing

Garments principally made of cloth could also incorporate fur or leather embellishments such as linings and facings. Other garments were made entirely of animal skins, such as hats and gloves, whilst leather was also used for shoes and boots and for gloves and mittens. The animal skins used for clothing varied widely in quality and thus in cost. Although by the end of the medieval period skins were readily available as a by-product of meat, dairy and wool production, the time spent on treating and curing raised the cost of the final product, as did the subsequent working of the skin into a form which could be worn. Thorold Rogers suggested that the cheapest animal skin linings came from sheep and cited a range of purchases which totalled 13s 6d for a hundred skins (equating to just over 1½d for a single skin).[33] Skins which were more highly prized were those of other domestically farmed animals, including horseskin, calfskin, coney and coltskin, together with the skins of domestic wild animals such as fox or cat.[34] The furs which were held in the highest regard were imports such as sable, ermine, Baltic squirrel, *lettice* and budge, although domestic otter and beaver skins were also coveted as were the softer, flatter skins of the legs of lambs, known as shanks.[35]

Changes during the period

The consumption of cloth and clothing underwent some subtle but important changes in the post-Black Death period. In particular, Dyer suggested that people generally owned an increasing number of garments and replaced clothing items more frequently and cited the increased number of tailors working in both rural and urban settings as evidence in support of this claim.[36] Occupational and surname evidence from the poll tax returns of 1379–81 indicated that tailors were present in even small towns so that four can be identified as operating in Thetford and three in Mildenhall.[37] This increase in the number of clothes owned was partly due to the rising incomes of the lower orders, but also by a growing preference for shorter, close-fitting clothes. As less fabric was needed for these new styles, clothes generally cost less.[38] Higher income levels combined with the need to purchase reduced amounts of fabric allowed people to purchase more items of clothing and also encouraged the use of better fabrics. For the majority of the population, this largely resulted in a wider use of higher-quality woollen cloths such as blanket (with an average cost of 1s 5¾d per yard in the period from 1447 to 1550), kersey (an average of 1s 3¾d per ell), russet, say (1s 5¼d per yard) and better-quality worsted (which varied widely in price from between 5½d and 6s per yard).[39] Many consumers also chose to spend more on linen fabrics such as lockram (for undergarments and shirts), buckram (for linings and domestic cloth) and fine linen (for bedding). In addition, towards the end of the fourteenth century, there was an increased tendency for the gentry and wealthy merchant classes to adopt garments made from luxury fabrics such as velvet, damask, silk, satin, sarcenet and camlet which had previously been the preserve of the aristocracy and nobility.[40] This was partly due to the increase in the availability of silk and silk products following the development of its production in Italy and Spain.[41] It also reflected the growing tendency of these groups to emulate the clothing worn by the noble classes and, perhaps more importantly, to distinguish themselves from the lower groups of society through the use of cloth which signified wealth and status. In addition to changes in the quality of the cloth chosen for garments, affluent consumers increasingly chose to wear garments of richer, darker colours as a means of distinguishing themselves and their clothing from the drab, faded items worn by the poorer groups of society. Demand and fashion led to an increase in the range of substances available as dyes in the late medieval period with deeper shades of green, blue, violet and black becoming especially favoured.[42]

The period also saw an increase in the use of fur, both for whole garments and for trimmings and linings, although many furs still remained prohibitively expensive to all but the wealthiest groups of society. Prior to the Black Death, imported furs would not have been available to anyone outside of the nobility, however, by the late fifteenth century, squirrel skins from northern Europe such as *miniver* and *gris* were available to a far wider section of society, principally for lining garments.[43] Although their increased adoption by members of the gentry and merchant classes saw a decline in the regard with which they were held, they remained expensive, luxury items and Elspeth Veale estimated that a lining of best-quality *gris* would have cost as much as £4 3s 4d in 1407.[44] As *miniver* and *gris* became less esteemed by the higher ranks, the skins of choice became sable, pine marten and budge, whilst lynx, black *genette* and fox were also considered highly fashionable.[45] For those further down the social scale, the period saw the increased adoption of domestic furs.

Sumptuary legislation

The wider adoption of better-quality cloth and finer garments was not universally popular. Chroniclers and moralists regularly complained about the immodesty of new fashions and the fact that these were no longer confined to the nobility and gentry but were increasingly being adopted by the lower classes.[46] In his *Chronicon* covering the years 1377 to 1395, Henry Knighton wrote that:

> for the lesser people were so puffed up in those days in their dress and their belongings, and they flourished and prospered so in various ways, that one might scarcely distinguish one from another for the splendour of their dress and adornments: not a humble man from a great man, not a needy from a rich man, not a servant from his master, not a priest from another man, but each imitating the other, and striving to shine in some new fashion and to outdo his superior in the splendour of his pomp and habit.[47]

In his poem entitled *The Regiment of Princes* written in 1412, Thomas Hoccleve criticised the lower classes for copying the extravagant fashions of the rich including the comment that: 'Sumtyme afer men mighten lordes knowe By hir array from othir folk, but now A man shal studie and musen a long throwe Which is which'.[48]

Criticism of dress by writers was also reflected in the series of sumptuary laws which sought to regulate behaviour in eating and dining practices and celebratory customs as well as clothing.[49] These laws encompassed a variety of objectives, however, most commentators agreed that the main one was to preserve class distinctions and, in particular, to restrict the wearing of certain clothing according to social status.[50] Whilst some sumptuary legislation in England had been passed prior to 1350, the amount and scope of the enactments increased in the post-Black Death era and continued beyond the Tudor period. For example, sumptuary legislation passed in 1363 forbade the wearing of cloth which cost more than two marks by grooms, servants of the lords and those of misteries and craftsmen, whilst yeomen and handicraftsmen were not permitted to wear cloth worth more than 40s for the whole cloth. Those people engaged in occupations relating to animal husbandry were ordered to wear only blanket cloth and russet costing 12d a yard. The wives and children of grooms, servants of lords, members of misteries and craftsmen were not to wear veils or kerchiefs costing more than 12d, whilst the legislation also ordered those people engaged in animal husbandry to wear only girdles of linen. A graduated scale stated that social groups earning between 40s and £500 a year were only entitled to wear predominantly domestic skins such as lamb, coney, cat or fox.[51] Further sumptuary legislation was passed in 1463/64, 1483, 1510, 1514 and 1533 and whilst it is impossible to measure how effective the laws were in curbing consumption within the realm, the ongoing persistence with such legislation suggests that it was both required and considered to be worthwhile.

Testamentary evidence – fifteenth and sixteenth centuries

Testamentary clothing bequests provide evidence of clothing items owned by individuals. As the clothes bequeathed were often described in some detail, it is possible to identify some of the fabrics used and also the various colours of such items. Many bequests indicated increased preferences for better-quality cloth, clothing items of dark colours and items which incorporated animal skins. Clothing was owned by everyone, irrespective of time, sex or rank and, unsurprisingly, around 24 per cent of wills included at least one bequest of an item of clothing. However, although clothing bequests were spread across all of the social tiers of the testamentary sample, some observations can be made: firstly, women tended to bequeath clothes more frequently than men with 40 per cent of female testators referring to an item of clothing whereas only 22 per cent of male testators did so; secondly, members of the gentry were less inclined to bequeath items of clothing than members of the higher-status, intermediate-status or yeoman groups; and thirdly, men who held low-status occupations and husbandmen bequeathed fewer items of clothing than men in higher-status groups.[52]

Most testamentary bequests of clothing items were of good-quality outer- or overgarments such as the gown of musterdevillers and the lined murrey gown which Emma Boteler of St Albans gave in 1471, and 'my Chamlet gown, my velvet doblet and damaske jakett' gifted by John Wheteley of Burwell in 1538.[53] Undergarments and clothing variously described as old or worn were also given: William Burden, the former prior of Thetford Priory, bequeathed 'my gowne that I use to were every day', whilst John Dalton of Thetford gave his apprentice 'a paier of old hose'.[54] In some instances these bequeathed items were even referred to as having already been acquired from someone else and were consequently bequests to at least a third owner and wearer.

The clothing items most frequently bequeathed by male testators were, without doubt, gowns such as the murrey gown with the silver print given by John Teryngham of Northampton in 1484 or the 'best furred gowne' given by William Aylnoth of Coggeshall in 1503.[55] As with these examples, many of these were described with additional detail and it is apparent from Table 4.1 that male gowns were made from a very wide variety of cloths, could be of a range of (usually dark) colours and were frequently lined, often with fur. Doublets were also often given and, again, were of a variety of fabrics and colours, such as the doublet of black fustian given by the yeoman John Barkere of Cowlinge in 1470 and the red satin doublet given by the yeoman William Cordell of Chingford in 1565.[56] Headcoverings in the form of caps, hats and hoods were bequeathed less frequently, as were outergarments such as jackets and coats, but Robert Wyot of Exning gave his best hood in 1444 and Alexander Samkyn his best cap in 1560.[57] Undergarments such as shirts and hose were given less frequently and in most cases were given by male testators to servants and apprentices as in the earlier example.

The clothing items bequeathed by female testators predominantly consisted of the garment known as a kirtle and the head covering known as a kerchief (also referred to as a 'kercher' or headkerchief). As with male gowns, kirtles were of a range of predominantly dark colours: Agnes Dunston of Thetford gave a green kirtle in 1483; and Margaret Kyng bequeathed two murrey kirtles in 1479.[58] Russet was one of only two fabrics referred to for kirtles; however, this term was also used to describe a grey or dull red so this may describe the colour rather than the fabric. The 'kerchers' worn by women were frequently bequeathed by them but the fact that they were rarely identified as being of a particular colour or fabric suggested that the majority were of undyed linen. Indeed, those bequeathed by Margerie Huggane of Godmanchester in 1558 are described as 'flaxen kerchers'.[59] Any further description of kerchiefs usually related to the use to which they were put so that in 1568 Katherine Childerston bequeathed a 'halldaye kercher' and a 'working day kercher'.[60] Bequests of outergarments by women testators were also common and in particular bequests of the hooded cloak known as a 'hewk' such as that bequeathed in 1466 by Joan Aleyn of Brandon Ferry.[61] Other clothing bequests included smocks, tunics, hats and aprons, although these were given far less commonly. Towards the middle of the sixteenth century bequests of kirtles become fewer in number and gowns were given such as the best gown and old gown bequeathed by Kateryn George of Thetford in 1523.[62] A few sixteenth-century wills also bequeathed petticoats including the 'petye cote' and 'smocke' given by Agnes Manninge of Thetford to her sister Evie in 1547.[63] This reflected the changing pattern of women's clothing referred to by John Styles (see p.114).

A sizeable number of the garments referred to in the wills were identified as incorporating fur, usually as a lining although trimmings were also popular. Almost all of the skins that were identified are those of domestic animals, particularly lambskin, although other references included otter, fox and coney such as William Benyngton's will in which he bequeathed 'both my blewe gownes one faced with foxe and the other faced with russelles'.[64] Very few wills referred to linings or trimmings made from imported furs although Joan Swanley of St Albans left her best gown edged with 'menyvere and letyse' and her black gown edged with the fur of 'blaklambe'; whilst John Cutt, merchant of Briston, Norfolk, gave a 'gowne furred with Jennyttes'.[65] (See Table 4.1.)

TABLE 4.1 Clothing items, fabrics and colours recorded in wills, 1370–1579

Male garments Item	Fabric	Colour
Gown	Russet, musterdevillers, worsted, scarlet, Bristol red, frieze, chamlet, ray	Black, violet, blue, puke, green, sanguine, murrey, crimson, blue medley, striped, muted, tawny
Doublet	Fustian, velvet, fence, satin, Bruges satin, camlet, sarcenet, buckskin, tawny, worsted, leather	Black, white, grey, red
Hose	Kersey	Black, white
Shirt		
Tunic	Blanket	
Smock		
Jacket	Worsted, damask, russet, velvet	Black, blue, tawny, violet
Jerkin	Velvet, camlet, leather	
Coat	Blanket, frieze, camlet, russet, musterdevillers, leather, velvet, worsted	Grey, blue, black, motley
Hat	Worsted, straw, silk	
Cap	Russet, velvet, felt	
Hood	Velvet, scarlet, damask, sarcenet, ray	
Female garments		
Kirtle	Russet, worsted	Green, red, violet, black, blue, murrey
Gown	Russet, musterdevillers	Green, black, blue, sanguine, murrey, violet
Kerchief (headkerchief, kercher)	Scarlet, flaxen	
Tunic	Russet	Violet, sanguine
Petticoat	Russet	Red, white
Smock	Flax	
Cloak (also referred to as 'hewk' or 'frende')		Blue, murrey, sanguine
Coat		Red
Hat	Silk	
Hood	Silk	
Apron	Flax	
Accessories to garments		
Girdle	Silver, silk	Blue, black, red, ruby
Linings	Lambskin, camlet, shanks, budge, otter, fox, coney, russelles, seeth, fitches, miniver, lettys, lamb, fur, frieze, genette, satin	Black, white, yellow

Probate evidence – sixteenth century

Probate inventories can also be used for the second half of the sixteenth century to provide evidence of the clothing items that were owned by individuals. Nearly all of the male garments referred to in Table 4.1 were also recorded in the Surrey inventories; the only exceptions were tunics and hoods. Doublets were the most common item of clothing recorded (14 per cent) followed closely by coats (13 per cent) and hose and shirts (both 12 per cent). Doublets were made from various materials including leather, chamlet, fustian and worsted. Nicolas Walker (1566), a yeoman and smith from Kingston upon Thames, had no clothing recorded in his inventory but his accompanying will recorded bequests of a doublet of doe's leather, his best cloak and jacket and a fox-furred gown. Gowns were recorded in 9 per cent of the inventories. William Beston (1579), a gentleman from Southwark, had an old gown faced with fox and furred and another faced with budge and lined with white cotton. Hats recorded in 11 per cent of inventories included felt, silk, taffeta and one which was faced or lined with velvet. The remaining items were jerkins in 7 per cent, caps 5 per cent and smocks, recorded in only 3 per cent of inventories.

Clothing from the seventeenth century

In the seventeenth century, men's clothing for middle ranks consisted of doublets, hose or breeches, stockings, jerkins and coats. Women's clothing for middle ranks comprised underlinen, smock and petticoat, gown, 'crosse cloths', apron, neckerchief and coat.[66] According to Styles, plebeian clothing followed the trends of high fashion but were made from different materials and worn in different circumstances. In particular, there was a clear distinction between best and working clothes.[67] For Tim Hitchcock, the significant item of clothing for the poor was their body linen, shirts, stockings and shifts that lay next to the skin and acted as underwear. They protected the wearer from the coarse fabrics and dirt of everyday life and labour and saved expensive outer garments from stains and smells.[68]

Contemporary writers frequently referred to relatively high standards of clothing worn by English people and this judgement extended to most social groups. Charles Davenant wrote in 1698 that 'there is no country in the world where the inferior rank of men were better clothed'.[69] In the late 1720s, Daniel Defoe wrote that 'no people in Europe wear and consume so great a quantity of linen, and that quantity so fine in its quality, as the English do'.[70] Overseas visitors, Pehr Kalm, Pierre Grosley and Karl Moritz, included the labouring poor in their positive view of dress that covered the period between the 1740s and 1780s.[71]

Margaret Spufford suggested that there was a significant improvement in the nation's clothing and that the seventeenth century witnessed 'the great re-clothing of rural England'. The extent to which this improvement could be afforded by all ranks is debateable; Keith Wrightson argued that the 'swelling ranks of the middling sort' had surplus income to spend on a range of domestic goods and better clothing.[72] The account book of Richard Latham, a Lancashire yeoman, provided an insight into spending by a family whose annual income (around £30) fell below that of most middle-ranking households.[73] Latham's account book covered the years from 1724 (just after his marriage) to 1767 (the year of his death). He had eight children, including seven daughters, and spent between 6–8 per cent of his overall spending on clothing.[74] This is not a straightforward calculation as some clothing was made in the household and spending varied considerably between individual years.[75] For example, in 1747 he spent considerable sums on clothing including gowns for daughters Rachel and Ann, cloaks (8s 11d each), shoes (3s) and coats. Payments for cloth and to a tailor to make up the clothing were recorded.[76] In 1742, a new gown for daughter Betty had cost just over £1 and in the previous year payments were recorded for new shoes, but also for mending old shoes.[77]

As Styles pointed out, Latham's income and spending on clothes was not dissimilar to the working-class budgets calculated by Frederick Eden and David Davies and analysed by Sara Horrell.[78] Gregory King had calculated that even 'the poorer sort' spent about 18 per cent of their income on clothes, but King's conclusions about the poor are contested by those supporting the pessimist case.[79] Horrell's findings from household budgets suggested that very little money, only £2 per annum, was available for clothing, other household goods and any discretionary spending.[80] Clothes worn by labourers and their families were typically old, shabby and made from coarse materials. Styles suggested several reasons why the pessimist case was overstated. Davies' and Eden's budgets were mainly for families with large numbers of young dependent children and Eden's budgets mainly related to the war years of 1794–96, a period of high inflation, falling wages and reduced opportunities for work.[81] Location as well as rank was also important. According to Eden, except for shoes and hats, almost every article of clothing worn by labourers in the north was manufactured at home. By contrast, in midland and southern counties, labourers bought most of their clothes from shopkeepers.[82]

After food, clothing continued to be the second largest item of household expenditure. Towards the end of the seventeenth century, King priced the nation's total expenditure on clothes at over £10 million, a quarter of national income.[83] In terms of value, half of the sum of £10 million was accounted for by five items of clothing: shoes, shirts and smocks, coats for men, stockings and petticoats and waistcoats. The value of shoes purchased was £1 million per annum and this represented about 12 million pairs or just over two pairs of shoes a year for the average person.[84] Shoes wore out and had to be replaced.[85] However, Negley Harte argued that King's figures represented only new clothing and must have excluded the extensive exchange of secondhand clothing in 1688.[86] Expenditure on clothing was therefore considerably higher than King's calculations. Giorgio Riello suggested that in terms of the McKendrick thesis of a consumer revolution in the third quarter of the eighteenth century, clothing was the single most important category of material culture in the explanation of expanding consumption.[87]

Tailors

There were 90 tailors in the inventory collection, just over 1 per cent of the total. Tailors tended to have low inventory values: 18 were under £10 and a further 16 were under £20. Clothing tradesmen could be both producers and retailers of clothes and the extent that clothes were made for stock may have influenced their inventory values from which interpretations about their relative status are often made. Styles suggested that there were regional differences in the supply of ready-made clothing which was more widely available in London, the Home Counties, other parts of south and East Anglia than in the north such as Latham's Lancashire.[88] Unlike cordwainers, there was little evidence of stocks of cloth or ready-made clothes in the 90 tailors' inventories and tailors with the highest inventories generally had substantial debts due to them at the time of their death. Barrie Trinder and Nancy Cox concluded from this evidence that customers usually provided their own materials from which tailors made clothes.[89]

Ready-made and secondhand clothing

Increasingly, ready-made clothing was sold both new and secondhand. Hoh-Cheung Mui and Lorna H. Mui argued that shops selling new clothing were the most common of the smaller shops which were growing in number in the eighteenth century.[90] Most were termed drapers, but others included haberdashers, hatters, hosiers and milliners, breeches and stay makers and tailors.[91] Criminal records also provided evidence of the availability of shops selling ready-made clothes which were often bought with stolen money. These purchases were usually made in shops located in larger towns and included coats, waistcoats and stockings.[92] Sellers of secondhand clothes included pawnbrokers, disposing of unredeemed clothing, and itinerant sales-persons. These itinerant clothes sellers were depicted by Paul Sandby in some of his eighteenth-century watercolours.[93] Bernard Capp argued that buying secondhand clothes was common amongst lower social groups and predominantly undertaken by females.[94] Beverly Lemire suggested that both the purchase of secondhand clothes and their sale was not confined to the poor but that there was an extensive secondhand trade that included many buyers from middling groups as well as labourers.[95] Samuel Pepys was not averse to buying secondhand clothes and recorded in his diary in June 1667 that his new silk 'Camelott suit' had been made from an old cloak.[96] Both the clergyman Ralph Josselin and the diarist James Boswell sold clothes to raise funds for certain purposes.[97]

Not all clothing was obtained by legal means.[98] Miles Lambert argued that poor consumers in Yorkshire regularly recycled secondhand clothing by legal

and illicit means.[99] Capp suggested that women buying secondhand clothes had
little regard for the provenance of these clothes and that they were often
stolen.[100] Sources used by historians can give a biased impression of the scale,
but theft of clothing did appear to be widespread in early modern England.[101]
In Essex, John Beattie found that clothing and household linen constituted
14 per cent of all thefts between 1620 and 1680.[102] In the following century,
clothing and textiles were the most commonly stolen goods in reported larcenies
in Surrey.[103] In London, too, over two in five cases (42 per cent) of house-
breaking and burglary in selected years in the period 1750–1821 involved the
theft of clothing. By the 1770s, there was a marked transition in the items of
clothing stolen. Cloaks, waistcoats, sleeves, shawls and petticoats were increasingly stolen as housebreakers and burglars followed trends in fashion.[104] Stolen
clothes could be sold to pawnbrokers, tailors and members of the public.[105]

Changes from the seventeenth century

Clothing changed over time and this could occur in at least four ways: the purpose of clothing, the types of garments worn, their style and the material from
which they were made. Cecil Willett and Phillis Cunnington argued that from
the seventeenth century, a fundamental difference between male and female
clothing emerged. Male garments were designed mainly to express social rank
whereas female clothing was designed to attract.[106] Evidence from probate
documents only provided very limited information about types of garments and
little about style or materials; however, they do indicate that there were significant modifications to the actual items that were being worn as fashions and
trends changed. Whilst doublets were often referred to in wills and inventories
from the fifteenth and sixteenth centuries, references gradually disappeared in
the seventeenth century although William Baker, a gardener from Marlborough,
still owned one in 1669 as did a Huntingdon butcher in 1674. Men increasingly
chose to wear long coats and waistcoats rather than the doublet.

Styles argued that between the mid-sixteenth and the early-eighteenth centuries the types of clothing worn by 'ordinary' people changed. For women,
gowns and mantuas replaced kirtles and for men, coat, waistcoat and breeches
replaced doublet and hose. Towards the end of the eighteenth century, men's
jackets became more common and breeches were replaced by trousers.[107]
Towards the end of our period, what Frank Trentmann has called the clothing
revolution was in full swing.[108] Cotton was increasingly used for clothing such
as gowns, petticoats and stockings at the end of the seventeenth century.
Cotton came in a variety of qualities with the middling sort favouring light
calicoes whilst lower classes purchased cheaper cottons.[109] The increasing use
of cotton was demonstrated in an analysis of the materials from which clothing
stolen after 1750 was made. However, shirts and shifts were still made from
linen suggesting that cotton was not yet making inroads into undergarment
production.[110]

Evidence from probate inventories

Despite the scale of spending on clothing, Spufford claimed that the subject had been neglected by historians.[111] However, Riello argued that recent emphasis on the history of consumption has led to the development of 'fashion studies' that has drawn together scholars from a wide range of disciplines. One result of this interdisciplinary research has been that museum curators have spent greater amounts of time in archives and historians have spent more time in museum galleries. However, archives have not always yielded information on clothing. Spufford lamented that it was 'impossible to trace the spread of the humble shirt or indeed any other clothing' in *probate inventories* 'since items of clothing are so rarely appraised in England'.[112] Riello endorsed Spufford's pessimism that clothing was rarely listed in detail in inventories.[113] Nevertheless, clothing was recorded in probate inventories including both the production and sale of clothing by tradesmen, cordwainers, glovers and shopkeepers and personal clothing owned by individuals.

Most studies of probate inventories have been of the period after the Restoration in 1660 when the extent to which clothing was separately identified in inventories significantly diminished. This study includes data from four counties with more than a hundred inventories dated prior to 1660: Huntingdonshire, Surrey, Cheshire and Wiltshire. This provides insights into valuations of personal clothing and variation by social rank. By the second half of the seventeenth century, clothing was usually jointly recorded with 'money in the purse'. This is consistent with Spufford's suggestion that as garments became more commonplace during the century, appraisers increasingly overlooked them when inventories were compiled.[114] Lionel Munby agreed and argued that only clothing worthy of special mention was recorded in inventories.[115]

More than half (57 per cent) of Huntingdonshire inventories dated before 1660 recorded clothing separately (Table 4.2).

TABLE 4.2 Clothing recorded in Huntingdonshire probate inventories

Period	Probate inventories	Record clothes separately	
	No.	No.	%
1601–1629	144	96	67
1630–1659	160	77	48
Sub Total	304	173	57
1660–1689	384	35	9
1690–1719	308	17	6
1720–1749	280	6	2
1750–1800	143	1	1
Grand Total	1419	232	16

Of the 173 Huntingdonshire inventories which recorded clothing separately during the period 1601–59, 22 people (13 per cent) had clothing valued at £5 or more. Huntingdonshire data showed a strong relationship between the value of clothes and overall inventory values. The 22 people with clothing valued at £5 or over in Huntingdonshire for the period 1601–59 had a median inventory value of £188 compared to a median of £27 for all inventoried persons in that period. Most collections of clothes valued at £5 and above were found in more urban locations. This is similar to the findings of Carl Estabrook who found that proportionately more urban dwellers than villagers spent 'lavish amounts' on clothing.[116] Females were more likely to own high value collections of clothes than males. Analysis of high value clothing by rank was limited because of very small sample sizes. In Huntingdonshire, seven out of eight gentry with clothing separately recorded in their inventory owned clothes valued at more than £5 but no husbandman or labourer did. Styles argued that what differed between clothing owned by the wealthy and the poor was not types of garment but the number of items and their value.[117]

By the seventeenth century, inventories provided little evidence of the kind of clothing owned. However, one early example was John Sheppard, a husbandman from Bristol, whose inventory valued at £35 was dated 1609. He owned two doublets, a jerkin, three pairs of breeches, a mandilion, two pairs of stockings, two cloaks, two waistcoats, two shirts, three caps, a hat, a pair of shoes, a coat and a girdle valued at a total of £2.[118] Such references are especially valuable as the survival of actual clothes from middling and lower ranks in earlier periods is rare.[119] John Sheppard's clothing can be compared with the late example of Francis Gregory, a cutler from Marlborough, who died in 1748. Gregory had no doublet or cloak but coats and waistcoats. He also owned breeches, a hat, shoes, stockings, shirts and neckcloths. It appears he had only recently acquired a pair of new breeches which were valued at 6s.[120]

These comparatively rare glimpses of clothing worn by relatively poor persons must be interpreted carefully as they represent used clothing of an unknown age.[121] Although no claim for representativeness can be made, the scarce examples tend to support the optimist case about the ability of the less affluent to clothe themselves. In 1674, a Huntingdon butcher whose total inventory was valued at only £9 2s had clothing similar to that outlined by Keith Wrightson and David Levine for middle rank persons.[122] His inventory listed clothing valued at £1 1s 6d which included a great coat, doublet and breeches (10s), shirts and handkerchiefs (4s), a hat (2s 6d), a pair of boots (1s 6d), a pair of shoes (6d) and a pair of stockings (6d). Mease, a labourer from Huntingdonshire, had the highest value of clothing of any labourer in the sample.[123] These were valued at £3 10s in 1635. They included a cloak, a coat, three pairs of breeches, a doublet, a waistcoat, two pairs of stockings, two pairs of shoes and two hats. Cranwell, a Huntingdonshire labourer who died in 1628, had two doublets valued at 6s 8d.[124] Boyden, another Huntingdonshire labourer, had two coats, three waistcoats, five shirts, a pair of breeches, two pairs of shoes, a pair of boots, an unspecified hat and a straw hat in 1754.[125] More than a century later, Boyden, like Francis Gregory, did not have a cloak or doublet recorded in his inventory reflecting Styles' argument that such clothes were no longer fashionable.[126]

The four most common items of female clothing recorded in inventories of those of middle rank were hat, gown, petticoat and smock. Gowns were worn over a petticoat and made of various materials ranging from silk to stuff, but typically cotton or linen. Differences in materials were reflected in their price. Silk gowns were typically twice the price of linen or cotton gowns and perhaps six times the price of stuff gowns.[127] Evidence about clothing from probate inventories is frustrating because even when garments were specified, essential information about materials was often omitted. For example, Spufford suggested that gowns were the most expensive item of clothing worn by females with median values of 10s 8d in Lincolnshire and 19s 6d in Kent.[128] However, no details about the materials used were provided, almost certainly because they were not recorded. In Huntingdonshire, Grace Coxe's five gowns were valued at £8 13s 4d, an average of £1 14s 8d each.[129] The valuation made in 1638 suggested that they were high-quality gowns and may have been silk. A century later, in 1740, Mary Normanson of Spaldwick owned four gowns, a hood and cloak, stays, flaxen shifts, aprons, handkerchiefs, shoes and clogs, aprons, girdles, gloves, hose, hats, apron and hoop petticoat valued at £8 17s 6d. However, in 1760 (8 May) Sarah Hurst recorded spending £8 on a single silk gown which she considered to be not extravagant as she only bought one every five years.[130] This is consistent with the view of Jane Whittle and Elizabeth Griffiths that gowns were not purchased very frequently but were durable items that lasted a number of years and could be adjusted and remade.[131]

Other items of display and apparel

Boots and shoes

This chapter has focussed on the garments that were worn by people during the late medieval and early modern periods and how these changed over the period as dress assumed a wider significance. However, certain other items were also worn, and a brief consideration will be given to some of these. These items were not subject to such a level of change during the period.

As has been noted, although animal skins were in wide supply as a by-product of meat and dairy production, the input of labour and materials required to turn raw hides into leather and then fashion the prepared leather into shoes or boots raised the cost of the final product. Thorold Rogers estimated that for the late medieval period, a pair of shoes cost an average of 6½d per pair with boots costing between 8d and 2s 6d; however, boots and shoes bought by Thetford Priory included a pair of shoes bought for the kitchen boy in 1499/1500 and which cost just 4d, boots and shoes bought in 1504/05 for novices at a cost of just under 10d per pair, whilst shoes bought for boys in the priory's school in 1521/22 cost just over 7d per pair.[132] Despite these lower values, these costs still suggest that, bought as new, even the meanest footwear might be difficult for the very poorest families to afford so that shoes and boots were regularly passed down amongst families and frequently repaired. Although shoes and boots were regularly handed on, they are only infrequently bequeathed although the Chingford husbandman Alexander Grene gave three sets of footwear which he described as being high shoes and slack-heeled shoes as well as a pair of boots.[133]

Cordwainers both produced and sold shoes. Production of shoes took place in cordwainers' workshops which were part of the family house and selling shoes typically took place in the front of the building. Over time, the standardisation of sizing for shoes facilitated the emergence of ready-made shoes. Based on probate inventory evidence, Styles suggested that standardised sizing for shoes was in operation during the civil war.[134] Although Wrightson found evidence of large numbers of ready-made shoes in the inventory of John Collingwood in Newcastle in 1636, Riello's recent major study of the shoe industry in 'the long eighteenth century' contained very little evidence from before 1750 particularly from outside London.[135] However, Jon Stobart found that out of 70 rural shoemaker's inventories from Cheshire from the period 1701–60, only three listed made-up shoes. The value of this stock was £1 18s 8d, £5 19s and £6 10s respectively, thus, the total stock of the three shoemakers was about 150 pairs of shoes. Stobart concluded that in rural Cheshire shoemakers mostly made shoes to order and that ready-made shoes were relatively rare in this period.[136] One of Riello's limited pieces of evidence from outside London came from the records of a shoemaker in Chelmsford, who in 1760 left a stock of 320 pairs of shoes and 31 pairs of boots mainly for the ready-to-wear market.[137]

Cordwainers' inventories provided evidence of the emerging ready-made market for shoes in the provinces and at a relatively early date although they could be frustrating in merely recording 'shop goods'. Others provided more detailed insights into the extent to which stocks of ready-made shoes were accumulated. A cordwainer's probate inventory from St Ives, Huntingdonshire recorded a large stock of ready-made shoes in 1675 so that 'All the boots and shoes ready made' in Bentley's inventory were valued at £27.[138] Using King's assumption of an average figure of 20d for a pair of shoes, Bentley's stock of shoes possibly represented more than three hundred pairs of shoes, depending upon their gender mix, size and quality.[139] In addition, Bentley had 'thirteen dozen and six pair of child shoes, white, yellow and red' valued at 5d a pair and sole leather and upper leather valued at £25 18s 10d. Excluding the substantial leather stocks, Bentley had enough shoes in stock for the annual shoe requirements of over 20 per cent of the population of St Ives. Noble, another St Ives cordwainer, had a range of nearly 200 pairs of ready-made boots and shoes in his inventory in 1717 ranging from boots at 7s 9d a pair to children's shoes at 1s 3d a pair. His stock of 23 backs and eight hides in his warehouse was valued at £48.[140]

Gloves

Late-medieval and early-modern people wore gloves, mittens and gauntlets for protection and decoration in many different contexts. They were made for men, women and children, for workers, falconers, fighters, preachers and lovers. Surviving examples show that they were made from various materials including wool, textiles, metals and leather and could be lavishly decorated.[141] Thorold Rogers suggested that for the late medieval period, gloves could cost anything upwards of 1d a pair, depending on their quality and the use to which they would be put.[142] Gloves purchased by Thetford Priory in 1519/20 were bought for 1d per pair.[143]

However, by the end of the seventeenth century, King suggested that gloves were about a shilling a pair and this was consistent with the price of gloves provided at funerals and recorded in probate accounts.[144] By contrast, probate inventories revealed that gloves increased in valuation over time but did not reach King's shilling a pair. John Fleming, a glover who died in Marlborough in 1612, owned nine pairs of gloves valued in total at 1s 6d, a mean of 2d a pair.[145] John Dale, a yeoman from Marlborough, owned four pairs of gloves in 1682 valued at 1s 6d, a mean of 4½d.[146] In 1683, Mary Hurle, a widow, had eight dozen and a half of male and female gloves valued at 8s a dozen or a mean of 8d a pair. No distinction was made in the price between male and female gloves in this valuation.[147] The 11 dozen gloves and 24 gross of buttons in Richard Bull's inventory was valued at £4 4s, meaning that the gloves could not have exceeded a mean of 7½d a pair in 1765.

Glovers were not confined to making gloves. For example, Richard Bull of Kimbolton was described as a glover and breeches maker in 1765.[148] Glovers often had relatively high inventory values as a result of owning high stocks of gloves and hides. John Inman who died in Hull in 1727 had an inventory value of £313. Inman's stocks of gloves and hides were valued at £269.[149] Stocks in Richard Day's shop in 1710 included gloves at £29 but also breeches, stays and stomachers (£13), as well as substantial stocks of leather (£40).[150]

Hats

Various forms of headgear were also worn by both sexes during the late medieval and early modern periods. Headcoverings were worn outside by both men and women whilst men also wore caps and women wore kerchiefs or kerchers when inside the house. Items of headgear were frequently bequeathed and these bequests demonstrate that hats, hoods and caps were made from a wide range of fabrics (see Table 4.1). Many of these were luxury cloths (which probably indicates that the item had some value and was worth bequeathing) such as silk, velvet and scarlet; for example, the Thetford cleric John Wurlych gave a scarlet hood in 1460 and the widow Alicia Hunte of Bradfield left a silk hood in 1487.[151] Headcoverings made from cheaper fabrics were also bequeathed; William Curteys of Mildenhall gave a straw hat in 1473 and Thomas Fysshepole of St Albans left 'my hatte and my typpet of worsted' in 1478.[152] The colours of hats and hoods were often described and indicated that these items were usually of dark colours such as the murrey hoods which John Payes, fletcher of St Albans, gave in 1478.[153] As has been noted earlier, women frequently bequeathed the 'kerchers' or kerchiefs which they used to cover their heads inside the house. Whilst various forms of hoods were commonly worn by both sexes during the medieval period, their use appears to have slowly died out from the end of the fifteenth century. There are frequent references to hoods in wills from the fifteenth century but only a handful from the sixteenth with the final reference that of Isabell Love, widow of Thetford, who left her daughter 'my best hoode' in 1513.[154] There were no hoods recorded in the Surrey inventories for the second half of the eighteenth century.

Hats and other headcoverings were acquired from a range of sources during the late medieval period. Simple kerchers were probably made by the women who wore them from purchased linen, whilst basic caps and hats were bought from regional mercers or from chapmen and pedlars, such as those acquired by Thetford Priory from the Roberdes family of local mercers.[155] Better-quality headgear was acquired in a number of different ways. Some may have been purchased from hatters or cappers who operated in some of the larger provincial towns, such as the capper Robert Testwood of Northampton whose will has been included in this study, whilst others may have been obtained in London from hatmakers or haberdashers.[156]

Hatters were making hats for stock, at least by the seventeenth century. A sample of 25 hatters had a median valuation of stocks of hats at £35 4s by 1710. In one extreme case, a milliner in Norfolk had stocks worth £300 when he died in 1720.[157] Valuations of hats in probate inventories suggested that the typical hatter might have 350 hats in stock and the Norwich milliner's stocks could represent up to 3,000 hats. For example, in Redcliffe, Bristol, the hatter John Trueman had 46 grey hats at 3s per hat in 1635.[158] In 1662/63 Edward Jones had 24 felt hats worth £2 8s, a mean of 2s per hat.[159] In 1672, the inventory of the widow Joan Herring recorded six dozen hats at £7 10s, a mean of just over 2s per hat.[160] Hats could be considerably more expensive; the Marlborough yeoman, John Dale, owned a new hat and two old hats valued in total at 15s in 1683.[161]

Haberdashers also sold hats of various types and colours. Sometimes stocks in the shop were summarized and a single valuation given; for example, William Stockwell, a haberdasher in Marlborough, had an inventory in 1630 that contained a valuation of wares in the shop totaling £42 17s 4d.[162] On the other hand, the haberdasher, Humphrey Ellis, had 38 coloured hats in his shop in Bristol in 1609. These were of various qualities and prices ranging from as low as 2d each to as much as 2s. He also had black felt hats at 2s 9d and others at 2s.[163]

Of the 33 feltmakers in the collection, over four in five were located in Gloucestershire and all the rest were in neighbouring counties. John Smith's studies of the Bristol Apprentice Register for the years 1593–1609 found 50 feltmakers working in Bristol but there was a large migration of feltmaking into the Frampton Cotterell area by the early eighteenth century.[164] In the mid-eighteenth century, the Whit Monday Frampton Cotterell feltmakers' procession comprised substantial numbers. Feltmakers did not generally produce completed hats but felted 'bodies' ready for shaping, dyeing and finishing. These were sent to the hatmakers of Bristol and London, in Bermondsey and Cripplegate.[165] Feltmakers, like many trades, could also be engaged in agriculture; Thomas Hollister's inventory (1679) recorded ten kine, four yearlings, one two-year beast, five weaned calves, one mare and two pigs valued in total at £42.[166] Tools were recorded in feltmakers' inventories but references to stocks of hats were rare. An exception was John Sommurhill who had five dozen hats valued at £2 10s representing a mean of 10d a hat in 1691.[167] The lower valuation of hats in hatters' inventories is probably a reflection of their unfinished nature.

Jewellery

Haberdashery goods such as hats and gloves not only served a practical purpose but could be used as items of personal display. More blatant adornment came in the form of various items of jewellery including rings, brooches and badges which could be made from a range of metals but were most commonly made from silver.[168] Small silver goods such as these were produced by regional specialists who lived and worked in several provincial towns and although these craftsmen were termed 'goldsmiths', their main trade was in silver plate and jewellery rather than gold.

Jewellery was occasionally bequeathed, particularly items which were either of silver, or which incorporated some silver, including rings, brooches and necklaces. Whilst most bequests of jewellery were to family members, prior to the Reformation these items were also often given to statuary in churches. In 1471, John West of St Albans gave a silver 'browche' to the image of the Blessed Virgin Mary in the chapel of Our Lady of the Pew in Westminster Abbey.[169] Silver appears to have been a material associated with remembrance (see also Chapter 5) and whilst silver spoons were the items most often given during the medieval period for this purpose, by the late sixteenth century a number of wills included gifts of silver rings or bequests of money with which silver rings of remembrance were to be bought. In 1574, John Barratt of Canewdon bequeathed 10s apiece to the overseers of his will 'to make them rings with a death's head for remembrance', and in 1621, Lady Anne Drury of Hardwick House in Suffolk gave 'tenne pounds a peece to all my brothers to buye them ringes, and twentie pounds to be bestowed in ringes of ten shillinges amongest my freindes'.[170] Whilst bequests of silver jewellery were infrequent, references to gold items were almost negligible and all of the wills that included gold items were those of higher-status individuals: the wealthy clothier John Baret of Bury St. Edmunds, who made his will in 1463, owned a number of gold items including three gold rings, of which one was set with an emerald and a ruby, and a gold badge; whilst in 1505 Estelyne Irby, the widow of a Thetford gentleman, gave her daughter 'my golde ryng that I was maryed with unto my last husband'.[171]

Jewellery was rarely recorded in early modern probate inventories and was usually owned by people of high status. The most common item was a ring made of either silver or gold. Thomas Crush (1686), a gentleman from Essex, had five gold rings valued at £4.[172] Richard Benthall, esquire, of Benthall Hall, Benthall left five old gold rings valued at £2 in 1720.[173] Tymothy Bulckley, gentleman, of Smeatonwood, who died in 1630, left his wearing apparel, ring, sword and money in his purse together valued at £13 6s 8d.[174] More modest examples included Jone Burgies, a widow who died in Kingston upon Thames in 1558, who owned a pair of silver hooks, a little silver pin and a silver ring valued in total at 1s 10d.[175] Katherine Mower, a widow who died in Cranleigh, Surrey in 1603, had two silver pins and hooks valued at 2s. Katherine Mower also owned a gold ring valued at 13s 4d.[176] Silver gilt pins were worn in the hair and a surviving sixteenth-century example can be seen in the Norris Museum, St Ives, Huntingdonshire.[177]

Conclusion

This chapter has shown that the late medieval and early modern periods saw a gradual change in the role and status of clothing. Prior to 1350, clothing for everyone outside of the aristocracy and nobility served a largely practical purpose as a means of covering the body and providing warmth and protection against the elements. However, in the post-Black Death period, clothing acquired a wider significance and for a much larger proportion of society. Clothing became a means of displaying status and wealth and dress became subject to changes in taste. Increasingly consumers changed their preferences in terms of the physical garments that they wore, the cut and style of these garments, the cloth used to make such items and the colours used for clothing. In the first instance, garments for both men and women became more fitted. As less cloth was needed and at a time when wages were rising, people could afford to purchase more items of clothing. Many consumers chose to purchase garments made from better-quality fabrics or which incorporated fur and other more expensive trimmings. Cloth which incorporated darker dyes also became desirable and was worn by those who could afford to do so. Initially, this wider adoption of new styles, cloths and colours was resented by the nobility and led to the increased use of sumptuary laws as a means of preserving social distinctions. As time progressed, however, sumptuary legislation was redirected and became a device for regulating England's economy through limiting foreign trade and encouraging the domestic economy, rather than as a means of social regulation.

The period saw other changes. In the late medieval period, only a few items of clothing could be purchased ready-made. Instead, lengths of cloth were purchased or woven within the household and then made up into garments either domestically, or through the services of a local seamstress or tailor. With the growth of shops, clothes could increasingly be acquired ready-made, although this trend seems to have been more significant in London and the south and east of the country than in the north of England. For example, probate inventory evidence showed that ready-made shoes were being produced in large numbers in Huntingdonshire. At the same time, much clothing was secondhand and could be purchased as such, passed on from friends and family, or even acquired through illicit means.

Notes

1   S. Newton, *Fashion in the Age of the Black Prince* (Woodbridge: Boydell Press, 1980).
2   F. Braudel, *Civilization and Capitalism, 15th–18th Century: Volume 1, The Structures of Everyday Life, the Limits of the Possible* (London: Fontana, 1981), p.317.
3   K. Dauteuille, 'Household materials and social networks in Norwich 1371–1500: a study of testamentary evidence' (unpublished PhD thesis, University of Cambridge, 2003), p.126.
4   *Ibid.*, p.126; I. Mortimer, *The Time Traveller's Guide to Medieval England: A Handbook for Visitors to the Fourteenth Century* (London: Bodley Head, 2008), pp.107, 117.
5   An example from the late medieval period was a woollen tunic found in a fifteenth-century coal mine at Coleorton in Leicestershire, R. Hartley, 'Coleorton', *Current Archaeology*, 134 (1993), p.77; R. Hartley, 'Tudor miners of Coleorton, Leicestershire' in T.D. Ford and L. Willies (eds), *Mining Before Powder* (Matlock Bath: The Peak District Mines Historical Society, 1994), pp.91–101.
6   A petticoat was a short garment, with or without sleeves, worn by both men and women, C. Cunnington and P. Cunnington, *A Handbook of English Mediaeval Costume* (London: Faber & Faber, 1969); the gown was a long-sleeved overgarment which could vary in length between the sexes: gowns worn by men could range from those worn just above the knee to full length, whilst those worn by women were always full length to the ground.
7   Dauteuille, 'Household materials', pp.127, 130–33.
8   *Ibid.*, p.136.
9   J. Singman, *Daily Life in Medieval Europe* (Connecticut and London: Greenwood Press, 1999), p.36.
10 J. Thorold Rogers, *A History of Agriculture and Prices in England from the Year after the Oxford Parliament (1279) to the Commencement of the Continental War (1793): Vol. IV 1401–1582* (Oxford: Clarendon Press, 1882), pp.567–68.
11 J. Thorold Rogers, *A History of Agriculture and Prices in England from the Year after the Oxford Parliament (1279) to the Commencement of the Continental War (1793): Vol. I 1279–1400* (Oxford: Clarendon Press, 1866), pp.568, 570, 575–76; Dauteuille, 'Household materials', pp.123 and 161; Newton, *Fashion in the Age of the Black Prince*, p.69.
12 F. Piponnier and P. Mane, *Dress in the Middle Ages* (Yale: Yale University Press, 1997) p.16.
13 *Ibid.*, pp.16–18.
14 Thorold Rogers, *A History of Agriculture and Prices: Vol. IV*, p.570.
15 Damask was the name given to reversible, patterned fabrics which could be made from a variety of fibres including silk, linen and wool. However, true damasks were made of silk; http://en.wikipedia.org/wiki/Damask [last accessed 8 June 2014].

Sarcenet is a thin soft silk fabric, camlet was originally an eastern fabric made from camel hair but was subsequently made from various combinations of materials including wool, silk, hair and even linen.

16 The sumptuary legislation of 1461/62 forbade the wearing of cloth of gold to anyone below the rank of lord and this was reiterated in the legislation passed in 1510.

17 Piponnier and Mane, *Dress in the Middle Ages*, p.20.

18 C. Dyer, *Standards of Living in the Later Middle Ages: Social Change in England, c.1200–1520* (Cambridge: Cambridge University Press, 1989), p.78.

19 W. Childs, 'Luxury imports to England in the fourteenth century', in C. Given-Wilson, A. Kettle and L. Scales (eds), *War, Government and Aristocracy in the British Isles, c. 1150–1500: Essays in Honour of Michael Prestwich* (Woodbridge: Boydell Press, 2008), p.270.

20 Piponnier and Mane, *Dress in the Middle Ages*, pp.16–17; Singman, *Daily Life in Medieval Europe*, p.37.

21 Dyer, *Standards of Living*, p.79.

22 D. Dymond (ed.), *The Register of Thetford Priory, Part II: 1518–1540: Norfolk Record Society Vol. LX* (Oxford: Oxford University Press, 1995 and 1996), pp.709, 726, 741.

23 *Ibid.*, p.585.

24 M. Casson and J. Lee, 'The origin and development of markets: a business history perspective', in *Business History Review*, 85 (2011), p.32; 'The Noumbre of Weyghtes', BL, Cotton MS Vespasian E.IX, ff.97v-98 cited in J. Davis, '"Men as march with fote packes"': pedlars and freedom of movement in late medieval England', in P. Horden (ed.), *Freedom of Movement in the Middle Ages: Proceedings of the 2003 Harlaxton Symposium* (Donington: Shaun Tyas, 2007), p.137.

25 Casson and Lee, 'The origin and development of markets', p.15.

26 SROB 1476/1/1, 33 and 35.

27 Casson and Lee, 'The origin and development of markets', pp.424, 552, 647, 652.

28 Dyer, *Standards of Living*, p.79.

29 Piponnier and Mane, *Dress in the Middle Ages*, pp.16–17; Singman, *Daily Life in Medieval Europe*, p.9.

30 J. Davis, 'Marketing secondhand goods in late medieval England', *Journal of Historical Research in Marketing*, 2 (3) (2010), p.271.

31 SROB Acc. 359/3; R. Gray and D. Stubbings, *Cambridge Street-Names: Their Origins and Associations* (Cambridge: Cambridge University Press, 2000), p.12.

32 SROB Newton 16 (Mancer).

33 Thorold Rogers, *A History of Agriculture and Prices: Vol. I*, p.582.

34 Conies (adult rabbits) were farmed in warrens during this period and their meat and skin were viewed as a rare and much prized delicacy until the late fourteenth century. They became increasingly less highly regarded in the fifteenth and sixteenth centuries as they adapted to the English climate, increased rapidly in numbers and began to colonise the countryside, M. Bailey, 'The rabbit and the medieval East Anglian economy', *Agricultural History Review*, 36 (1998), pp.1–20.

35 Ermine was the name given to the winter coat of the stoat; *lettice* was the skin of the snow-weasel; budge was black lambskin imported from south-west Europe; E. Veale, *The English Fur Trade* (London: London Record Society, 2003), pp.23, 134, 142, 148, 167, 216, 220.

36 C. Dyer, *Making a Living in the Middle Ages: The People of Britain, 850–1520* (London: Penguin Books Ltd, 2003), p.296.

37 C. Fenwick, *The Poll Taxes of 1377, 1379 and 1381: Part Two Lincolnshire – Westmorland* (Oxford: Oxford University Press, 2001), pp.131–32, 516.

38 C. Dyer, *An Age of Transition? Economy and Society in England in the Later Middle Ages* (Oxford: Oxford University Press, 2007), p.135.

39 Thorold Rogers, *A History of Agriculture and Prices: Vol. IV*, pp.567–70.

40 Childs, 'Luxury imports to England in the fourteenth century', pp.269, 281, 283.

41 Piponnier and Mane, *Dress in the Middle Ages*, pp.19–20.

42 *Ibid.*, pp.16–17.

43 Veale, *English Fur Trade*, pp.133, 137.

44 *Ibid.*, pp.132, 135.

45 Sable was the skin of a northern variety of marten, *genette* was the name given to civet cat; *Ibid.*, pp.134, 136, 219.

46 M. Kowaleski, 'A consumer economy', in R. Horrox and W.M. Ormrod (eds), *A Social History of England 1200–1500* (Cambridge: Cambridge University Press, 2006), p.248.

47 G. Martin (ed.), *Knighton's Chronicle: 1337-1396* (Oxford: Clarendon Press, 1995), p.599, reference from previous edition cited in F. Baldwin, *Sumptuary Legislation and Personal Regulation in England* (Baltimore: Johns Hopkins Press, 1926), p.69.

48 C. Blyth (ed.), *Thomas Hoccleve: The Regiment of Princes* (Kalamazoo: Medieval Institute Publications, 1999), p.52, poem originally cited in Baldwin, *Sumptuary Legislation*, p.74 and quoted in J. Strutt, *A Complete View of the Dress and Habits of the People of England from the Establishment of the Saxons in Britain to the Present Time: Vol. II* (London: Tabard Press, 1842), pp.138–39.

49 Baldwin, *Sumptuary Legislation*, pp.9, 27–29, 30–32, 47–51, 102–6, 110–13, 114–17, 140–45, 147–48, 149–50, 157–61, 167–68.

50 *Ibid.*; Kowaleski, 'A consumer economy', p.248.

51 Baldwin, *Sumptuary Legislation*, pp.47–51; Veale, *English Fur Trade*, pp.4–5.

52 For discussion of status groups see Chapter 8. No clothing bequests were made by the men who identified themselves as labourers but as this was such a small number, it is inappropriate to draw conclusions from this.

53 S. Flood (ed.), *St Albans Wills, 1471–1500: Hertfordshire Record Publications Vol. IX* (Hertfordshire: Hertfordshire Record Society, 1993), p.12; TNA PROB 11/27/394 (Wheteley).

54 NRO NCC Attmere 330 (Burden); NRO ANW Bakon 374 (Dalton).

55 TNA PCC PROB 11/7/167 (Teryngham); TNA PCC PROB 11/14/745 (Aylnoth).

56 SROB Baldwyne 468 (Barkere); ERO MS9171/15 235 (Cordell).

57 SROB Baldwyne 52 (Wyot); ERO MS9171/15 35 (Samkyn).

58 SROB NRO ANW Fuller alias Roper 66 (Dunston); Flood (ed.), *St Albans Wills*, p.55.

59 HA 11/250.

60 SROB IC500/1/2/82 (Childerston).

61 NRO NCC Cobald 119 (Aleyn).

62 NRO ANW Randes 190 (George).

63 NRO ANW Aleyn 115 (Manninge).

64 TNA PCC PROB 11/33/98 (Benyngton).

65 Will of Joan Swanley, widow, of St Albans, in Flood (ed.), *St Albans Wills*, p.13; i.e. *genette*, TNA PCC PROB 11/57/286 (Cutt).

66 K. Wrightson and D. Levine, *Poverty and Piety in an English Village: Terling, 1525–1700* (Oxford: Clarendon Press, 1995), p.38.

67 J. Styles, *The Dress of the People: Everyday Fashion in Eighteenth-Century England* (New Haven and London: Yale University Press, 2007), pp.323–24.

68 T. Hitchcock, *Down and Out in Eighteenth-Century London* (London: Bloomsbury Publishing, 2004), p.98.

69 N.B. Harte 'The economics of clothing in the late seventeenth century', *Textile History*, 22 (1991), p.288.

70 M. Spufford, *The Great Reclothing of Rural England: Petty Chapman and Their Wares in the Seventeenth Century* (London: A&C Black, 1984), pp.114–26.

71 Styles, *Dress of the People*, pp.78, 224; K.D.M. Snell, *Parish and Belonging: Community, Identity and Welfare in England and Wales, 1700–1900* (Cambridge:

Cambridge University Press, 2006), p.52; Karl Moritz was a Lutheran pastor from Berlin.

72 K. Wrightson, *Earthly Necessities: Economic Lives in Early Modern Britain, 1470–1750* (New Haven: Yale University Press, 2000), p.241.

73 L. Weatherill, *Consumer Behaviour and Material Culture in Britain 1660–1760* (London: Routledge, 1996), p.98.

74 Styles, *Dress of the People*, pp.230–31.

75 L. Weatherill (ed.), *The Account Book of Richard Latham, 1724–1767* (Oxford: Oxford University Press, 1990), p.xxi.

76 *Ibid.*, pp.67–69.

77 *Ibid.*, pp.46, 51.

78 Styles, *Dress of the People*, p.230.

79 Harte, 'The economics of clothing', p.291.

80 S. Horrell, 'Home demand and British industrialisation', *Journal of Economic History*, 56 (3) (1996), p.582.

81 J. Styles, 'Custom or consumption? Plebeian fashion in eighteenth-century England' in M. Berg and E. Eger (eds), *Luxury in the Eighteenth Century: Debates, Desires and Delectable Goods* (Basingstoke: Palgrave Macmillan, 2003), p.106.

82 J. Styles, 'Clothing the North: the supply of non-elite clothing in the eighteenth-century North of England', *Textile History*, 25 (2) (1994), p.139; Styles, *Dress of the People*, p.139.

83 T. Arkle, 'Illuminations and distortions: Gregory King's Scheme calculated for the year 1688 and the social structure of later Stuart England', *Economic History Review*, 59 (2006), p.46.

84 G. Riello, *A Foot in the Past: Consumers, Producers and Footwear in the Long Eighteenth Century* (Oxford: Oxford University Press, 2006) p.20; Harte, 'The economics of clothing', pp.288, 293.

85 H.C. Mui and L.H. Mui, *Shops and Shopkeeping in Eighteenth-Century England* (London: Routledge, 1989), p.240.

86 Harte, 'The economics of clothing', pp.287, 293.

87 Riello, *Foot in the Past*, pp.5–9.

88 Styles, 'Clothing the North', p.160.

89 B. Trinder and J. Cox, *Yeomen and Colliers in Telford: Probate Inventories for Dawley, Lilleshall, Wellington and Wrockwardine:1660–1750* (Chichester: Phillimore, 1980), p.65.

90 Mui and Mui, *Shops and Shopkeeping*, p.289.

91 *Ibid.*, pp.6, 57.

92 Styles, *Dress of the People*, p.161.

93 See, for example, 'Old Clothes to Sell' 1759 Nottingham Castle Museum, www.londonlives.org/static/StBotolphAldgate.jsp [last accessed 1 November 2016].

94 B. Capp, *When Gossips Meet: Women, Family and Neighbourhood in Early Modern England* (Oxford: Oxford University Press, 2003), p.65.

95 B. Lemire, 'Peddling fashion: salesmen, pawnbrokers, taylors, thieves and the second-hand clothes trade in England, *c.*1700–1800', *Textile History*, 22 (1991), p.67; B. Lemire, *Dress, Culture and Commerce; The English Clothing Trade Before the Factory 1660–1800* (Basingstoke: Macmillan, 1997), p.124.

96 H. Clifford, 'Precious metalwork in early modern England', in M. Berg and H. Clifford (eds), *Consumers and Luxury: Consumer Culture in Europe* (Manchester: Manchester University Press, 1999), p.153.

97 B. Lemire, 'The theft of clothes and popular consumerism in Early Modern England', *Journal of Social History*, 24 (1990), p.270.

98 E. Cockayne, *Hubbub: Filth, Noise, and Stench in England, 1600–1770* (New Haven: Yale University Press, 2007), pp.77–78; B. Lemire, 'Peddling fashion', p.68.

99 M. Lambert, 'Cast-off wearing apparel: the consumption and distribution of second-hand clothing in northern England during the long eighteenth century', *Textile History*, 35 (2004), p.21.
100 Capp, *When Gossips Meet*, p.65; A. Green 'Consumption and material culture', in K. Wrightson (ed.), *A Social History of England, 1500–1750* (Cambridge: Cambridge University Press, 2017), p.244.
101 H. Shore, 'Crime, criminal networks and the survival strategies of the poor in early eighteenth-century London', in S. King and A. Tomkins (eds), *The Poor in England 1700–1850: An Economy of Makeshifts* (Manchester: Manchester University Press, 2003), p.150.
102 J. Beattie, *Crime and the Courts in England, 1660–1800* (Oxford: Clarendon Press, 1986).
103 Lemire, 'Peddling fashion', p.77; Lemire, *Dress, Culture and Commerce*, p.125.
104 S. Horrell, J. Humphries and K. Sneath, 'Cupidity and Crime' in M. Casson and N. Hashimzade (eds), *Large Databases in Economic History* (London: Routledge, 2013), pp.259–60.
105 Styles, *Dress of the People*, pp.162–63.
106 C. Willett and P. Cunnington, *The History of Underclothes* (New York: Dover Publications, 1992), p.53.
107 Styles, *Dress of the People*, pp.6, 45, 87.
108 F. Trentmann, *Empire of Things: How We Became a World of Consumers, from the Fifteenth Century to the Twenty-First* (London: Allen Lane, 2016), pp.67–68.
109 G. Riello, *Cotton: The Fabric that Made the Modern World*, (Cambridge: Cambridge University Press, 2013), pp.127–29.
110 Horrell et al., 'Cupidity and Crime', p.260.
111 M. Spufford, 'The cost of apparel in seventeenth-century England and the accuracy of Gregory King', *Economic History Review*, 53 (2000), p.677.
112 M. Spufford, 'The limitations of the probate inventory', in J.A. Chartres and D. Hey (eds), *English Rural Society, 1500–1800: Essays in Honour of Joan Thirsk* (Cambridge: Cambridge University Press, 1990), p.149.
113 Riello, *Foot in the Past*, p.19.
114 Spufford, *Great Reclothing*, p.126.
115 L. Munby, *Life and Death in King's Langley* (Kings Langley: Kings Langley Local History and Museum Society, 1981), p.xxx.
116 C. Estabrook, *Urbane and Rustic England: Cultural Ties and Social Spheres in the Provinces 1660–1780* (Manchester: Manchester University Press, 1998), p.153.
117 Styles, *Dress of the People*, p.32.
118 J. Moore (ed.), *Clifton and Westbury Probate Inventories, 1609–1761* (Bristol: Avon Local History Association, 1981), p.1.
119 Styles, *Dress of the People*, p.12.
120 L. Williams and S. Thomson (eds), *Marlborough Probate Inventories, 1591–1775: Wiltshire Record Society Vol. 59* (Chippenham: Wiltshire Record Society, 2007), p.303.
121 Harte, 'The economics of clothing', p.286.
122 HA AH18/8/10.
123 HA AH18/13/99.
124 HA AH18/3/130.
125 HA AH18/2/809.
126 Styles, *Dress of the People*, p.6.
127 Styles, *Dress of the People*, pp.32–35.
128 Spufford, 'The cost of apparel', p.694.
129 HA AH18/3/182
130 S.C. Djabri (ed.), *The Diaries of Sarah Hurst 1759–1762* (Horsham: Horsham Museum Society, 2003), p.93.

131 J. Whittle and E. Griffiths, *Consumption and Gender in the Early Seventeenth-Century Household: The World of Alice Le Strange* (Oxford: Oxford University Press, 2012), p.128.

132 Thorold Rogers, *A History of Agriculture and Prices: Vol. IV*, pp.580–81; D. Dymond (ed.), *The Register of Thetford Priory: Part 1 1482–1517: Norfolk Record Society Vol. LIX* (Oxford: Oxford University Press, 1994), pp.84, 197; Dymond (ed.), *Thetford Priory: Part II*, pp.372, 414.

133 F. Emmison, *Elizabethan Wills of South-West Essex* (Waddesdon: Kylin Press, 1983), p.24.

134 J. Styles, 'Product innovation in early modern London', *Past and Present*, 168 (2000), pp.159–60; Riello, *Foot in the Past*, p.48.

135 K. Wrightson, *Ralph Tailor's Summer: A Scrivener, his City and the Plague* (Yale: Yale University Press, 2011), p.122; N. Cox, 'A foot in the past: consumers, producers and footwear in the long eighteenth century by Giorgio Riello', *Economic History Review*, 60 (2007), pp.405–6.

136 J. Stobart, 'The economic and social worlds of rural craftsmen-retailers in eighteenth century Cheshire', *Agricultural History Review*, 52 (2004), p.150.

137 Riello, *Foot in the Past*, p.95.

138 HA AH18/2/197.

139 Riello, *Foot in the Past*, p.20; Harte, 'The economics of clothing', p.293.

140 HA AH18/14/153.

141 A. Willemsen, 'Taking up the glove: finds, uses and meanings of gloves, mittens and gauntlets in western Europe, *c.* AD 1300–1700', *Post Medieval Archaeology*, 49 (1) (2015), pp.1–36.

142 Thorold Rogers, *A History of Agriculture and Prices: Vol. IV*, pp.580–81.

143 Dymond (ed.), *Thetford Priory: Part II*, p.411.

144 Spufford, 'The cost of apparel', p. 694.

145 Williams and Thomson, *Marlborough Probate Inventories*, p.30.

146 *Ibid.*, p.165.

147 *Ibid.*, p.168.

148 HA AH18/2/833.

149 Borthwick Institute for Archives, York.

150 HA AH18/4/206.

151 NRO NCC Betyns 72 (Wurlych); SROB Hervye 419 (Hunte).

152 SROB Hervye 6 (Curteys); Flood (ed.), *St Albans Wills*, p.42.

153 *Ibid.*, p.40.

154 Dymond (ed.), *Thetford Priory: Part II*, pp.648, 652.

155 NRO NCC Johnson 235 (Love).

156 D. Edwards, M. Forrest, J. Minchinton, M. Shaw, B. Tyndall and P. Wallis (trans. and ed.), *Early Northampton Wills Preserved in Northamptonshire Record Office: Northamptonshire Record Society Vol. XLII* (Northampton: Northamptonshire Record Society, 2005), p.225; The Haberdashers' Livery Company had been granted a charter of incorporation in 1448 but its members were predominantly engaged in the sale of small wares until it was joined in 1502 by the hatmakers' fraternity. From this date, two distinct types of haberdasher emerged, those who specialised in hats and those who continued to specialise in small wares – The Haberdashers' Livery Company –www.haberdashers.co.uk/content.php?p=company-history [last accessed 28 February 2017].

157 J. Parker, 'Retailers' records as evidence for a "consumer revolution" *c.*1660–1780' (unpublished undergraduate dissertation, University of Cambridge, 2016).

158 E. and S. George (eds), *Bristol Probate Inventories, Part 1 1542–1650: Bristol Record Society's Publication Vol. 54* (Bristol: Bristol Record Society, 2002), p.93.

159 Trinder and Cox, *Yeomen and Colliers*, p.65.

160 Williams and Thomson, *Marlborough Probate Inventories*, p.139.

161 *Ibid.*, p.165.
162 *Ibid.*, p.62.
163 George and George, *Bristol Probate Inventories, Part I*, p.14.
164 J.S. Moore, *The Goods and Chattels of our Forefathers: Frampton Cotterell and District Probate Inventories: 1539–1804* (Chichester: Phillimore, 1976), p.16.
165 C. Heal, 'The forgotten Gloucestershire hatters of 1841', *Journal of the Bristol and Avon Family History Society*, 2007.
166 Moore, *Goods and Chattels*, p.111.
167 *Ibid.*, p.144.
168 Dauteuille, 'Household materials', p.136.
169 Will of John West of St. Albans, 9 October 1471 in Flood (ed.), *St Albans Wills*, p.10; NRO NCC Brigges 28 (Howton).
170 Will of John Barratt of Canewdon yeoman, 16 April 1574 in F. Emmison (ed.), *Elizabethan Life: Wills of Essex Gentry and Yeoman* (Chelmsford: Essex County Council for the Essex Record Office, 1980), pp.86–87; will of Lady Anne Drury of Hardwicke, 1621 in S. Tymms (ed.), *Wills and Inventories from the Registers of the Commissary of Bury St Edmunds and the Archdeacon of Sudbury* (London: Camden Society, 1850), pp.166–68.
171 Will of John Baret of Bury St. Edmunds in Tymms, *Wills and Inventories*, p.37; TNA PROB 11/14 Holgrave (Irby).
172 F. Steer, *Farm and Cottage Inventories of Mid-Essex 1635–1749* (Chichester: Phillimore, 1969), p.177ff.
173 B. Trinder and J. Cox, *Miners and Mariners of the Severn Gorge: Probate Inventories for Benthall, Broseley, Little Wenlock and Madeley, 1660–1764* (Chichester: Phillimore, 2000), p.132.
174 P. Pixton (ed.), *Wrenbury Wills and Inventories, 1542–1661: Record Society of Lancashire and Cheshire Vol. 144* (Chester: Record Society of Lancashire and Cheshire, 2009), p.258.
175 D.M. Herridge (trans.), *Surrey Probate Inventories, 1558–1603: Surrey Record Society Vol. 39* (Woking: Surrey Record Society, 2005), p.2.
176 Herridge, *Surrey Probate Inventories*, pp.425–26.
177 Norris Museum, St Ives, Cambridgeshire, SAVNM2014.10.

5

THE HOME ENVIRONMENT

Medieval houses were simple, functional single-storey dwellings but from the mid-sixteenth century the development of methods of controlling smoke from domestic fires had a huge impact on the development of housing and led to a swift stylistic change in domestic architecture, referred to by W.G. Hoskins as the 'rebuilding of rural England'.[1] Internal forms of houses could now be adapted to incorporate new features which particularly included the insertion of chimney stacks, ceilings and upper floors, but also comprised storeyed end bays and jetties which both enabled the available living space to be increased and facilitated the development of separated rooms and the loss of the hall area.[2] Less soot and grime within the domestic environment meant that houses became more comfortable and people began to take more pride in both the interior and exterior of their houses. Features were incorporated which not only made houses more conducive to agreeable living, but also reflected the social standing of the household. Internally, oak panelling known as wainscotting became popular, walls were painted and decorative plasterwork was often incorporated, all of which were regarded as an indication of status (Photo 5.1). Floorboards started to be used which were generally wooden but might also be of stone, especially in higher-status dwellings. The growing importance of the home was also reflected in a desire for more and quality furnishings which, again, invariably incorporated a desire for comfort with a need to display status.

As with clothing, many items of furniture were acquired secondhand. Wills contain numerous references to items which had been bought from a previous owner, such as the 'hutche which I bought of a woman of Maundon', given by the widow Margaret Newmane of Bishop's Stortford in 1570.[3] Very many others ask for items to be sold and the money used for various purposes such that it is evident that there was a ready market for used goods. This is reflected

PHOTO 5.1 Wall painting, Godmanchester, c.1620

in other sources; in Parson Woodforde's diary he recorded the purchase in 1789 of '2 large second hand double flapped Mohogany Tables, also one second hand Mohogany dressing Table with drawers'.[4] Parson Woodforde may have read advertisements about the sale of secondhand furniture in the *Norwich Mercury*; in a study of newspaper advertising from 1765 to 1805, covering York, Stamford, Bath and Norwich, Dinah Reed found that auctions of real estate and property increased considerably in the second half of the eighteenth century and especially the auctioning of whole households of goods (see Figure 5.1).[5] From around 30 such advertisements per year in the 1770s, the numbers rose in Bath and Norwich to over 100 by 1800. Such sales of household furniture may have been prompted by death, bankruptcy, the need to move away or 'giving up housekeeping'. The auctions mostly took place in the residence and may have lasted many days.

Beds and bedding

The earliest form of bedding used by *homo sapiens* more than 70,000 years ago was discovered in 2011 in South Africa. Sleeping mats made of plant material were used by hunter-gatherers at Sibudu Cave, a rock shelter in a cliff face above the Tongati River.[6] By the medieval period in England there was not a great advance, for when medieval people 'hit the hay' it was often a literal event for their bed was frequently of hay or straw.

Most people still slept on pallet beds which consisted of straw or straw-filled mattresses covered with a single sheet of coarse linen, a coverlet of worsted, fustian or a sheepskin and a log pillow.[7] In his study of Worcestershire peasantry in the later Middle Ages, R.K. Field noted that none of the *principalia* lists of

To be SOLD by AUCTION,
(By Mr. *SNOW*,)
On Monday the 13th of June Inst. upon the Premises at Edith Weston, in the County of Rutland,

THE Neat and Genuine HOUSHOLD FURNI-
TURE of a GENTLEMAN leaving the Country; comprising
Four-post and Tent Bedsteads, decorated with Crimson Silk Damask,
Linen, and other Hangings; exceeding fine Goose Feather-Beds and
Bedding; a variety of Mahogany Furniture, consisting of Bureaus,
Tables, Chairs, &c. &c.; Pier and other Glasses; Wilton and other
Carpeting; Bath Stoves; Variety of Kitchen Furniture; Yellow
and Stone Wares, &c. &c. and a number of other valuable Articles; all
of which is in very good Condition, and have been purchased new
about six Months since.

₊ The Sale to begin at Ten o'Clock.

‖‡‖ Catalogues may be had at the Falcon, Uppingham; Crown,
and George Inns, Oakham; Swan, Melton Mowbray; and of the
AUCTIONEER, at Stamford.

FIGURE 5.1 Newspaper entry advertising an auction of secondhand furniture and other items

Source: Image courtesy of the British Newspaper Archive

household items used for his study referred to beds but that five cottagers had a *tignum*, which was probably a rough, pallet-style bed made from wood.[8] As late as 1587, William Harrison referred to the old men dwelling in his village remembering that:

> our fathers, yea, and we ourselves, also, have lien full oft upon straw pallets, on rough mats covered only with a sheet, under coverlets made of dagswain or hapharlots (I use their own terms), and a good round log under their heads instead of a bolster or pillow.[9]

Sleeping arrangements had improved during the late medieval period with the growing use of items such as sheets, blankets, coverlets, bedcloths, bedboards, flock mattresses, bolsters and pillows. Testamentary evidence confirmed this increased use with 22 per cent of the wills including a reference to one or more of these bedding items with pairs of sheets being a particularly popular bequest. Bequests of beds and sheets were also the most common specified item (after money and 'the residue of the estate') in wills from Stratford on Avon in the period between 1530–1650.[10]

Although most people still lay down to sleep on fairly rudimentary beds, the most comfortable and desirable form of a late medieval bed was a 'featherbed' or *lectum plumalem*, in the form of a mattress filled with feathers. The featherbed was usually set inside a wooden frame and frequently included a tester and curtains, which gave some degree of privacy as well as keeping out drafts.[11] Evidence suggested that new featherbeds were not purchased as complete items but as a set of individual components acquired separately and made up and assembled to form the bed. In 1532/33, Thetford Priory accounts recorded that ticking for a mattress cost 8s whilst just short of 7lb of feathers amounted to an additional 1s and a task referred to as driving was charged at 1s per featherbed (presumably the making up and stuffing of the mattress) so that the total cost of a feather mattress was 10s.[12] Other items were needed to make the bed complete; a coverlet of tapestry-work cost the priory 10s 4d, a tester with curtains cost 11s, a painted cloth cost 5s, three pillowbeers were bought at 9d per pillow and sheets cost 5s for the canvas and 4d for the making up.[13] Added together, the total cost of a featherbed with all of its accoutrements came to £2 4s 1d, a considerable sum for the late medieval period. James Thorold Rogers also listed featherbeds in his survey of prices which ranged from 15s in 1543 (probably for just a feather mattress without the other components) to 36s 8d in 1506.[14] The rising demand for featherbeds led to the use of less desirable materials to supplement feathers and subsequently to the 1552 'Act for the true stuffynge of Feather-Beds Mattresses and Cushions' which ordered that featherbeds be stuffed only with 'dry pulled Feathers, or clean Down only, without mingling of scalded Feathers, Fen-down, Thistle-down, Sand, Lime, Gravel, Hair or any other unlawful or corrupt Stuff'.[15]

In the seventeenth century, featherbeds were frequently valued by weight. For example, Henry Stanworth, a cordwainer from Wellington, had a featherbed which weighed 56lb when he died in 1685. It was valued at 6d a pound, which should result in a valuation of £1 8s but the valuation was calculated to be £1 10s 4d.[16] Whilst the featherbed remained the most highly regarded mattress, other materials were used to stuff mattresses. Down beds were rare and generally tended to be a mark of high status, whilst most lower-status households used flockbeds (wool-stuffed mattresses) or even continued to use straw, although inventory evidence showed that even down mattresses could be owned by the relatively poor.[17] Lucy Worsley suggested that female servants in the kitchen were allowed to keep feathers of the birds they plucked for the table and could save them up for a marital featherbed.[18]

During the early modern period, sleeping places increasingly moved upstairs with the creation of designated upstairs chambers for sleeping. Householders experienced an increase in their comfort and privacy as servants remained downstairs.[19] Not only were the beds within these chambers more commodious, but other pleasing furnishings were added, including cushions and window curtains.[20] The increased role of the bed chamber was such that Jane Whittle and Elizabeth Griffiths contended that beds were the symbolic centre of the early modern household in the same way that hearths had been in the medieval period.[21] Such essential aspects of early modern lives as morning prayers would have taken place in the bedchamber.[22]

Although featherbeds were regarded as exclusive, luxury items throughout the medieval period, by the second half of the sixteenth century, they were becoming more common and 42 per cent of the inventoried population of Surrey owned one. In urban areas such as Southampton and Ipswich, ownership of featherbeds reached 85 per cent and 84 per cent of the inventoried population respectively. Whilst the gentry had the highest level of ownership, a quarter of inventoried labourers owned featherbeds by the second half of the eighteenth century. Joseph Harley found that around a third of pauper inventories in Dorset, Kent and Norfolk recorded feather-beds after 1770.[23] In Shefford, Bedfordshire, an inventory of the main poor house taken in 1812 revealed that one of the beds in the four bedrooms was a featherbed.[24]

Bed frames also varied widely in cost and style (Photo 5.2). Keith Wrightson and David Levine suggested that in the 1660s and 1670s 'high beds' complete with curtains appeared among the 'wealthier people' of Terling.[25] High-quality joined beds, made by a skilled carpenter or joiner, were morticed and tenoned.[26]

a)

b)

c)

d)

PHOTO 5.2 Beds: a) parlour chamber (image courtesy of Ford Green Hall, Stoke); b) reconstructed seventeenth-century bed (image courtesy of the Weald and Downland Museum); c) a trundle bed under a tester bed with hanging curtains (image courtesy of the Weald and Downland Museum); d) cradle (image courtesy of Ford Green Hall, Stoke).

Those of humbler status often had much lower-quality boarded beds with solid panels at the head or at both ends. Trundle beds were low framed, often with castors enabling them to be rolled under bedsteads during the day. Children or personal servants frequently used trundle beds.[27] Cradles varied in design but were mostly low, box-like structures of panelled wood on rockers with hoods that protected young children from draughts. Beds were often shared; Tara Hamling and Catherine Richardson cited the example of the son of a household sharing a bed with a servant, whilst Nehemiah Wallington shared a bed with an apprentice.[28]

The mean number of beds per household was three in 1,218 probate inventories that recorded beds in Huntingdonshire and 2.9 in 1,230 inventories in Yorkshire. If household size remained at about 4.25 persons and married couples shared a bed, then it appears that sharing of beds by others was not commonplace among the inventoried population, other than perhaps for small children.

Sheets

In the late medieval period, sheets were regarded as prestige items and were increasingly purchased by those who could afford to do so. Households purchased the fabric required for sheets and then either paid for someone to make this up into sheets or did it themselves within the domestic environment. As they required a large amount of fabric (those recorded in the accounts of Thetford Priory generally used around seven and a half yards of linen for one pair of sheets), even basic sheets could be quite costly. The cheapest linen sheets purchased by Thetford Priory cost 1s 7d a pair for the fabric and an additional 2d for the making, whilst other sheets cost 5s per pair which probably indicates that they were of finer quality linen.[29] Sheets were also common bequests in the wills used for this study. They came in a variety of qualities or cloth in the medieval period so that those referred to include a 'flaxyn schett', 'hempinge shetes', 'curse sheetes' and 'hardene sheates' although no values were given.[30]

Sheets continued to be a status commodity in the early modern period so that Barrie Trinder and Nancy Cox regarded the capacity to change bed linen as one of the best indicators of steadily rising standards of comfort in the seventeenth century.[31] They found that in Telford the ratio of single sheets to beds rose from 1.4 in 1660–69 to 4.8 in 1740–49, whilst Margaret Spufford suggested that the number of sheets per bed had risen to five by the turn of the eighteenth century.[32] The range of different qualities found in wills from the late medieval period was also evident in probate inventories, from fine Holland to coarse harden sheets. Holland sheets could be more than three times the valuation of coarse sheets. Spufford suggested that gentry preferred Holland sheets but as with mattresses, the relationship of sheet quality to rank was not a simple one since even labourers could own Holland sheets. A labourer, William Clarke from Little Paxton in Huntingdonshire, owned 12 pairs of sheets in 1646 which included Holland, flaxen, hempteare and harden sheets.[33]

One problem in identifying the incidence of sheet ownership was that some probate inventories referred only to a general heading 'linen' whereas others separately identified sheets. Mark Overton *et al.* found very different recording practices between Cornwall and Kent. In Kent, 92 per cent of inventories recorded sheets separately in 1600–29 and there was only a slight fall to 86 per cent by 1690–1719. In the final 30-year period (1720–49) 80 per cent of inventories recorded sheets. In Cornwall, only 52 per cent of inventories recorded sheets in 1600–29 and this fell to just 13 per cent by 1720–49.[34]

Coverlets

In addition to sheets, people increasingly began to use coverlets on their beds in the medieval period. These were mostly made of relatively basic fabrics, such as worsted, or sheepskin, however, as people began to adorn their domestic dwellings, the most affluent members of society increasingly chose household possessions which combined practicality with extravagance and bed coverlets were one such item. For the affluent, these were often made of quality fabrics, such as velvet and damask, and decorated either by painting or tapestry-work, whilst the most desirable were those made or lined with fur, with the most exclusive being those of ermine, squirrel or even leopard.[35] Within wills, bed coverlets were often identified by their colours so that Agnes Dunston left a coverlet of sanguine colours (red), a white coverlet with green flowers as well as a third coverlet described simply as '*vetus*' (old).[36]

Bed curtains and hangings

Curtains and hangings around the bed provided some level of privacy at a time when most members of the household slept in close proximity to one another and, in addition, were valuable in keeping out draughts and the cold. English wills refer to the bequest of bed curtains from as early as the eleventh century, and by the end of the medieval period they were often associated with featherbeds so that, together with the bed itself, they were regarded as luxury items.[37] As a result, they could be expensive so that a tester with curtains bought by Thetford Priory cost 11s.[38] They were often made from quality fabrics and could be stained or incorporate tapestry work and embroidery; the gentleman Thomas Stotevile of Dalham described bed hangings which he bequeathed with a featherbed in 1466 as being 'of the philosoferes steyned (stained [with images] of philosophers)' and in 1579 Rafe Marsham, merchant of Norwich, gave 'one Testor for a bed of the Duke of Suffolk armes'.[39] As with featherbeds, bed curtains or hangings were far more likely to be bequeathed by wealthy testators and rarely appeared in the wills of husbandmen or craftsmen.

Ownership of bed curtains rose to a peak of at least 35 per cent of the inventoried population in 1660–89 and then declined to at least 18 per cent by the second half of the eighteenth century. Once again ownership was highest in urban centres and gentry and high-status occupations were most likely to own them. Between 14 per cent and 16 per cent of inventoried labourers owned bed curtains between 1660 and 1749.

Establishing the incidence of ownership of beds and their furniture presents challenges to the historian. Sheets may be lost from sight within the general heading of linen but the common phrase 'beds with their furniture' may also have reduced the numbers of featherbeds, hangings or other items of bedding. The results of incidence of ownership indicated by analysis of probate inventory data are therefore the minimum level and may be considerably higher. However, there was no indication that the method of recording differed significantly by rank and so comparisons of ownership between ranks are not necessarily invalid.

Tables

For most households in the late Middle Ages, domestic space was limited and consequently, if a table was owned, it was not a permanent fixture but consisted of a wooden board supported on folding trestles which enabled it to be erected where and when it was required, and taken down and stored against a wall when it was not.[40] Many of the tables bequeathed in late medieval wills can be identified as being of this type so that, for example, Isabella Sprot of St Albans gave her trestles and boards in 1487 and Agnes Sunbury of Loughton referred to her folding table in 1563.[41] In the fifteenth century these tables were often recorded merely as 'boards' and gave rise to the expression 'board and lodging' provided by inns. The poor even owned table boards without trestles. An inventory in the Warwickshire sample (John Morice, 1697) had a table board without trestles and Nat Alcock suggested that the board probably rested on upturned pails.[42] Permanent tables, known as a table dormant, did exist but were generally only associated with higher-status households so that in the Prologue to *The Canterbury Tales*, Chaucer could write of the Franklin, obsessed with *gentilesse*, that:

> His table dormant in his halle always
> Stood redy covered al the longe day.[43]

As domestic space increased from the sixteenth century onwards, tables dormant were more commonly owned by lower-status households where they were located in the hall, often with forms for seating (Photo 5.3). Again, this change in tables was reflected in testamentary bequests so that by the mid-sixteenth century tables were often referred to as being long or great or were defined as being joined tables so that Agnes Sunbury bequeathed a long table in addition to her folding table referred to earlier, and Matthew Dale of East

PHOTO 5.3 Medieval table
Source: Image courtesy of Ford Green Hall, Stoke

Hanningfield gave his 'great jointed table' in 1586.[44] Such tables could be made of various materials including oak, elm and mahogany, whilst in 1571, Richard Bould of Royston bequeathed to his wife 'ij plankes of walnuttry to make her a tabull'.[45] By the seventeenth century, various other types of table were being used so that probate inventories of this time included references to side tables, card tables and tea tables as well as dining tables. Gate-leg dining tables appeared in the seventeenth century from about 1640 and were located in the parlour.[46]

Prior to the sixteenth century, most household activities took place within the hall and this included the eating of family meals.[47] As houses became more elaborate, a subordinate parlour area was often divided off from the hall and this became the space in which people took their meals. In time, this area became a room in its own right and a definite addition to the layout of the house rather than simply a sub-division of existing space.[48] By the second half of the sixteenth century, tables were often referred to in wills as being in the parlour such as the 'table that standeth in the parlour' given in 1566 by the Essex yeoman Thomas Harryson.[49] The practice of eating in the parlour seems to have continued for some time so that John Robinson argued that in the late seventeenth and early eighteenth centuries, people generally ate meals in the parlour. Robinson maintained that private dining rooms only emerged in the 1730s when dining rooms began to appear in great country houses and suggested that the dining room at Houghton Hall was one of the earliest surviving dining rooms.[50] Robinson's dating of the emergence of dining rooms appears to be rather late. Stana Nenadic argued that the term 'dining room' was commonly used in middle-rank houses with more than three rooms in Glasgow and Edinburgh in the 1720s, and when Celia Fiennes visited Lord Orford's house, Chippenham Park, Cambridgeshire, in 1698, she found a dining room.[51] Lord Petre's inventory listed a dining room at Ingatestone Hall in Essex as early as 1601.[52] Rooms recorded as dining rooms appeared in the sample of Yorkshire probate inventories as early as 1690: two were in houses owned by gentlemen who died in 1690, and three dining rooms were recorded in 1694 in houses belonging to a gentleman, a merchant and a widow.

By the eighteenth century, dining rooms were recorded in nearly 3 per cent of Yorkshire probate inventories. Although gentry only represented 3 per cent of Yorkshire inventories which recorded rooms, a third of these dining rooms were in gentry houses. Other ranks that had a dining room included one husbandman, Beale. However, Beale's inventory value at £162 in 1735 was significantly above the median for a husbandman. No labourers had a separate dining room.

Seating

In a survey of chair ownership in France, Daniel Roche suggested that in the Middle Ages the chair was an attribute of the sacred, reserved for kings and holy images. Common people sat anywhere, on the ground, on the ledges of the fireplace, on cushions, coffers or benches, depending on rank and in striking proximity to each other.[53] Christopher Dyer argued that before the sixteenth century, peasant houses were commonly furnished with a single chair at the head of the table on which the male head of the household sat, whilst the wife, children and any servants sat on benches beside the table.[54] The phrase 'taking the chair' and the role of a chairperson reflected the concept of the chair as a sign of authority. Bequests contained in medieval wills suggested that chairs were not in common possession as these were rarely bequeathed. Instead, testamentary evidence suggests that furniture for sitting largely consisted of benches, commonly referred to as forms, or stools. Stools were also often given and from the mid-sixteenth century, they were often identified as being joined stools which were typically framed with mortise and tenon joints and fixed by dowels or pegs without glue.[55]

The low level of ownership of chairs was probably related to the cost of such items since basic chairs recorded by Thorold Rogers included one purchased in 1410 for 1s 2d and one bought in 1431 at a cost of 1s 6d, whilst a 'cypress' chair bought in 1477 cost 3s and a wainscot chair acquired in 1532 was bought for 8s.[56] By contrast, forms could be roughly made from almost any wood so that whilst the priory accounts did not record payments for completed items, a craftsman was paid just 1s in 1516/17 for making four forms.[57]

From the sixteenth century, chairs became much more frequent bequests in wills, although forms and stools still predominated. From this time onwards, the chair increasingly dominated the social space. Although the furniture of most households remained rudimentary items which could be roughly made and easily mended, in the latter seventeenth century, decorative woods and fine cabinet making became more fashionable.[58] Leading furniture makers such as Chippendale and Hepplewhite produced furniture for the elite but popular design manuals introduced patterns and designs to a wider consuming public.[59] Many sorts of chairs ranging from leather covered chairs, turkey-work chairs and joined chairs to more basic boarded seating were recorded in probate inventories.[60] Senior members of the household and significant guests were seated on high-backed chairs, whilst other family members sat on stools and forms (Photo 5.4). Turkey-work replaced needlework as the fashionable upholstery after the Restoration in 1660. Originally an expensive importation from the Near East, an English imitation was produced.[61]

PHOTO 5.4 Chairs and stool

Source: Images courtesy of Ford Green Hall, Stoke.

Cupboards

Cupboards were originally shelves for plates and cups, i.e. a cup board. Again, although they were referred to infrequently in wills from the fifteenth century, they appeared with increased regularity from the sixteenth so that by the middle of the century, Richard Feaste, butcher of Much Hadham, bequeathed 'a cubborde wich standethe at my chamber doore and all that standeth upon the said cubbord' and Agnes Smithe of Godmanchester referred to 'my cubberd as yt standes in the hall'.[62] As the century progressed, cupboards were often described in a way which reflects other changes that were taking place at this time so that in 1565 William Holbrooke of Waltham Holy Cross could give his cupboard of joined work and in 1566 Thomas Harryson of Loughton identified his cupboard as being in the parlour.[63] In time, plates were displayed in court cupboards which had several shelves and William Harrison suggested that many farmers had learned to garnish their cupboards with plates (see p.144, Pewter). These basic cupboards had open shelving; those with their shelves enclosed with doors were known as press cupboards and were usually more expensive (Photo 5.5). Richard Gylman, a gentleman from Bletchingley Surrey who died in 1571, had a joined press valued at £2, whereas his joined court cupboard was valued at only 5s.

PHOTO 5.5 Press cupboard

Source: Image courtesy of Ford Green Hall, Stoke

Chests

The late medieval period saw the increased adoption of chests and coffers which were used for storage as well as seats, although possession of such items largely remained the preserve of higher and middling social groups and such items were not commonly owned by people of lower status.[64] Medieval chests were wooden receptacles with flat lids, usually made to stand on the floor. They were often carved and inlaid with a plain lid and could be made of various woods including cypress, deal, fir, elm, juniper and oak, although spruce seems to have been particularly common. Chests and coffers recorded in wills sometimes included details of the wood from which they were made; for example, the 'gret spruce chest standyg' in the halle' given by John Tyrle to his wife, Alice in 1482.[65] Others incorporated carving as with the coffer of 'kervinge' work bequeathed by William Allen in 1536 and some were painted so that in 1482 Robert Pynhorn records his chest as being 'lez peynted'.[66]

Sixteenth-century Surrey inventories sometimes used the term chest with descriptive additions such as with a lock and key or descriptions of size (large or small) or the material from which it was made. William Beston, a Southwark gentleman who died in 1579, had a Danske chest valued at 6s.[67] The term coffer for wooden receptacles for storing clothes and valuables appeared less frequently. In the seventeenth century, the chest was still commonly used for storing clothing, linen and valuables (Photo 5.6). Adjectives used to describe chests appearing in inventories included boarded, dansk, dower, great, ironbound, joined, mule, settle, plain, small, turned and wainscot.

From the sixteenth century onwards, as people started to own more household goods, chests with drawers appeared and started to replace traditional chests. These new items of furniture made it easier to retrieve goods from storage and Overton *et al.* suggested that the adoption of chests of drawers was an important example of increasing consumption linked with improved standards of living. Overton *et al.* calculated that by the earlier part of the eighteenth century, the majority of Kent inventories recorded chests with drawers.[68]

More than four in five inventories in the present sample recorded chests of some kind and ownership was widespread across the social spectrum and throughout the 250-year period. The description of chests in these inventories was frequently inadequate. Chests of drawers were among the types of chest recorded. Whilst minimum numbers of chests with drawers can be calculated, it is questionable whether sufficiently precise quantification of types of chests is possible.

Pewter

Pewter, an alloy of mainly tin and lead, was produced in considerable quantities in Roman Britain and it is believed that pewter was exported from Britain to the continent.[69] Pewter had been used by the church from the early Middle

PHOTO 5.6 Replica of a boarded chest
Source: Image courtesy of the Weald and Downland Museum

Ages and it remained the largest consumer of pewter until the Reformation.[70] John Hatcher and Theodore Barker suggested that pewter items began to appear in the households of the nobility from the fourteenth century and were increasingly being adopted by the gentility, merchants and larger landowners by the late fourteenth and fifteenth centuries.[71]

London was the centre of the English industry but pewter was also produced in many larger provincial towns including York and Norwich.[72] In smaller towns, demand for pewter was limited and pewterers often combined making and supplying pewter items with other metal-related activities, so that the pewterer Thomas Chirch of Bury St Edmunds was also a bellfounder and gunmaker.[73] The limited demand for pewter products outside of London is reflected in the fact that only a handful of pewterers operated within Norfolk and Suffolk at this time. Only one pewterer was listed within the Suffolk Hundred of Babergh in 1522, despite the area including two towns which stood at 13th and 46th places respectively in the ranking of provincial towns by taxable wealth in 1524 (Lavenham and Long Melford), and the large town of Sudbury.[74] Even in Norwich, which stood in first place in the ranking and was thus the richest town by taxable wealth, only two pewterers were admitted the freedom of the city between 1500 and 1529, and only three from 1530 to 1558.[75]

This lack of supply and apparent limited demand was possibly due to cost. Pewter items bought by Thetford Priory ranged from a pewter salt bought in 1510/11 which cost 6d, to 5s for two pewter pots bought in 1518/19 and for a pewter basin and laver bought in 1518/19.[76] Testamentary evidence suggested that pewter ownership was rising during the late fifteenth and early sixteenth centuries and wills contained a variety of pewter bequests including platters, chargers, dishes, basins, pots, chafers and salt cellars. William Harrison identified that it was often sold by a count known as a 'garnish' which comprised twelve platters, twelve dishes and saucers and this was often reflected in wills; for example, John Withall gave 'half a garnishe of pewter vessell'.[77] Many people purchased pewter at Stourbridge Fair; by 1589, the fair lasted from August 24 to September 29, with the 1589 charter stating that it 'far surpassed the greatest of and most celebrated fairs of all England'.[78] Following his visit to Stourbridge Fair in the early eighteenth century, Daniel Defoe described the huge variety of merchandise, with stalls including 'goldsmiths, toyshops, brasiers, turners, milliners, haberdashers, hatters, mercers, drapers, pewterers, china-warehouses, and in a word all trades that can be named in London'.[79]

Pewter goods recorded in probate inventories included both goods for eating and drinking as well as chamber pots, basons, ewers, pottingers, skinkers and candlesticks (Photo 5.7). Barrie Trinder and Nancy Cox examined the incidence of pewter in

PHOTO 5.7 Pewter tableware from Pendean farmhouse
Source: Image courtesy of the Weald and Downland Museum

more than 800 Telford inventories from the seventeenth and eighteenth centuries and found that well over two thirds (72.7 per cent) recorded pewter.[80] However, many items recorded in probate inventories frequently did not specify the material of construction, so that their data understated the true incidence of pewter ownership which was very high indeed, although the incidence of pewter was higher than this in the inventory collection in the present volume. It exceeded 80 per cent in all periods until the second half of the eighteenth century when it fell to 71 per cent. Thus, probate inventory evidence provided some support to Hatcher and Barker's assertion of a decline of pewter after 1740.[81] High levels of pewter ownership were found amongst all ranks until the latter half of the eighteenth century when a considerably lower percentage of inventoried husbandmen owned pewter.

In probate inventories, pewter was frequently valued by weight without specifying the items, thus creating a problem for analysis. For example, the inventory of Margerye Clarke, a Surrey widow who died in 1602, had pewter valued at 5d per pound and brass at 4d a pound. Trinder and Cox found that values ranged from 6d to 8d a pound in the latter seventeenth and early eighteenth centuries, although pewter dishes in one inventory dated 1711 recorded pewter dishes at 10d a pound.[82] In William South's inventory of 1658 (Writtle, Essex), pewter was valued at 12d a pound. Pewter was also often recorded with brass so the entry, 'the brass and pewter [valued] £4 11s' in the yeoman John Clarke's inventory dated 1648 was not untypical, except for its relatively high valuation.

Pictures

The growing emphasis on personal space within houses from the fifteenth century onwards saw an increased adoption of household goods which decorated or subdivided living areas, or which combined both functions. Internal adornments adopted in the fifteenth century included wainscoting and painted or embroidered wall hangings which could also be used as room dividers and thereby combined both decorative and practical elements. The most desirable of these hangings were made of imported embroidered tapestry but these were rare and most wall hangings were made of cheaper cloth, such as worsted, and any image was painted or stained.[83] Thetford Priory bought a set of hangings for the prior's parlour which cost £1 plus an additional 14s 4d for painting and staining.[84] Whilst the type of cloth is not specified, the amount of fabric required for such a purpose suggested that a relatively inexpensive cloth was being used. The wills describe some of the images painted on similar cloths; for example, in his will of 1498, Robert Deane, smith, bequeathed his 'paynted cloth' with the image of the Blessed Virgin Mary on it.[85]

In the sixteenth century, the most common artworks were hangings which were recorded in 5 per cent of Surrey inventories covering the period 1558–1603 and were more common than paintings, pictures or maps.[86] Images in homes also took the form of paintings on canvas, wood or even walls. Tara

Hamling and Catherine Richardson found that painted cloths were more commonly recorded than pictures in Kent inventories from Faversham, Sandwich and Canterbury in the second half of the sixteenth century.[87] Some indication of the themes of paintings used to decorate walls in the sixteenth century can be gleaned from the Southampton inventories. They included portraits such as 'our lady', the king and the emperor, as well as narratives: 'a story of shipes' and two Flanders stories.[88] In Surrey, 'a pycture of the Savyor' was owned in 1563 by John Hull, a gentleman, which was valued at 2s 6d.[89] The seventeenth-century inventory of John Roseworme of Bristol (1675) was appraised by John Bevill and George Bennett who were painters.[90] Roseworme owned 18 pictures of the 'better sort' valued in total at £18. In addition, he had eight 'landskips' (landscapes) and six 'faces ordinary' and eight 'better' (presumably portraits).[91] However, these examples were rare exceptions, and it was unusual to find any descriptive material about pictures recorded in inventories. Most pictures were of low value, typically worth about 6d.

Prints and maps were occasionally listed together with pictures. For example, 1 per cent of both Surrey and Marlborough inventories recorded maps and these were owned by people of relatively high status: a linen draper, an apothecary, a barber and a vintner in Marlborough and a parson, a gentlewoman and a haberdasher in Surrey.[92] No details of these maps were given but it is clear that some were hung on the wall as they were described as framed. Catherine Delano Smith explored a very rich and untypical source for ownership of maps, the sixteenth-century probate inventories from the Vice-Chancellor's Court in Cambridge where the owners were mainly members of the university. Delano Smith found a sample of no less than 52 inventories which had recorded maps and atlases. It was clear that not all of these maps were owned solely for academic purposes and were a fashionable domestic decoration. At least half of these maps were hung on the wall and many of their valuations were not dissimilar to those found in Marlborough and Surrey.[93]

Susan Foister found that 'works of art' were recorded in about 10 per cent of sixteenth-century inventories but as Robert Tittler pointed out, 'works of art' could include a variety of objects including wall hangings.[94] Tittler suggested that areas proximate to London were exceptional in the extent to which they owned pictures in the century prior to the civil war and that in the country as a whole picture ownership remained quite small.[95] Henry French combined pictures and maps and considered hangings separately in his analysis of household items in inventories from various parts of England. By the mid-seventeenth century, pictures and maps were much more commonly found in households and in north-west England they were recorded in 15 per cent of French's category of non-officer households and 20 per cent of officer households.[96]

Overton *et al.* found that 'pictures', defined as portraits, landscapes and prints, increased in popularity in Kent from around the second decade of the eighteenth century. Ownership of pictures rose to 25 per cent of Kent inventories in

1720–49 whereas in Cornwall picture ownership did not exceed 4 per cent until the 1740s.[97] Similar trends were found by the present study which also found that pictures were much more common in urban areas. Pictures were recorded in no less than 60 per cent of inventories in Bristol after 1720.

Silver

London was the centre of the true goldsmiths who were responsible for the production of gold items as well as more substantial silver goods. Their standards were closely regulated by the Goldsmiths' Company who, in addition, exercised an increasingly restrictive control over provincial goldsmiths so as to benefit London craftsmen.[98] In 1372, London goldsmiths were given the authority to visit fairs to inspect and assay the work that was being sold and from 1478 'hall marking' was introduced which required that all gold and silver objects be taken to Goldsmiths' Hall in London to be assayed and 'hallmarked'.[99] As a consequence of these controls, the London goldsmiths ensured that their reputation for producing the finest metalwork with assured standards of gold purity was secured. As other jewellery items of quality were imported into London from the continent, particularly Italy, wealthy clients came to London to purchase gold and larger silver items, or sent agents to the capital on their behalf. The exclusivity of gold itself and items made from gold was reflected in its cost; James Thorold Rogers noted that gold cost between 30s and 32s per ounce, whilst three gold rings bought by Magdalen College in 1554 cost 13s 4d each.[100]

Items made of silver were the most commonly possessed luxury item throughout the Middle Ages. When people chose to spend money on luxuries, their purchases tended to be of durable and long-lasting goods and silver was a popular investment since it was a commodity that could last for generations (often with some remodelling). Possession conveyed the impression of wealth and status and it was a means of storing equity until it was needed. In 1470, Margaret Paston sent her son John certain items of family silver which were referred to as having been passed to her by her husband, who had himself received them from his father.[101] The items were sent for John to sell as he and his brother were in need of money; this incident reflected the perception of silver as an asset to be liquidated when required.

The most prestigious silver possessions were pieces of silver tableware, commonly used in noble households throughout the medieval period, although the cost of silver tableware was such that outside of the nobility, possession was restricted to the very wealthiest gentry and merchant families and even then its use was reserved for guests and senior members of the household.[102] Further down the social scale, Dyer suggested that yeomen were likely to own at least a set of silver spoons, but that silver was rarely found in peasant households, whilst Jeremy Goldberg also suggested that by the end of the thirteenth century, possession of silver spoons was associated with bourgeois identity.[103] Testamentary evidence for the medieval period confirmed this pattern of ownership. Although silver was referred to in just 9 per cent of wills (the luxury item most commonly referred to as being owned), possession was largely the preserve of the gentry, those in high-status occupations, widows, yeomen and, less frequently, those in intermediate-status occupations. Almost all of the silver bequests were small articles, such as spoons, rings and belt adornments, rather than substantial pieces. The most common bequest was of spoons which were usually gifted in sets of varying numbers, although they were also often left as single items as a form of remembrance so that Thomas Stotevile left the wife of his former servant 'j gilte spone for a remembrennce the more to thenk on me'.[104] Whilst most of the wills simply referred to silver spoons, a few references suggested that spoons could be ornate, such as the reference in the will of William Aylnoth to 'three spones of silver that be knopped on the ende lyke acornes'.[105] Other household items were decorated with silver rather than made from it: John Bakhot bequeathed a bowl with a gilt top to his son Richard, whilst Laurence Smyth left two mazers 'bonnde with silver overgilt' to his two sons.[106]

The wills contained very few bequests of more substantial household items which were made of silver rather than simply embellished. A small number of testators bequeathed silver salt cellars and an even smaller number gave items which were probably used as serving dishes or even religious items such as the silver goblet and chalice included in the will of the chaplain Richard Roger of Thetford.[107] Once again, wider ownership of such items was limited by cost; one further will that referred to larger items was that of the Mildenhall mercer William Bakhote which valued the cost of the bequest of a silver basin and two silver cruets at £3 6s 8d.[108] Evidence from Thetford Priory accounts confirmed that substantial silver household items were well beyond the financial reach of all but a small minority of the population. Silver items purchased by the priory included a silver and gilt salt purchased in 1511/12 at a cost of £3 7s 6d; a gilt salt bought in 1520/21 for £6; and 'le stondyng gilte cuppe with a cover' bought for £6 4s 9d in 1520/21.[109] Other evidence from the Breckland region also showed that high prices were paid for silver; in 1515, the churchwardens of Mildenhall paid 10s 5d for two and a half ounces of silver which were fashioned into a censer and in 1538 they received £1 10s 8d from Antony Yorewly, goldsmith of Cambridge, for nine ounces of silver.[110]

Whilst testamentary evidence suggested limited ownership of substantial goods, silver additions to other items were more common, for example, the most commonly bequeathed silver item of adornment were girdles which incorporated silver embellishments such as the 'girdle of silk, harnessed with silver' given to his son by the Newmarket barker John Ray.[111] Most prayer-beads referred to in the sample of wills were of semi-precious materials, but a few also incorporated silver; Thomas Cake bequeathed a pair of beads with silver rings on them and Agnes Breye gave her daughter 'my bedes of coral with a hart of silver and gilt ther upon hanging'.[112] Other embellished items could be even simpler; the Thetford widow Joan Fickeis bequeathed 'a rebonde of silk with ij aglettes of silver' which would have been used as a tie on an item of clothing.[113]

The incidence of goods made of silver recorded in probate inventories did not change greatly throughout the early modern period. In the second half of the sixteenth century, 14 per cent of inventories recorded silver. In only one of the next six selected time periods did ownership fall outside the range 19 per cent to 21 per cent. However, ownership of silver goods in urban centres was very much higher. In Southampton, in the second half of the sixteenth century, 45 per cent of probate inventories recorded items made of silver. In Bristol, more than half of all inventories in the period 1630 to 1719 recorded silver. This reached 80 per cent by the second half of the eighteenth century. As with testamentary evidence, silver spoons were the most commonly recorded item of silver in probate inventories (Photo 5.8). In Surrey, there were 20 references to silver but in 18 of these cases, silver spoons were one of the silver items. There were also five salts and two salt cellars, five silver goblets, one silver cup, three silver bowls and three mazers edged with silver. In Southampton, there were 50 references to silver and 36 related to silver spoons. The most expensive item was a salt which weighed over 66 ounces.

Silver was a clear indicator of status; silver items communicated wealth among the upper echelons of the middling sort, however, Hamling and Richardson identified a tension between spirituality and material wealth expressed in the house of John Carter, vicar of Bramfield, Suffolk. Carter never used silver plate in his house and his plain table attracted attention as it defied the expectations of tableware appropriate to his social status.[114] This is borne out by inventory evidence; hardly any labourers owned silver but 50 per cent or more of all gentry inventories recorded silver goods in all seven periods between 1550 and 1800. Silver remained expensive for people of low social rank. The six silver spoons in Thomas Warner's inventory of 1571 were valued at 4s 4d each. In 1606, Jane Ward's 20 silver spoons were also valued at 4s 4d each, based on their weight of 1 ounce per spoon. Mary Aderne's substantial collection of silver in Stockport 1619 was valued at between 4s 10d and 5s 2d per ounce. Nearly half a century later, Deborah Prior's silver spoons were still valued at 5s per ounce in 1662.[115]

PHOTO 5.8 Seventeenth-century silver spoon made by Thomas Punchard
Source: Image courtesy of Totnes Museum, Devon

James Woodforde recorded in his eighteenth-century diary that he bought a dozen large silver tablespoons and half a dozen silver dessert spoons for £10 which he regarded as a 'great bargain'.[116]

Silver spoons continued to have a significance as items of commemoration and remembrance and were often given as a christening present. Lawrence Williams, a merchant from Southampton whose inventory was dated 1574, had two silver spoons pertaining to John Williams that were given him by his godfather.[117] Maxine Berg found that women in Birmingham and Sheffield purchased silver spoons in the eighteenth century and had them engraved with family names. For Berg, these spoons were cultural symbols of family connections and bearers of memory.[118]

Books

For most of the Middle Ages, books took the form of bound and covered codices which were hand-written on parchment made from animal skins. Production was slow and laborious so that books were expensive. Most books were devotional works and written in Latin rather than the vernacular and this, combined with their high cost, meant that they were rarely owned by anyone other than members of the clergy and the upper orders of medieval society. The production of paper, made from fibres of cellulose pulp dried together into flexible sheets, had reached Baghdad from China by the end of the eighth century but it was not widely adopted in Europe. In England, paper was used but it was imported and thus expensive and parchment remained the material of choice for books. Thetford Priory bought both parchment and paper for its uses but whereas parchment could be obtained within the region, paper was acquired as an import and from London. The first English paper mill was established in 1490 but was not a commercial success. Paper only replaced parchment when the printing press became firmly established; although printed parchment documents do exist, parchment could not be produced in sufficient quantities to meet the increased demand for printed books.

In 1453, Johannes Gutenberg invented movable metal type and printing spread rapidly through Western Europe from this time. This led to a substantial increase in the availability of books although production was still dominated by devotional works.[119] Although many of these were translations of religious texts primarily intended for religious orders or intellectuals, primers became increasingly popular and affordable amongst literate lay people.[120] In an inventory of his books which he made around 1479, the affluent gentleman John Paston II listed the books in his possession.[121] Paston owned various religious texts, but also a range of secular books written in English including a number of works by both Geoffrey Chaucer and John Lydgate. He also referred to books which had been printed by William

Caxton including 'a boke jn preente of þe Pleye of þe ...', which has been identified as *The Game of Chess*, first printed in 1474.[122] Nevertheless, Paston was highly untypical; from her analysis of wills Margaret Deanesley demonstrated that most of the books owned were religious texts in Latin and that secular books, and those written in the vernacular, were rare.[123] The testamentary evidence used for this study largely supported Deanesley's claim as it suggested that book ownership was largely confined to members of the clergy and that texts owned were almost always religious texts in Latin; for example, John Berton of Mildenhall bequeathed a small psalter with *placebo* and *dirige* in 1441 and John Upryght of Exning left a pocket breviary in 1445.[124] Printed books were still largely theological and in Latin, although one bequest from this period was specified as being of a printed book, the 'porteous in print' given by Sir George Gatynbe, a Mildenhall priest.[125] Only a handful of bequests of books were by people who could definitely be identified as being other than clergymen and most of these also had a high social standing and the texts related to their occupation. Edward Eyr, master of the grammar school in Thetford, gave all his grammar books to his son John in 1424 and in 1479 the lawyer George Armestrong of St Albans owned a number of legal texts.[126] Whilst various factors may have contributed to the scarce ownership of books, including low levels of literacy and even limited contemporary use of spectacles, it is probable that the cost of books remained a significant check on ownership even within the higher tier income group. In 1443, King's Hall, Cambridge, bought 27 volumes from the executors of John Paston at the substantial cost of £8 17s 4d.[127] Books purchased by the churchwardens of Mildenhall at the Reformation included a Bible bought in 1545/46 at a cost of 18s (with an additional 1s 4d for bossing and 6d for carriage), a 'boke of the new order' which cost 6s in 1549 and 'iiij salters ij bokes of the new order' which came to a total of 15s 4d.[128]

The initial impact of the Protestant Reformation on ownership of books was probably limited. Shortly after the publication of the Great Bible in 1539, Henry VIII restricted Bible reading to those of noble birth.[129] However, the tide was unlikely to be stemmed for long. More than four out of five books printed in England were now in the vernacular.[130] Examples started to appear in probate inventories in the 1550s. John Staveley, a grocer from Southampton, owned both a 'gret bybyll and a lytyll bybell' in 1559 and together they were valued at 18s. Protestantism was a book religion and the distinguishing mark of converts was to be well learned in the scriptures. Even illiterates were encouraged to own a Bible so that any literate visitors might read it to them.[131] In the early seventeenth century, following the publication of the new Authorised Version, Bible boxes became a popular household item for the safe storage of the book. Some had a sloping top, used as a bookrest for daily Bible readings, whilst others were rectangular boxes with decoration at the front, as depicted in Photo 5.9.[132]

PHOTO 5.9 Seventeenth-century Bible box
Source: Image courtesy of the Museum of Cambridge

English printed-book production grew at 2.6 per cent a year between 1500 and 1650.[133] Throughout the early modern period book consumption *per capita* in Britain was second only to the Netherlands.[134]

John Plumb saw the growth of the market in printed materials as an important element in the development of a consumer society. In the sixteenth century, books were expensive, predominantly theological or classical and bought mainly by lawyers, clergymen, gentry or prosperous merchants. The civil war of the mid-seventeenth century brought a growth in pamphlets and ballads but for Plumb the

TABLE 5.1 Book consumption

Per capita (thousand)	1551–1600	1601–50	1651–1700	1701–50	1751–1800
Netherlands	34	139	259	391	488
Sweden	1	40	59	84	209
Britain	27	80	192	168	192

Source: B. A'Hearn, 'The British Industrial Revolution in a European Mirror', in R. Floud J. Humphries and P. Johnson (eds.) *The Cambridge Economic History of Modern Britain, Volume I 1700-1870* (Cambridge, 2014) p.42.

real growth in printed materials did not take off until the last decade of the seventeenth century.[135] Conversely, Spufford suggested that growth in popular literature took place earlier. Spufford argued that Registers of the Stationers' Company from their opening in 1557–58 showed that there was a widespread popular as well as educated market for books, with ballad titles particularly popular.[136]

Ian Green compiled a database of 'best-selling' Protestant titles from the 1530s onwards, which focussed on those books published in at least five editions. His sample comprised over 300 titles between the 1560s and 1640 and a further 426 titles between 1641 and 1700 and included Bibles, psalters, books of homilies, catechisms, sermons, treatises and devotional works.[137] Susan Doran and Christopher Durston cited some of the most popular books of religious and moral instruction including Lewis Bayly's *The Practice of Piety* and Richard Allestree's *The Whole Duty of Man*.[138] *The Practice of Piety*, a devotional Puritan handbook, was one of the best-selling books in the seventeenth century.[139] Alec Ryrie suggested that it was the most successful devotional handbook of all and over 50 editions were produced between its publication in 1612 and 1640.[140]

The collapse of the Licensing Act in 1695 stimulated book publishing and the number of new books published increased significantly.[141] James Raven maintained that prior to 1700 up to about 1,800 different printed titles were produced annually. By 1800, over 6,000 titles were produced each year.[142] Raven was not convinced that this implied a much-expanded readership, but that those already reading books were buying more.[143] For Plumb the change was total. Print 'had been exploited in all its possibilities' and was reaching out and responding to an ever-widening market.[144] Religious literature continued to be the largest subject area in the eighteenth century, but other topics included 'social sciences', literature, history and geography as well as practical subjects like cookery and gardening.[145]

Inventory evidence suggested that Bibles, catechisms, conduct books and devotional works were still the most common books being published although by the eighteenth century the influence of the Enlightenment was such that new material was becoming more widely owned. The only book title other than the Bible specified in the Surrey inventory collection for the sixteenth century was *Calvens Institucions*, owned by the clothier Thomas Warner in Farnham in 1571.[146] By the seventeenth century, inventories started to record several individuals with valuable and substantial libraries. Benjamin Taylor, vicar of Madeley, Shropshire, had books valued at £100 in 1704 as did Robert Lowther, a gentleman from Pontefract in 1720.[147] Robert Ogden, the clerk rector of Broseley in Shropshire, had a study of books valued at £90 10s in 1679.[148] Thomas Palmer, vicar of St Mary Redcliffe and St Thomas Redcliffe in Bristol, had books valued at £60 in 1640; George Williamson, Clerk in Bristol (1685), also had books valued at £60; and Henry Wood, vicar of Wellington (1712), had a study of books valued at £45.[149] The value of these libraries is put into perspective by the work of Elizabeth Leedham Green. She analysed 20 seventeenth-century inventories relating to Cambridge containing books, several of which contained significant libraries. The most valuable library was that of Tyndall (1614), chancellor of Lichfield Cathedral, who had over 190 volumes valued at £47.[150]

Most of these substantial libraries belonged to clergy. The extent to which clergy owned books is exemplified by the collection of Sussex clergy inventories edited by Annabelle Hughes. Of 177 clergy inventories, only six failed to record books. The median value of the libraries was £5, but ten libraries were worth more than £50. Giles Moore, rector of Horsted Keynes in Sussex, had books valued at £100 in 1679 as did Thomas Pelling, vicar of Rottingdean in 1732. At the other end of the spectrum was Samuel Dowlin, vicar of Sherston Magna in Wiltshire until he was deprived in 1638. He died in West Grinstead in 1644 when he owned just an old Bible and a book of Cotton's sermons valued together at 3s.[151]

The most commonly listed title in the inventory collections was still a Bible. John Foxe's *Actes and Monuments*, known as *Foxe's Book of Martyrs*, was also popular and cited several times in probate inventories. John George, a yeoman who died in Writtle in 1638, had one valued at £2. Lewis Bayly's *The Practice of Piety*, Richard Allestree's *The Whole Duty of Man* and an unknown author's *The Christian Warfare* make occasional appearances.[152] However, titles of books were rarely recorded. One notable list was that of Alexander Kerswell, a woollen draper of Bristol, whose inventory was dated 1644. He owned two copies of the *Book of Martyrs* (valued together at £3) as well as Stowe's *Survey of London*, Josephus' *History of the Jewish War*, Withers' *Plain Man's Pathway to Heaven* and other books in French. Ann Goodeere, a twice-married widow of Ipswich (1628), had '*Eusebuss the Rhennists Testament, Mr Perkins upon the 5th of St Mathewe and the songe of Solomon.*'[153] On occasions an accompanying will provided more details than the inventory. Dorothy Cotton, a spinster in Cheshire (1647), bequeathed to her cousin *Mr Perkins' Works* in three volumes, *Mr Grantam's Works*, *The Doctrine of the Gospel*, two of Dr Preston's books and Mr Ball's *Treatise of Faith*.[154] A clergyman in St Ives, Huntingdonshire, who died in 1678, had 82 books valued at £19 1s 4d and all the titles were recorded in his inventory. Recording of book titles other than the Bible was even rarer in the eighteenth century. An exception was Francis Gregory from Marlborough, Wiltshire who had three Oxford almanacks valued together at just 1s in 1748.

The purpose of probate inventories as a source means that very low value items were not always recorded or else grouped with other items. The incidence of books being recorded in probate inventories rose from 8 per cent in the sixteenth century to 28 per cent around the mid-seventeenth century but recording of books fell away again to just 11 per cent by the latter half of the eighteenth century. This trend does not reflect decreasing book ownership but as books became more widespread and prices fell, they were less likely to be recorded in inventories by appraisers.[155]

This is illustrated by two diaries which revealed the reading habits of literate members of the 'middling sort' in the second half of the eighteenth century. Thomas Turner, a shopkeeper from East Hoathly in Sussex, kept a diary covering the years 1754 to 1765. The entry for 3 December 1757 revealed his enjoyment of reading: 'How pleasant this day hath been–to have been almost continual busy, and then after the hurry of the day to enjoy the pleasure of the even [ing] in reading'. Although inventories provided relatively few titles of books owned, qualitative sources such as diaries gave details of reading habits. Turner's reading matter included classics such as Homer's *Odyssey* and Josephus' *Antiquities*, Shakespeare's *Macbeth* and *Merry Wives of Windsor*, religious literature from Milton's *Paradise Lost* to Tillotson's sermons and various newspapers such as *London Magazine*, *Tatler*, *Universal Magazine* and *The Lewes Journal*. Turner spent substantial sums on buying books including 12s for Ainsworth's *Dictionary* and 4s 6d for Locke's *On Human Understanding*.[156] Sarah Hurst, also from Sussex (Horsham), kept a diary for a similar period to that of Turner (1759–62).[157] The daughter of a tailor, Sarah read widely and enjoyed comparable material to Turner, from classical works (Horace, Pliny and Lucian) to Shakespeare's plays and various magazines including *The Connoisseur*, *The Gentleman's Magazine*, *The Lady's Magazine* and *The Christian's Magazine*. She also read French literature, poetry and spiritual works.

Clocks and watches

Clocks

The earliest clocks depended on the sun or water. Egyptians produced the *gnomon*, a stick that cast a shadow revealing the time of day, and Greeks and Romans improved this simple device into sundials. Water clocks were based on the principle of dripping water through a tiny hole in the mechanism. However, the sun was often obscured by cloud and water sometimes froze. Europeans led the way in developing mechanical clocks in the late thirteenth century with the invention of the escapement. This transformed a falling weight into short movements of equal length, but these early clocks were very inaccurate.[158] Early mechanical clocks known as turret clocks were found on public buildings, in particular monasteries, churches and town halls. A majority of documented parishes possessed working clocks at some stage between 1400 and 1700 and whilst the wills used for this study contain no references to domestic clocks, they included a handful of bequests towards church clocks, such as the £3 which Edward Rows gave for a clock bell at Dennington church in 1506.[159] Domestic clocks were very rare in England before the seventeenth century as they were very high-end, exclusive goods. Henry V had a chamber clock among his possessions in 1422 and the Edgcumbe family, who lived at Cothele near Saltash in Cornwall, owned a 'faceless household clock with a verge escapement' in 1493.[160] The clock remains in the house, now owned by the National Trust, and it is still in operation.

The introduction of lantern clocks early in the seventeenth century initiated important changes in the social and economic use of time. Lantern clocks were shaped like an old hand-held lantern, with a single hand and verge and balance escapement. Lantern clocks were superseded by pendulum clocks, and particularly longcase clocks which protected the pendulum (Photo 5.10). The first pendulum clocks were controlled by a 'bob' pendulum which were more accurate than verge and balance clocks. Pendulum clocks could last for eight days and beyond and occasional references were made to eight-day clocks in probate inventories.[161] Spring-driven bracket or mantel clocks had the advantage that they were also potentially portable which enabled the owner to take it to their chamber to determine the time on awaking and many bracket clocks had handles so they could be carried. After 1675, bracket clocks became more elaborate in their decoration and by the eighteenth century, had become more commonly owned.[162]

According to Paul Glennie and Nigel Thrift, the 'horological revolution' in the later-seventeenth century resulted in a 'massive' increase in the production of domestic clocks and watches.[163] Examples of seventeenth- and eighteenth-century clocks can be seen in many museums and houses but Glennie and Thrift warned that surviving examples, particularly from the seventeenth century, usually originated from the upper levels of the domestic market. Clocks recorded in probate inventories were frequently likely to be plainer and less expensive.[164]

David Landes argued that Britain became dominant in clock manufacture because it was free of guild restrictions and because Protestant French clockmakers fled to Britain after the revocation of the Edict of Nantes in 1685.[165] Clockmakers were concentrated in London but at the end of the seventeenth century clockmakers started to be established in other parts of the country. According to Landes, by the end of the eighteenth century a transformation had occurred and England had become a nation of timekeepers.

Clocks were relatively expensive goods. The median valuation of a clock in the probate inventory collection was £1 10s. This was based on 605 clocks where a separate value was recorded in the inventory. There was little change in nominal values over the period with the median clock value being £1 10s in both periods 1690–1719 and 1720–49 and only rising to £1 11s 4d by the second half of the eighteenth century. This is consistent with a much smaller sample of clocks recorded in probate inventories in the archdeaconry of Lewes in East Sussex. Glennie and Thrift found that the median value of 52 timepieces in the 1730s was also £1 10s.[166]

Higher wages in the second half of the eighteenth century and particularly in the last decade meant that clocks became relatively more affordable, although rapidly rising food prices and rents were putting pressure on household budgets. Craig Muldrew calculated that a year's rent for labouring families was about 30s in the late seventeenth century rising to between £2 and £4 by the late 1760s.[167] The purchase of a clock therefore typically could involve the outlay of up to a year's rent. Samuel Roberts, a clockmaker from Montgomeryshire, kept his *Register of Clocks* for the period 1755–74, giving details of nearly 300 clocks and their prices.[168] Most were sold for between 41s and 50s and his customers ranged from clergy to coopers and weavers. The register reveals how Roberts

a)

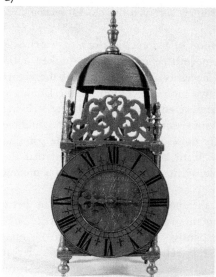

b)

c)

PHOTO 5.10 Clocks: a) unconverted weight-driven eighteenth-century English lantern clock by John Maynard of Long Melford in Suffolk (image courtesy of Alamy); b) longcase clock (image courtesy of the Clockmakers' Museum); c) bracket clock (image courtesy of Ford Green Hall, Stoke).

sought to make his clocks more affordable by establishing a 'clock club' into which members paid 6d a week. His customers received the clocks *seriatim* after drawing lots.

Gerald Whitrow argued that the possession of a domestic clock or watch was still restricted to the wealthy in the seventeenth century and was looked upon more as a sign of affluence than a social necessity.[169] By the end of the eighteenth century, John Styles argued that it was not uncommon for the labouring poor to own clocks and they became familiar adornments of labourers' living rooms.[170] Styles believed that at least some contemporary paintings could be used as evidence for ownership of specific possessions. Styles cited the painting entitled *Poor Old Woman's Comfort* by William Bigg and commented that the teapot, tea bowl and saucer, the side table, chair and clock suggested a modest degree of material comfort.[171]

Norman Pounds argued that clocks did not penetrate lower than petty burgesses and yeomen.[172] Pounds' argument was based on cost and he suggested that clocks remained relatively expensive until they began to be mass produced in the nineteenth century.[173] E.P. Thompson also maintained that no labourer could have afforded a clock in the mid-eighteenth century. Thompson agreed with the Chancellor of the Exchequer's argument when he introduced a tax on clocks at 5s per clock; in the parliamentary debate, the Chancellor referred to clocks as a luxury.[174] Berg suggested that clocks were semi-luxuries; items considered worth saving for. They were not so expensive that only elites could afford them and they were not so common that they counted among the possessions of labouring classes.[175] However, Peter King found that in north Essex one in five paupers, people who required support from the parish, owned a clock in the years 1711–69. This increased to 38 per cent of the sample in the period 1770–1812.[176] Joseph Harley found that in Kent, half of his sample of pauper inventories recorded a clock after 1770.[177]

Probate inventory evidence revealed that Pounds' and Thompson's assertions were incorrect, since nearly half (46 per cent) of inventoried households owned a clock by the second half of the eighteenth century. In middle England, clock ownership was widespread with 55 per cent of Huntingdonshire inventoried households owning clocks, 51 per cent in Dorset and 43 per cent in Yorkshire. In relatively affluent Kent, clocks were to be found in more than three quarters (77 per cent) of inventoried households. Furthermore, no less than 40 per cent of inventoried labourers in the sample owned a clock.

Watches

Using evidence from Old Bailey trials, Styles argued that watch ownership was increasing rapidly in the eighteenth century.[178] The database of Old Bailey cases compiled by Sara Horrell, Jane Humphries and Ken Sneath for selected years in the period 1750–1821 found 72 watches (1.5 per cent) and 16 clocks (0.3 per cent) out of a total of 4,542 individual items stolen.[179] Only one of these watches was recorded as stolen prior to 1770. Morgan Kelly and Cormac Ó Gráda recently analysed all watches recorded as stolen in the Old Bailey trials records between the years 1685 and 1850 and found that of 7,273 watches recorded, only 92 were stolen before 1710 and 55 per cent of the total were stolen after 1809.[180] Alison Backhouse found that 197 watches but only three clocks were recorded in a York pawnbroker's pledge book in the years 1777–78. However, Styles found that out of 117 cases of watch theft between 1640 and 1800 in north of England assize trials, only seven (6 per cent) dated from before 1750.[181] Putting all this evidence together suggests that watch ownership spread outwards from London and did not reach much of the provinces until later in the eighteenth century.

Watches were rarely recorded in probate inventories. For example, in Marlborough, eight inventories recorded watches (1.7 per cent) and only two were recorded before 1733. Relatively valuable watches could be owned by lower-status tradesmen. Edward Cox, a carrier in Broseley, Shropshire, owned a watch valued at £3 in 1714. His total inventory was valued at £25 11s.[182] However, inventory evidence showed a wide range of inventory values within occupational groups (see Chapter 8, Table 8.8b). A baker in Marlborough, William Flower, owned a silver watch valued at £2 2s in 1740 but his inventory, which included debts and money exceeding £300, suggested that he had a successful business.[183] The value of these watches can now be put in context following the study of Old Bailey Records by Kelly and Ó Gráda. They found that the average price of a silver watch fell from around £6 in 1710 to around £2 by 1809.[184]

Window curtains

The type of windows that a building contained usually reflected the status of that building, and that of the owner. Windows in medieval cottages were small rectangular openings framed in wood with vertical slats which reduced the amount of air entering the building but also the amount of light. Windows were usually shuttered rather than glazed because of the high cost of glass.[185] Before the sixteenth century, most windows were constructed from timber frames with unglazed openings; these could be closed with either sliding or folding wooden shutters, oiled cloth or paper, or even thin sheets of horn.[186] When windows were glazed, they evidently had some value since they are occasionally bequeathed in wills; Richard Josselyne, esquire of Sawbridgeworth, gave his son 'all the glasse in everie of the wyndowes of my Mannour of hyde hall'.[187]

Window curtains prevented drafts from windows and provided privacy. As windows were shuttered rather than glazed in the late medieval period, window curtains were not required as shutters largely performed the same purpose and,

PHOTO 5.11 Window shutters[188]
Source: Image courtesy of the Weald and Downland Museum

unsurprisingly, the wills used for this study did not record any ownership of window curtains. However, by the end of the seventeenth century, window curtains were increasingly being used in place of shutters as a means of displaying taste and status. For Beverley Lemire, window curtains were visible signals, fluttering flags of relative affluence that marked the windows of the genteel and the aspirants to their standing, in city, town or village.[189] The earliest reference to window curtains in Telford inventories studied by Trinder and Cox was in 1696 and these curtains were found in the best chamber of a mercer.[190] By contrast, Weatherill found that 7 per cent of her sample of inventories recorded window curtains at the beginning of the period 1675–1725 and this rose to 21 per cent by the end of this period.[191] Window curtains were much more commonly owned in urban households. No less than 67 per cent of inventoried households in Bristol owned window curtains by the second half of the eighteenth century. Window curtains appeared much earlier in Huntingdonshire as they were recorded in the possessions of the vicar of Kimbolton who died in 1637. Some Stockport probate inventories recorded window sheets in the late sixteenth and early seventeenth centuries, however, it is not clear what these sheets were, and they could refer to the oiled cloths or sheets of horn that covered medieval windows.[192]

Looking glasses (mirrors)

Mirrors have a long history with finds at Catal Hoyuk, Anatolia, confirming that they were used from the early Neolithic period.[193] In our period, mirrors were not only used for viewing oneself (mirrors used for this purpose were generally known as looking glasses), but were a means of enhancing and magnifying artificial lighting. During the Middle Ages, small metallic mirrors of steel or silver were the only ones in use in England. Surviving examples invariably incorporated a candleholder, as in the example shown in Photo 5.12a, so that their main purpose was to magnify candlelight rather than reflect images. 'Pennyware' looking glasses were also imported from Germany although they were very inefficient and only reflected about 20 per cent of the light.[194]

Around 1500, a new process of silvering cold flat plates of glass by applying thin sheets of tin foil with mercury as the cementing medium was developed and adopted by Venetian looking glass makers.[195] In 1567, Jean Carré, known as 'the father of glassmaking', arrived in England from the Netherlands. Production of glass quickly developed and by 1618 Sir Robert Mansell, who had obtained the monopoly of glassmaking in England, was employing Venetian workers to produce looking glasses.[196]

Margaret Ezell suggested that during the latter part of the seventeenth century, the terms 'mirror', 'looking glass' and 'glass' were used interchangeably to indicate a reflective surface, however, the word 'mirror' was generally used to refer to any

a) b)

PHOTO 5.12 Mirrors: a) late medieval mirror or light reflector (image courtesy of and reproduced with kind permission of the Metropolitan Museum of Art, New York © The Metropolitan Museum); b) eighteenth-century mirror (image courtesy of the Museum of Cambridge)

highly polished metal surface which was a widely available domestic object. Looking glasses were more typically associated with glass plates with reflective coatings and therefore the term 'looking glass' more closely accords with modern conceptions of a mirror.[197] Mirrors could be held in the hand or mounted on the wall and so ranged in size, quality and price (Photo 5.12b). Shakespeare's *The Winter's Tale* written in 1611 refers to Autolycus, a pedlar, who carried looking glasses among his wares.[198] Such looking glasses were likely to be cheap compared to the small looking glass that Samuel Pepys recorded his wife purchasing in 1664 at a cost of £5 5s.[199] Carl Estabrook sought to recreate the life patterns of Joseph Marks in the city of Bristol from his probate inventory of 1746. Estabrook envisaged Marks dressing and performing morning ablutions before the mirror in his kitchen.[200]

Mirrors continued to be used to create an impression of light and space within the home, whilst Berg argued that the main point of mirrors was not to make domestic life easier or more comfortable but to display genteel taste.[201] Mirrors and looking glasses also had other socio-cultural meanings including magic and myth that went beyond their role as a consumer good.[202] Ezell examined cultural accretions surrounding the looking glass in the early modern period and argued that the cultural symbolism of the mirror was to produce reflection in the viewer and not just a simple mirror image. People believed that looking in a mirror produced a vision of the future. They were also used by so-called 'cunning men and women' to find lost objects. A mirror could repel witches, as witches could not bear to see their own reflection. Furthermore, mirrors had the ability to absorb so were often covered in a room where a person was dying in case their soul became trapped in the mirror.[203]

Mirrors, or looking glasses, came in various qualities and were owned by people of most social ranks. Ann Smart Martin found that Britain supplied most mirrors exported to the American colonies in the eighteenth century. Ownership of these mirrors extended right down the social scale and were even purchased by slaves.[204] As with clocks, there were no references to mirrors in the wills which suggested that these items were not commonly owned in the late fifteenth and sixteenth centuries; however, ownership seems to have expanded rapidly in the seventeenth century. Ownership of mirrors increased from about one in 20 inventoried households in the first half of the seventeenth century to almost one in three by the second half of the eighteenth century. Over the same timespan, whilst no inventoried labourer in our sample owned a mirror at the beginning, one in five had a mirror by the end. Most urban inventoried households possessed a mirror and nearly three quarters of the inventoried households in Bristol owned one.

Fuel

Fuel also constituted an important consumption item for most households. The fuel most commonly burned in medieval hearths was wood, but this was not always easy or cheap to obtain. This was particularly the case in towns where inhabitants had to purchase most, if not all, of their fuel requirements and where the expense incurred in transporting a bulk commodity from the place of origin was reflected in the final cost. The difficulty in obtaining wood supplies is illustrated by an example from the accounts of Thetford Priory. The priory was located in the Breckland region where poor soils resulted in sparse woodland and a limited local supply of wood so that most requirements were sourced from outside the region; the difficulty in obtaining these supplies is reflected in the account entries. In 1500/01, the priory bought in excess of 121 loads of timber and wood costing £5 from Fakenham, a distance of six miles from Thetford. An additional £1 18s 4d was spent on 'fellyng and makyng' and £3 3s 10d on transporting the wood to the priory. Carriage costs alone added 64 per cent to the original cost of the wood.[205]

Other fuels were also used, particularly by the poorer classes. Around the fen-edge in eastern England peat turves were cut out in blocks from the fenland turbaries and dried out before being burned as a source of heat. Sedge, a rush-like plant which grew widely in the Fens, was also burned, whilst Mark Bailey indicated that gorse, heather and broom could also be used.[206]

Fuel was frequently bequeathed which reflected the enhanced value that restricted availability gave to this basic commodity. In 1452, Robert Tyd of Mildenhall bequeathed to his wife for her fire a thousand sedge (*segge*) and six thousand turves (*turbar*), whilst in 1494, John Hadnaham left his wife ten hundred 'toorf' and two hundred 'thakke'.[207] In her study of Norwich testators Karine Dauteuille noted that firewood was often bequeathed to the poor which demonstrates that it was not readily available to the lower social groups and this was evident in the wills used for this study.[208] In 1503, Sybil Tyllis of Thetford requested that 'ther be distribute amongst poor ffolke in wynter or ageyns Crystemesse an hundred wood', and that her 'coles be distribute amonge poor folke to every man a pekke as fere as they may extende'.[209] Consequently, for the poorest classes, fires were limited to the very coldest times of the year whilst in other households it seems unlikely that a fire would have burned continuously, even in winter months, but would only be lit when required. Philippe Ariès and Georges Duby suggested that the practice in France was for fires to be lit only when they were needed to warm or dry out individuals that had come in from the outside.[210]

The rise in population from 3 million to 5.2 million in the century preceding the introduction of the Hearth Tax, adverse weather conditions and the growth of the economy all led to increased demand for fuel.[211] The rising price of wood meant that there was a demand for other sources of fuel.[212] William Harrison and Arthur Standish both testified to the increasing use of domestic coal.[213] Tom Arkell suggested that a heating revolution was taking place in later seventeenth-century Warwickshire when wood was being replaced by coal.[214]

Analysis of a sample of over 1,400 Huntingdonshire inventories found that by far the most common references to fuel were to firewood, but 'sesses' (another peat-based fuel) and turves were frequently recorded in the Fens. For example, Robert Engerson, a blacksmith from Ramsey, had 80,000 turves and 60,000 sesses in 1691.[215] Thomas Barley, a husbandman also from Ramsey, had 18,000 turves in 1678.[216] Very few inventories recorded coal stocks but coal was owned by those of relatively lowly status, such as Edward Green, a weaver.[217] Joan Bailife, a widow whose goods were appraised in 1687, had both a parcel of turf and a parcel of coal valued in total at 5s 4d.[218] There were also occasional references to grates particularly in kitchens, which Arkell interpreted as indicating the presence of coal.[219] Elizabeth Cooper, a widow who died in Elton in 1675, had a coal grate in her hall, parlour and her kitchen. In her hall, she also had a fire shovel and tongs.[220] Bridget Dean, who died in Kimbolton in 1642, had cooking implements in her hall including tongs which indicated that she was cooking with coal.[221] In one case, ownership of coal was a commercial undertaking. Robert Lord of St Ives died in 1650 leaving 12 cauldrons of coal.[222] He came from a family of watermen, which suggested that it was a load of coal brought up the river from King's Lynn for onward sale.

This evidence about the use of fuel in Huntingdonshire needs to be carefully interpreted. Limited references to coal stocks in probate inventories might have indicated that Huntingdonshire was not experiencing the heating revolution that Arkell claimed for Warwickshire although Amanda Vickery emphasised that the advent of the coal-fuelled chimneyed cooking hearth was widespread and a hugely significant development in the early modern period.[223] However, Huntingdonshire's proximity to the Fens, with its abundance of turf, was such that peat could be acquired easily and much more cheaply than coal. In some areas, the use of wood and peat for cooking persisted into the twentieth century.[224] Nevertheless, the presence of a fire shovel, tongs, bellows, grate or warming pan (see p.168) in an inventory all pointed to more widespread use of coal than initial indications suggested.

Artificial lighting

Rushlights and candles

Rushlights and candles have been used for lighting since prehistory and were the commonest form of lighting throughout both the medieval and early modern periods. Various types of lighting equipment were available to late medieval households such as rushlight holders, lamps, torches, lanterns, candle-holders and prickets.[225] These were used in conjunction with a range of fuels including vegetable oils, tallow (animal fat) and beeswax.[226] The relative costs of these different lighting options varied widely. According to John Caspall, beeswax could cost more than 17 times the price of the same quantity of tallow in the fourteenth century, however, the prices paid for wax by Thetford Priory in the late fifteenth and early sixteenth centuries was only usually around six times as much as it paid for tallow; whereas the priory paid between 1d and 1½d per pound for tallow, wax cost between 4½d and 7¼d per pound.[227]

The cheapest lighting option for households was that of basic rushlights made from dipping the dried pith of the rush plant in tallow and then burning it in special holders. Rushlights were relatively inexpensive, easy to obtain and could be purchased throughout England or even made domestically so that they were regarded as the poor person's source of light.[228] They could be lit at both the bottom and the top to increase the light, hence the origin of the term, 'burning the candle at both ends'. Vegetable oils, including hemp, rape and olive, burned in metal or pottery oil lamps were a further cheap lighting option with vegetable oils costing an average of 1s 2½d per gallon during the late medieval period.[229] Tallow candles were a slightly more expensive form of domestic lighting. Tallow cost an average of 1s 11½d for a dozen pounds in the thirteenth and fourteenth centuries, but had dropped in price to an average of only 1s 3¾d for the same amount in the period from 1401 to 1530, a time which also saw an increase in domestic use of tallow.[230] Tallow candles were often made in the household with wicks supplied by chandlers but could also be made by the chandler himself who charged a sum for this service in addition to the charges made for the cost of the materials. Wick yarn was also required for both oil lamps and for candles and this cost between 3s 9d and almost 10s for a dozen pounds, although it seems likely that most consumers would have purchased much smaller amounts.[231]

The preferred luxury fuel for lighting was beeswax which was used in a solid form for candles as well as in a liquid form to fill cresset lamps, open stone bowls in which the lighted wick floated in wax.[232] Beeswax did not smell foul or emit soot and smoke unlike tallow but cost considerably more. Thorold Rogers noted that wax cost an average price of 6s 6d for a dozen pounds in the period from 1400 to 1540 and suggested that the use of wax was almost exclusively reserved for religious purposes and only used domestically in the households of monarchs and nobles.[233]

Candlesticks

Lighting fuel could be burned in a variety of holders including oil lamps and rush-light holders (Photo 5.13). However, extant evidence suggested that various forms of candlestick, including sockets and prickets, were most commonly used both in the late medieval and early modern periods (although this may simply reflect the fact that these were more expensive and thus more likely both to be recorded in wills and inventories and also to be owned by the more affluent people who made these records). Most candlesticks recorded in late medieval wills were referred to as being made of latten, for example Henry Houghton of Thetford distinguished between his 'best candilstykke of laten and a wrytyngg (writing) candilstykke'.[234] Thorold Rogers noted that these cost between 1s 4d and 1s 8d a pair although four latten candlesticks purchased by Thetford Priory in 1521/22 cost 3s 9d.[235] Other testamentary bequests were of pewter and Craig Muldrew suggested that candlesticks in the sixteenth century were mostly made from pewter and were

PHOTO 5.13 Rushlight holder with a candle

Source: Image courtesy of Ford Green Hall, Stoke

high-quality display items. Sixteenth-century inventories from Surrey did not support Muldrew's contention; pewter candlesticks were in the minority and most were made of brass and latten where the material was specified. By the eighteenth century, as a result of advances in metalworking, they tended to be made of tin and iron.[236] Luxury candlesticks were made of silver.

Bernard and Therle Hughes suggested that only from the days of George I did candles light the house of even the most prosperous wage-earner; previously open flame lamps and rushlights had sufficed.[237] Testamentary and probate evidence showed that this was incorrect. Even the earliest wills used for this study contain bequests of candlesticks and whilst these were predominantly the testaments of people of status, by the end of the sixteenth century this was no longer the case. John Plomer, shoemaker of Buntingford, owned a latten candlestick in 1574 and in 1635 Richard Dawnce, a weaver who died in Marlborough with a probate valuation of just £13, owned two candlesticks.[238] This increase in the references to candlesticks in probate documents coincides with a decline in the cost of tallow candles; Thorold Rogers noted that candles were much cheaper in the fifteenth century than in the fourteenth, and that they kept falling from the last decade of the fifteenth century.[239] Francis Steer noted that although a tinder box was an essential feature of every kitchen before matches came into common use, only one was recorded in his collection of mid-Essex inventories. He concluded that their low value meant that appraisers had not bothered to record them.[240]

Lanterns

Lanterns facilitated the portability of lighting. During the Roman period bronze lanterns with windows to facilitate the transmission of light were in use. They had holes in their roofs to help ventilate the candle flame. Outdoor lanterns were used in the medieval period in England to avoid the many hazards that darkness provided.[241] An early fourteenth-century reference to the beneficial use of lanterns is found in Geoffrey Chaucer's *The Legend of Dido, Queen of Carthage*: 'and I shal, as I can, Folow thy lantern, as thou gost biforn'.[242] However, no references to lanterns have been found in the testamentary bequests which probably reflect the fact that they were relatively inexpensive and not considered to be an appropriate item for a bequest. Lanterns came in the shape of a tankard with a domed roof and a handle (Photo 5.14). The case was transparent to protect the candle flame. References to lanterns in probate inventories frequently used the term lanthorn and were so named because they had thin strips of animal horn instead of glass in the lantern. Lantern windows continued to be made of horn and the use of glass was very slow to be adopted.

PHOTO 5.14 Lantern

Source: Image courtesy of Ford Green Hall, Stoke

Thomas Whetebreade, who died in Marlborough in 1601, had a lantern in his hall valued at just 2d.[243] A century later, Isaac Martin, a cooper, had no less than eight, valued in total at 8s.[244] Just 6 per cent of inventories in Marlborough recorded a lantern.

Warming pans

Warming pans were made of brass or copper, with a long handle for inserting the pan between the sheets to warm the bed (Photo 5.15). The pan was usually kept near the hearth where it could easily be filled with glowing coals or wood embers. Great care had to be taken to ensure that sheets were not damaged by the warming pan. The process of warming the bed was described by Elizabeth Harris in the case of William Priddle who was accused but found not guilty of raping her in a trial at the Old Bailey in 1775. A servant girl brought the warming pan up to the bedroom after filling it with coals from the dining room. Giving evidence, Elizabeth stated that she then warmed the bed a 'full half an hour' which normally involved moving the pan swiftly between the sheets using the

PHOTO 5.15 Warming pan

Source: Image courtesy of Dorset County Museum

long handle before the occupant got into the bed. In this case the defendant allegedly attacked Elizabeth Harris. The evidence stated that it was normal practice for the maid servant to warm William Priddle's bed every night.[245]

It has not been possible to identify clearly any warming pans in wills before 1579 (whilst pans are frequently mentioned it has been assumed that these were for cooking rather than warming beds). Only one in ten of the inventoried population owned warming pans until around 1630 but by the second half of the eighteenth century they were to be found in half of inventoried households. Warming pans stolen in London in the 1730s were typically ascribed a value of 2s.[246] By the third quarter of the eighteenth century, the typical valuation had increased to 5s; in a case in 1764 which involved Henry Horner, employed by the warming pan maker Richard Woolley of Crooked Lane, two warming pans cited in the case were valued together at 10s.[247]

Leisure goods

The rare references to musical instruments are perhaps a reminder that life at least for the more affluent was not all work but that there were opportunities for leisure activities too. In the present inventory sample, musical instruments were nearly always owned by gentry and more affluent professionals and tradesmen. One of the most commonly recorded instruments was a pair of virginals. A virginal was an instrument like an early organ but was referred to as a pair when it had two keyboards. John Hull, gentleman from Hambledon in Surrey, had a pair of virginals valued at 10s in 1563, whilst Rafe Marsham, merchant of Norwich, bequeathed 'virginalles' in his will of 1579.[248] In Shropshire, Richard Clowes, a gentleman from Great Dawley (1679), had a pair of virginals; Mennes Langley, a gentleman from Broseley (1699), owned a flute; and Richard Phillips, gentleman from Wellington (1705), had three violins worth £1 2s 6d, a steel bow valued at 9d, three flutes (floats) valued at 2s 9d and five sets of chimes (10s 4d).[249] In Huntingdon, Thomas King, a Doctor of Physick (1664), owned an 'organ, a bandore and a harpsicall' valued in total at £20.[250] Alexander Reynoldson, a grocer from Writtle (Essex) who died in 1671, had an old pair of virginals valued at 5s.[251] William Birch (1716), apothecary and surgeon, had a spinet valued with four chairs and a table at £1.[252] A barber, John Glen (1662), had one pair of virginals and the frame they stand upon valued at £1 10s.[253] In 1788, a Madeley Wood collier was in possession of a barrel organ that he wanted his executors to sell in order to pay off his debts.[254] A further source for exploring the ownership of musical instruments is the Proceedings of the Old Bailey which has published cases of theft of various musical instruments online.[255]

Cathedral cities such as Bristol and Lincoln were exceptional in the number of instruments owned and were not at all representative of other parts of the country. Estabrook's study of Bristol and its environs identified a range of instruments including harpsichords, viols, dulcimers and percussion instruments.[256] In

1668, Thomas Adeane, the organist of the Cathedral Church, owned a pair of virginals valued at £1 and three viols (bass, tenor and treble) valued at £1 for the three.[257] In 1678, John Bevill, Arms Painter, owned a new organ, an old broken organ and a pair of virginals. The new organ was valued at no less than £20.[258] A clearly prosperous saddeler, Francis Little from Bristol (inventory value £489), also owned a pair of virginals in 1681.[259] In Lincoln, from 590 inventories there were two bass viols, three citterns, a cornet, two dulcimers, three harpsicords, a lute, two organs, a sackbut, two spinnets, a triangle, five viols, a voil bandero, eight violins and ten virginals.[260] Four inventories recorded the occupation of the deceased as musician. William Norris (1702), steward of the choristers and singing master of The Close Lincoln, had a harpsicord and frame valued at £3.[261]

Apart from musical instruments, inventories also provided rare glimpses of other leisure activities that were enjoyed. Stephen Willoughby from Marlborough had a billiard table, sticks and balls in his billiard room valued at £8 8s in 1746. His inventory also included a deal table, backgammon table and a draught board.[262]

Forgotten goods

It has already been noted that many goods were not referred to in wills. Other goods were briefly referred to in both wills and probate inventories but were disguised in such common phrases as 'things forgotten', 'ostilments' or, in Yorkshire, 'hustlement'. John Bedell suggested that archaeology might shed light on the extent to which certain goods were omitted from or were underreported in probate or other records. For example, archaeological excavations in Colonial America noted the ubiquity of ceramics whereas interpretations of probate inventories related to these sites indicated either that ceramics were significantly less common than archaeological finds suggested or that ownership patterns changed over time.[263]

Smoking was a common leisure activity but was not strongly evidenced in probate records. Tobacco bowls, dishes, tongs, boxes and pots were rarely recorded.[264] Although tobacco pipes were commonly owned consumer goods, they were only recorded in the stock of shopkeepers' goods and that of a vintner.[265] Visits to local museums confirm that these are often one of the commonest items found in their collections (Photo 5.16). For Jan de Vries, tobacco pipes were the first throwaway consumer item.[266]

The introduction of tobacco to England in the late sixteenth century soon led to the rapid development of the smoking-pipe industry. Tobacco, like sugar, was originally an expensive luxury but fell in price from between 20s to 40s a pound during the reign of James I to no more than 1s in the second half of the seventeenth century, so that its consumption became increasingly popular amongst the lower classes.[267] This cost is broadly consistent with a fraud case tried at the Old Bailey in 1685 in which 6lb of tobacco was valued at 7s.[268] Daniell Bridges' inventory dated 1725 recorded a large cask of tobacco which

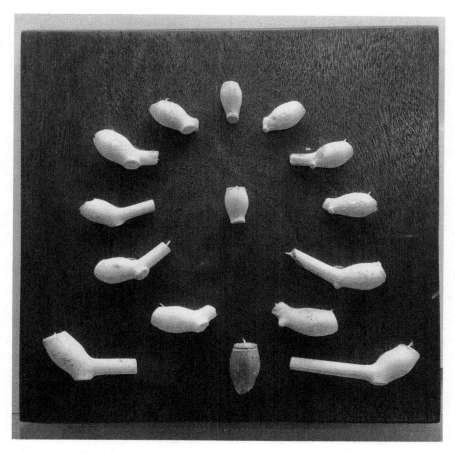

PHOTO 5.16 Clay pipes

Source: Image courtesy of the Museum of Cambridge

weighed about 130lb and this was valued at £6 10s, i.e. a shilling a pound.[269] Bridges' inventory also suggested that the quantity of tobacco held by a shopkeeper in Wiltshire was very large. John Fowler, a linen draper in Marlborough who was buried in 1722, had tobacco valued at no less than £87 in his cellar.[270] At a shilling a pound, Fowler's tobacco would have weighed 1740lb.

Legal imports of tobacco for home consumption increased rapidly after the 1630s and reached 1lb *per capita* in 1672 and over 2lb by the 1690s. As Carole Shammas observed, tobacco became a mass-consumption item. Data for the eighteenth century suggested a sharp downturn in tobacco consumption but high tariffs introduced in 1685 led to a large increase in smuggling tobacco. Robert Nash calculated that legal and illegal tobacco together actually remained in excess of 2lb *per capita* over most of the first half of the eighteenth century.[271]

Manufacture of clay pipes expanded along with the increase in tobacco consumption. Inventory evidence provides insights into pipe manufacturing. The inventory of Thomas Roden, a tobacco pipemaker from Broseley, was exhibited in 1723 and recorded details of his tools and the moulds used in pipe manufacture which were described as peak heal, broad heel, short and hunting moulds.[272] The tobacco pipemaker Thomas Hartshorne from Benthall died in 1743; his old tobacco pipe tools were valued at 12s 6d.[273] Richard Benthall's inventory dated 1720 included pipemakers' clay valued at £2 6s 10½d.[274]

A further 'forgotten good' which was an important consumption item in the late medieval and early modern periods was religious practice, an activity which is usually neglected in consumption studies; modern perceptions being very different from those of earlier periods. The significance of 'religious consumption' in the lives of people in the medieval and early modern periods is explored in the following chapter.

Notes

1 W.G. Hoskins, 'The rebuilding of rural England, 1570–1640', *Past and Present*, 4 (1953), pp.44–59.
2 J. Grenville, *Medieval Housing* (Leicester: Leicester University Press, 1999), p.146.
3 ERO D/ABW 27/71 (Newmane).
4 D. Hughes (ed.), *The Diary of a Country Parson, the Revd James Woodforde* (London: Folio Society, 1992), p.295; Extract from *Lincoln, Rutland and Stamford Mercury*, Friday 10 June 1785.
5 D. Reed, 'To what extent does the newspaper advertising of goods (specifically those related to dress and household goods) in the second half of the eighteenth century reflect a consumer revolution in England?' (unpublished dissertation for the Advanced Diploma in Local and Regional History, University of Cambridge, 2018).
6 http://news.sciencemag.org/2011/12/earliest-human-beds-found-south-africa [last accessed 3 November 2017].
7 G. Edelen (ed.), *The Description of England: The Classic Contemporary Account of Tudor Social Life by William Harrison* (London: Constable Company, Ltd, 1994), p.201.
8 *Principalia* were principal goods attached to a customary tenement deemed to belong to the lord and therefore listed on the transfer of a customary holding; R.K. Field, 'Worcestershire peasant buildings, household goods and farming equipment in the later Middle Ages', *Medieval Archaeology*, 9 (1965), p.123.
9 Dagswain and hap-harlots were coverlets of coarse, shaggy material; Edelen (ed.), *Description of England*, p.201.
10 T. Hamling and C. Richardson, *A Day at Home in Early Modern England: Material Culture and Domestic Life, 1500–1700* (New Haven: Yale University Press, 2017), p.243.
11 K. Dauteuille, 'Household materials and social networks in Norwich 1371–1500: a study of testamentary evidence' (unpublished PhD thesis, University of Cambridge, 2003), p.159.
12 D. Dymond (ed.), *The Register of Thetford Priory, Part II: 1518–1540: Norfolk Record Society Vol. LX* (Oxford: Oxford University Press, 1995 and 1996), pp.597, 602, 608.
13 D. Dymond (ed.), *The Register of Thetford Priory: Part 1 1482–1517: Norfolk Record Society Vol. LIX* (Oxford: Oxford University Press, 1994), p.223; Dymond (ed.), *Thetford Priory: Part II*, pp.597, 601.
14 J. Thorold Rogers, *A History of Agriculture and Prices in England from the Year after the Oxford Parliament (1279) to the Commencement of the Continental War (1793): Vol. IV 1401–1582* (Oxford: Clarendon Press, 1882), p.576.

15 J. Raithby (ed.), *The Statutes at Large of England and of Great Britain: From Magna Carta to the Union of the Kingdoms of Great Britain and Ireland, Vol. III* (London: G. Eyre and A. Strahan, 1811), p.594.

16 B. Trinder and J. Cox, *Yeomen and Colliers in Telford: Probate Inventories for Dawley, Lilleshall, Wellington and Wrockwardine:1660–1750* (Chichester: Phillimore, 1980), p.274.

17 R.P. Garrard, 'English probate inventories and their use in studying the significance of the domestic interior 1570-1700', in A. Van Der Woude and A. Schuurman (eds), *Probate Inventories: A New Source for the Historical Study of Wealth, Material Culture and Agricultural Development* (Wageningen Hes & De Graff Publishing, 1980), p.58.

18 L. Worsley, *If Walls Could Talk: An Intimate History of the Home* (London: Faber & Faber, 2012), p.10.

19 Hamling and Richardson, *Day at Home*, p.29.

20 *Ibid.*, p.51.

21 J. Whittle and E. Griffiths, *Consumption and Gender in the Early Seventeenth-Century Household: The World of Alice Le Strange* (Oxford: Oxford University Press, 2012), p.133.

22 Hamling and Richardson, *Day at Home*, pp.44–46.

23 J. Harley, 'Material lives of the English poor: a regional perspective 1670–1834' (unpublished PhD thesis, University of Leicester, 2016), pp.85–87.

24 S. Williams, *Poverty, Gender and Life-Cycle under the English Poor Law 1760–1834* (Woodbridge: Boydell & Brewer, 2013), p.49.

25 K. Wrightson and D. Levine, *Poverty and Piety in an English Village: Terling, 1525–1700* (Oxford: Clarendon Press, 1995), p.38.

26 D. Banks, *Ludlow Furniture 1660–1760* (Ludlow: Ludlow Historical Research Group, 1984), p.12.

27 F. Steer, *Farm and Cottage Inventories of Mid-Essex 1635–1749* (Chichester: Phillimore, 1969), p.17.

28 Hamling and Richardson, *Day at Home*, p.43; P. Seaver, *Wallington's World: A Puritan Artisan in Seventeenth-Century London* (Stanford: Stanford University Press, 1985), p.76.

29 Dymond (ed.), *Thetford Priory: Part II*, pp.481, 633.

30 CA VC 5:66 (Vyncentt); NRO ANW Athowe 95 (Fickeis); NRO ANF Liber 3a (Bemond) 5 (Houghton); HA 11/327 (Richmond).

31 Trinder and Cox, *Yeomen and Colliers*, pp.36–37.

32 *Ibid.*, p.37; M. Spufford, *The Great Reclothing of Rural England* (London: Bloomsbury Publishing, 1984), p.115.

33 HA, AH18/3/224.

34 M. Overton, J. Whittle, D. Dean and A. Hann, *Production and Consumption in English Households 1600–1750* (Abingdon: Routledge, 2004), p.109.

35 E. Veale, *The English Fur Trade* (London: London Record Society, 2003), p.15.

36 NRO ANW Fuller alias Roper 66 (Dunston).

37 R. Gilchrist, *Medieval Life: Archaeology and the Life Course* (Woodbridge: Boydell Press, 2014), p.128.

38 Dymond (ed.), *Thetford Priory: Part II*, p.597.

39 TNA PROB/11/5 (Stotevile); TNA PCC PROB 11/61/559 (Marsham).

40 Field, 'Worcestershire peasant buildings', p.122.

41 S. Flood (ed.), St Albans Wills, 1471–1500: Hertfordshire Record Publications Vol. IX(Hertfordshire: Hertfordshire Record Publications, 1993), p.88; F.G. Emmison, *Elizabethan Wills of South-West Essex* (Waddesdon: Kylin Press, 1983), p.10.

42 N.W. Alcock, *People at Home: Living in a Warwickshire Village, 1500–1800* (Chichester: Phillimore, 1993), pp.62, 121.

43 M. Filbee, *Dictionary of Country Furniture* (London: The Connoisseur, 1977), p.164. G. Chaucer, *The Canterbury Tales* (The General Prologue, lines 353–54) (London: Penguin Group, 2005), p.16.

44 Emmison, *Elizabethan Wills of South-West Essex*, p.10.
45 ERO D/ABW 4/298 (Bould).
46 P. Philp and G. Walkling, *Antique Furniture Expert* (London: Tiger Books, 1991), p.163; Worsley, *If Walls Could Talk*, p.177.
47 M. Johnson, *English Houses, 1300–1800: Vernacular Architecture, Social Life* (Harlow: Pearson Education Ltd, 2010), pp.68–74.
48 *Ibid.*, pp.98–99.
49 Emmison, *Elizabethan Wills of South-West Essex*, p.27.
50 J.M. Robinson, *The Regency Country House: From the Archives of Country Life* (London: Aurum Press, 2005), p.20.
51 S. Nenadic, 'Middle-rank consumers and domestic culture in Edinburgh and Glasgow 1720–1740', *Past and Present*, 145 (1994), p.140; J. Hillaby (ed.), *The Journeys of Celia Fiennes* (London: Macdonald, 1983), p.183.
52 Garrard, 'English probate inventories', p.59.
53 D. Roche, *A History of Everyday Things: The Birth of Consumption in France, 1600–1800* (Cambridge: Cambridge University Press, 2000), p.173.
54 C. Dyer, *An Age of Transition? Economy and Society in England in the Later Middle Ages* (Oxford: Clarendon Press, 2007), p.137.
55 Filbee, *Dictionary of Country Furniture*, p.161.
56 Thorold Rogers, *History of Agriculture and Prices: Vol. IV*, p.609.
57 Dymond (ed.), *Thetford Priory: Part I*, p.342.
58 Whittle and Griffiths, *Consumption and Gender*, p.138.
59 M. Berg, *Luxury and Pleasure in Eighteenth-Century Britain* (Oxford: Oxford University Press, 2005), p.114.
60 Turkey-work is woollen material woven in the same way as a Turkish carpet. J. Bristow, *Local Historian's Glossary* (Nottingham: Continuing Education Press, 1990), p.202.
61 J.A. Johnson, 'Furniture and furnishings in seventeenth-century Lincoln', *Lincolnshire History and Archaeology*, 35 (2000), p.11.
62 ERO D/ABW 14/164 (Feaste); HA 1/47 (Smithe).
63 Emmison, *Elizabethan Wills of South-West Essex*, p.27.
64 Dauteuille, 'Household materials', p.173; Overton *et al.*, *Production and Consumption*, p.90.
65 NRO ANW Fuller alias Roper fo.34 (Tyrle).
66 SROB Longe 229 (Allen); SROB Hervye 307 (Pynhorn).
67 D.M. Herridge (trans.), *Surrey Probate Inventories, 1558–1603: Surrey Record Society Vol. 39* (Woking: Surrey Record Society, 2005, p.15.
68 Overton *et al.*, *Production and Consumption*, pp.90–92; S. Broadberry, B. Campbell, A. Klein, M. Overton and B. van Leeuwen, *British Economic Growth, 1270–1870* (Cambridge: Cambridge University Press, 2015), p.298.
69 J. Laing, *Art and Society in Roman Britain* (Stroud: Sutton Publishing Ltd, 1997), p.63.
70 J. Hatcher and T. Barker, *A History of British Pewter* (London: Longman, 1974), pp.24, 30.
71 *Ibid.*, pp.50–59.
72 *Ibid.*, pp.40, 124.
73 R. Gottfried, *Bury St Edmunds and the Urban Crisis: 1290–1539* (Guildford: Princeton University Press, 1982), p.40.
74 J. Patten, 'Village and town: an occupational study', *Agricultural History Review*, xx (1972), p.14, cited in Hatcher and Barker, *British Pewter*, p.123; A. Dyer, *Decline and Growth in English Towns: 1400–1640* (Cambridge: Cambridge University Press, 1991), pp.62–63.
75 Hatcher and Barker, *British Pewter*, p.124.

76 Dymond (ed.), *Thetford Priory: Part I*, p.274; Dymond (ed.), *Thetford Priory: Part II*, pp.350, 488.

77 TNA PCC PROB 11/22/268 (Withall).

78 C. Dyer, 'The consumer and the market in the later Middle Ages', *Economic History Review*, 42 (1989), p.310.

79 D. Defoe, *Tour Through the Whole Island of Great Britain*, Volume 1, Letter 1 (1724). www.visionofbritain.org.uk/text/contents_page.jsp?t_id=Defoe [last accessed 12 August 2019].

80 Trinder and Cox, *Yeomen and Colliers*, p.106.

81 Hatcher and Barker, *British Pewter*, p.279.

82 Trinder and Cox, *Yeomen and Colliers*, p.106.

83 Dauteuille, 'Household materials', p.172.

84 Dymond (ed.), *Thetford Priory: Part II*, pp.374, 376, 416.

85 Flood (ed.), *St Albans Wills, 1471–1500*, p.151.

86 D.M. Herridge (trans.), *Surrey Probate Inventories, 1558–1603: Surrey Record Society Vol. 39* (Woking: Surrey Record Society, 2005), p.476.

87 Hamling and Richardson, *Day at Home*, p.123.

88 E. Roberts and K. Parker (eds), *Southampton Probate Inventories 1447–1575, Volume 1: Southampton Records Series Vol. XXXIX* (Southampton: Southampton University Press 1992), p.xxiv.

89 Herridge, *Surrey Probate Inventories*, p.42.

90 A. Jennet Rogers who is bound to John Bevill, painter, Bristol is an emigrant to Barbados in 1657. P. Coldham, *The Complete Book of Emigrants 1607–1660* (Baltimore: Genealogical Publishing Co., 1987), p.338.

91 E. and S. George (eds), *Bristol Probate Inventories, Part 2 1657–1689 Bristol Record Society's Publication Vol. 57* (Bristol: Bristol Record Society, 2005), p.78.

92 L. Williams and S. Thomson (eds), *Marlborough Probate Inventories, 1591–1775: Wiltshire Record Society Vol. 59* (Chippenham: Wiltshire Record Society, 2007), pp.351, 361, 395.

93 C.D. Smith, 'Map ownership in sixteenth-century Cambridge: the evidence of probate inventories', *Imago Mundi*, 47(1), (1995), pp.67–93.

94 S. Foister 'Paintings and other works of art in sixteenth-century English inventories', *Burlington Magazine*, cxxiii (1981), p.273ff.

95 R. Tittler, *Portraits, Painters and Publics in Provincial England, 1540–1640* (Oxford: Oxford University Press, 2013), p.48.

96 French defined 'officers' as those who can be identified positively as having served in parish or borough office in the relevant period, H. French, *The Middle Sort of People in Provincial England, 1600–1750* (Oxford: Oxford University Press, 2007), pp. 153–54.

97 Overton et al., *Production and Consumption*, pp.111–13.

98 C. Dyer, *Making a Living in the Middle Ages: The People of Britain, 850–1520* (London: Penguin Books, 2003), p.305.

99 J. Cherry, *Medieval Goldsmiths* (London: British Museum Press, 2011), pp.69–70.

100 Thorold Rogers, *History of Agriculture and Prices: Vol. IV*, pp.474, 612.

101 N. Davis (ed.), *Paston Letters and Papers of the Fifteenth Century: Part I* (Oxford: Oxford University Press, 1971), p.350.

102 Hatcher and Barker, *British Pewter*, p.107.

103 C. Dyer, *Standards of Living in the Later Middle Ages: Social Change in England, c. 1200–1520* (Cambridge: Cambridge University Press, 1989), p.173; J. Goldberg, 'The fashioning of bourgeois domesticity in later medieval England: a material culture perspective', in M. Kowaleski and J. Goldberg (eds), *Medieval Domesticity: Home, Housing and Household in Medieval England* (Cambridge: Cambridge University Press, 2011), p.127.

104 TNA PROB 11/5 Godyn 20.

105 TNA PROB 11/14/745 (Aylnoth).
106 SROB Baldwyne 379 (Bakhot); SROB Hawlee 325 (Smyth).
107 NRO NCC Caston 130 (Roger).
108 SROB Baldwyne 303 (Bakhote).
109 Dymond (ed.), *Thetford Priory: Part I*, p.284; Dymond (ed.), *Thetford Priory: Part II*, pp. 388, 571.
110 J. Middleton-Stewart (ed.), *Records of the Churchwardens of Mildenhall: Collections, 1446–1454, Accounts, 1503–1553* (Woodbridge: Boydell Press, 2011), pp.64, 84.
111 SROB Baldwyne 298 (Ray).
112 SROB Baldwyne 205 (Cake), NRO NCC Johnson 108 (Breye).
113 NRO ANW Athowe 95 (Fickeis); J. Tiramani, 'Pins and aglets', in T. Hamling and C. Richardson (eds), *Everyday Objects: Medieval and Early Modern Material Culture and its Meanings* (Farnham: Ashgate, 2010), p.90.
114 Hamling and Richardson, *Day at Home*, p.135.
115 Williams and Thomson (eds), *Marlborough Probate Inventories*, p.109.
116 M. Finn, 'Men's things: masculine possession in the consumer revolution', *Social History*, 25 (2000), p.141.
117 Roberts and Parker, *Southampton Probate Inventories*, p.410.
118 M. Berg, 'Women's consumption and the industrial classes', *Journal of Social History*, 30 (1996), p.427.
119 Twenty million books were printed before 1500 and between 140 and 200 million in the following century, D. Headrick, *Technology: A World History* (Oxford: Oxford University Press, 2009), pp.84–85.
120 R. Swanson, *Church and Society in Late Medieval England* (Oxford: Basil Blackwell, 1989), p.210; E. Duffy, *The Stripping of the Altars: Traditional Religion in England, 1400–1580* (Yale: Yale University Press, 2005), p.211ff.
121 Davis (ed.), *Paston Letters*, pp.517–18.
122 G. Lester, 'The books of a fifteenth-century English gentleman, Sir John Paston', *Neuphilologische Mitteilungen*, 88 (2) (1987), p.204.
123 M. Deanesley, 'Vernacular books in England in the fourteenth and fifteenth centuries', *Modern Language Review*, 15 (4) (1920), pp.349–50.
124 NRO NCC Doke 164 (Berton alias Wotts); NRO NCC Wylbey 56 (Upryght).
125 A 'porteous' was a portable breviary which contained all the texts for the celebration of divine office; NRO NCC Ryxe 146 (Gatynbe).
126 NRO NCC Hirning 125 (Eyr); Flood (ed.), *St Albans Wills*, p.58.
127 John Paston was the father or the aforementioned John Paston II; Thorold Rogers, *History of Agriculture and Prices: Vol. IV*, p.600.
128 Middleton-Stewart (ed.), *Records of the Churchwardens of Mildenhall*, pp.99, 109.
129 The Act for the Advancement of True Religion, 34 & 35 Henry VIII, c.1.
130 I. Mortimer, *Human Race: Ten Centuries of Change on Earth* (London: Random House, 2015), pp.13–34.
131 A. Ryrie, *Being Protestant in Reformation Britain* (Oxford: Oxford University Press, 2015), pp.260–62.
132 Filbee, *Dictionary of Country Furniture*, pp.35–37.
133 Broadberry et al., *British Economic Growth*, p.154.
134 B. A'Hearn, 'The British industrial revolution in a European mirror' in R. Floud, J. Humphries and P. Johnson (eds), *The Cambridge Economic History of Modern Britain* (Cambridge: Cambridge University Press, 2014), p.42.
135 J.H. Plumb, 'The commercialisation of leisure in eighteenth century England', in N. McKendrick, J. Brewer and J.H. Plumb (eds), *The Birth of a Consumer Society: The Commercialization of Eighteenth-Century England* (London: Hutchinson, 1983), pp.267–68.
136 M. Spufford, *Small Books and Pleasant Histories: Popular Fiction and its Readership in Seventeenth-Century England* (Cambridge: Cambridge University Press, 1981), p.10.

137 I. Green, *Print and Protestantism in Early Modern England* (Oxford: Oxford University Press, 2000), p.180ff.

138 S. Doran and C. Durston, *Princes, Pastors and People: The Church and Religion in England, 1500–1689* (London: Routledge, 2002), pp.187–88.

139 W. St Clair, *The Reading Nation in the Romantic Period* (Cambridge: Cambridge University Press, 2004), p.306; J. Tiller, 'Lewis Bayly', in J. Douglas, (ed.), *New International Dictionary of the Christian Church* (Zondervan: Grand Rapids, 1974), p.113.

140 Ryrie, *Being Protestant in Reformation Britain*, p.22.

141 D. McKittrick, 'Ovid with a Littleton; the cost of English books in the early seventeenth century', *Transactions of the Cambridge Bibliographical Society*, XI (1997), p.190.

142 J. Raven, 'The book trades', in I. Rivers (ed.), *Books and their Readers in Eighteenth-Century England: New Essays* (London: Continuum, 2001), p.2.

143 J. Raven, *Judging New Wealth: Popular Publishing and Responses to Commerce, 1750–1800* (Oxford: Clarendon Press, 1992), p.56.

144 Plumb, 'The commercialisation of leisure', pp.268–72.

145 J. Brewer, *The Pleasures of the Imagination: English Culture in the Eighteenth Century* (London: Routledge, 1997), p.171.

146 Herridge, *Surrey Probate Inventories*, p.87.

147 A. Hughes (ed.), *Sussex Clergy Inventories, 1600–1750* (Lewes: Sussex Record Society, 2009), p.112; B. Trinder and J. Cox, *Miners and Mariners of the Severn Gorge: Probate Inventories for Benthall, Broseley, Little Wenlock and Madeley, 1660–1764* (Chichester: Phillimore, 2000), p.287.

148 Trinder and Cox, *Miners and Mariners*, p.163.

149 E. and S. George (eds), *Bristol Probate Inventories, Part 1 1542–1650: Bristol Record Society's Publication Vol. 54* (Bristol: Bristol Record Society, 2002), p.117; George and George, *Bristol Probate Inventories, Part 2*, p.147; Trinder and Cox, *Yeomen and Colliers*, p.344.

150 E. Leedham Green, *Books in Cambridge Inventories* (Cambridge: Cambridge University Press, 1986), pp.560–69.

151 Hughes, *Sussex Clergy Inventories*, pp.98–99, 112–14, 170–72.

152 *The Christian Warfare* was a book owned by G. Weston, a mariner, in 1637 and therefore seems too early to be the similarly titled volume by William Gurnall.

153 This is probably William Perkins (1558–RY1602), a Puritan scholar whose works included *A Godly and Learned Exposition upon Christ's Sermon in the Mount*.

154 P. Pixton (ed.), *Wrenbury Wills and Inventories, 1542–1661: Record Society of Lancashire and Cheshire Vol. 144* (Chester: Record Society of Lancashire and Cheshire, 2009), p.392.

155 M. Spufford, 'The limitations of the probate inventory', in J.A. Chartres and D. Hey (eds), *English Rural Society, 1500–1800: Essays in Honour of Joan Thirsk* (Cambridge: Cambridge University Press, 1990), p.149.

156 D. Vaisey (ed.), *The Diary of a Village Shopkeeper 1754–1765: Thomas Turner* (London: Folio Society, 1998).

157 S. Djabri (ed.), *The Diaries of Sarah Hurst 1759–1762* (Horsham: Horsham Museum Society, 2003).

158 Headrick, *Technology*, pp.63–64.

159 P. Glennie and N. Thrift, *Shaping the Day: A History of Timekeeping in England and Wales 1300–1800* (Oxford: Oxford University Press, 2009), p.153; TNA PROB PCC 15/157 (Rows).

160 Mortimer, *Human Race*, pp.118–19.

161 A. Smith, *A Collector's Guide to Antique Clocks and Watches* (London: Leopard, 1996), p.90.

162 D. Roberts, *The Bracket Clock* (Newton Abbott: David&Charles, 1982), p.48ff.

163 Glennie and Thrift, *Shaping the Day*, p.24.

164 *Ibid.*, p.169.

165 D.S. Landes, *Revolution in Time: Clocks and the Making of the Modern World* (London: Belknap Press, 1983), pp.219–23.

166 Glennie and Thrift, *Shaping the Day*, p.170.

167 C. Muldrew, *Food, Energy and the Creation of Industriousness* (Cambridge: Cambridge University Press, 2011), p.163.

168 A.C. Davies, 'Rural clockmaking in eighteenth-century Wales: Samuel Roberts of Llanfair Caereinion, 1755–1774', *The Business History Review*, 59 (1985), pp.49–50.

169 G.J. Whitrow, *Time in History: Views of Time from Prehistory to the Present Day* (Oxford: Oxford University Press, 1989), p.112.

170 J. Styles, 'Georgian Britain' in M. Snodin and J. Styles (eds), *Design and the Decorative Art: Britain 1500–1900* (London: V&A Publishing, 2001), p.182.

171 Styles, 'Georgian Britain', p.181.

172 N.J.G. Pounds, *Hearth and Home: A History of Material Culture* (Bloomington: Indiana University Press, 1989), p.201; Styles, 'Georgian Britain', p.182.

173 Pounds, *Hearth and Home*, p.201.

174 E.P. Thompson, 'Time, work-discipline and industrial capitalism', *Past and Present*, 38 (1967), p.76.

175 M. Berg and H. Clifford, *Consumers and Luxury; Consumer Culture in Europe 1660–1850* (Manchester: Manchester University Press, 1999), p.69.

176 P. King, 'Pauper inventories and the material lives of the poor in the eighteenth and early nineteenth centuries', in T. Hitchcock, P. King and P. Sharpe (eds), *Chronicling Poverty: The Voices and Strategies of the English Poor, 1640–1840* (Basingstoke: Macmillan, 1997), p.179; Glennie and Thrift, *Shaping the Day*, p.168.

177 Harley, 'Material lives of the English poor', p.196.

178 J. Styles, *The Dress of the People: Everyday Fashion in Eighteenth-Century England* (New Haven: Yale University Press, 2008), p.343.

179 S, Horrell, J. Humphries and K. Sneath, 'Consumption conundrums unravelled', *Economic History Review*, 68 (2015), p.256.

180 M. Kelly and C. Ó Gráda, 'Adam Smith, watch prices and the Industrial Revolution', *Quaterly Journal of Economics*, 131 (4) (2016), p.5.

181 Styles, *Dress of the People*, p.97.

182 Trinder and Cox, *Miners and Mariners*, p.184.

183 Williams and Thomson (eds), *Marlborough Probate Inventories*, p.292.

184 Kelly and Ó Gráda, 'Adam Smith, watch prices and the Industrial Revolution', p.7.

185 N.J.G. Pounds, *The Culture of the English People: Iron Age to the Industrial Revolution* (Cambridge: Cambridge University Press, 1994), p.118.

186 Historic Window Guide, http://tewkesbury.gov.uk/CHttpHandler.ashx?id=872 [last accessed 2 December 2015].

187 ERO D/ABW 21/95 (Josselyne).

188 These window shutters were from a late fifteenth-century hall house in North Cray, Kent, now located at the Weald and Downland Museum.

189 B. Lemire, *Fashion's Favourite: The Cotton Trade and the Consumer in Britain* (Oxford: Oxford University Press, 1991), p.82.

190 Trinder and Cox, *Yeomen and Colliers*, pp.99, 307.

191 L. Weatherill, *Consumer Behaviour and Material Culture in Britain 1660–1760* (London: Routledge, 1996), p.26.

192 For example. John Smyth Baker, 1595/6, C.B. Phillips and J.H. Smith (eds), *Stockport Probate Records, 1578–1619: Publications of the Record Society of Lancashire and Cheshire Vol. CXXIV* (Gloucester: Record Society of Lancashire and Cheshire, 1985), p.21.

193 J. Enoch, 'Archaeological optics: the very first known mirrors and lenses', *Journal of Modern Optics*, 54 (2007), pp.1221–39.

194 Mortimer, *Human Race*, p.120.

195 E.S. Godfrey, *The Development of English Glassmaking 1560–1640* (Oxford: Clarendon Press, 1975), p.235.

196 G. Child, *World Mirrors 1650–1900* (London: Sotheby's Publications, 1990), pp.12–18.

197 M.J.M. Ezell, 'Looking glass histories', *Journal of British Studies*, 43 (2004), pp.322–24.

198 Spufford, *Small Books and Pleasant Histories*, p.116.

199 B. Goldberg, *The Mirror and Man* (Charlottesville: University Press of Virginia, 1985), p.169.

200 C. Estabrook, *Urbane and Rustic England: Cultural Ties and Social Spheres in the Provinces 1660–1780* (Manchester: Manchester University Press, 1998), p.128.

201 J.M. Ellis, 'Consumption and wealth', in L.K.J. Glassey (ed.), *The Reigns of Charles II and James VII and II* (Basingstoke: Macmillan, 1997), pp.200–1; Berg, *Luxury and Pleasure*, p.115.

202 F. Dikoter, 'Objects and agency', in K. Harvey (ed.), *History and Material Culture: A Student's Guide to Approaching Alternative Sources* (Abingdon: Routledge, 2018), pp.211–12.

203 Ezell, 'Looking glass histories', pp.324–28.

204 A.S. Martin, *Buying into the World of Goods* (Baltimore: Johns Hopkins University Press, 2008), p.173ff.

205 *Ibid.*, pp.35, 133.

206 M. Bailey, *A Marginal Economy? East Anglian Breckland in the Later Middle Ages* (Cambridge: Cambridge University Press, 1989), pp.163–64.

207 SROB Baldwyne 128 (Tyd); SROB Boner 75 (Hadnaham).

208 Dauteuille, 'Household materials', p.171.

209 NCC Popy 286 (Tyllis), 'coles' is assumed to refer to wood charcoal.

210 P. Ariès and G. Duby (eds), *A History of Private Life: Vol. II, Revelations of the Medieval World* (Cambridge, Massachusetts: Belknap Press, 1988), pp.349, 500.

211 E.A. Wrigley, R.S. Davies, J.E. Oeppen and R.S. Schofield, *English Population History from Family Reconstitution 1580–1837* (Cambridge: Cambridge University Press, 1997), p.614.

212 M. Spufford, 'Chimneys, wood and coal', in P. Barnwell and M. Airs (eds), *Houses and the Hearth Tax: The Later Stuart House and Society* (York: Council for British Archaeology, 2006), p.23.

213 Edelen (ed.), *Description of England*, pp.363–64; A. Standish, *New Directions of Experience to the Commons* (London: [publisher not identified], 1613).

214 T. Arkell (ed.) with N. Alcock, *Warwickshire Hearth Tax Returns: Michaelmas 1670 with Coventry Lady Day* (Stratford: Dugdale Society, 2010), p.108.

215 HA, AH18/5/109.

216 HA, AH18/2/224.

217 HA, AH18/7/8.

218 HA, AH18/2/353.

219 Arkell (ed.), *Warwickshire Hearth Tax Returns*, p.108.

220 HA, AH18/3/292.

221 HA, AH18/4/67.

222 HA, AH18/12/105.

223 A. Vickery, *Behind Closed Doors: At Home in Georgian England* (New Haven: Yale University Press, 2009), p.265.

224 S. Pennell, 'Material culture in seventeenth-century Britain: the matter of domestic consumption', in F. Trentmann (ed.), *The Oxford Handbook of the History of Consumption* (Oxford: Oxford University Press, 2012), p.69.

225 G. Egan, 'Lighting equipment' in G. Egan with J. Bayley, *The Medieval Household: Daily Living c.1150–c.1450* (London: Museum of London, Stationery Office, 1988), pp.126–51.

226 Dauteuille, 'Household materials', p.169.
227 J. Caspall, *Fire and Light in the Home Pre-1820* (Woodbridge: Antique Collectors' Club, 1987), p.43; Dymond (ed.), *Thetford Priory: Parts I and II*.
228 J. Thorold Rogers, *A History of Agriculture and Prices in England from the Year after the Oxford Parliament (1279) to the Commencement of the Continental War (1793): Vol. 1 1259–1400* (Oxford: Clarendon Press, 1866), p.416
229 Thorold Rogers, *History of Agriculture and Prices: Vol. IV*, p.366.
230 Thorold Rogers identifies that tallow candles were frequently bought by the dozen pounds; Thorold Rogers, *History of Agriculture and Prices: Vol. IV*, p.367; Egan, 'Lighting equipment', p.126.
231 *Ibid.*, p.368.
232 Dyer, *Standards of Living*, p.74.
233 Thorold Rogers, *History of Agriculture and Prices: Vol. IV*, p.365.
234 NRO ANF Liber 3a (Bemond) 5 (Houghton).
235 Thorold Rogers, *History of Agriculture and Prices: Vol. IV*, p.611; Dymond (ed.), *Thetford Priory: Part II*, p.413.
236 Muldrew, *Food, Energy and the Creation of Industriousness*, p.196.
237 B. and T. Hughes, *Three Centuries of English Domestic Silver* (London: Lutterworth Press, 1952), p.69.
238 ERO D/ABW 28/349 (Plomer); Williams and Thomson (eds), *Marlborough Probate Inventories*, p.76.
239 Thorold Rogers, *History of Agriculture and Prices: Vol. IV*, p.367.
240 Steer, *Farm and Cottage Inventories*, p.21.
241 Caspall, *Fire and Light*, p.223.
242 G. Chaucer, *The Legend of Good Women* (London: Createspace Independent Publishing Platform, 2015), p.15.
243 Williams and Thomson (eds), *Marlborough Probate Inventories*, p.15.
244 *Ibid.*, p.242.
245 The Proceedings of the Old Bailey: William Priddle t17750218-1 www.oldbaileyon line.org/; Victoria and Albert Museum, Warming Pan Museum Number 1462-1870, http://collections.vam.ac.uk/item/O77414/warming-pan-unknown/[last accessed 24 January 2016].
246 The Proceedings of the Old Bailey www.oldbaileyonline.org/: Anne Smith t17371012-11; James Dillon t17371012-24; Edward Smith t17380222-61 [last accessed 24 January 2016].
247 For example, The Proceedings of the Old Bailey www.oldbaileyonline.org/: Benjamin Thornton and Mary Gibbons t17710220-80 [last accessed 24 January 2016]; The Proceedings of the Old Bailey www.oldbaileyonline.org/: t17640502-72 [last accessed 24 January 2016].
248 Herridge, *Surrey Inventories*, p.41; TNA PCC PROB 11/61/559 (Marsham).
249 Trinder and Cox, *Yeomen and Colliers*, pp.168, 327; Trinder and Cox, *Miners and Mariners*, p.176.
250 HA, AH18/11/82.
251 Steer, *Farm and Cottage Inventories*, p.120.
252 Trinder and Cox, *Yeomen and Colliers*, p.348.
253 J.A. Johnston (ed.), *Probate Inventories of Lincoln Citizens, 1661–1714: Lincoln Record Society Vol. 80* (Woodbridge: Boydell & Brewer, 1991), p.3.
254 Trinder and Cox, *Miners and Mariners*, p.71.
255 The Proceedings of the Old Bailey www.oldbaileyonline.org/see for example Reference Number: t17321206-36.
256 Estabrook, *Urbane and Rustic England*, p.135.
257 A bass viol was a large stringed instrument played with a curved bow; George and George, *Bristol Probate Inventories, Part 2*, p.35.
258 *Ibid.*, p.89.

259 *Ibid.*, p.123.
260 Johnston (ed.), *Probate Inventories of Lincoln*, p.lxxiii.
261 *Ibid.*, p.121.
262 Williams and Thomson (eds), *Marlborough Probate Inventories*, p.298.
263 J. Bedell, 'Archaeology and probate inventories in the study of eighteenth-century life', *Journal of Interdisciplinary History*, xxx1 (2000), pp. 231–33.
264 Tobacco boxes for storing tobacco were usually made of wood and of low value. Much rarer, silver tobacco boxes were of considerable value. Among the goods stolen from Richard Bycott of Sohoe-fields in 1684 was a silver tobacco box valued at 30 s. The Proceedings of the Old Bailey www.oldbaileyonline.org/Reference Number t16841008-9.
265 Stephen Willoughby, Vintner in Marlborough who died in 1746, had a small box with tobacco and a box with pipes in the bar. Williams and Thomson (eds), *Marlborough Probate Inventories*, p.296.
266 J. de Vries, *The Industrious Revolution: Consumer Behaviour and the Household Economy, 1650 to the Present* (Cambridge: Cambridge University Press, 2008), p.157.
267 R. Findlay and K. O'Rourke, *Power and Plenty: Trade, War and the World Economy in the Second Millennium* (Princeton: Princeton University Press, 2007), p.259; Pennell, 'Material culture in seventeenth-century Britain', p.74.
268 The Proceedings of the Old Bailey www.oldbaileyonline.org/t16850826-4.
269 Steer, *Farm and Cottage Inventories*, p.258.
270 Williams and Thomson (eds), *Marlborough Probate Inventories*, p.277.
271 C. Shammas, *The Pre-Industrial Consumer in England and America* (Oxford: Clarendon Press, 1990), pp.96–98.
272 Trinder and Cox, *Miners and Mariners*, pp.191–92.
273 *Ibid.*, p.141.
274 *Ibid.*, pp.136, 141.

6

RELIGIOUS CONSUMPTION

One area of expenditure is often neglected in the calculations of household expenditure patterns and living standards made by economic historians. Expenditure on religion, in its various manifestations, was a further area of consumption, particularly in the late medieval period, which could absorb a significant proportion of household income and further restrict the amount available for expenditure on other commodities and material goods. Religion dominated daily life in both the late medieval and early modern periods such that often considerable amounts were spent on a very wide variety of goods and services. In this and subsequent periods, religious expenditure can also be viewed as a form of conspicuous consumption and a further way in which an individual could express social status.

Many of the religious payments made can be regarded as being involuntary and included various sums payable by both individuals and collectively by the community to the various tiers of the Roman Catholic and, subsequently, Anglican Church such as tithe payments and payments to the parish priest to perform spiritual functions relating to rites of passage.[1] However, particularly in the pre-Reformation period, there also existed an enormous range and scope for money to be spent on items of religious consumption such that there was a 'substantial spiritual economy based on voluntary donations'.[2] Whilst much of this expenditure was on non-physical items such as prayers, masses, pilgrimages and gild membership, much was also on tangible, material items.

Religious consumption in the pre-Reformation period

The parish church

In the late Middle Ages, the main focus of voluntary payments was on the parish church. Members of the parish were responsible for the maintenance of the structure of the church (with the exception of the chancel which was looked after by the owners of the rectorial land within the parish) and this maintenance included repairs to the actual building as well as to vestments, bells, pews, books, the church organ and the church clock. In addition to the ongoing maintenance of the fabric, many communities undertook substantial reconstructions of their parish church, especially during the late fourteenth, fifteenth and early sixteenth centuries, the 'great age of parish church rebuilding'.[3] Whilst these rebuilding schemes were often driven by one main benefactor, or a small group of significant benefactors, they also relied heavily on contributions from members of the local community which were often raised through weekly donation schemes and community activities such as church ales, plays, May ales and May games.

Many testamentary bequests reflect the responsibility that parishioners had towards the maintenance and glorification of their parish churches. In Godmanchester, a small town in Huntingdonshire, Henry Smyth left £10 for a set of liturgical vestments to be made, William Pelman bequeathed 6s 8d to buy a cloth for the high altar and John Aldred gave 3s 4d to the bells.[4] In 1491, Thomas Frost gave 6s 8d for a Day of Judgement painting over the rood and this painting was almost certainly undertaken in conjunction with other church rebuilding known to have taken place around this date.[5] Bequests such as these were often recorded within the church environment, partly as a means of ensuring that the benefactors were included in the prayers of parishioners, but also as a reminder of their wealth and generosity. Many of these physical records have remained; for example, the names of the key contributors to the rebuilding of Holy Trinity Church in Long Melford are still visible, picked out in the flint and limestone flushwork above the clerestory as inscribed pleas (Photo 6.1).

A memorial brass of a man wearing a long, fur-lined gown with a purse and dated *c.* 1520 has survived in Godmanchester's parish church (Photo 6.2). It has been suggested that the man depicted may have been the donor of the rood screen.

In addition to the main altar, medieval churches included a number of separate chancel altars and side altars which were often used by gilds and perpetual chantries. These were invariably richly decorated with a variety of paintings, plate, embroidered coverings, hangings and lights while the clergy themselves wore elaborate clothing. The community sought to ensure that these were all of the finest materials available, as inferior materials were only used in the poorest parishes.[6] Such liturgical items were provided by parishioners either through gifts of the articles themselves, or by sums of money which enabled the articles to be acquired. An inventory of St Mary's Church, Mildenhall, taken in 1508, showed that the church possessed a total of 17 copes made from a variety of expensive cloths including cloth of gold, cloth of tissue, white damask, red damask, blue velvet and red velvet.[7] Parishioners were also keen to give offerings to the statues, images and relics situated within medieval churches and these gifts took various forms including straightforward monetary offerings, donations

PHOTO 6.1 Holy Trinity Church, Long Melford, Suffolk substantially rebuilt in the fifteenth century. Names of main benefactors are picked out in the flint and limestone flushwork on the church.

of money or objects designed to adorn the relevant icon and payments to support lights before them. Women, in particular, frequently gifted their prayer beads to images within the church.

Payments relating to the parish church also included a range of other items for which smaller amounts were given. These included donations relating to certain religious ceremonies such as the making, maintenance, lighting and watching of the sepulchre for Holy Week and Easter, gifts to the parish box and contributions towards payments to parochial officers.[8] Payments were also made for a 'quetheword', the announcement of the death of a parishioner which was supported by a bequest or legacy to the parish church.[9] The Mildenhall churchwardens' accounts showed that this was a popular tradition as they contained regular and ongoing payments for quethewords with the amounts paid by the executors of the deceased for this service ranging considerably from 4d to £1.[10] Other parishioners paid to be included on the bede roll, the list of deceased parishioners regularly prayed for within the church. Richard Mores of Chippenham asked that the profits of five roods of land be used so that the vicar of Chippenham could pray for him and his friends 'every sonday in his bede rool'.[11] In addition, the practice of renting or purchasing pews began in the fourteenth century and was a further source of income for the church and

PHOTO 6.2 Memorial brass of a civilian dated *c.* 1520

expenditure for members of the community.[12] Seating within the church began to reflect the social hierarchy of the local community with the gentry and burgesses within towns paying to secure pews located at the front of the nave and nearest to the altar.[13] People from the next social tier took the pews behind the parish elite and so on with the lowest peasants or labourers sitting at the back of the nave and furthest from the altar. People often expressed a desire to be buried close to their seating so that references to the practice often appear in wills; Edward Ballys of Thetford asked to be buried 'in the chappell of Saynt Anne within the churche of Seynt peter before my seat'.[14]

During the seventeenth century seat reservation and appropriation in churches increased. Christopher Marsh argued that the urge to own and pass on a pew was widespread and it was not uncommon for the gentry to place locks on their pews and a few even attempted to sell their seats to others.[15] David Palliser argued that, as typified in Myddle, post-Reformation seating normally reflected the social hierarchy of the parish whether measured by wealth, ancestry or office.[16] David Underdown found that in Trinity Church, Dorchester leading male parishioners sat in rows in the middle aisle, with eminent men at the front and poorer men towards the back.[17] Gwyneth Nair uncovered a seating plan of Highley church dated 1775 where large pews at the front were reserved for particular farms rather than individuals, with a careful gradation to smaller pews for lesser properties and finally 'cottage seats' at the back.[18] Conflicts over church seating were principally about social status; Amanda Flather's study of Essex church seating revealed battles between neighbours and presentments by churchwardens indicating that hierarchy of rank and degree was an area of constant contest and continually shifting boundaries.[19]

Marsh accepted that arguments about church seating could be about issues of status but suggested that they also reflected religious concerns. Location of pews and benches within 'God's house' was important because they allowed people to sit, kneel or stand to hear divine service and sermon. Proximity to the pulpit was a prestigious pew and Marsh suggested that the most sought-after seats in Sutton, Ely were those at the front of the southernmost column of seats. One godly gentleman from Almondbury in West Riding constructed his new pew in order to hear sermons. On this basis, the claims for seating upon churchwardens by the deaf might take precedence over wealth.[20] Marsh's argument is a reminder to exercise due care in examining sources from a world with very different mentalities from our own. Even if social status was the principal source of conflict over church seating, religious concerns about sacred space might also have been important to many people in the early modern period.

Personal religious consumption

Religious consumption also encompassed purchasing personal or household items of a religious nature, such as prayer beads, liturgical texts, statuary and other relics which were bought and collected by the laity as well as by the church.[21] Prayer beads (widely known as paternosters) had been used since at least the eleventh century but became increasingly common from the early fifteenth century with the development of the belief that they contained indulgences which were released to the wearer once an appropriate number of devotions had been recited.[22] They served both religious and display purposes and were often owned by women, particularly widows, as the only form of jewellery which was considered appropriate for them to wear.[23] These items could be made from a range of materials from precious metals, such as gold or silver, through to simple wood or bone; however, jet, amber and coral were especially popular materials as they were all regarded as having various additional quasi-religious apotropaic properties.[24] Personal items also included pardons or indulgences which were freely available and widely purchased in both their hand-written and, subsequently, printed forms.[25] These were not only obtained by individuals but were frequently acquired by parishes and gilds. Quasi-religious personal items were also in existence such as manuscript prayer rolls which were worn as girdles to secure safe childbirth.[26]

The popularity of saints in the late medieval period led many consumers to purchase statues or other hagiographical images such as the 'Saynte John's heed'
referred to by John Flecher of Thetford in his will of 1499 (Photo 6.3a).[27] Small
alabaster statuaries such as these became popular in the late Middle Ages and were
commonly produced in England from the fourteenth century, particularly in and
around alabaster quarries in Nottingham, York and Burton-on-Trent. They were
especially coveted throughout Europe as items of personal devotion such that England became a major centre for the production of these objects and they were
exported in large numbers.[28] Ironically, many of these exports have survived whilst
those that remained in England were largely destroyed during the Reformation.

Whilst late medieval churches commonly possessed relics, they could also be
found in the possession of wealthy households. These were often contained
within reliquaries, particularly the enamel caskets made in Limoges, and could
also be incorporated into items of adornment and worn on the person. Other
items regarded as having similar powers were in more common ownership; pil-
grims to religious shrines frequently purchased *ampullae* filled with holy water or
oil thought to be capable of bestowing holy miracles in much the same way as
a relic. Once again, these were frequently worn around the neck (Photo 6.3b).

Prior to the Reformation, fear of purgatory loomed large in the hearts of lay
people as they approached death. Whilst all Christians might hope to go to
heaven, only saints were admitted to heaven immediately. Ordinary souls had to
first suffer physical torment in preparation for heaven. The medieval mind was

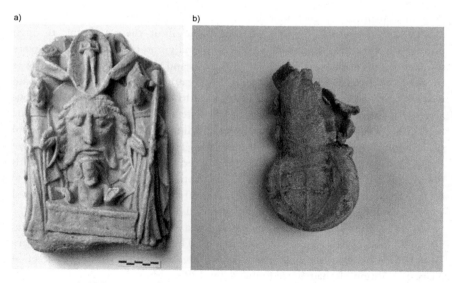

PHOTO 6.3   a) Alabaster panel with head of St John the Baptist, date unknown (image
by courtesy and reproduced by kind permission of the Salisbury Museum © The Salisbury Museum); b) incomplete medieval lead-alloy pilgrim *ampulla*, *c.* 1300–1500

fixated with the need to ensure that souls passed safely from this world to the next. As they prepared their wills, the soon to be deceased were anxious to take the appropriate steps; in particular, most wills contained a clause to the effect that 'tithes and offerings negligently forgotten' should be paid by the executors since spiritual and material debts left undischarged resulted in a longer period in purgatory. Similarly important were payments for masses to be sung to aid the release of the soul from purgatory since the prayers of the living could also reduce the time spent in purgatory. As a result, for most people, the greatest area of personal religious consumption was on making provision for the soul in the period after death in an attempt to secure a reduction of time spent in purgatory and to ensure ultimate salvation.

Chantries and gilds

For wealthier members of society, this desire to secure prayers after death was also reflected in founding or supporting chantries. Chantries could be in the form of a service chantry which ran for a specified number of years or a perpetual chantry intended to run for eternity and which usually utilised the rent from an endowment of property to provide an ongoing income for a stipendiary chaplain or chaplains to perform a daily Mass for the soul of the founder. Wills indicated that service chantries were a popular form of religious consumption as they contained numerous bequests for chantries which were mostly for one year (usually at a cost of eight marks) but could be for as little as a quarter-year or for as long as ten years. The investment required to establish perpetual chantries was such that they were only founded by the very wealthy.

One way in which the less affluent could limit their suffering through prayer was through membership of a socio-religious gild. These gilds were founded on a parish basis for religious reasons and, in particular, as a response to the role played by the doctrine of purgatory. They enabled men and women to come together on a voluntary basis to undertake a range of religious and social functions but particularly to regulate the devotional lives of members in activities which they believed would limit both their own penitential suffering and those of deceased gild members. These devotional activities were frequently coordinated by gild priests appointed and funded by the gild. Gilds became deeply integrated into their communities and consequently into local society and there may have been as many as 30 thousand gilds in late medieval England although the spread and density varied quite widely.[29]

Evidence from Godmanchester demonstrated how significant both chantries and gilds were to late medieval communities. The Chantry of the Blessed Mary (also known as Roode's Chantry) was associated with the parish church of St Mary the Virgin. It had been founded by 1297, although no details about its foundation appear to have survived, and it became the focus of a number of endowments of land in the town including a gift of 31 acres of land and four acres of meadow from Roger de Strateshill in 1307. The chantry appointed a priest to pray in the parish church and its close association with the town was such that this priest was bound to pray 'for the good state, welfare and prosperity of the Bayliffs of this town, and all the Comynalty of the same, fundars of the Chauntre'.[30] Any chantry chapel was probably on the north side of the church since in his will of 1515, John Stukeley gave 40s 'to a cowcher to lye before the Charntry preest on the north syde'.[31] At least six socio-religious gilds are also known to have existed at one time or another within the town and this abundance of gilds is reflected in other settlements. Testamentary bequests confirmed the importance of these gilds to the residents of Godmanchester; for example, Thomas Robyns left half a quarter of barley each to the gilds of St John the Baptist and Corpus Christi in his will of 1306 and Thomas Froste left half an acre of meadow to the Gild of Corpus Christi.[32]

Funerals and associated rituals

Religious expenditure was also a means by which the testator could exhibit status, albeit after death, and significant amounts could be spent on funerals and associated rituals. Both wills and probate accounts provide a wealth of evidence about funerals and the range of different aspects that these encompassed. The standard pattern for a late medieval funeral service was the saying of the Office of the Dead, consisting of the *placebo* and *dirige*, which was said on the day of the funeral. For those who could afford it, this basic service was supplemented by other commemorations and in particular celebration of anniversaries or obits which re-enacted the Office of the Dead with requiem Masses.[33] The most popular form of *post mortem* commemoration was a trental, the celebration of 30 masses on consecutive days, which could be said either in the parish church or, more frequently, in a religious house. Burial at this time was a highly ritualised ceremony; people were anxious to secure a decent Christian burial both for themselves and their loved ones so that this rite could also be an expensive occasion. Before the burial service, expenditure was required on wax candles, known as 'soul candles', a shroud for the body (which could range from a simple linen shroud to clothing of an appropriate rank or even embalming) and a coffin (although for the less affluent members of society this was just used for the funeral service as the body would be removed from it before being buried).[34] The burial service itself usually began with a procession to accompany the body to church which was in itself a display of prestige and would include as many people and of the highest rank together with as many ecclesiastics as possible with all of the processors expected to be attired in mourning clothes.[35] The coffin was either carried in the procession by pall-bearers or pulled along on a cart and the procession was accompanied with torches and bells whilst gild banners would also be displayed if the deceased was a gild member.[36] Once inside the church, the body would be placed on a wheeled bier or hearse which would be covered by a hearse cloth or 'pall' and taken before the altar for the Office of the Dead.[37] The body was then interred and this could be either within the church itself or outside in the churchyard. Funeral sermons were said as the actual burial was taking place whilst memorial sermons took place on various times after death (usually on the seventh day, 30th day and on the anniversary of death).

Whilst the basic structure of a late medieval burial was relatively standard, many people were keen to make special provisions for the event to ensure that the ceremony reflected their status and, perhaps more importantly, to secure the progress of the soul through purgatory. Some of these provisions were likely to have been made and paid for during life without any formal record being made so that the deceased's family did not have to incur the expense, however, many wills contained records of these arrangements in the form of bequests which reflected the testator's desire for a proper burial. John Ray of Newmarket gave 12 marks for the expenses of obsequies and mass on the day of his burial and for commemorations on his seventh and 30th days, and Thomas Hull bequeathed 'to the byeng of a vestiment to be for the church of Myldenhale xxvjs viijd for a preste to sing in it the tyme of my service and after to remayn to the sayed church off Myldenhale for ever'.[38] Margaret Carman made provision in her will for her body to lie on a bier cloth costing 12d and for an undercloth at a cost of 8d.[39]

Burial could be within the churchyard, within the church itself or within the precincts of a religious house. Burial within the church or in a religious house was largely reserved for higher-status individuals with the optimum location being before the altar so that the deceased would be remembered during Mass.[40] Many wealthy testators used their wills to stipulate the actual location of their burial; for example, the yeoman Symon Folkys requested 'to be buried in the church of seynt Peter thappostelle bifore thymage of seynt Cristofer'.[41] A cost was associated with burial within the church and most testators who requested such a burial bequeathed sums of money to facilitate it. John Judy, who asked to be buried in the Holy Trinity chapel of St Cuthbert's Church in Thetford, left 20s 'to the sayde churche to thentent that I maye be so liconsed ther to be buried for the reysing of a stone ther to leye it ageyn and breking of the erth for my sepulture' while the Mildenhall churchwarden's accounts recorded a number of payments of 6s 8d for 'berying ... in the church'.[42]

The practice of erecting some form of memorial at the burial place had been largely reserved for the very wealthy, however, from the 1460s onwards commemorative brasses were increasingly adopted by people lower down the social scale and in time grave markers in the form of gravestones were also erected within the churchyard.[43] Prior to the Reformation, only a handful of the testators made provision for the erection of a memorial but when they did this, it was an expensive undertaking. John Withall of Newmarket asked that 'myn executours shall bye and provide a grave stone to the value of xxs to be laide upon my grave' and Richard Mores of Chippenham requested that his 'close at

Chevelay be sold to bye two stones to be layde on my faders grave and the other on myn'.[44] A very few of the wealthiest members of society also paid for other physical reminders within the parish church such as inscriptions around the church, the incorporation of a coat-of-arms or merchant's mark in service books, vestments, stained glass or fonts, or even memorial tombs.[45]

Pious bequests

Most examples of religious consumption previously discussed can be considered to be professions of piety. However, late medieval Christians believed that on their own these were insufficient to secure God's grace and that they would also be judged by their benevolence towards the poor and the weak.[46] As a consequence, those who could afford to do so made pious and charitable gifts in accordance with the seven corporal acts of mercy.[47] Significance was attached to all of these acts but particular emphasis was placed on giving alms to the poor. Once again, evidence for such gifts made during life was lacking but wills contained abundant evidence of *post mortem* doles to the poor of various forms including money, clothing, fuel or bread and ale. As the prayers of the deserving poor were considered to be highly beneficial to the soul, many wills encouraged their attendance at funerals through doles which would be distributed at the burial service; for example, Robert Master stipulated in his will that 'there be distributid at my buriall to the prestes and clerkes and to poore folkes in bred and drinke xs' and William Fullere asked his executors to give 13d in alms to the poor on his burial day and on his seventh- and 30-day anniversaries.[48] The practice of giving to the poor survived the Reformation so that in 1551 William Sewster of Godmanchester gave money to be distributed to the poor of Godmanchester, Ashwell, Steeple Morden, Guilden Morden and Abington.[49]

Gifts such as these can clearly be regarded as acts of charity but other categories of charitable donations, such as to bridges and highways and for educational purposes, initially appeared to have been rather more secular. However, benefactors clearly regarded their offerings as analogous to other charitable gifts and considered that they had a religious significance. Eamon Duffy observed that testators made no distinction between gifts of this nature and other works of mercy and this was reflected in testamentary bequests.[50] Bequests to build or maintain roads and bridges in particular were frequent and often of a personal nature in that the highways to which the bequests were made would have been travelled by the testator. Godmanchester wills frequently included bequests for repair and upkeep of roads; John Stukeley gave 20s to every street 'to the reparacions of highways', and William Frost left 40s to repair Arnying Street. Again, bequests such as these continued beyond the Reformation so that in 1540, William Bennet left 26s 8d to repair the road from John Godwyn's bridge to the west end of West Street and in 1545, William Frere left 6s 8d to repair the road in West Street and a further 6s 8d to repair the road in Post Street from the Cross to the Court Hall. Charitable donations for educational purposes could include bequests to educational buildings, to scholars generally or to specific, named individuals.[51]

It is impossible to calculate how much most late medieval people would have spent on ensuring that, post death, their body and soul were properly provided for, however, an inventory has survived from 1484 which recorded the costs associated with the testament and funeral costs of Agnes Mayr of St Albans.[52] This lists expenditure on a range of items which were typical of those made during this period by an affluent person at death including bequests to religious houses, for the maintenance of lights, for inclusion on the bede roll, for a trental, masses and *diriges*, to an anchorite, to priests and clerks, and for food, drink and clothing for poor people. The total amount paid on funeral and other death expenses was recorded as £6 4s 4d, a considerable sum for the period.

Religious consumption in the early modern period

The Reformation brought an end to much religious expenditure associated with the rituals and practices of Roman Catholicism, particularly those which related to belief in purgatory, but also to those connected more generally to relics, pardons and the cult of saints. The Thirty-nine Articles of Religion, the defining statements of doctrine of the Church of England established in 1563, included as Article XXII the assertion that:

> the Romish Doctrine concerning Purgatory, Pardons, Worshipping and Adoration, as well of Images as of Relics, and also Invocation of Saints, is a fond thing, vainly invented, and grounded upon no warranty of Scripture, but rather repugnant to the Word of God.[53]

Many areas associated with religious expenditure traditionally made during life disappeared, such as the socio-religious gilds or pilgrimages to places which held relics or had other associations with saints. However, the largest decline in expenditure was probably on observances associated with death and came about as a combination of the loss of many of the death ceremonies associated with Roman Catholicism and the decline of belief in the practice of purgatory. Payments were no longer made for masses and prayers for the soul and such items as testamentary bequests to religious houses for prayers, to priests to celebrate trentals or to the parish church for inclusion on the bede roll disappeared.

The early modern funeral

However, although expenditure relating to death sacraments and observances dropped away, it is apparent that funeral costs in the early modern period became increasingly significant to the extent that Thomas Laqueur argued that funerals actually became a consumption good.[54] Whilst there was an important difference between funerals and other consumption goods in that the main consumer was a deceased person, many people expressed their wishes about their funeral arrangements before death. These wishes ranged from precise details to general principles to be followed. Nigel Llewellyn cited one devout working person's desire to be 'simply not sumptuously … buried, I require no more'.[55] In practice, the actual purchaser of funeral goods was usually the executor or administrator of the estate and they may have an important influence on the funeral arrangements despite the wishes of the deceased. In a purely material sense, it is worth remembering that the more that was spent on the deceased's funeral, the less remained to be distributed to legatees. The substantial proportions of movable assets spent on funerals showed that consumption could have a broader meaning than merely material goods; it was also about exhibiting status and religious concerns including the desire for a decent Christian burial.

Details about the cost of such funeral rituals can be found in probate accounts. Amy Erickson suggested that funeral amounts were generally between £1 and £2 but varied widely with an individual's wealth. Erickson did not attach dates to her estimates of funeral costs, but she was likely to be referring to the period for which most probate accounts survive, i.e. about 1590–1690.[56] The mean cost of a Huntingdonshire funeral recorded in 249 probate accounts in the quarter century 1675–1700 was £5 and the median £3. The cost of individual funerals ranged from 7s 6d to £106. The range is a crude measure of dispersion and a more useful measure, the standard deviation, was £7.89 (CV=1.58) in Huntingdonshire.

Laqueur argued that there was almost no relationship between costs of seventeenth-century and early eighteenth-century funerals and the size of the deceased's estate and suggested that in this period funerals were a demonstration of status quite independent of their economic position. For Laqueur this situation had changed by the nineteenth century when funerals had become a consumption good. Money now made the man and death became the occasion for a final accounting, a stocktaking of worldly success. Those of relatively low status could have a lavish funeral if they could afford it.[57] Evidence from Huntingdonshire does not support Laqueur's contention that there was almost no relationship between costs of early modern funerals and the size of the deceased's estate. Huntingdonshire accounts showed a significant positive correlation between funeral costs and inventory values (p<0.01). The strength of the relationship was moderate (Pearson correlation coefficient 0.310). These findings concurred with those of Peter Earle who suggested that 'the invasion of commerce into the rites of passage' took place in the seventeenth century when a consumer-oriented mentality drove 'ordinary ranks' to imitate elite society and provided the emerging undertakers with an untapped market.[58] Increased expenditure on funerals led the pamphleteer T.T. Merchant to complain that 'persons of ordinary rank may for the value of fifty pounds make as great a figure as the nobility and the gentry did formerly.'[59] Carl Estabrook suggested that expenditure was related to location and that there was an urban/rural divide in relation to the amounts that people spend on funerals. He noted that in Bristol and its surrounding villages, the funeral expenses of ordinary urban dwellers often exceeded those of the most substantial yeomen.[60]

Despite these exceptions, the elite sought to distinguish themselves from the masses in their funeral customs. For many people, the body would be carried to the grave in a communal parish coffin and then removed for burial just in its shroud.[61] A parish coffin dated from around 1645 can still be seen in the parish church at Easingwold, Yorkshire and there are other later examples still in existence.[62] Cressy commented that people of rank preferred their own personal coffins and 'would not be seen dead' in the common parish box, although it was only the wealthy that could look forward to decomposing in their own wooden box.[63] However, details of funeral expenditure recorded in Huntingdonshire probate accounts did not accord with Cressy's argument because most accounts included expenditure on a coffin with the median value of Huntingdonshire coffins between 1676 and 1688 being 10s. An excavation of a Quaker burial ground in 2006 at Hemingford Grey in Huntingdonshire also suggested that the use of coffins was widespread since all of the bodies interred between 1687 and 1721 were buried in coffins.[64]

Other evidence suggested that the practice of burying bodies in coffins became increasingly widespread; in Kent a coffin was always used for pauper burials from the mid-seventeenth century, whilst paupers in Devon were usually provided with coffins at a cost of 7s 6d at the end of the eighteenth century.[65] In Great Gransden, Huntingdonshire, Overseers of the Poor accounts recorded a coffin costing 10s which was provided for 'an old beggar man found dead under a haycock' in 1680.[66] Overseers of the Poor in both Godmanchester and Kimbolton also provided coffins for some pauper funerals.[67] In Godmanchester, the price of seven coffins for paupers in the three-year period 1787–89 was lower than comparative prices for those recorded in probate accounts. Five coffins cost 9s and the other two cost 6s. In the eighteenth century, coffins were made of wood but covered with fabric, usually baize. Upholstery pins were nailed to the surface of the coffin in various patterns and the coffin was finished with stamped metal motifs which were cheap to produce. Coffins finished in polished wood did not become fashionable until the introduction of French polishing in the mid-nineteenth century.

Funeral expenditure could be on a range of other items and not simply the coffin, particularly for the social elite who wished to ensure that their funerals were set apart from those of the majority of the population; for these people, the funeral ritual adhered strictly to the hierarchical niceties of genteel funerary decorum. Significant amounts could be expended on mourning clothes, particularly pairs of gloves and hatbands which were given to mourners to maintain perceptions of status.[68] The most expensive funeral in the Huntingdonshire probate accounts at £106 5s 10d was that of a clergyman, Francis Barnard of Wyton in 1682.[69] The cost of Barnard's funeral represented 36 per cent of his inventory value. At £5, his coffin was ten times the common sum of 10s and his burial linen was a further £5. Gloves provided for mourners at Barnard's funeral cost £39 15s 8d.[70] This sum is put into perspective by comparison with John Berridge's funeral at Upton in 1722 when 14 pairs of gloves were provided at a cost of 1s per pair.[71] A horse and related charges for Barnard's burial was £4 13s whereas a horse for Francis Marchant's funeral at Stanground in the same year, 1682, cost only 10s.

Parish bells tolled when a person was dying and rang again when the funeral service took place. Tolling of the bell was variously interpreted by Protestant and Catholic but after the restoration of the monarchy in 1660 it symbolised the rehabilitation of the ceremonies of the Church of England. Joyce Jeffries, an elderly single Herefordshire gentlewoman, paid 3s 6d for ringing five peals at the burial of her cousin about 1640 and the Catholic squire William Blundell had ringers to the value of 4s towards the end of the seventeenth century.[72] The range of payments for bell ringing was illustrated in Huntingdonshire where the cost of digging James Cooper's grave and ringing the bell was 2s in 1681 whereas in the following year John Peachey, a gentleman from Needingworth, had ringers costing 10s. Bells also tolled for the poorest in society; in 1789, Overseers of the Poor in Godmanchester provided beer costing 3s and 2s 10d for the toll bearers at the funerals of John Ray and a deceased person recorded as Bright.[73]

Cressy commented that strictly there was no fee for a Christian burial but custom required payment of fees to the church. Only men dying with goods valued at £6 13s 4d or more were required to pay mortuary fees and then only when constrained to do so by local custom. The fee was assessed on a sliding scale from 3s 4d to 10s.[74] John Dickenson's mortuary payment was 10s but Peacock's mortuary in 1682 was only 7s 6d despite the value of their goods being almost the same.[75]

Cressy also suggested that the incidence of funeral sermons was related to social rank, with a simple service without sermon sufficient for most ordinary burials.[76] But for Harold Mytum, sermons became more common from the seventeenth century onwards and followed a set pattern.[77] A text would be expounded to remind mourners of their own mortality and this would be followed by a biography of the deceased. This description of the deceased's character was awaited with keen anticipation; the preacher carefully selected what was good from the person's life and drew a veil over the rest so that he could both satisfy the expectations of the congregation and his own conscience.[78] Clare Gittings suggested that income from funeral sermons was a lucrative business for clergymen. She argued that the usual fee was 10s prior to the Restoration and £1 thereafter, although Ian Mortimer found that most funeral sermons in Berkshire cost 6s 8d or 10s with the higher charge twice as common as the lower. Mortimer speculated that the two figures depended on whether the incumbent preached or whether an external preacher spoke.[79] In Huntingdonshire, fees for funeral sermons were almost always 10s in the last quarter of the seventeenth century and not the higher fee of £1 suggested by Gittings.

One aspect of the funeral ceremony which survived from the medieval period into the early modern was the preparation of the body for burial which involved washing, winding and watching. Neighbouring women and female servants were frequently employed to clean and dress a corpse.[80] Winding the corpse in a sheet or burial shroud was the minimum requirement for a decent burial for only animals were buried naked. Legislation in 1678 required all bodies to be buried in wool in order to support the domestic industry. This was reflected in payments in probate accounts where woollen cloth was expressly recorded although costs varied widely.[81] The woollen sheet for Atkins of Holywell in 1681 cost as much as 18s, whereas cloth to wind the body of James Cooper of Stanground in the same year was only 6s. Overseers of the Poor accounts for Great Gransden recorded affidavits which were sworn to affirm that five paupers were buried in wool in 1678. However, these accounts also recorded two cases where the body was buried in linen: Andrew Lilly in 1682 and Mary Griffin in 1683. Each case incurred a fine of £5, of which half went to the informer and the other half to the poor of the parish.

Cressy argued that the custom of sitting up all night watching the body applied to both rich and poor. The intention was to safeguard the body and to ensure that there was somebody present if the corpse revived. In the late seventeenth century, John Aubrey reported the practice in Yorkshire of watching and sitting up all night until the body was interred while drinking beer, taking tobacco and sometimes engaging in 'mimical plays and sports'.[82] In 1720, women were paid 2s 6d for laying out Henry Careless, a waterman from Godmanchester, and a further 3s 6d was paid for watching the body, victuals and drink for the watchers and for the fire and candle.[83]

William Gouge, one of the most widely read conduct book writers in the seventeenth century, argued in his *Domesticall Duties* that it was the duty of children to bring the bodies of their deceased parents for burial with 'decency and honour'.[84] Testators in Huntingdonshire frequently expressed their concern that their body was given a 'decent Christian burial'. The *Directory of Publique Worship* of 1645, which superseded the Canon of 1603 and lasted until 1660, reflected Puritan teaching that corpses should be immediately interred without any ceremony.[85] The Puritan rector Samuel Hurlstone stipulated in his will of 1616 that his body should be buried 'without any delay after my death, without popish pomp, vain compliments and ringing'.[86] However, being buried 'without pomp' could be variously interpreted. The significant levels of expenditure on funerals recorded in probate accounts could be viewed as avoidance of meanness rather than vanity and ostentation. One example of desire for a simple funeral was that of John Brown of Broughton. His will commended his soul into the hands of Jesus Christ and humbly hoped that he would take care of it. His loving wife Mary Brown was enjoined to bury his body in 'a frugal manner'.[87]

Mortimer found that many individuals in the Berkshire probate accounts were buried within the building of their church although this does not appear to have been the case in either Huntingdonshire or Yorkshire where there were only two references in extant probate accounts to burial inside a church.[88] Both were gentlemen, which conformed to the late medieval preference for those of higher estate to be buried within the church building. The will of Matthew Burgh, gentleman and alderman, required his body to be buried in the parish church of St Augustine in Hedon, Yorkshire, and Robert Ramsden, gentleman, was buried in the parish church of Halifax in 1757. The usual place of burial was the Anglican parish churchyard. Although the unbaptised or suicides were not legally provided for, even these were often buried in an unconsecrated part of the churchyard.[89]

As has been noted, by the end of the medieval period the practice of erecting gravestones was becoming more common and was no longer the preserve of high-status individuals. However, the survival of medieval gravestones is very rare and even the numbers of gravestones that can be dated to the seventeenth century are small. H. Mytum and Kate Chapman argued that this was partly due to erosion of inscriptions of early memorials or because broken stones have been removed. They also suggested that stones may sink into the ground and many early stones are partially buried so that their form and date cannot be easily ascertained.[90] One of the earliest known gravestones in a Huntingdonshire churchyard is that of William Bandol, a yeoman who died in Stilton in 1613 (Photo 6.4).

PHOTO 6.4 Gravestone of William Bandol, 1613

The Huntingdonshire probate accounts revealed that the median expenditure on headstones was 4s 6d in the 1670s but £1 11s 3d in the second half of the eighteenth century. The diary of Thomas Marchant provided an insight into how the costs of headstones were calculated. The diary recorded that the tombstone for Marchant's father cost 3s a foot in 1714 plus 7s 6d for 'squaring him and working the edges' and a further penny a letter for the inscription.[91] Tombstones for the middle ranks varied considerably in both price and quality. John Shawforth, a yeoman from Wheldrake, Yorkshire had a tombstone costing over £12 in 1793. Tombstones were also erected for those of relatively low status. Henry Apthorp, a butcher from St Ives, had a gravestone which cost £2 2s in 1783 and setting his gravestone was a further 6s 8d. His funeral cost £8 4s 9d, 41 per cent of his movable assets. One of the oldest dateable gravestones in Godmanchester churchyard is that of Robert Vinter who died in 1723.[92] The inscription reads, 'Here lyeth the Body of Robert Vinter who dyed February 16th 1723 aged 49' (Photo 6.5).

PHOTO 6.5 Gravestone of Robert Vinter, 1723

Vinter's inventory revealed that he was a tailor with moveable goods valued at £34 8s 6d. Although there was no probate account to give details of his funeral it also probably represented a significant proportion of his assets. When Vinter died he was only 49 years old but perhaps saddest of all is that his moveable goods included three barrels of beer in his buttery worth 16s which he had not got around to drinking!

Evidence suggested that in addition to expenditure on the funeral service and burial, costs could also be incurred on providing appropriate hospitality for mourners. Alan Macfarlane wrote that although seventeenth-century funerals were dignified occasions filled with processions, tears, solemn gestures and lengthy sermons, they were also occasions for feasting and exchange of gifts.[93] Gittings argued that the most striking feature of funeral details contained in probate accounts was the amount of money spent on food and drink.[94] It commonly amounted to half the cost of burying someone and could be as much as three quarters or more of total costs.[95] The amount spent on food and drink for mourners amounted to more than half the total cost of burying someone in over two thirds of Huntingdonshire probate accounts although expenditure varied widely and was not necessarily related to social rank. A barber from Godmanchester, John Dickenson, had goods worth £47 15s when he died in 1676. His funeral cost over £6, which made it more expensive than half of the gentry funerals for which there were surviving records. Two thirds of the cost of Dickenson's funeral was spent on food and drink which included £2 10s on bread and cakes and £1 12s 6d on a hogshead of beer.[96] At Mary Harrison's funeral in St Ives in 1679, £8 was spent on bread, beer and cakes for mourners. An indication of the amount of food that could be purchased for such sums was revealed by Joane Lord's probate account; expenditure on her funeral included 20 dozen cakes at £1 10s and 20 dozen loaves at £1 2s. Although the amounts were significantly smaller than those provided for these funerals, the Overseers of the Poor in Godmanchester and Kimbolton also provided beer for mourners at paupers' funerals. Hospitality for mourners was not necessarily limited to food and drink; tobacco and pipes costing 10s were provided at the funeral of William Proud of Ramsey in 1676.[97]

The relatively poor could also have a decent Christian burial. The limited evidence from probate accounts showed that in Huntingdonshire, the median cost of a funeral for inventoried husbandmen and labourers was no lower than that of the population with surviving probate accounts. The very poorest in society could have a dignified funeral and the use of coffins was widespread.

Conclusion

In the medieval period, death was at the centre of everyday life. A major concern of this life was to prepare for the next and the funeral was therefore an important part of the ritual. Prior to the Reformation, it was commonly believed that the soul entered purgatory at death and people invested considerable sums in hastening the time spent suffering its pains. The Reformation initiated major changes in belief but expenditure on rituals associated with death continued to absorb a relatively high proportion of the deceased's resources. Expenditure on funerals showed that consumption could have a broader meaning than merely material goods. It was also about exhibiting status and religious concerns including the desire for a decent Christian burial. When writing *Martin Chuzzlewit* in 1843, Charles Dickens could still pose the question, 'Why do people spend more money upon a death, Mrs Gamp, than upon a birth?' But the past is indeed a foreign country. Contemporary society focusses on this world and has little confidence in a future judgement. Consumption expenditure at rites of passage has as a result shifted to weddings and their associated hen nights and stag nights rather than funerals.

Notes

1 R. Swanson, *Church and Society in Late Medieval England* (Oxford: Oxford University Press, 1989), p.210.
2 *Ibid.*, p.225.
3 C. Dyer, *Making a Living in the Middle Ages: The People of Britain, 850–1520* (London: Penguin Books, 2003), p.300; B. Kümin, 'The secular legacy of the late medieval English parish', in C. Burgess and E. Duffy (eds), *The Parish in Late Medieval England: Proceedings of the 2002 Harlaxton Symposium* (Harlaxton: Shaun Tyas, 2002), p.100.
4 TNA PROB 11/15/15 (Smyth); HA HK 2455/4/1 (Pelman); TNA PROB 11/15/607 (Aldred).
5 HA, wills of the Archdeaconry of Huntingdonshire, Reg. i, fols 30, 54 (Frost).
6 J. Middleton-Stewart (ed.), *Records of the Churchwardens of Mildenhall: Collections, 1446–1454, Accounts, 1503–1553* (Woodbridge: Boydell Press, 2011), p.xxxvi.
7 *Ibid.*, p.xxxv.
8 E. Duffy, *The Stripping of the Altars: Traditional Religion in England, 1400–1580* (Yale: Yale University Press, 2005), p.31; Middleton-Stewart (ed.), *Records of the Churchwardens of Mildenhall*, p.xliii.
9 *Ibid.*, p.xliv.
10 *Ibid.*, pp.50, 58, 61, 65, 66, 67, 86.
11 TNA PCC PROB 11/14/316 (Mores).
12 Swanson, *Church and Society*, p.258.
13 R. Gilchrist, *Medieval Life: Archaeology and the Life Course* (Woodbridge: Boydell Press, 2014), p.175.
14 NRO NCC Attmere 74 (Ballys).
15 C. Marsh, 'Sacred space in England, 1560–1640: the view from the pew', *The Journal of Ecclesiastical History*, 53 (2002), pp.299–301.
16 D. Palliser, *Towns and Local Communities in Medieval and Early Modern England* (Aldershot: Ashgate, 2006), p.20.
17 D. Underdown, *Fire from Heaven: Life in an English Town in the Seventeenth Century* (Yale: Yale University Press, 1992), p.39.
18 G. Nair, *Highley: The Development of a Community, 1500–1880* (Oxford: Basil Blackwell, 2009), pp.131–33.
19 A. Flather, *The Politics of Place: A Study of Church Seating in Essex c.1580–1640* (Leicester: Leicester Friends of the Department of English Local History, 1999), pp.25, 54.
20 Marsh, 'Sacred space in England', pp.287–307.

21 Swanson, *Church and Society*, p.290; Gilchrist, *Medieval Life*, p.156.
22 R. Swanson, 'Treasuring merit/craving indulgence: accounting for salvation in pre-Reformation England', *Inaugural Lecture delivered on 19 November 2002 in the University of Birmingham* (Birmingham: University of Birmingham, 2003), p.5.
23 Gilchrist, *Medieval Life*, p.96.
24 Swanson, 'Treasuring merit/craving indulgence', p.179; Gilchrist, *Medieval Life*, pp.141, 143, 166.
25 Swanson, 'Treasuring merit/craving indulgence', p.6.
26 Swanson, *Church and Society*, p.255; Gilchrist, *Medieval Life*, p.138.
27 NRO NCC Sayve 13 (Flecher).
28 N. Ramsey, 'Alabaster', in J. Blair and N. Ramsey (eds), *English Medieval Industries: Craftsmen, Techniques, Products* (London: Hambledon Press, 1991), p.38.
29 P. Clark, *British Clubs and Society, 1580–1800: The Origins of an Associational World* (Oxford: Oxford University Press, 2001), p.20.
30 R. Fox, *History of Godmanchester* (London: Baldwin, 1831), p.263.
31 TNA PROB 11/18/92 (Stukeley).
32 Fox, *History of Godmanchester*, pp.268–69.
33 Middleton-Stewart (ed.), *Records of the Churchwardens of Mildenhall*, p.lii.
34 C. Daniell, *Death and Burial in Medieval England* (London: Routledge, 1998), pp.43–44.
35 *Ibid.*, pp.45–47.
36 *Ibid.*, pp.45–48.
37 *Ibid.*, pp.47–48.
38 SROB Baldwyne 298 (Ray); TNA PCC PROB 11/22/339 (Hall) cited in Middleton-Stewart (ed.), *Records of the Churchwardens of Mildenhall*, p.xxxvi.
39 NRO ANW Randes 321 (Carman).
40 N. Rogers, '*Hic Iacet*...: the location of monuments in late medieval parish churches', in Burgess and Duffy (eds), *Parish in Late Medieval England*, p.263.
41 TNA PCC PROB 11/15/718 (Folkys).
42 NRO NCC Godsalve 296 (Judy); Middleton-Stewart (ed.), *Records of the Churchwardens of Mildenhall*, p.49; Rogers noted that the charge levied for opening a grave in the church was usually 6s 8d; Rogers, '*Hic Iacet*', p.262.
43 Duffy, *Stripping of the Altars*, p.332.
44 TNA PCC PROB 11/22/268 (Withall); TNA PCC PROB 11/14/316 (Mores).
45 Rogers, '*Hic Iacet*', p.261.
46 Duffy, *Stripping of the Altars*, p.357.
47 The seven corporal acts of mercy are feeding the hungry, giving drink to the thirsty, giving hospitality to the stranger, visiting the sick, clothing the naked, ransoming prisoners and burying the dead.
48 NRO ANW Bakon 7 (Master); SROB Hervye 175 (Fullere).
49 TNA PCC PROB 11/34/316 (Sewster).
50 Duffy, *Stripping of the Altars*, p.367.
51 Swanson, *Church and Society*, p.304.
52 S. Flood (ed.), *St Albans Wills, 1471–1500: Hertfordshire Record Publications Vol. IX* (Hertfordshire: Hertfordshire Record Publications, 1993), pp.71–72.
53 Many of these issues had been addressed in the first official doctrinal formulary of the Church of England, the Ten Articles of 1536. However, the language used was rather more circumspect; Duffy, *Stripping of the Altars*, pp.392–93.
54 T. Laqueur, 'Bodies, death and pauper funerals', *Representations*, 1 (1983), pp.109–15.
55 N. Llewellyn, *Funeral Monuments in Post-Reformation England* (Cambridge: Cambridge University Press, 2000), pp.237–39.
56 A.L. Erickson, 'Using probate accounts', in T. Arkell, N. Evans and N. Goose (eds), *When Death Do Us Part: Understanding and Interpreting the Probate Records of Early Modern England* (Oxford: Leopard's Head Press, 2000), p.108.

57 Laqueur, 'Bodies, death and pauper funerals', pp.109–15.
58 P. Earle, *The Making of the English Middle Class: Business, Society and Family Life in London, 1660–1730* (London: Methuen, 1991), p.79.
59 P.S. Fritz, 'The undertaking trade in England: its origins and early development, 1660–1830', *Eighteenth-Century Studies*, 28 (1994–1995), p.246.
60 C. Estabrook, *Urbane and Rustic England: Cultural Ties and Social Spheres in the Provinces 1660–1780* (Manchester: Manchester University Press, 1998), p.153.
61 C. Gittings, 'Sacred and secular: 1558–1660', in P. Jupp and C. Gittings (eds), *Death in England: An Illustrated History* (Manchester: Manchester University Press, 1999), p.157; D. Cressy, *Birth, Marriage and Death: Ritual Religion and the Life-Cycle in Tudor and Stuart England* (Oxford: Oxford University Press, 1997), pp.432–43.
62 J. Litten, *The English Way of Death: The Common Funeral Since 1450* (London: Robert Hale, 1991), p.97.
63 Cressy, *Birth, Marriage and Death*, pp.430–44.
64 M. Pitts, 'Compassion revealed in Quaker finds', *British Archaeology*, 95 (2007), p.6.
65 C. Gittings, *Death, Burial and the Individual in Early Modern England* (London: Croom Helm, 1984), p.61; P. Sharpe. *Population and Society in an East Devon Parish: Reproducing Colyton 1540–1840* (Exeter: University of Exeter Press, 2002), p.298.
66 HA HP 36/12/1, Great Gransden Overseers of the Poor accounts.
67 HA HP 34/12/2/1, Godmanchester Overseers of the Poor accounts; HA HP 52/12/5, Kimbolton Overseers of the Poor accounts.
68 M. Finn, 'Men's things: masculine possession in the consumer revolution', *Social History*, 25 (2) (2000), p.148.
69 Francis Barnard was almost certainly a member of the prominent Barnard family of Brampton Park, Huntingdonshire. Edward, earl of Manchester, sold the manor of Houghton and Wyton to Robert Bernard of Brampton Park in 1651, W. Page, G. Proby and S. Inskip Ladds (eds), *Victoria County History, A History of the County of Huntingdon Volume 2* (London: St Catherine Press, 1932), p.179. Following his funeral on 19 December 1679, the Wyton parish register recorded that Francis Barnard's body was transferred to Brampton for burial, HA HP 101/1/1/1.
70 HA AH 19/2/100.
71 HA AH 19/4/28.
72 Cressy, *Birth, Marriage and Death*, pp.421–44.
73 HA AH 19/2/6; HA AH 19/2/95; HA HP 34/8.
74 *Ibid.*, pp.456–57.
75 HA AH 19/1/39; HA AH 19/2/98.
76 *Ibid.*, p.408.
77 H. Mytum, *Mortuary Monuments and Burial Grounds of the Historic Period* (Oxford: Oxford University Press, 1994), p.14.
78 R. Houlbrooke, 'The age of decency 1660–1760', in Jupp and Gittings, *Death in England*, p.188.
79 Gittings, *Death, Burial and the Individual*, p.138; I. Mortimer, *Berkshire Probate Accounts 1583–1712: The Berkshire Record Society* (Reading: Berkshire Record Office, 1999), pp.xix–xx.
80 Cressy, *Birth, Marriage and Death*, p.428.
81 C. Willett and P. Cunnington, *The History of Underclothes* (New York: Dover Publications Inc., 1992), p.55.
82 Cressy, *Birth, Marriage and Death*, p.427.
83 HA AH 19/4/25.
84 *Ibid.*, p.415.
85 R. Schofield, 'Monday's child is fair of face: favoured days for baptism, marriage and burial in pre-industrial England', *Continuity and Change*, 20 (2005), p.98.
86 J. Spurr, *The Post-Reformation: Religion, Politics and Society in Britain, 1603–1714* (Harlow: Longman, 2006), p.292.

87 HA AH 16 1752/14. The motivation for the frugal burial was not clear. Whilst John Brown was recorded as a labourer, the substantial bequests in his will did not suggest that frugality was economically determined. Brown had at least a measure of literacy for he signed the will and his soul was bequeathed into the hands of Jesus Christ in a strongly Protestant formulation.

88 Mortimer, *Berkshire Probate Accounts*, p.xix.

89 J. Morgan, 'The burial question in Leeds in the eighteenth and nineteenth centuries', in R. Houlbrooke (ed.), *Death, Ritual and Bereavement* (London: Routledge, 1989), p.95.

90 H. Mytum and K. Chapman, 'The origin of the graveyard headstone: some 17th-century examples in Bedfordshire', *Church Archaeology*, 7–9 (2006), p.67.

91 A. Bower (ed.), *A Fine Day in Hurstpierpoint – the Diary of Thomas Marchant 1714–1728* (Hurstpierpoint: Hurst History Study Group, 2005), p.8.

92 There are a number of gravestones in the churchyard where the inscription has disappeared and have not been dated.

93 A. Macfarlane, *The Family Life of Ralph Josselin, a Seventeenth-Century Clergyman: An Essay in Historical Anthropology* (New York: Norton, 1976), p.100.

94 C. Gittings, 'Probate accounts: a neglected source', *The Local Historian*, 21 (1991), p.53.

95 Gittings, *Death, Burial and the Individual*, p.97.

96 HA AH 19.

97 *Ibid.*

7

WHEN AND WHERE DID THE CONSUMER REVOLUTION TAKE PLACE?

At the beginning of the period covered by this study, England was a heavily rural country with limited urbanisation and an economy predominantly based on agriculture. There was a very low level of domestic industry associated with both agricultural production (such as rudimentary tools, ropes and harnesses for animals, ploughs and carts, etc.) and some household necessities.[1] By 1800, the country had been transformed. An industrial revolution was taking place, even if contemporaries were unaware of it, and the homes of much of the population boasted a range of goods that were not to be found in them a century earlier. This chapter addresses the key questions of when consumer change took place and whether there was a consumer *revolution* or gradual change over a long period of time.

In their highly influential work in which they suggested that a consumer revolution began in the eighteenth century, Neil McKendrick, John Brewer and Jack Plumb referred to the expansion of consumption as being 'the necessary analogue to the industrial revolution, the necessary convulsion on the demand side of the equation to match the convulsion on the supply side'.[2] In doing so, they defined that for a 'consumer revolution' to have taken place there needed to be significant and dramatic changes to levels of demand. Such increased levels of demand would have manifested themselves in a variety of different ways: in particular, any 'revolution' should be seen to have impacted on all levels of society so that an increased ownership of consumer goods reached down the social scale and affected the lives of most and not just the wealthy; in addition, this increased consumption should have encompassed ownership of a wide level of goods and included better-quality and luxury goods as well as simple necessities; and, finally, this increased level of demand would be reflected back into the supply side so that it was apparent that suppliers had responded to increased levels of demand by expanding the range and types of goods available to consumers.[3]

On the basis of the evidence presented in this study, there was little to suggest that the dramatic changes to levels of ownership indicative of a 'consumer revolution' occurred in the late medieval period, as there was no evidence that a significantly increased ownership of consumer goods had spread down the social scale and engulfed all social groups. Despite this, consumption patterns were changing although this largely related to significant dietary improvements. However, increasingly, material goods were purchased by middle-tier income households and more frequently by higher-tier income households in the form of bedding and cooking utensils and, subsequently, furniture and furnishings. More luxury goods were also being purchased although ownership of these items remained largely exclusive to higher-tier income households. This extension in consumption was gradual and piecemeal and in itself did not justify the term 'revolution'; it was a period of gestation before much greater change.[4]

McKendrick called for 'detailed quantitative work' on probate inventories to provide evidence on English consumption patterns. Two major studies following his call were provided by Lorna Weatherill in 1988 and Mark Overton, Jane Whittle, Darron Dean and Andrew Hann in 2004. Weatherill's study, *Consumer Behaviour and Material Culture, 1660–1760*, was based on 2,902 probate inventories from eight regions.[5] Overton *et al.*'s *Production and Consumption in English Households, 1600–1750* covered Cornwall and Kent but was based on a much larger sample of about 8,000 inventories, approximately 4,000 from each county.[6] Neither study supported the McKendrick thesis of a consumer revolution in the latter part of the eighteenth century. They found that there was a widespread expansion of consumer goods in the seventeenth and first half of the eighteenth centuries rather than in the latter part of the eighteenth century.

There were issues associated with both of these studies. Both rejected McKendrick's postulated 'consumer revolution', yet Weatherill's study only covered the period up to 1725 and the study by Overton *et al.* only covered the period to 1750. Their research did not, therefore, cover the vital period after 1750. Furthermore, Overton *et al.* had few primary sources for Kent in the 1730s and 1740; for example, only 27 inventories survived from their 28 Kent parishes in the 1740s, less than 1 per cent of their total sample.[7] A further problem related to people at the lower end of the social scale, because of the inherent bias in using probate inventories; they largely relate to 'the middling sort'. Labourers were significantly underrepresented. Weatherill recognised this and did not attempt a study of society as a whole but people of middle rank. She had only 26 labourers in her sample of 2,902 inventories and Overton *et al.* also had a very low percentage of labourers.[8] The present study seeks to address these problems by the inclusion in the selected sample of over 1,100 inventories covering the second half of the eighteenth century and also over 350 labourers' inventories.

Overton *et al.*'s study charted the beginnings of consumer change in the early modern period. In the first third of the seventeenth century, very few of the selected consumer goods were to be found even in Kent. By the period 1660–89, 18 per cent of inventoried persons owned clocks and looking glasses in Kent (Tables 7.1 and 7.4). By choosing Kent and Cornwall, Overton *et al.* revealed the opposite ends of the consumption spectrum in England. Kent was in the vanguard of the new consumer society which was largely absent from Cornwall. Joyce Ellis was therefore correct to suggest that the term 'consumer revolution' was inappropriate for the years between 1660 and 1688, since the bulk of the population were not yet regular consumers of a wide range of goods.[9] However, towards the end of the seventeenth century, wider ownership of certain goods began to take place and this was captured by Weatherill's study which commenced in 1675.

This volume presents new evidence from agricultural counties, Huntingdon-shire and Dorset, from Yorkshire in the heartland of industrial change and 13 other locations both urban and rural. For the first time, it sheds light on the vital period after 1750. In Huntingdonshire, consumer change began around the turn of the century and took place largely in the eighteenth century. Not all consumer goods followed the same chronologies of change; ownership of warm-ing pans rose steadily from just 3 per cent in the sixteenth century to a half of all inventories by the end of the study period (Table 7.9). Some goods such as looking glasses began to be more widely owned in the first half of the eight-eenth century (Table 7.4). When Kent was included in the analysis, ownership of pictures trebled after 1690 and they were commonly found on the walls of homes in urban centres such as Bristol, where they were recorded in nearly two thirds of inventories (Table 7.5).

The 'take off' in ownership of other goods like clocks, knives and forks and goods associated with hot drinks did not occur in Huntingdonshire, Dorset and Yorkshire until the second half of the eighteenth century, during the period of 'McKendricks's consumer revolution'. After 1750, approaching half (46 per cent) of the entire sample of probate inventories recorded a clock. Only inventoried people in Gloucestershire and Shropshire had ownership levels for clocks below 40 per cent. Huntingdonshire (55 per cent) and Dorset (51 per cent) had very similar levels of ownership for clocks by the second half of the eighteenth century as Kent had achieved a generation before. The new evidence also showed that ownership of clocks continued to rise in Kent, rapidly reaching more than three quarters (77 per cent) of the inventoried population by the end of the century (Table 7.1). The new data presented in this chapter and Chapter 9 supports Maxine Berg's suggestion that clocks were not so expensive that only elites could afford them. It contradicts assertions by Norman Pounds that clocks did not penetrate lower than petty burgesses and yeomen until much later and by E. P. Thompson that no labourer could have afforded a clock in the mid-eighteenth century.[10] However, it must be recognised that, as Sara Pennell

TABLE 7.1 Ownership of clocks over time and by location

	1551–99	1600–29	1630–59	1660–89	1690–1719	1720–49	1750–1800
	%	%	%	%	%	%	%
Huntingdonshire	N/A	0	1	2	13	22	55
Yorkshire	N/A	N/A	N/A	N/A	16	27	43
Dorset	N/A	0	0	1	9	13	51
Bristol	N/A	0	0	12	9	35	53
Southampton	0	N/A	N/A	N/A	N/A	N/A	N/A
Lincoln	N/A	N/A	N/A	10	11	N/A	N/A
Ipswich	0	3	N/A	N/A	N/A	N/A	N/A
Marlborough	0	2	0	0	3	19	N/A
Gloucs	N/A	0	0	5	19	27	32
Essex	N/A	N/A	0	8	26	26	N/A
Cheshire	0	1	5	N/A	N/A	N/A	N/A
Surrey	0	0	N/A	N/A	N/A	N/A	N/A
Warwickshire	0	0	0	33	10	60	N/A
Shropshire	N/A	N/A	N/A	7	18	39	39
Sussex	N/A	0	0	2	6	60	N/A
All 15 locations*	0	0	1	4	14	25	46
Cornwall	N/A	0	0	1	2	9	N/A
Kent	N/A	1	1	18	41	54	77
Bucks-PC	N/A	N/A	N/A	33	39	N/A	N/A

* excluding Kent, Cornwall and Bucks

pointed out, aggregating different types of consumer goods using quantitative analysis obscures the differences between them, including their age and quality.[11] Unfortunately, probate sources only rarely specified this information.

For knives and forks, again Huntingdonshire had exactly the same level of ownership post-1750 as the inventoried population of Kent after 1720. After 1750, levels in Kent more than doubled and the very rapid growth in Dorset reached almost the same level as Kent (Table 7.2). Ownership of goods associated with new hot drinks (tea and coffee) quadrupled. Even in Kent and Bristol, areas where ownership of these goods had been relatively high, it roughly tripled amongst the inventoried population after 1750. In Dorset, ownership of these goods rose from 2 per cent in 1720–49 to 47 per cent after 1750 (Table 7.3).[12]

The new evidence, when added to that for Kent and Cornwall, calculated by Overton *et al.*, showed a consumption pattern for these goods beginning in the richer south-east of England and spreading out to the rest of the country during the eighteenth century. Urban centres were exceptions to this pattern and the impact of urbanisation upon consumption is explored towards the end of this chapter. Whilst McKendrick was a little too narrow in confining change to the third quarter of the eighteenth century, the evidence revealed very rapid growth in ownership of important new consumer goods amongst the inventoried population in the second half of the century. The following tables summarise the results from the inventory analysis of other goods with different patterns of change.

Ownership of looking glasses and pictures roughly doubled in the eighteenth century but the increase in ownership largely took place in the earlier part of the century (Tables 7.4 and 7.5). These levels of ownership were generally lower than that found by Henry French in the north-west of England, and by Weatherill in London and East Kent, except in urban locations.[13] Ownership of looking glasses and window curtains (Table 7.6) was particularly high in the more urban communities of Bristol, Lincoln and Marlborough. There was a gradual increase in ownership of warming pans to reach 50 per cent of inventoried persons by the second half of the eighteenth century (Table 7.9). The highest levels of ownership were in Marlborough, Shropshire and Dorset.

Some more traditional goods showed little change in ownership. Pewter was owned by around 80 per cent of inventoried persons from the sixteenth until the mid-eighteenth centuries. After 1750, recording of pewter started to fall which is consistent with Hatcher and Barker's suggestion that ownership began to fall from the mid-century.[14] Hatcher and Barker ascribed this fall, at least in part, to the rise of the pottery industry associated with the consumption of hot drinks, however, ownership of pewter would still have been 79 per cent if the spectacular fall in Gloucestershire were to be excluded from the overall results (Table 7.7).[15]

TABLE 7.2 Ownership of knives and forks over time and by location

	1551–99	1600–29	1630–59	1660–89	1690–1719	1720–49	1750–1800
	%	%	%	%	%	%	%
Huntingdonshire	N/A	0	0	0	3	3	13
Yorkshire	N/A	N/A	N/A	N/A	1	1	7
Dorset	N/A	0	0	0	1	2	30
Bristol	N/A	0	0	0	5	26	40
Southampton	0	N/A	N/A	N/A	N/A	N/A	N/A
Lincoln	N/A	N/A	N/A	12	5	N/A	N/A
Ipswich	0	0	N/A	N/A	N/A	N/A	N/A
Marlborough	0	0	0	0	2	15	N/A
Gloucs	N/A	0	0	1	1	1	0
Essex	N/A	N/A	0	1	2	10	N/A
Cheshire	0	0	0	N/A	N/A	N/A	N/A
Surrey	0	0	N/A	N/A	N/A	N/A	N/A
Warwickshire	0	0	0	0	0	0	0
Shropshire	N/A	N/A	N/A	0	4	6	0
Sussex	N/A	0	0	0	0	10	N/A
All 15 locations	0	0	1	2	2	3	12
Cornwall	N/A	0	0	0	0	3	N/A
Kent	N/A	0	0	1	5	13	34
Bucks–PC	N/A	N/A	N/A	2	16	N/A	N/A

TABLE 7.3 Ownership of hot drinks over time and by location

	1551–99	1600–29	1630–59	1660–89	1690–1719	1720–49	1750–1800
	%	%	%	%	%	%	%
Huntingdonshire	N/A	0	0	0	4	12	31
Yorkshire	N/A	N/A	N/A	N/A	0	4	16
Dorset	N/A	0	0	0	0	2	47
Bristol	N/A	0	0	2	2	26	73
Southampton	0	N/A	N/A	N/A	N/A	N/A	N/A
Lincoln	N/A	N/A	N/A	5	11	N/A	N/A
Ipswich	0	0	N/A	N/A	N/A	N/A	N/A
Marlborough	0	0	0	0	3	30	N/A
Gloucs	N/A	0	0	0	1	1	18
Essex	N/A	N/A	0	0	0	16	N/A
Cheshire	0	0	0	N/A	N/A	N/A	N/A
Surrey	0	0	N/A	N/A	N/A	N/A	N/A
Warwickshire	0	0	0	0	0	20	N/A
Shropshire	N/A	N/A	N/A	0	1	4	4
Sussex	N/A	0	0	0	0	5	N/A
All 15 locations	0	0	0	0	1	6	25
Cornwall	N/A	0	0	0	0	6	N/A
Kent	N/A	0	0	0	4	27	73
Bucks-PC	N/A	N/A	N/A	1	19	N/A	N/A

TABLE 7.4 Ownership of looking glasses over time and by location

	1551–99	1600–29	1630–59	1660–89	1690–1719	1720–49	1750–1800
	%	%	%	%	%	%	%
Huntingdonshire	N/A	3	1	6	27	39	42
Yorkshire	N/A	N/A	N/A	N/A	19	22	20
Dorset	N/A	5	0	6	17	17	45
Bristol	N/A	17	27	53	60	71	73
Southampton	12	N/A	N/A	N/A	N/A	N/A	N/A
Lincoln	N/A	N/A	N/A	44	58	N/A	N/A
Ipswich	10	14	0	N/A	N/A	N/A	N/A
Marlborough	0	6	5	18	27	63	N/A
Gloucs	N/A	3	3	10	16	19	23
Essex	N/A	N/A	0	11	36	29	N/A
Cheshire	0	3	5	N/A	N/A	N/A	N/A
Surrey	1	0	N/A	N/A	N/A	N/A	N/A
Warwickshire	0	0	0	50	10	30	N/A
Shropshire	N/A	N/A	N/A	12	23	28	30
Sussex	N/A	0	0	5	6	25	N/A
All 15 locations	3	5	5	14	23	26	30
Cornwall	N/A	1	1	4	4	8	N/A
Kent	N/A	3	10	18	36	52	55
Bucks-PC	N/A	N/A	N/A	28	61	N/A	N/A

TABLE 7.5 Ownership of pictures over time and by location

	1551–99	1600–29	1630–59	1660–89	1690–1719	1720–49	1750–1800
	%	%	%	%	%	%	%
Huntingdonshire	N/A	3	1	1	4	18	20
Yorkshire	N/A	N/A	N/A	N/A	7	11	9
Dorset	N/A	1	0	2	2	2	18
Bristol	N/A	11	24	30	19	65	60
Southampton	8	N/A	N/A	N/A	N/A	N/A	N/A
Lincoln	N/A	N/A	N/A	20	42	N/A	N/A
Ipswich	3	8	N/A	N/A	N/A	N/A	N/A
Marlborough	0	0	0	2	8	48	N/A
Gloucs	N/A	3	0	6	2	2	9
Essex	N/A	N/A	0	2	0	6	N/A
Cheshire	0	6	5	N/A	N/A	N/A	N/A
Surrey	1	4	N/A	N/A	N/A	N/A	N/A
Warwickshire	0	0	0	17	0	30	N/A
Shropshire	N/A	N/A	N/A	1	8	20	17
Sussex	N/A	0	0	0	0	5	N/A
All 15 locations	2	4	4	5	6	12	14
Cornwall	N/A	0	0	0	1	4	N/A
Kent	N/A	2	6	5	6	25	31
Bucks-PC	N/A	N/A	N/A	13	39	N/A	N/A

TABLE 7.6 Ownership of window curtains over time and by location

	1551–99	1600–29	1630–59	1660–89	1690–1719	1720–49	1750–1800
	%	%	%	%	%	%	%
Huntingdonshire	N/A	1	6	4	12	14	13
Yorkshire	N/A	N/A	N/A	N/A	8	6	3
Dorset	N/A	1	0	0	3	2	13
Bristol	N/A	4	18	12	19	45	67
Southampton	14	N/A	N/A	N/A	N/A	N/A	N/A
Lincoln	N/A	N/A	N/A	22	42	N/A	N/A
Ipswich	0	0	N/A	N/A	N/A	N/A	N/A
Marlborough	0	6	2	4	9	48	N/A
Gloucs	N/A	0	0	2	3	4	0
Essex	N/A	N/A	0	5	20	23	N/A
Cheshire	6	7	9	N/A	N/A	N/A	N/A
Surrey	3	4	N/A	N/A	N/A	N/A	N/A
Warwickshire	0	0	0	0	0	20	N/A
Shropshire	N/A	N/A	N/A	1	6	8	4
Sussex	N/A	0	0	2	6	0	N/A
All 15 locations	4	3	5	4	8	9	8
Cornwall	N/A	0	0	0	1	1	N/A
Kent	N/A	6	8	11	16	22	38
Bucks-PC	N/A	N/A	N/A	22	45	N/A	N/A

TABLE 7.7 Ownership of pewter over time and by location

	1551–99	1600–29	1630–59	1660–89	1690–1719	1720–49	1750–1800
	%	%	%	%	%	%	%
Huntingdonshire	N/A	80	78	81	82	79	63
Dorset	N/A	43	65	75	88	89	80
Bristol	N/A	89	92	92	78	77	73
Southampton	76	N/A	N/A	N/A	N/A	N/A	N/A
Lincoln	N/A	N/A	N/A	90	84	N/A	N/A
Ipswich	90	78	N/A	N/A	N/A	N/A	N/A
Marlborough	83	74	82	90	88	81	N/A
Gloucs	N/A	78	83	86	88	69	32
Essex	N/A	N/A	77	88	88	81	N/A
Cheshire	94	95	98	N/A	N/A	N/A	N/A
Surrey	80	98	N/A	N/A	N/A	N/A	N/A
Warwickshire	67	56	83	83	70	90	N/A
Shropshire	N/A	N/A	N/A	93	83	84	83
Sussex	N/A	82	77	88	88	95	N/A
14 locations	80	80	82	86	85	84	71
Cornwall	N/A	46	71	87	90	95	N/A
Kent	N/A	94	93	94	95	90	83
Bucks-PC	N/A	N/A	N/A	92	94	N/A	N/A

Ownership of silver remained fairly constant at around a fifth of the inventoried population after 1600, although ownership was much higher in the urban areas of Bristol, Lincoln and Marlborough (Table 7.13). Levels of ownership were similar to Weatherill's results with much higher ownership in urban centres than rural locations.[16] Between 40 and 50 per cent of inventories recorded featherbeds during the study period (Table 7.11) although much higher levels of ownership of featherbeds were recorded in the latter sixteenth and early seventeenth centuries in the urban centres of Southampton and Ipswich. Bed curtains were recorded in just over a third of inventories after 1660 but ownership fell back again during the eighteenth century (Table 7.10).

Some data required careful interpretation. Recording of books rose towards a peak in the mid-seventeenth century and then fell back to almost sixteenth-century levels (Table 7.8). This was very unlikely to reflect changes in book ownership in the light of the rapid increase in the production of books, particularly after the collapse of the Licensing Act in 1695 (Chapter 5). It is probably a failure to record books separately as prices fell and they became more commonly owned.

Increasing ownership of chairs and more rapidly falling ownership of stools and forms were revealed in probate inventory data (Tables 7.14, 7.15 and 7.16). Whilst two thirds of inventories (67 per cent) recorded forms in the second half of the sixteenth century, less than one in ten (7 per cent) did so by the second half of the eighteenth century. Ownership of stools more than halved (from 49 per cent to 23 per cent) over the same period. The tables only record incidence of ownership. This is not the only measure of change. As Overton *et al.* pointed out, people owned greater numbers of chairs rising from a median of one to six in Cornwall and from three to 13 in Kent between 1600–29 and 1720–49.[17] Similarly in Huntingdonshire, chair ownership rose from two to a median of ten by 1720–49.

Below county level, there were wide variations in ownership of goods. Lawrence Robinson carried out a study of Whitehaven and Workington in Weatherill's poorest county, Cumbria.[18] Although the sample of inventories was small, there were much higher levels of ownership of goods in Whitehaven than in Workington. For example, looking glasses were recorded in 30 per cent of inventories in Whitehaven compared to only 5 per cent in Workington for the years 1676 to 1686. In Sear and Sneath's sample of inventories, 542 related to the years 1676 to 1686 and 19 per cent of these inventories recorded looking glasses. Thus, on the measure of looking glass ownership, Whitehaven was considerably above average. Consumer goods and pockets of relative affluence could therefore exist in even the poorest regions. Overton *et al.* also found that material wealth varied quite widely between parishes in Cornwall. Some of the poorest parishes were mining areas and there was a general tendency for east Cornwall to be richer than the west of the county. However, where a low proportion of households were involved in commercial agriculture, they tended to be poorer.[19]

TABLE 7.8 Ownership of books over time and by location

	1551–99	1600–29	1630–59	1660–89	1690–1719	1720–49	1750–1800
	%	%	%	%	%	%	%
Huntingdonshire	N/A	11	21	11	12	11	4
Yorkshire	N/A	N/A	N/A	N/A	16	10	8
Dorset	N/A	12	25	15	15	12	21
Bristol	N/A	50	56	37	34	48	67
Southampton	12	N/A	N/A	N/A	N/A	N/A	N/A
Lincoln	N/A	N/A	N/A	37	21	N/A	N/A
Ipswich	19	50	N/A	N/A	N/A	N/A	N/A
Marlborough	0	19	26	31	24	37	N/A
Gloucs	N/A	11	24	12	13	12	5
Essex	N/A	N/A	12	22	34	3	N/A
Cheshire	18	17	43	N/A	N/A	N/A	N/A
Surrey	6	13	N/A	N/A	N/A	N/A	N/A
Warwickshire	8	11	33	33	10	10	N/A
Shropshire	N/A	N/A	N/A	17	26	14	4
Sussex	N/A	12	10	14	13	0	N/A
All 15 locations	8	18	28	19	17	12	11
Cornwall	N/A	9	10	8	6	8	N/A
Kent	N/A	19	31	25	25	20	25
Bucks–PC	N/A	N/A	N/A	42	52	N/A	N/A

TABLE 7.9 Ownership of warning pans over time and by location

	1551–99	1600–29	1630–59	1660–89	1690–1719	1720–49	1750–1800
	%	%	%	%	%	%	%
Huntingdonshire	N/A	18	23	36	41	46	38
Dorset	N/A	1	2	25	41	43	59
Bristol	N/A	7	32	42	50	55	47
Southampton	1	N/A	N/A	N/A	N/A	N/A	N/A
Lincoln	N/A	N/A	N/A	56	47	N/A	N/A
Ipswich	10	39	N/A	N/A	N/A	N/A	N/A
Marlborough	0	17	37	44	39	67	N/A
Gloucs	N/A	3	3	17	24	32	23
Essex	N/A	N/A	27	46	50	48	N/A
Cheshire	0	2	14	N/A	N/A	N/A	N/A
Surrey	4	13	N/A	N/A	N/A	N/A	N/A
Warwickshire	0	0	50	83	40	70	N/A
Shropshire	N/A	N/A	N/A	26	32	42	65
Sussex	N/A	24	16	40	44	75	N/A
14 locations	3	10	20	35	38	45	50
Bucks-PC	N/A	N/A	N/A	37	61	N/A	N/A

TABLE 7.10 Ownership of bed curtains over time and by location

	1551–99	1600–29	1630–59	1660–89	1690–1719	1720–49	1750–1800
	%	%	%	%	%	%	%
Huntingdonshire	N/A	9	18	30	44	40	32
Yorkshire	N/A	N/A	N/A	N/A	23	19	9
Dorset	N/A	1	0	14	17	10	22
Bristol	N/A	54	79	74	64	65	33
Southampton	67	N/A	N/A	N/A	N/A	N/A	N/A
Lincoln	N/A	N/A	N/A	68	68	N/A	N/A
Ipswich	19	39	N/A	N/A	N/A	N/A	N/A
Marlborough	17	13	9	34	46	67	N/A
Gloucs	N/A	14	14	22	21	13	23
Essex	N/A	N/A	31	58	76	48	N/A
Cheshire	6	8	20	N/A	N/A	N/A	N/A
Surrey	10	15	N/A	N/A	N/A	N/A	N/A
Warwickshire	8	11	50	67	50	60	N/A
Shropshire	N/A	N/A	N/A	20	21	28	61
Sussex	N/A	0	3	30	31	20	N/A
All 15 locations	21	14	22	35	31	24	18
Kent	N/A	N/A	N/A	N/A	N/A	N/A	18
Bucks-PC	N/A	N/A	N/A	73	68	N/A	N/A

TABLE 7.11 Ownership of featherbeds over time and by location

	1551–99	1600–29	1630–59	1660–89	1690–1719	1720–49	1750–1800
	%	%	%	%	%	%	%
Huntingdonshire	N/A	34	46	46	52	58	40
Dorset	N/A	36	63	44	48	42	46
Bristol	N/A	59	76	66	55	52	60
Southampton	85	N/A	N/A	N/A	N/A	N/A	N/A
Lincoln	N/A	N/A	N/A	73	74	N/A	N/A
Ipswich	84	86	N/A	N/A	N/A	N/A	N/A
Marlborough	39	37	40	54	45	44	N/A
Gloucs	N/A	39	31	33	27	9	9
Essex	N/A	N/A	65	76	76	48	N/A
Cheshire	47	25	23	N/A	N/A	N/A	N/A
Surrey	42	52	N/A	N/A	N/A	N/A	N/A
Warwickshire	42	56	50	50	40	60	N/A
Shropshire	N/A	N/A	N/A	51	44	39	52
Sussex	N/A	35	52	60	44	55	N/A
14 locations	53	41	48	52	46	42	43
Cornwall	N/A	33	32	29	28	26	N/A
Kent	N/A	44	48	55	62	51	N/A
Bucks-PC	N/A	N/A	N/A	71	65	N/A	N/A

TABLE 7.12 Ownership of chests over time and by location

	1551–99	1600–29	1630–59	1660–89	1690–1719	1720–49	1750–1800
	%	%	%	%	%	%	%
Huntingdonshire	N/A	82	82	75	76	79	61
Dorset	N/A	97	79	88	80	82	80
Bristol	N/A	83	87	76	62	74	73
Southampton	96	N/A	N/A	N/A	N/A	N/A	N/A
Lincoln	N/A	N/A	N/A	83	89	N/A	N/A
Ipswich	97	94	N/A	N/A	N/A	N/A	N/A
Marlborough	89	91	96	87	83	96	N/A
Gloucs	N/A	76	85	79	76	56	27
Essex	N/A	N/A	92	70	64	48	N/A
Cheshire	76	83	75	N/A	N/A	N/A	N/A
Surrey	80	91	N/A	N/A	N/A	N/A	N/A
Warwickshire	92	89	67	100	80	100	N/A
Shropshire	N/A	N/A	N/A	84	85	86	87
Sussex	N/A	76	87	86	100	90	N/A
14 locations	84	86	84	80	78	79	71
Bucks-PC	N/A	N/A	N/A	83	83	N/A	N/A

TABLE 7.13 Ownership of silver over time and by location

	1551–99	1600–29	1630–59	1660–89	1690–1719	1720–49	1750–1800
	%	%	%	%	%	%	%
Huntingdonshire	N/A	10	8	9	19	16	26
Yorkshire	N/A	N/A	N/A	N/A	22	14	14
Dorset	N/A	11	15	10	18	16	32
Bristol	N/A	28	61	52	55	48	80
Southampton	45	N/A	N/A	N/A	N/A	N/A	N/A
Lincoln	N/A	N/A	N/A	51	42	N/A	N/A
Ipswich	19	42	N/A	N/A	N/A	N/A	N/A
Marlborough	17	19	19	15	20	41	N/A
Gloucs	N/A	14	17	21	19	14	9
Essex	N/A	N/A	12	20	18	19	N/A
Cheshire	18	34	45	N/A	N/A	N/A	N/A
Surrey	4	11	N/A	N/A	N/A	N/A	N/A
Warwickshire	16	11	17	17	10	20	N/A
Shropshire	N/A	N/A	N/A	19	11	10	4
Sussex	N/A	6	0	21	13	25	N/A
All 15 locations	14	19	21	19	20	16	21
Kent	N/A	N/A	N/A	N/A	N/A	N/A	43
Bucks–PC	N/A	N/A	N/A	50	55	N/A	N/A

TABLE 7.14 Ownership of chairs over time and by location

	1551–99	1600–29	1630–59	1660–89	1690–1719	1720–49	1750–1800
	%	%	%	%	%	%	%
Huntingdonshire	N/A	66	63	73	81	80	71
Yorkshire	N/A	N/A	N/A	N/A	78	74	60
Dorset	N/A	35	47	53	67	65	75
Bristol	N/A	67	87	89	79	77	80
Southampton	81	N/A	N/A	N/A	N/A	N/A	N/A
Lincoln	N/A	N/A	N/A	93	89	N/A	N/A
Ipswich	84	86	N/A	N/A	N/A	N/A	N/A
Marlborough	56	56	56	78	68	89	N/A
Gloucs	N/A	48	56	68	67	49	23
Essex	N/A	N/A	81	87	92	77	N/A
Cheshire	47	71	82	N/A	N/A	N/A	N/A
Surrey	48	74	N/A	N/A	N/A	N/A	N/A
Warwickshire	83	78	50	83	80	90	N/A
Shropshire	N/A	N/A	N/A	75	77	81	91
Sussex	N/A	47	45	84	81	90	N/A
All 15 locations	57	61	64	75	75	73	65
Bucks-PC	N/A	N/A	N/A	87	94	N/A	N/A

TABLE 7.15 Ownership of stools over time and by location

	1551–99	1600–29	1630–59	1660–89	1690–1719	1720–49	1750–1800
	%	%	%	%	%	%	%
Huntingdonshire	N/A	61	51	49	39	24	17
Yorkshire	N/A	N/A	N/A	N/A	50	33	20
Dorset	N/A	47	50	41	38	34	39
Bristol	N/A	80	82	73	50	19	20
Southampton	69	N/A	N/A	N/A	N/A	N/A	N/A
Lincoln	N/A	N/A	N/A	78	53	N/A	N/A
Ipswich	68	81	N/A	N/A	N/A	N/A	N/A
Marlborough	44	52	65	78	59	63	N/A
Gloucs	N/A	46	49	57	53	34	14
Essex	N/A	N/A	73	73	52	52	N/A
Cheshire	41	67	86	N/A	N/A	N/A	N/A
Surrey	44	59	N/A	N/A	N/A	N/A	N/A
Warwickshire	16	33	50	83	60	40	N/A
Shropshire	N/A	N/A	N/A	57	49	26	13
Sussex	N/A	35	29	60	69	50	N/A
All 15 locations	49	59	59	59	47	32	23
Cornwall	N/A	32	27	27	19	9	N/A
Kent	N/A	59	65	72	70	62	N/A
Bucks-PC	N/A	N/A	N/A	79	77	N/A	N/A

TABLE 7.16 Ownership of forms over time and by location

	1551–99	1600–29	1630–59	1660–89	1690–1719	1720–49	1750–1800
	%	%	%	%	%	%	%
Huntingdonshire	N/A	65	55	38	19	7	3
Yorkshire	N/A	N/A	N/A	N/A	41	23	5
Dorset	N/A	51	52	44	34	33	15
Bristol	N/A	50	26	21	2	0	0
Southampton	70	N/A	N/A	N/A	N/A	N/A	N/A
Lincoln	N/A	N/A	N/A	54	11	N/A	N/A
Ipswich	87	56	N/A	N/A	N/A	N/A	N/A
Marlborough	83	56	53	34	15	11	N/A
Gloucs	N/A	64	66	45	19	6	0
Essex	N/A	N/A	69	69	66	26	N/A
Cheshire	65	57	68	N/A	N/A	N/A	N/A
Surrey	63	76	N/A	N/A	N/A	N/A	N/A
Warwickshire	75	89	50	83	60	50	N/A
Shropshire	N/A	N/A	N/A	60	52	31	4
Sussex	N/A	71	68	49	56	75	N/A
All 15 locations	67	60	55	44	32	22	7
Bucks-PC	N/A	N/A	N/A	42	42	N/A	N/A

Urbanisation

As this chapter has already demonstrated, an important factor influencing owner-ship levels below the level of the county was the degree of urbanisation. This supports the historiography in Chapter 1 which suggested that consumer demand was strongest in towns for the medieval period and into the early modern period.[20] Goods were far less frequently recorded in probate records in areas distant from London, such as Cumbria and Cornwall.[21]

Carl Estabrook argued that patterns of material culture conformed to distinct urban and rural conventions; for example, urban dwellers were five times more likely to own window curtains than those who lived in rural parishes. Weatherill also found that whereas window curtains were recorded in 40 per cent of inventories in London, they were only found in 1 per cent of Cumbrian inventories.[22] The urban–rural divide was not confined to window curtains; the likelihood of finding a musical instrument was significantly greater in an urban home than a rural one.[23] Overton et al. also found that urban parishes in Kent and Cornwall generally had higher rates of adoption of new goods than rural ones. For example, over 40 per cent of probate inventories in Milton, Kent had goods that were associated with hot drinks in 1700–49 compared with very small percentages in the most remote rural areas.[24] Overton et al. defined six of their 51 parishes as urban. In Kent, Canterbury had 7,000 inhabitants, Milton just over 800 in 1663/64 and Folkestone 500 in 1671. However, Overton et al. wrote that 'it is doubtful whether our three urban parishes in Cornwall (Madron, Tregony and St Stephens by Saltash) can be considered urban at all' as the parishes did not consist of built-up areas although they did have the lowest commercial agricultural production in their sample.[25]

Further evidence on patterns of ownership of consumer goods in urban areas came from Yorkshire. However, categorising communities as urban was not straightforward and there were also significant changes in the degree of urbanisa-tion over time. For example, Halifax remained a relatively insignificant Pennine backwater in the period up to 1500. By the turn of the nineteenth century, the parish of Halifax had a population of more than 60,000 (Table 7.17).

TABLE 7.17 Population of Halifax township and parish

Year	TOWNSHIP	PARISH
1439	313	1,000
1548		8,500
1566	2,600	
1630		20,000
1641–42	4,400	
1743	5,000	31,000
1764	6,360	41,220
1801	8,886	63,434

TABLE 7.18 Selected consumer goods in Yorkshire over time and by parish

	Knives and forks			Clocks		
	1690–1719	*1720–49*	*1750–1800*	*1690–1719*	*1720–49*	*1750–1800*
	%	%	%	%	%	%
Halifax	1	0	9	28	35	58
Hull	0	0	17	3	29	14
Bradford	0	8	10	38	31	33
Huddersfield	0	0	6	6	57	35
Almondbury	0	0	3	13	27	53
Wakefield	0	5	21	17	24	64
Birstall	0	5	14	41	47	57
Kirkburton	0	0	18	7	57	59
Rydale	0	0	0	6	14	22
Yorkshire	1	1	7	16	27	43

	Window curtains			Looking glasses		
	1690–1719	*1720–49*	*1750–1800*	*1690–1719*	*1720–49*	*1750–1800*
	%	%	%	%	%	%
Halifax	5	5	3	16	20	18
Hull	28	21	9	58	74	39
Bradford	8	8	0	23	18	5
Huddersfield	0	0	6	0	7	15
Almondbury	4	8	0	13	15	16
Wakefield	21	13	21	29	34	64
Birstall	0	16	0	24	26	38
Kirkburton	0	14	5	7	14	27
Rydale	0	2	0	16	4	8
Yorkshire	8	6	3	19	22	20

	Silver			Hot drinks		
	1690–1719	*1720–49*	*1750–1800*	*1690–1719*	*1720–49*	*1750–1800*
	%	%	%	%	%	%
Halifax	23	9	18	0	0	16
Hull	70	50	41	3	18	59
Bradford	18	13	10	0	3	0
Huddersfield	0	0	6	0	0	6
Almondbury	4	8	6	0	0	6
Wakefield	38	29	57	0	11	64
Birstall	18	21	7	0	5	7

(Continued)

TABLE 7.18 (Cont.)

	Silver			Hot drinks		
	1690–1719	1720–49	1750–1800	1690–1719	1720–49	1750–1800
	%	%	%	%	%	%
Kirkburton	0	0	9	0	0	14
Rydale	6	7	3	0	2	4
Yorkshire	22	14	14	0	4	16

Similarly, Bradford was a small market town with a population of just over 1,000 (or just over 2,000 when the neighbouring townships of Bowling, Horton and Manningham are included) at the beginning of the eighteenth century.[26] Leigh Shaw-Taylor and Amanda Jones estimated that Bradford's population rose from 11,436 in 1785 to 30,669 in 1819.[27]

Ownership of certain goods was higher in more urbanised communities in Yorkshire (Table 7.18). Eight parishes provided over half (51 per cent) of the total inventories in the Yorkshire sample. Seven of these parishes were in Pontefract Deanery in the West Riding, the heartland of industrial change. The eighth, Hull in East Yorkshire, was important because of its links with West Yorkshire and its role in the export of textiles. By contrast, Rydale Deanery in North Riding was a mainly rural area with its economy dominated by agriculture. More than half the inventoried population of Halifax, Birstall, Almondbury, Kirkburton and Wakefield owned clocks in the second half of the eighteenth century compared with just 22 per cent in rural Rydale. Rydale generally had much lower ownership of consumer goods than in urbanised West Yorkshire parishes. Wakefield had particularly high levels of ownership of looking glasses, goods associated with hot drinks and silver.

Conclusion

On the basis of the evidence presented elsewhere in this study, there is little to suggest that the dramatic changes to levels of ownership indicative of a 'consumer revolution' occurred in the late medieval period, as there was no evidence to show that a significantly increased ownership of consumer goods had spread down the social scale and engulfed all social groups. Despite this, it is evident that consumption patterns were changing.

These first stirrings of consumer change in the late medieval period focussed on London and the south-east and gradually spread outwards to other areas of England. Pennell was correct to emphasise continuities rather than dramatic change in consumption patterns. Overton et al. identified Kent as being in the vanguard of the new consumer society which was emerging in the mid-

seventeenth century. Towards the end of the seventeenth century, wider ownership of certain goods began to take place. In much of rural England, such as
Huntingdonshire, Dorset and some areas of Yorkshire like Rydale and Holderness, the rapidly increasing ownership of goods like clocks, knives and forks and
goods associated with hot drinks mainly occurred in the second half of the
eighteenth century, during the period of McKendrick's 'consumer revolution'.
The new inventories for Kent also revealed a continued upward trajectory of
ownership of these goods in this period. McKendrick's thesis was therefore not
without merit, although we trust that the much wider chronology covered in
this volume places the changes in a better perspective.

Urbanisation was an important factor in consumption. Ownership of certain
goods in cities like Bristol and Lincoln, towns like Marlborough and the rapidly
urbanising areas of West Yorkshire tended to be much higher than in rural
areas. As we shall see in Chapter 9, increased ownership of certain goods
extended quite widely throughout society. But before we can consider how
ownership of consumer goods related to social rank, we must first explore the
nature of social status.

Notes

1   E.A. Wrigley, *The Path to Sustained Growth: England's Transition from an Organic Econ-
    omy to an Industrial Revolution* (Cambridge: Cambridge University Press, 2016), p.1.
2   N. McKendrick, J. Brewer and J. Plumb, *The Birth of a Consumer Society: The Com-
    mercialization of Eighteenth-Century England* (London: Hutchison, 1982), p.9.
3   *Ibid.*, pp.9–33.
4   *Ibid.*, p.13.
5   L. Weatherill, *Consumer Behaviour and Material Culture in Britain 1660–1760* (London:
    Routledge, 1996), p.3.
6   M. Overton, J. Whittle, D. Dean and A. Hann, *Production and Consumption in English
    Households 1600–1750* (Abingdon: Routledge, 2004), pp.28–31.
7   *Ibid.*, p.180.
8   Weatherill, *Consumer Behaviour*, p.210; Overton *et al.*, *Production and Consumption*,
    p.22.
9   J.M. Ellis, 'Consumption and wealth', in L.K.J. Glassey (ed.), *The Reigns of Charles II
    and James VII and II* (Basingstoke: Macmillan, 1997), p.210.
10 N.J.G. Pounds, *Hearth and Home: A History of Material Culture* (Bloomington: Indiana
    University Press, 1989), p.201; J. Styles, 'Georgian Britain' in M. Snodin and
    J. Styles, (eds), *Design and the Decorative Art: Britain 1500–1900* (London: V&A Pub-
    lishing, 2001), p.182; E.P. Thompson 'Time, work-discipline, and industrial capital-
    ism', *Past & Present*, 38 (1967), pp. 56–97. See Chapter 9 for ownership of clocks by
    labourers in the eighteenth century.
11 S. Pennell, 'Mundane materiality, or, should small things still be forgotten?', in
    K. Harvey (ed.), *History and Material Culture* (London: Routledge, 2018), pp.221–39.
12 Goods which included the word tea and coffee in the inventory: e.g. tea cups,
    teapots, coffee cups, coffee pots and tea tables.
13 H. French, *The Middle Sort of People in Provincial England, 1600–1750* (Oxford:
    Oxford University Press, 2007), pp.153–54; Weatherill, *Consumer Behaviour*, p.49.
14 J. Hatcher and T. Barker, *A History of British Pewter* (London: Longman, 1974),
    p.279ff.

15 *Ibid.*, p.281.
16 Weatherill, *Consumer Behaviour*, p.76.
17 Overton *et al.*, *Production and Consumption*, p.91.
18 L. Robinson, 'Consumerism in late seventeenth-century Cumbria: comparing Workington and Whitehaven 1676–1686', *The Local Historian*, 45 (2015), pp.195–210.
19 Overton *et al.*, *Production and Consumption*, p.153.
20 M. Kowaleski, 'A consumer economy', in R. Horrox and W.M. Ormrod (eds), *A Social History of England 1200–1500* (Cambridge: Cambridge University Press, 2006), pp.239, 242, 247–49, 252–53; C. Dyer, *Making a Living in the Middle Ages: The People of Britain 850–1520* (London: Penguin Books Ltd, 2003), pp.305, 307, 322–44, 356–57.
21 Weatherill, *Consumer Behaviour*, p.60; Overton *et al.*, *Production and Consumption*, p.171.
22 Weatherill, *Consumer Behaviour*, p.44.
23 C. Estabrook, *Urbane and Rustic England: Cultural Ties and Social Spheres in the Provinces 1660–1780* (Manchester: Manchester University Press, 1998), pp.132–49.
24 Overton *et al.*, *Production and Consumption*, pp.157–60.
25 *Ibid.*, pp.147–48.
26 E. Willmott, 'Occupations in eighteenth century Bradford', *The Bradford Antiquary*, 4 (1989), pp.67–77.
27 L. Shaw-Taylor and A. Jones 'An industrialising region? The West-Riding of Yorkshire *c.*1755–1871', www.geog.cam.ac.uk/research/projects/occupations/abstracts/paper2.pdf p.6. [last accessed 10 September 2016].

8

SOCIAL GROUPS

An important theme of this study is an assessment of how far changing consumption patterns permeated through the various rankings of society. For this, it is important to understand the social hierarchy that existed in late medieval and early modern England and this chapter will aim to establish the structure of this social hierarchy. Firstly, some contemporary perceptions of society during these periods will be reviewed; secondly, some of the relevant historiography which has shaped the debate about social structure will be considered; thirdly, for the inventoried population, the social structure devised by Lorna Weatherill will be introduced; fourthly, the occupations of those people for whom testamentary evidence has been used for this study (dated between 1430 and 1579) will be placed into rankings which give an indication of social status and, finally, the chapter will explore some of the social status designations and occupations used for the social structures.[1] Grouping occupations and constructing rankings in this manner provides a framework by which the impact of social status on consumer behaviour can be assessed and changes over the period in question can be considered in detail.

Contemporary perceptions of social status

Contemporary interpretations of medieval society did exist, but these varied according to the purpose for which they were intended and were generally very broad-based. In the words of Stephen Rigby, 'contemporaries did *not* merely employ *one* scheme for describing the social hierarchy but adopted different perspectives according to their specific purposes'.[2] In particular, most commentators emphasised the social function of different groups rather than their economic role or their comparative status.

Medieval commentators generally considered society to be divided into the well-recognised three estates of *oratores*, *bellatores* and *laboratores*, all interdependent of one another so that, for example, Wulstan of York stated in 1008 that:

> Every lawful throne which stands perfectly upright, stands on three pillars: one is oratores, and the second is laboratores and the third is bellatores. 'Oratores' are prayer-men, who must serve God and earnestly intercede both day and night for the entire nation. 'Laboratores' are workmen, who must supply that by which the entire nation shall live. 'Bellatores' are soldiers, who must defend the land by fighting with weapons.[3]

By the beginning of the early modern period, in 1587, William Harrison could write that 'we in England divide our people commonly into four sorts, as gentlemen, citizens or burgesses, yeomen, and artificers or labourers' and this was reiterated in 1583 by Sir Thomas Smith with his classifications of gentlemen (containing nobles and esquires as well as gentlemen), citizens and burgesses, yeomen and 'the fourth sort of men which does not rule … day labourers, poore husbandmen, yea marchantes or retailers which have no free lande, copiholders, and all artificers'.[4] No comprehensive analysis of the social order of England was undertaken until that of the late seventeenth century made by Gregory King, who was the first to consider the social divisions of the vast majority of the population, namely labourers and artificers who came below the status of yeoman, such as smallholders, labourers and paupers.[5]

The Domesday Book sub-divided rural society in the Middle Ages into four main groups: *liberi homines* and *sochemanni* (free peasants who held varying amounts of land and who formed about 14 per cent of the recorded rural population); *villani* (unfree peasants who were the wealthiest of the lord's tenants, often holding between 30 and 40 acres of land, and who comprised around 41 per cent); *bordarii* and *cotarii* (unfree peasants who usually held only a few acres or even no land and who constituted around 32 per cent of the population); and *servi* (slaves who made up 11 per cent of the population). However, contemporaries did not always make such distinctions between the different groups that made up rural society: in his *Vox Clamatis* of 1381, the poet and landlord John Gower used the term '*seruiles rustici* [lowly peasants]' to describe all the workers who revolted against the freemen and nobles of the realm and sought increased wages after the Black Death; whilst William Langland referred to all men 'þat lyven with here handes' as 'laborers'.[6]

In towns, society was generally considered to be divided into three groups of powerful, middling and lesser townspeople and this was often formally acknowledged by municipal authorities so that, for example, Lynn's records referred to the *potentiores*, *mediocres* and *inferiores*.[7] One group of contemporary sources which provide a wider definition of the urban hierarchy of occupations in the late medieval period are the instructions for the annual Corpus Christi processions which took place in a number of English towns.[8] The procession of the priest displaying the holy sacrament was accompanied by townspeople in a strict, hierarchical order with the lowest crafts represented at the beginning and the highest crafts at the end.[9] Instructions for these processions stipulated the order in which various urban crafts were to process and were therefore a broad commentary on the relative social status of the different crafts as perceived by contemporary society. For example, in 1437, the mayor, bailiffs, citizens and community of Winchester agreed that lights should be carried in due order in the Corpus Christi procession in advance of the priests and that carpenters and tilers should go in the first section, smiths and barbers in the second, cooks and butchers in the third, shoemakers in the fourth, tanners and coverlet-weavers in the fifth, the fraternity of St. Thomas and tailors' assistants in the sixth, fishermen and skinners in the seventh, vintners and the fraternity of St Anne in the eighth, weavers in the ninth, fullers in the tenth, dyers in the eleventh, mercers in the twelfth, and wives in the thirteenth.[10] Although the extant instructions refer to processions which took place within larger towns, the order of crafts does appear to reflect the status that existed within smaller towns and, where appropriate, rural locations. However, in this context, it is worth noting that these orders were not fixed and could vary between towns and over time.

Social status in the late Middle Ages

Social hierarchy has been extensively debated by historians whose discussions have covered much ground and encompassed a number of theories.[11] In relation to medieval England, studies have focussed on three broad perspectives: the 'dichotomic' conception of society in which social structure is viewed in terms of binary oppositions; the social 'gradation' in which society is seen as a graded hierarchy of groups; and the 'functional' perspective in which society is seen as one which consists of a number of functionally interdependent social groups.[12] For example, for the Marxist and Marxist-influenced historians such as Rodney Hilton and Zvi Razi, late medieval society could be expressed in a range of binary terms: lord and peasant (in the rural setting); artisans and mercantile elite (in the urban environment); or, simply, exploiter and exploited.[13] Other historians rejected such a clearly defined social polarisation and saw medieval society as a 'spectrum of quantitative differences of wealth' so that status comprised a series of degrees of social rank.[14] Status was defined in terms of the lifestyle and the prestige which was afforded to an individual as perceived by others.[15] The 'Toronto school' in particular emphasised that the medieval peasantry should not simply be defined as 'an exploited mass' but as a series of separate village communities which consisted of a wide range of sub-groups and different social 'classes'.[16] In *The Community of the Vill*, Edward Britton allocated the peasant families of pre-Black Death Broughton to one of four social groups depending on the official activities of the male members of each family and demonstrated that this was indicative of social and economic status.[17]

Mark Bailey has also written widely on the structure of rural society in the Middle Ages and how this changed during the late medieval period.[18] He noted that the peasant class could be sub-divided in a variety of different ways such as by the personal status of the individual (free or unfree), or by the size and nature of their holdings.[19] This resulted in a range of different terms such as 'bordars', 'sokemen' and 'villeins'.[20] As manorial power waned, particularly in the period between *c.* 1350 and *c.* 1500, the relationship between lords and peasants was fundamentally altered and, in particular, land tenures moved from villein tenure to copyholds.[21] The feudal terms used to describe the various ranks of the medieval peasantry were no longer applicable and new terms emerged, such as 'yeoman' and 'husbandman', which emphasised the relationship between holdings and social status. This revised structure was further complicated by the entrance of new players into the land market in the form of 'freemen, townsfolk, artisans, even lesser lords'.[22] Keith Lilley noted that the close relationship between holdings and social status also existed within the urban environment.[23] Urban property-holding mirrored urban social hierarchies so that personal wealth and status were reflected in the amount, type, location and tenure-type of property held to the extent that it could 'reinforce an individual's place in the medieval urban social hierarchy'.[24] Many of the theories and interpretations of social structure in the late medieval period have been explored and analysed in some detail by Rigby in his work on late medieval society.[25]

Historians generally acknowledged that important social changes were taking place during the late medieval period. Some historians suggested that, regardless of these changes, late medieval society remained rigidly hierarchical so that people had a clear understanding of the divisions and gradings that existed and of their position within that hierarchy. For example, Maurice Keen referred to medieval England as being a 'deference society' with an 'ordered graduation' in which everyone knew their place and how they should treat those above and below them within the social hierarchy.[26] Other writers rejected these claims of harmony and acquiescence; in his article on the Corpus Christi celebrations, Mervyn James argued that whilst the ritual was intended to affirm 'social wholeness and social differentiation', it was often the specific focus of conflict so that the York and Chester processions were subject to lawsuits, riots and even bloodshed as the craft gilds competed fiercely for precedence of position within the procession and the esteem this could bring.[27]

Whilst the relationship between the different groups in society remains open to debate and interpretation, many historians concurred with a basic definition of late medieval society as a series of gradations. This consisted of the king at the top followed by a nobility which included both lay and spiritual peers responsible for advising the king and who held large estates throughout the country (although the influence and wealth of individual members of this group varied considerably). Below the nobility was the gentry class which had emerged from the lesser nobility during the first half of the fourteenth century and which, as with the nobility, was a diverse group headed by knights but also included esquires, gentlemen and a few gentlewomen.[28] Below the gentry came 'the people', consisting of yeomen, husbandmen, smaller freeholders and copyholders, merchants, craftsmen, shopkeepers and labourers.[29]

Social status in the early modern period

Many historians have focussed attention on terms used by people in early modern England. Keith Wrightson explored concepts of estates, degrees and sorts. As the economy expanded professional groups, tradesmen and yeomen increased their wealth and the medieval language of estates gave way to degrees and 'sorts' as a wider variation of degrees and occupational groups emerged.[30] The designation of people into broad groupings such as 'better sort' or 'meaner sort' was based on wealth.[31] Henry French also explored how individuals understood their position in society, how they identified with others and how they generated a sense of belonging together. French found that in the late seventeenth century at village level, terms such as 'better sort' were frequently used by people who were not poor but also did not have the status to call themselves gentry.[32] Although individuals were the key to understanding social identity, French argued that historical individuals were born into a 'dense web of social and behavioural constraints'. The autonomy of individuals was heavily circumscribed by pre-existing value systems.[33]

Craig Muldrew endorsed the importance of morality in the way individuals viewed self-identity within society. Virtuous living enhanced a person's reputation on which obtaining credit depended and which could be crucial for survival.[34] Early modern England was a competitive society where households strove to be successful. The terms 'better sort' and 'meaner sort' were words of judgement, for the former were successful whereas the latter were not.[35] The language of sorts reflected contemporary social tensions as society became more polarised.[36] Gwyneth Nair highlighted contemporary use of the terms by an example from the parish register of Highley in 1678. Giles Rawlins, the vicar, left money to be 'set forth yearlie by the Churchwardens for the best use of the poor of the Parish at the discretion ... of the best sort of the said parish'.[37] In Highley, the churchwardens were among the best sort for they were economically successful.

Those who comprised the 'middling sort' were not easy to define.[38] As Margaret Hunt wrote, the composition of the middling sort 'is and must remain somewhat vague'.[39] One problem was the absence of legal and fiscal definition of social position, apart from peers and those on poor relief.[40] Maxine Berg argued that the most common criteria for membership of 'the middling classes' in the mid-eighteenth century were minimum incomes of £40–£50 per year and liability for payment of the poor rates.[41] For Shani D'Cruze they were independent trading households.[42] A working definition of the middling sort was that they fell between the landed elite and the poor and were broadly synonymous with the inventoried population.

Two local studies demonstrated how in different ways the 'middling sort' was changing in the early modern period. John Smail suggested that society in Halifax, Yorkshire became more polarised. In the latter part of the seventeenth century, Halifax had been 'a community of the middling sort'. The community included simple clothiers, independent rural artisans, small landowners and a few substantial yeomen. By the mid-eighteenth century, a new group of merchants and manufacturers had emerged to form the elite in the community. Independent clothiers had been reduced to the status of semi-independent wage labourers.[43] Highley in Shropshire was a rural community dominated by agriculture until mining emerged towards the end of the eighteenth century.[44] Nair's study of Highley suggested that enclosure was a pivotal point in changing relationships between social groups. Prior to enclosure, wealth was not the sole criterion of social influence and settled residence and personal reputation were also important. For Nair, the open-field system of agriculture imposed a degree of cooperation between neighbours and communal activity acted to blunt the divisions of financial hierarchy. Following enclosure, society became more polarised and there was a firmer delineation between social groups. Nair argued that social advancement became even more difficult. Those who combined a smallholding with another occupation were more likely to be farmers on the way down than artisans on the way up.[45]

Alexandra Shepard also contended that society was becoming increasingly polarised. Shepard analysed how people rated themselves by analysing the language of self-description of court witnesses in early modern England. She examined over 13,000 witness statements covering the years 1550–1728. Most witnesses based their view of themselves upon a broad financial estimate of moveable wealth rather than land. Shepard argued that whilst these worth assessments were often rounded figures and sometimes imprecise, they nevertheless represented meaningful data.[46] 'Worth' for the court was net wealth after outstanding debts had been deducted.[47] During the century after 1550, disparities in worth between gentry and yeomen on the one hand, and the majority of tradespeople, artisans and labourers on the other, widened markedly with yeomen in particular recording the most spectacular rise. Shepard also noted variations in the 'worth' of yeomen by region, with those in York having a much lower worth than those in Canterbury, Chichester, Lewes, Chester and Richmond.[48]

In a rapidly changing society, establishing a person's place in the social hierarchy was very contentious. Mark Overton argued that the most important determinant of status was possession, and particularly ownership of land.[49] Anthony Fletcher and John Stevenson suggested that several criteria determined social rank including birth, wealth, occupation and lifestyle.[50] These criteria were often in conflict and one area where this conflict was frequently revealed was in church seating arrangements as outlined in Chapter 6.

A person's place in the social hierarchy was contentious because an individual's circumstance could change. If Keith Wrightson was correct that relative status related to wealth, this opened the door to both upward and downward social mobility.[51] For example, Richard Hall's examination of Yorkshire Deeds Registers highlighted Stephen Read from Hedon who was recorded as a tailor in 1727, a merchant tailor by the end of that year and a gentleman by 1729 when he became mayor.[52] A family's status could change rapidly. There was little financial security in the early modern period because people were vulnerable to sickness, fire, bad harvests and other threats. Probate inventories revealed that debts due to the deceased were a large element in a person's movable assets. Non-payment of debts could therefore threaten the economic viability of households. Muldrew drew attention to Richard Gough's descriptions of individuals and families in the parish of Myddle who were experiencing economic decline; increasing indebtedness inevitably meant loss of reputation. Muldrew suggested that downward economic mobility was not an uncommon experience. The continued presence of elite families in local communities was less in the early modern period than in twentieth century societies in England.[53]

Social structure for the late medieval and early modern periods

Given the constraints and problems associated with defining social status and structures in both the late medieval and early modern periods, the grouping of social and occupational groups and subsequent use of these to construct a social order presents a considerable challenge. For the early modern period, Weatherill responded by developing a social hierarchy based on Vivien Brodsky Elliott's study of marriage partners.[54] Weatherill's structure assimilated the social structures that existed in both rural and urban settings so that the traditionally rural groupings of gentry, husbandmen and labourers were ranked alongside the predominantly urban occupational groups of tradesmen and craftsmen. For Weatherill, 'gentry' status ranked above 'trades of high status', which included members of the clergy and professions. 'Trades of intermediate status', such as innkeepers, maltsters and tanners, ranked below this grouping and, in turn, ranked above 'yeomen; large farmers'. 'Trades of low status', for example bakers and cordwainers, ranked below 'yeomen', and were followed by the rankings of 'husbandmen; small farmers' and 'labourers'.[55] Three other status groups were included in the structure but did not form part of the ranking, those of 'widows; spinsters', 'tradesman: trades unknown' and 'occupation or status unknown'.

Weatherill's social hierarchy was constructed as a means of analysing the inventories used for her study and which were dated between 1675 and 1725.[56] Her structure has been adopted for use with the inventories used for this study to enable comparisons to be made between her inventory data and that used by the present study (dated between 1550 and 1749). However, the social hierarchy that existed for the period between 1430 and 1579, which has been investigated in this study using testamentary evidence, was broadly comparable with Weatherill's social hierarchy but not identical. As a result, a revised social structure for this period was constructed and is shown in Table 8.1. As with Weatherill's structure, it aims to assimilate the rankings which existed within both rural and urban settings into a social order based on nine social status groups of which seven are ranked. It is substantially based on the social hierarchy devised by Weatherill but incorporates evidence from the period in question. In particular, the instructions issued by various towns for the order in which craftsmen were to process on Corpus Christi Day, referred to on pp.231–32, was used as evidence of the perceived social status of late medieval urban society. Other sources included references to status and occupations within sumptuary legislation, observations by contemporary writers and commentators and the relative wealth of individuals holding certain occupations as reflected in their wills. Table 8.1 gives a broad definition of the occupations and groups represented by each of the social status groups, but a more detailed list of the occupations held by the people whose testamentary records were used for this study and the social status groups to which they were allocated is included in the Appendix.

As has been noted, Table 8.1 was heavily based on that devised by Weatherill. However, it was important that the ranking reflected the period between 1430 to 1579, rather than the period between 1660 and 1760. It could not be assumed, for example, that a baker in the late fourteenth century had the same social status as a baker in the eighteenth century despite having the same occupational designation and performing broadly similar tasks in the pursuit of their trade. It was evident from the outset that social status was flexible and that the perceived standing of an occupation could vary over time and between individuals. It was also recognised that the three categories of 'high-status', 'intermediate-status' and 'low-status' trades are somewhat artificial constraints and that at times there is a very fine distinction between these different groupings. In this connection, although the table does reflect the social structure of this period, it should be regarded as having a degree of fluidity.

In general, the evidence used to construct the table suggested that the social status of most trades and occupations was largely unchanged between the fourteenth and eighteenth centuries; for example, smiths were regularly placed at or towards the

TABLE 8.1 Social structure for the period 1430–1579

Social status groups	Occupations and status
1 **Gentry**	Esquires, gentlemen, knights.
2 **High-status trades**	Clerics, merchant trades, members of the professions.
3 **Intermediate-status trades**	Some victualling trades, e.g. butchers, fishmongers; crafts which required a greater outlay of capital, e.g. tanners, dyers, saddlers; tailors.
4 **Yeomen**	Men who held land in excess of 40 acres; occupations relating to estate management.
5 **Low-status trades**	Some victualling trades, e.g. bakers, cooks; crafts associated with the manufacture of cloth; craftsmen designated as one of the various types of smiths; men associated with building and woodworking; craftsmen who used prepared cloth or skins to make small clothing items.
6 **Husbandmen**	Men who held land between 15/20 and 40 acres.
7 **Labourers**	Agricultural labourers.
8 **Females**	Widows, married women and spinsters.
9 **Unknown**	Men for whom no occupational or status designation can be found.

front of the Corpus Christi processions (i.e. they were perceived as having low status) and Weatherill allocated blacksmiths to the category of 'trades of low status'; whilst mercers processed at or towards the back (i.e. they were perceived as having high status) and Weatherill allocated them to the category of 'trades of high status'. In a few cases where the social status remained unchanged, the name of the trade differed between the two periods and assumptions had to be made that the occupation was the same or very similar so that, for example, the occupation referred to as 'skepmaker' for the earlier period was seen as being the same as that of 'basketmaker' for Weatherill's period, whilst the occupation of 'furberer' was considered to be equivalent to that of 'armourer'. In these and other similar cases the different names given to these trades did not result in a change in status.

The status of some occupations did change (although it should be recognised that this would have been a gradual, piecemeal modification) so that the perception of status suggested by the Corpus Christi processions differed from that indicated by Weatherill for the seventeenth and eighteenth centuries. In almost all of these cases the evidence from the earlier period was used to rank the occupation although it should be noted that most variances only resulted in a change of ranking of just one agricultural or occupational group and/or affected a very small number of testators. For example, the occupation of 'tailor' was well regarded in the late medieval period and their position within the urban hierarchy was such that tailors were allocated positions towards the upper end of the Corpus Christi processions. By the end of the seventeenth century, the perception of their status had declined so that Weatherill allocated tailors to the category of low-status trades (this is explored in more detail later). Other occupations similarly declined in status so that clothiers were afforded high status in the late medieval period but were only given intermediate status by Weatherill for the early modern period. By contrast, some occupations rose in status: the inferior ranking afforded to barbers meant that they were generally placed towards the front of the Corpus Christi processions, yet Weatherill gave intermediate status to barbers and high status to barber-surgeons; whilst masons were generally ranked together with low-status craftsmen with building-related skills in the Corpus Christi processions, but had achieved intermediate status by the early modern period (although other craftsmen with skills relating to building largely retained the low status they had been afforded in the earlier period).[57]

In a very few cases Weatherill's rankings were used rather than those suggested by contemporary evidence. Two occupations ranked in this manner caused concern since although this only resulted in a change of ranking of one group, a number of testators held the occupations in question. The first of these was that of 'tanner' which was generally afforded low status in the Corpus Christi processions but was allocated to the category of 'trades of intermediate status' by Weatherill. Tanners were often quite wealthy but were poorly regarded because of the noxious nature of their trade and they were expected to operate on the margins of towns and other settlements. Weatherill's categorisation was followed since it was evident from the wills of the men who described themselves as 'tanner' that they were men of some wealth and social standing. The Northampton tanner John James bequeathed a gown furred with polecat and a piece of decorated silver with a cover together with £5 17s in cash bequests and domestic utensils to the value of £2 13s 4d.[58] The second significant occupation which was allocated according to Weatherill's ranking was that of 'butcher' although in this instance the reasoning behind the decision was rather more complicated and required some debate and consideration. The occupation was generally given low/inter-mediate status by the Corpus Christi procession rankings and was allocated to 'trades of low status' by Weatherill. The Corpus Christi rankings were almost certainly due to the fact that, like tanning, the trade was regarded as noisome whilst butchers themselves were often suspected of sharp practice and were generally litigious. However, the wills and other sources indicated that the testators who held the occupation of 'butcher' were generally wealthy men who held large amounts of land and had high social status within their communities. Edmund Ballys held very large amounts of land in and around the town of Thetford, had twice been mayor and paid 50s on goods in the 1524 Lay Subsidy.[59] Despite referring to themselves as 'butchers', these men were, in effect, operating as 'graziers', an occupation which Weatherill allocated to the category of 'yeomen/large farmers'. Consequently, it was decided to allocate butchers to the category of 'trades of intermediate status' which largely brought them in line with Weatherill's treatment of 'graziers'.

A few occupations did not appear in the instructions for the Corpus Christi processions and were not referred to by Weatherill in her list of occupations so that other evidence was needed to be able to allocate these to an appropriate social status group. For example, some will-makers held the occupations of 'forester', 'sheepreeve' and 'warrener', offices which were associated with different aspects of estate management. The holders of such offices were required to ensure that the landlord's rights were respected and enforced and were generally men of high local standing. Richard Almond and A.J. Pollard noted that the office of 'forester' was held by men of families below minor gentry who were 'yeomen by status as well as occupation' and this appears to have been the case with the other offices so that the sheepreeve Nicholas Bott also referred to himself as being a yeoman in his will of 1535.[60] Men holding these occupations were therefore included with the status group of 'yeomen'.

Occupational terms were applied in a general manner so that they included men who held varying levels of status and who undertook a range of different tasks; for example, the term 'smith' could be used to denote both a variety of types of metalworkers, from goldsmiths to blacksmiths, and a range of operations, from small village smithies to large-scale urban operations.[61] For this study, 'weaver' was frequently used to designate the occupations of testators and could be applied to men with very wide-ranging social backgrounds, although weavers were generally considered to have low status in the Corpus Christi processions and were allocated to the category of 'low-status trades' (which was consistent with Weatherill's classification of weaving as a trade of low status).[62] Whilst weaving was a very common craft in the late medieval and early modern periods, most weavers were poor out-workers whose assets did not necessitate the making of a will. Although this study included some wills made by weavers, these largely confirmed that their subjects were men of limited means as they were generally proved at the lowest level of church court and contained few bequests of either cash or goods. However, William Benyngton, who described himself in his will of 1549 as a linen-weaver, had his will proved in the Prerogative Court at Canterbury and left cash bequests to the value of £16 4s 11d, a considerable sum for the time.[63] This, and other evidence, suggested that despite describing himself as a weaver, Benyngton coordinated the work of weaving craftsmen rather than engaged actively in the craft.

A further issue shared by both this social structure and that produced by Weatherill was that whilst both assumed that status and wealth were correlated, this was not always the case. For example, many clerics came from gentry families and were viewed as having high social status within their communities, yet this did not necessarily mean that they enjoyed high levels of income. Whilst most of the wills of clerics used for this study included numerous bequests of both cash and goods, others contained very little and suggested that the testator did not have much to leave. Conversely, barkers were generally perceived to be occupations of, at best, intermediate status, yet the wills of some of the traders used for this study suggest that they were men of some affluence. In his will of 1467 proved in the Prerogative Court of Canterbury, the Thetford barker John Bernham left over 65 acres of land in and around Thetford and over five hundred wool fleeces in addition to cash bequests to the value of £13 4s 2d.[64]

A further concern which is mutual to both social structures is that no distinction was made between the different categories of females. Weatherill grouped widows and spinsters together when considering the ownership of goods and this was done for this social structure as it was not always possible to identify whether a female testator was a widow, spinster or a married woman who had made a will.[65] Nevertheless, Amy Froide argued that early modern England did not think of widows and spinsters in the same way and historians who considered them together left the unique experiences of single women unexamined.[66] Froide claimed that historians have given insufficient attention to single women and focus on them was fruitful and long overdue.

Although status descriptions or occupations recorded on wills and inventories usually represented the deceased's principal activity and minority activities were not often recorded, the categorisation of individuals was complicated by the issue of dual occupations. Again, this was an issue encountered for this social structure and that developed by Weatherill.[67] In many cases it was apparent that the testator was both practising a trade and engaging in agriculture, and in a few instances two separate trades or crafts were listed. Moira Long also found that dual occupations of fathers were occasionally recorded in Yorkshire baptism registers although usually only one occupation was given.[68] In these situations, the principal activity was taken to be the status or occupation that was recorded

first on the relevant document so that, for example, the occupation of John Ley-
cestr' of Northampton who referred to himself in his will of 1490 as 'mercer et
potycary' was designated as being a mercer.[69] In almost all cases, as with this
one, the different trades were from the same occupational ranking, or, in those
instances where an agricultural status and trade occupation were given, these
were of comparable rankings.

Whilst this study adopted Weatherill's structure without amendment for analysing
the inventories used for this study, some criticisms can be levelled at her work and,
in particular, at the categories that she allocated to certain occupations. Occupations
such as mariners, joiners and perhaps bakers, appear to have been inappropriately
categorised by Weatherill. For example, she placed mariners in her high-status
group of professionals along with merchants, drapers, mercers and apothecaries
but this appeared to be a surprising decision. Mariners' inventory values had a high
coefficient of variation and comprised a wide range of people from part-owners of
substantial boats to, much more commonly, lowly-paid seamen with few assets
other than the wages due to them when they died aboard ship.[70] Joiners were
placed in the higher category of 'trades of intermediate status' whereas carpenters
were categorised as 'trades of low status'.[71] Weatherill's own data gave little support
for this decision since it recorded joiners as having significantly lower overall inventory values (mean £48) than carpenters (mean £70) and in terms of household goods
alone, there was little difference with carpenters at £18 and joiners at £20.[72] The
data for this study (Table 8.8a) also gave little support for her decision. In the
present study for the same period (1675–1725), there was little difference between
carpenters with a mean of £62 (median £29) and 13 joiners (compared to Weatherill's sample of just four) with a mean of £63 (median £34).

Agricultural ranks

Gentry

The highest social group considered by this study was that of the 'gentry' which
comprised knights, esquires and gentlemen. The gentry initially emerged as
a distinct group in the late medieval period. Christine Carpenter argued that this
was as a reaction to the appearance of an aggressive, newly prosperous peasantry
which encouraged the well-born to establish hierarchical lines to confirm their
distinction from 'uppity peasants', so that the Statute of Additions of 1413 established the title of 'gentleman' for the lowest of the well-born.[73] Despite attending
court and parliament on an infrequent basis, the prime importance of members of
the gentry was within their own locality where they acted as sheriffs, justices of
the peace and representatives of the shire in parliament, or as commissioners for
raising loans or the investigation of crown rights.[74] Although there were certain
'indisputable qualifications' for gentry status such as the sovereign's commission,
a call to the bar or a university degree, there was a considerable degree of dispute
as to who should be accepted as a gentleman since gentry were not a legally

defined group. Felicity Heal and Clive Holmes argued that by the early modern period, flexible definitions of gentility were a necessary feature of the rather mobile society of England with the key determinants being land, lordship and local acknowledgement.[75] This was succinctly encapsulated in the early seventeenth century by Thomas Adams who wrote, 'first riches and then honour for it is lightly found ... reputation is measured by the acre'.[76] Land implied income from rents.

Given this imprecision of definition, it is not surprising that claims for gentility were often disputed. In his study of Lancashire gentry, B.G. Blackwood suggested that the term was often vague and meaningless because it was too readily used for town officials or even men of lower status who did not claim gentility so that, as a result, some historians have argued that herald's visitation lists held at the College of Arms are the most reliable guides to gentry status.[77] From 1530 to 1688, heraldic visitations operated under the crown as a means of regulating the gentry, and the kings of arms were empowered, under their commissions, to deface or remove bogus arms. The 'official badge of gentility' was the coat of arms but Sir Thomas Smith in *De Republica Anglorum* (1583) argued that 'the reputation of being a gentleman came first, with the confirmation by a king of arms following, if necessary, thereafter'.[78] Peter Coss warned that possession of a coat of arms was problematic as a test for gentry status as not all gentry were armigerous and heraldic visitations were intermittent.[79] John Bedells used heralds' visitation returns to assess the number of gentry in Huntingdonshire. The two visitations for Huntingdonshire in the seventeenth century were held in 1613 and 1684. The 1613 visitation accepted 60 families living in 48 different parishes in Huntingdonshire and 53 gentry families in 1684. These numbers suggested that gentry households represented just over 1 per cent of Huntingdonshire households.[80]

Wrightson argued that possession of gentility was a fundamental dividing line in society.[81] Two contemporaries offer definitions of this distinction: for William Harrison, an essential element of gentry status was that gentlemen were those who 'can live without manual labour', whilst Sir Thomas Overbury described the important difference between yeomen and gentlemen by writing that the yeoman, even though he be master, says not to his servants go to the field but let us go.[82] Despite the apparent clarity in how contemporaries perceived gentleman status, the ranks were increasingly fluid; the inventory evidence showed that those who termed themselves 'gentlemen' could have very different backgrounds and had a wide range of inventory values. This is further illustrated by a study of 185 feodary surveys for the 1520s which found that the median income for knights was £204, esquires had an annual income of £80, but lesser gentry only £17. It is also reflected in the gentry wills used for this study since whilst most were proved in the Prerogative Court of Canterbury, as with that of Richard Gaysley of Swaffham Prior, many were confirmed by lesser courts such as that of William Bassyngtwyte of Thetford which was proved in the Court of the Archdeaconry of Norwich.[83] Varying levels of wealth were also reflected in the totals of the cash amounts recorded in wills used for this study: the largest total for cash bequests was that of £302 contained in the will of Walter Porter of Thetford which was made in 1550; by contrast, William Bassyngtwyte, referred to previously, left total bequests of only £1 2s in his will of 1520, the smallest amount recorded in the will of a gentleman.[84] Generally, cash bequests of members of the gentry were no higher than those of members of certain occupational groups, and in particular mercers and drapers, and reflected the fact that wealth and an affluent lifestyle were not always typical features of gentry status.

Yeomen

The terms 'yeoman', 'husbandman' and 'labourer' were increasingly used from the end of the Middle Ages to replace those which had been associated with a feudal peasantry. The term 'yeoman' was applied to men with landholdings which were generally in excess of 40 acres and defined an intermediary social category between gentry and husbandman.[85] The growing tendency for contemporaries to see 'yeomen' as a separate and defined status was confirmed by the Statute of Additions of 1413 which made a clear distinction between those of gentle status, the gentry, and those of non-gentle status, the yeoman.[86] The typical yeoman held a level of influence and respect within their parish and often held offices for the manorial lord.[87] Other rural occupations relating to estate management also existed in the late medieval period, including those of steward, forester and warrener which were viewed as being of a similar status.[88]

During the early modern period, numbers of yeomen were increasing by both upward and downward mobility and the term yeoman incorporated diverse social groups.[89] Farm size remained important in identifying yeoman although Leigh Shaw-Taylor drew attention to examples of different interpretations by historians about thresholds for what might be considered small or large farms and how these thresholds changed over time.[90] Bailey's 40-acre definition for the late medieval period had, for Wrightson, increased to 'usually in excess of fifty acres' although he acknowledged that the size of holdings varied considerably and suggested that yeoman status was accorded to men who farmed 'a substantial acreage'.[91] By the seventeenth century, Wrightson and David Levine implied that farms of over 50 acres should be considered large.[92] By contrast, Margaret Spufford wrote of the disappearance of 'small' farms of up to 40 or 45 acres at Chippenham and Orwell in Cambridgeshire during the seventeenth century.[93] Gordon Mingay, writing about the eighteenth and nineteenth centuries, treated farms of up to 100 acres as 'small'.[94] The term 'yeoman' was also applied to men holding freehold lands worth 40s or more per annum although, again, this term became increasingly meaningless as a result of inflation.[95] Other definitions were more nebulous; Peter Laslett defined yeomen as the most successful of those who worked the land.[96] Weatherill asserted that yeomen were a distinct group from the gentry and that yeoman status was well recognised by contemporaries in the early modern period.[97]

As with those who held gentry status, the wills of yeomen used for this study suggest that these men had varying levels of affluence. Some were proved at the

Prerogative Court of Canterbury, but most were taken to the lesser courts. Similarly, the total of the monetary bequests contained within them varied widely; John Smyth of Ashley in Cambridgeshire bequeathed £160 in 1528, whilst the will of Thomas Hovell of nearby Cowlinge, made in 1473, contained no cash bequests.[98]

Between the third quarter of the sixteenth century and the second quarter of the seventeenth century, the relative wealth of yeomen improved strikingly. Shepard found that whereas the median worth of yeomen and husbandmen was not markedly dissimilar in the third quarter of the sixteenth century, the worth of yeomen rose more than fourteen-fold (ten-fold in real terms) over the century whilst the worth of husbandmen only doubled. According to Shepard's calculation the result was that yeomen came to be worth ten times that of husbandmen (Table 8.2).[99]

Median inventory values for the present study sample followed a similar but less pronounced trajectory over the same period, rising by about seven-fold for yeomen and over double for husbandmen. The amounts were always higher for inventory values than for worth, but calculation of worth involved a deduction of debts owed by court witnesses whereas inventory values did not. Furthermore, court witnesses represented a wider social range than those who left inventories.[100] Overton contended that probate inventory data excluded around 40 per cent of the population.[101] Even in the present study, where the sample included many more labourers' inventories, the number was not sufficient to challenge Overton's broad estimate. On the other hand, Shepard narrowed the social range of her sample of court witnesses by omitting those witnesses with little or no wealth from her worth calculations.[102] Both sets of data, inventory values and the worth of court witnesses, supported the contention that a widening wealth gap was opening between yeomen and husbandmen in the early seventeenth century.

However, there was also a wide range of inventory values during the seventeenth and early eighteenth centuries. James Sharpe argued that yeomen enjoyed

TABLE 8.2 Comparison of yeomen and husbandmen 'worth' and inventory values

	1550–74 Col 1	1625–49 Col 2	Increase Col. 2/Col 1
	£	£	%
Yeomen			
Median worth	7	100	1,429
Inventory values	17	125	735
Husbandmen			
	£	£	
Median worth	5	10	200
Inventory values	21	52	248

Source: Shepard Accounting for Oneself, p.69.

'massive variations of wealth' and that some yeomen might be 'very prosperous indeed'.[103] There was often no sharp distinction between lesser gentry and richer yeomen. At the opposite end of the scale, those classified as yeomen in probate inventories could have very low values of moveable goods. Wrightson and Levine came to similar conclusions; in their study of Whickham, they categorised more substantial farmers with minor gentry and placed lesser yeomen with craftsmen and tradesmen.[104] Weatherill's conclusions were not so emphatic. On the one hand, she argued that yeomen were a discrete group as their inventory values in the period 1675–1725 concentrated at a clear peak between £65 and £85. On the other hand, Weatherill recognised that there were a wide range of values and that it was not unusual to find a wealthy yeoman referred to as a gentleman on occasions whereas poorer yeomen, especially in the north-west of England, could sometimes refer to themselves as husbandmen.[105]

Sharpe's argument that yeomen were a heterogeneous group was based on data obtained by Francis Steer in Essex and Peter Ripley in the hinterland of Gloucester.[106] Data from additional counties in the present study have been added to Sharpe's data and have been included in Table 8.3.

The much larger dataset adds weight to Sharpe's conclusions. Only nine yeomen had inventoried wealth over £1,000 but 42 (5 per cent) yeomen out of 857 in the seven inventory collections had inventoried wealth between £500 and £1,000. Nearly three quarters (73 per cent) of all inventoried yeomen in the collection of inventories covering the period from 1601–1723 had inventory values below £500. At the opposite end of the scale were yeomen with inventoried wealth under £10, the lowest value inventory being a yeoman in Ramsey with a valuation of only £1 10s. None of the seven Huntingdonshire yeomen with inventories under £10 recorded any animals and only one had crops. In Yorkshire, five yeomen inventories were valued at under £10. Three recorded animals but none recorded crops. No yeoman in Mid-Essex had valuations under £10, but there were four in Dorset, four in Shropshire and ten in the other Gloucestershire parishes.

Husbandmen

The word 'husbandmen' was literally a person engaged in husbandry, tending animals and tilling the soil:[109] 'A husbandman is he which with discretion and good order tilleth the ground in his due seasons, making it fruitfull to bring forth corne, and plants, meete for the sustenance of man'.[110]

This social category saw fundamental revisions from the late fourteenth century as the increased availability of land saw previously landless labourers become landholders, smallholders increase their landholdings and existing landholders engross holdings and create sizeable estates.[111] As a result, the proportion of the population who could be described as 'husbandmen' increased substantially from this period onwards, as did the relative size of their holdings, which ranged from the small estates of formerly landless labourers to relatively large estates. It is evident that the

TABLE 8.3 Yeomen inventory values

	Mid-Essex (1638–1723)		Vale of Gloucs (1600–1700)		Other Gloucs (1609–1723)[107]		Yorkshire (1690–1719)	
	No.	%	No.	%	No.	%	No.	%
>£1,000	1	2	1	0	1	1	1	1
£500–£1,000	2	4	11	3	14	11	4	4
£250–£500	13	27	55	15	11	9	8	8
£100–£250	17	36	138	38	43	35	33	32
<£100	15	31	157	44	54	44	56	55
Totals	48	100	362	100	123	100	102	100

	Huntingdonshire (1609–1723)		Shropshire (1661–1723)		Dorset (1627–1723)		Totals	
	No.	%	No.	%	No.	%	No.	%
>£1,000	2	2	1	3	2	3	9	1
£500–£1,000	2	2	2	6	7	9	42	5
£250–£500	15	13	7	21	9	11	118	14
£100–£250	39	36	13	38	29	37	312	36
<£100	51	47	11	32	32	40	376	44
Totals	109	100	34	100	79	100	857	100

distinction between the designations of 'yeoman' and 'husbandman' were not always clear, particularly in the fifteenth and early sixteenth centuries. This is hardly surprising given that such titles were still emerging and that, as has been explored previously, the sizes of landholdings were increasing so that many husbandmen were acquiring levels of holdings which eventually became synonymous with yeomen rather than husbandmen. Despite this, the term was understood to be someone who cultivated land as a free tenant or small landowner holding land between 15/20 and 40 acres and therefore below the size of holdings normally ascribed to yeomen.[112]

Most husbandmen appear to have conformed to Sharpe's definition of a husbandman as a small-to-middling farmer for whom life was a struggle, who was always vulnerable to economic disaster, but who could expect to get by in all but the very worst years.[113] Almost all of the wills made by husbandmen included within the sample for this study contained limited bequests of cash and goods and only one was proved at the higher court of Canterbury, that of John Bavise of Everton in Huntingdonshire whose will was made in 1496.[114] It is possible to identify that Bavise's landholdings exceeded 40 acres, in common

PHOTO 8.1   Yeoman's farmhouse, Midhurst, 1609[108]
Source: Weald and Downland Museum

with some of the other testators who identified themselves as husbandman, so that these men would probably have been termed yeomen by later generations.

There is a continuous debate as to whether, from the mid-sixteenth century onwards, husbandmen were a homogenous or a heterogeneous group, both as regards how they differed from yeoman and in relation to their relative status when compared to labourers. Husbandmen typically worked smaller plots than yeomen which were defined by Wrightson as holdings supporting a family and producing a modest surplus in most years. These small holdings relied for the most part on family labour.[115] Barry Coward claimed that the differences between yeomen and husbandmen were substantial and that whereas yeomen were 'large farmers' who might be owner occupiers or tenants, husbandmen were much poorer and often farmed little more than 'smallholdings'.[116] Wrightson also drew a contrast between yeomen who as 'large-scale producers' were able to exploit economic opportunities and husbandmen who were less well placed as they 'simply produced too little'.[117]

Categorisation of the agricultural ranks of yeomen and husbandmen were further confused by the term 'farmer'. The occupational designation of 'farmer' did not appear in late medieval sources although 'farmers' did exist and were understood as being men who leased land, often the demesne lands of manorial lords so that, for example Stephen Draper, gentleman, of Thetford referred in his will to 'Robert

Ballye my fermor'.[118] However, the term was increasingly used as an occupational term in probate inventories which raises the question whether 'farmers' were synonymous with yeomen. Barry Trinder, who analysed inventories in Shropshire, did not recognise this as a problem as he found that the term farmer was almost unknown in the county's probate documents before 1750.[119] However, Weatherill found that the term 'farmer' was commonly used in her sample for the period 1675–1725 and she designated farmers with inventory values over £60 (60 per cent of total farmers in her sample) as yeomen and those with values under £60 (40 per cent of total farmers) as husbandmen.[120]

At the lower end of the social scale, it is also important to consider the extent to which husbandmen can be distinguished from labourers. Shephard showed that the median worth evaluations of husbandmen were five times that of labourers by the second quarter of the seventeenth century.[121] Shaw-Taylor examined Poll Tax returns for 1660 in Cheshire and found that husbandmen had an average tax rating three times that of labourers which led to his conclusion that husbandmen were a distinct social group from labourers.[122] On the other hand, Spufford identified two sharply defined groups in her examination of 24 inventories for Cambridgeshire husbandmen in the 1660s. The first group were husbandmen who farmed less than ten acres of arable land and who could hardly be distinguished from better-off labourers. The second more prosperous group farmed between 21 and 40 acres. They had a wide range of inventory values but the median was £30 or double that of labourers' inventories relating to the same period.[123] For Alan Everitt the difference between a poor husbandman and a better off labourer was also a grey area.[124]

Labourers

This section considers agricultural labourers, although not all those classified as 'labourers' were employed in the primary sector of the economy.[125] Prior to the Black Death, the landless and smallholding peasants who depended on wages to maintain themselves and their households created a ready supply of labour. The increased availability of land from the mid-fourteenth century allowed many waged labourers to either acquire or substantiate landholdings and consequently reduce or even curtail their need for waged labour. This, combined with the overall population decline of the fourteenth century, led to a significant decrease in the number of labourers although occupational designations in tax records suggested that they still formed a significant proportion of the population; for example, 161 of the 248 heads of households listed in the 1380 poll tax return for Mildenhall were classified as '*labor*'.[126] The lowest tiers of rural society in the late Middle Ages also included cottagers, rural craftsmen, paupers and vagrants although none of the wills used for this study could be identified as being of people who came from these groups.[127] Stephen Broadberry *et al.* estimated that these lowest tiers represented 22 per cent of all households in 1381, and that whereas the average income for English households was £6.6 per annum, these households earned an average of just £3 per annum.[128]

Although the labourers used for this study were all designated as such within their probate documents, it seems unlikely that they were strictly typical of contemporary labourers since members of this low-status occupational group generally had insufficient wealth, possessions or land to require the making of a will or inventory. For the wills, with only one exception, labourers did not bequeath much in the way of goods, property or cash and their wills were proved in the lowest level of ecclesiastical court. Only Thomas Crupens of Mildenhall, who made his will in 1525, was able to bequeath ten bullocks, 12 sheep and two horses in addition to his house and small monetary bequests which suggests that despite referring to himself as 'labourer', he was unusual for this occupational group.[129]

Gregory King estimated that 'labourers, cottagers and paupers' and their families comprised 46 per cent of the population in 1688.[130] He calculated that these groups decreased the wealth of the kingdom because their yearly expenditure exceeded their income. Nevertheless, the category of 'labourers, cottagers and paupers' embraced a wide range of people, from labourers who owned some land to paupers. For Wrightson, the most striking feature of King's calculation was the 'yawning gap' between the yearly income of the least well off of the 'middle sort' and those of labouring people.[131] King estimated the annual income of a farmer's family to be £42 10s, whereas families of labourers and servants had £15 and cottagers and paupers only £6 10s.[132] Whilst most labourers were agricultural labourers, labourers also worked in other sectors of the economy, although the distinction between labourers and petty craftsmen could be blurred, particularly in towns.[133]. Dual employments were also widespread; Sharpe found that 60 per cent of labourers on a Gloucestershire listing of 1608 were also carrying out other trades.[134]

Alan Everitt maintained that in this period no one had left more scanty records than labourers. No diaries, no letters, no account books, few lawsuits and a 'handful of wills and inventories'.[135] Overton et al. concluded their study by declaring, 'we can say nothing about the 40 per cent or so of the population that were exempt from most taxes and were unlikely to have an inventory'.[136] However, there are rather more surviving labourers' inventories than Everitt and Overton suggested although it must be recognised that inventoried labourers were likely to be more affluent than labourers as represented in the wider population.[137]

Muldrew analysed almost 1,000 labourers' inventories dating from 1550–1799 for Cambridgeshire, Cheshire, Hampshire, Kent, Lincolnshire and Norfolk. The inventories largely covered a chronological span of about 200 years although only 11 inventories related to the period after 1750. The median inventory values ranged from £12.94 in Norfolk to £22.37 in Hampshire (Table 8.4).[138] In the present sample, inventories for labourers from Huntingdonshire had a median inventory value of £17.26, close to that of neighbouring Cambridgeshire.

Most labourers did not work land on their own account but worked for other people; however, Wrightson suggested that more fortunate labourers might hold an acre or two or enjoy the benefits of customary common rights.[139] He estimated

TABLE 8.4 Labourers' inventory values

	1550–99	1600–49	1650–99	1700–49	Median Inv. Value
	No.	No.	No.	No.	
Cambs.	1	1	170	88	16.16
Cheshire	7	20	32	17	19.33
Hampshire	22	38	76	26	22.37
Kent	48	64	112	37	20.23
Lincolnshire	18	0	42	4	19.92
Norfolk	24	77	12	23	12.94
Sub total	120	200	444	195	18.49
Hunts	N/A	87	97	70	17.26
Totals	120	287	541	265	

Source: Muldrew, *Food, Energy and the Creation of Industriousness*, pp.172–73.

that a labourer's wage represented about 12d for a day's work in the seventeenth century but argued that wage rates varied regionally. For example, in Whickham, County Durham, agricultural labourers earned between 8d and 10d a day in the mid-eighteenth century.[140]

Three major factors influenced annual family income: regularity of employment, payments in kind and contributions of other family members. Demand for labour was seasonal and irregular with peak periods at lambing, harvesting and haymaking and slack periods from November to February. Labour markets were also highly localised and employment opportunities varied in different regions of the country.[141] Furthermore, labourers were not always paid in money so that Donald Woodward argued that Spufford's acceptance of such a dramatic fall in the labourer's economic position was misleading as labourers were often provided with food and drink at work.[142] Shaw-Taylor drew attention to the significance of common land in contributing to the livelihood of English labourers and suggested that the right to graze a cow, gather fuel, fatten a pig, glean after the harvest together with possession of a small garden could provide resources equal to the annual cash wages of a labourer.[143]

Professionals and tradesmen

High-status trades (HST)

The occupations viewed as having high social status in the late Middle Ages were the merchant trades of mercers, grocers and drapers, together with goldsmiths, and in that order of status.[145] Members of professions were also considered to be of high status including secular and regular clergy, doctors, lawyers and scriveners. Whilst men who followed professional careers did not necessarily possess substantial wealth, they were

PHOTO 8.2 Seventeenth-century labourer's cottage[144]
Source: Weald and Downland Museum

often from gentry families and retained close associations with other gentry or profes-sionals such that contemporary society perceived them to be of high status.

Household incomes for average households within this social status group were difficult to estimate as surviving records generally related to large households. One source which did provide a basic outline was the account book of William Saver-nak which detailed the expenses of a small household consisting of two chantry priests and their servant for seven years during the 1450s.[146] Although the accounts do not list receipts, K.L. Wood-Legh estimated that the yearly expenses of the household varied during these years between £22.65 and £11.77 with a mean of £15.75 and that these figures probably included an annual sum of £2 for chaplains' stipends.[147] This suggests that this small household of minor clergy probably had a mean income of around £13.75 (if it is assumed that their income was broadly in line with their expenditure), just over double the average house-hold income of £6.60 as calculated by Broadberry *et al.* for 1381.[148] However, once again, it seems likely that the wealth of members of this social status group varied widely. As with those who held gentry and yeoman status, the wills of men who held high-status occupations used for this study included those proved at the Prerogative Court of Canterbury as well as the lesser courts and monetary bequests ranged considerably. The total value of those made by John Parsey, a draper from Bury St. Edmunds, came to over £175, whilst some members of this group left no monetary bequests, although all of these were clerics such as the Thetford chaplain William Iskyn.[149]

A wide range in clerical incomes continued beyond the Reformation. Gregory King suggested that there were approximately 10,000 clergymen in England in 1688 with about 2,000 categorised as 'eminent' and 8,000 as 'lesser' clergymen.[150] By 1736, although the bishops of Durham and Winchester had incomes of £6,000 and £5,000 respectively, 5,600 of England's 11,000 livings fell below the 'poverty line' of £50 per annum.[151] Clergy income was not always easy to determine and could easily be misinterpreted. In 1650, a parliamentary survey valued the living of Earls Colne in Essex at only £24 plus £4 glebe.[152] However, the diary of Ralph Josselin, vicar, revealed that he received substantial income from other sources which included annual gifts from the living's patron, about £70 a year for teaching at Earls Colne school and approximately £70 a year from farming and leasing land. According to Alan Macfarlane's calculations, Josselin's income ranged between £160 and just over £200 a year in the period 1650 to 1683.[153]

Inventory values of clergy also suggested that the term clergyman did not represent a homogenous group. Clergy inventory values in Huntingdonshire ranged from £24 in 1678 to £709 in 1642. In Yorkshire, the lowest value was a curate with £37 in 1735 and the highest was £441 in 1690. The median value of Annabelle Hughes' substantial collection of 178 Sussex clergy inventories was £110 or £103 if the 24 PCC inventories are excluded.[154] Five clergy inventories exceeded £1,000 and 17 clergy inventories were valued at £20 or less with four of these under £6.

Shopkeepers had the highest median probate inventory values of occupational groups in the period 1675–1725 (£153). Weatherill found that mercers and drapers had much higher inventory values than those recorded as shopkeepers. Mercers (£341) had the highest mean values followed by drapers (£274), whereas those shopkeepers categorised by Weatherill as of intermediate status, general shopkeepers (£133), specialised shopkeepers (£92) and chandlers (£95) were much lower.[155] Hoh-Cheung Mui and Lorna H. Mui referred to the many 'mere shopkeepers' whose income and lifestyle placed them among the lower echelons of the middling groups.[156] The present study also found that drapers (£502) and mercers (£276) had high mean values but sample sizes at this level of disaggregation were relatively small. High inventory values were often the result of levels of stock in their shop rather than household goods or other personal assets. These stocks were frequently purchased on borrowed money. For example, the inventory of William Eastwood, a grocer in Wakefield, was valued at £1,200 in 1735 of which goods in his shop represented £992. Revealingly, his probate account recorded that he also owed a total of £992 in debts and therefore it would appear that his very substantial shop goods were financed on credit.

Intermediate-status trades (IST)

Trades that have been classed as having intermediate status were generally those that required a higher capital outlay on tools and materials, or on stock. These included some of the victualling trades, particularly those which were associated with the manufacture of ale, such as brewers, maltsters and innholders, shopkeepers, tanners and chandlers. Similarly, whilst most of the occupations associated with the manufacture of cloth were generally viewed as being of low status, dyers were categorised as having intermediate status and superior to other cloth-workers. Some types of dye were very expensive so that the dyeing tended to be undertaken by craftsmen operating their own independent, self-financed units whilst other stages of cloth manufacture were increasingly controlled by middlemen.

As has been noted, the status of a trade could change over time so that, for example, 'tailors' held intermediate status at the beginning of our period but were viewed as low status by the seventeenth century. It is evident from the instructions issued in Norwich in *c.* 1449 and *c.* 1453 for the processions on the crafts on Corpus Christi Day that tailors were accorded at least intermediate status, whilst evidence from the wills of men described as tailors used for this study confirmed that they were often men of some wealth.[157] John Michell, a tailor from Soham, Cambridgeshire, left over £5 in monetary gifts to various religious benefactors in and around Soham and had his will proved at the Prerogative Court of Canterbury.[158] By the early modern period, the median value of 26 tailors' inventories dating from 1675–1725 was only £22, one of the lowest of any occupational group and barely above that of labourers (£18) (Table 8.8a). A contributing factor towards lower inventory values was that tailoring required few tools and tailors did not have stocks of leather, ready-made shoes or gloves found in other clothing tradesmen's inventories.[159]

A possible explanation for this apparent discrepancy is that 'tailor' was initially used to describe someone who dealt in cloth rather than just, as was subsequently the case, someone who worked with cloth. In his will, John Michell also referred to his ownership of a close with tenters, as well as his woollen cloth at his home and at Ely and Newmarket. By the end of the early modern period, John Styles suggested that for many tailors, mending accounted for most of their orders. He cited an engraving which portrayed a humble stitch tailor in Westminster in 1784 who worked in shabby premises and advertised that he performed small jobs.[160] Nevertheless, the term could still be applied to men with varying economic circumstances and not all tailors were of lower status. Malcolm Smith described Samuel Pepys as a man of 'humble beginnings' for he was the son of a tailor; however, this was hardly a fitting description for John Pepys who ran a tailoring business serving London lawyers, whilst the Pepys family was well connected and counted Edward Montagu, the future earl of Sandwich, as a relative.[161]

Also of intermediate status were some of the trades and crafts associated with leather and skins, so that leather-dealers and tanners were viewed as being of intermediate status (a greater outlay of capital was also required for these occupations).[162] Tanners had one of the highest median inventory values and, like shopkeepers, often had high value stocks recorded in their inventories. Tanners made considerable investments in hides before achieving a return. The Negus family in Godmanchester, Huntingdonshire were tanners; W. Negus, who died in

1709, had hides and other stocks valued at £550 and J. Negus (died 1749) had hides, skins and bark in his 'tanyard' valued at £336. W. Negus was described as a gentleman in his inventory which at £1,351 was the highest valuation of any surviving Godmanchester inventory. Evidence from probate accounts did not suggest that tanners owed large amounts of money at their death despite the significant investments their occupation required.

Low-status trades (LST)

The majority of trades were designated as being of low status. In particular, most crafts were considered to be of this category including those associated with the manufacture of cloth, such as shearmen, weavers and fullers; most metalworkers, such as locksmiths, blacksmiths and armourers (but not those that worked with more valuable metals such as pewterers and goldsmiths); those connected to building and woodworking, for example, carpenters, coopers, fletchers and bricklayers; and crafts which used prepared skin to make clothing items, such as glovers or cordwainers. In addition, some of the victualling trades were viewed as being of low status, particularly bakers and cooks.

Almost all the wills used for this study made by men with low-status occupations were proved in the lesser courts. A very few contain large cash bequests such as that of the shearman Edward Briges of Walthamstow who left a total of £5 4s in 1565, but most leave few or no cash bequests beyond a small amount given to the high altar for forgotten tithes, as with the 4d given by the furberer William Plumer of St Albans in 1493.[163]

Median inventory values for most of the largest groups of occupations assigned lower status in our sample were similar, ranging from £29 to £39 in the period 1675–1725. Weatherill gave more widely varying mean values which might have been influenced by those towards the top and bottom of the distribution. The one exception was bakers which had higher values than other occupations and a case could be made for grouping them with intermediate trades.

Females

Women were underrepresented across all of the probate records used for this study, both wills and inventories, since the property of married women became the possession of their husband on marriage so that far fewer women than men made wills or inventories.[164] Common laws of coverture, based on the concept that a husband and wife were one person, meant that the wife was figuratively 'covered' by him and she had no independent legal identity at common law.[165] Until the Married Women's Property Act of 1882, a married woman could only make a will with her husband's consent.[166] As a result, most women who made wills or inventories were either widows with assets which had probably been bequeathed to them by deceased husbands, or spinsters who had never married but who held property which was likely to have been inherited from other family members.

It has been calculated that, factoring in the proportions of widows, only about half of all adult women in early modern England were married at any given point in time, so that 'single women', including both widows and spinsters, comprised a significant proportion of the population. Froide maintained that single women in late seventeenth-century England comprised at least a third of adult women.[167] Spinsters under 45 typically lived with their parents and provided care for them until their death.[168] Other occupations undertaken by spinsters included looking after bachelor brothers, whilst many single women in rural areas were employed in agriculture.[169] Alex Cowan argued that defining widows was not straightforward and that widowhood was a 'highly subjective condition'; in a review of Sandra Cavallo and Lyndan Warner's *Widowhood in Medieval and Early Modern Europe*, Cowan argued that the classic definition of widowhood as the phase of marriage following a partner's death was unsatisfactory. Contemporary documents were inconsistent in recording widowed status, and people were often unable to differentiate between women whose husbands had died and married women whose husbands had left them and moved away.[170] Bridget Hill went further and argued that women had a range of domestic and sexual relationships with men.[171]

Despite their underrepresentation in the sources used for this study, McKendrick expected that women would play a more central role in generating demand for goods.[172] For Jan de Vries also, the wife took a primary role as decision maker in consumption.[173] By contrast, Margot Finn argued that men were active both as participants and as initiating agents in a range of consumer activities which historians have frequently associated with women. For Finn, the diaries of James Woodforde, William Holland and Robert Sharp exemplify male acquisitive impulses unleashed by the consumer revolution.[174]

Around 13 per cent of the wills used for this study were made by women. In most cases, testators specifically identify themselves as 'widows' and almost certainly bequeathed assets received from deceased husbands. Some wills were made by married women, however, in many of these cases the will refers to a previous, deceased husband so that any bequests were probably items which were previously those of a former husband and which had not been passed on to a subsequent husband at marriage, such as landholdings used to maintain dependent children from the earlier marriage. Reference to a husband's consent was exceptional in probate records. A rare example was the will of Susannah Malsham, a wife from Kingston upon Hull who died in 1727. Her will stated in the introduction that she was making it with the consent of her husband.

Shepard's research suggested that there was a significant difference between the assets of widows and single women. Her analysis of court witnesses revealed that the 'worth' of widows was much higher than that of single women. For example, in the years 1625–49 the mean worth of widows (£16.71) was more than three times that of single women (£5.30).[175] The present study supported Shepard's findings and found that generally widows had a higher incidence of ownership of most items including bedding, seating, clocks and pewter.

Selected probate records by rank

The numbers of wills used for this study from each of these rankings, together with the dates to which they relate, are detailed in Table 8.5a.

Whilst the selected wills included those made by both male and female testators, there is a gender bias so that only 13.25 per cent of the total will sample were made by women and 86.75 per cent were made by men. This closely corresponds with the gender division of those people whose inventories have been used for this study. 'Gentry' testators represented 3.4 per cent of the wills, whilst the wills of men who can be identified as having 'high-status trades' comprised 7.9 per cent of the total. Men with 'intermediate-status trades' made up 6.4 per cent of testators and those with 'low-status trades' amounted to 10.2 per cent. For the agricultural rankings, 'yeomen' comprised 9.6 per cent of the testators, husbandmen 8.2 per cent and labourers only 1 per cent.

The occupations of just over 40 per cent of the testators have not been identified as they are not referred to within the will itself and cannot be reliably ascertained from other sources. The wills chosen include many that have been

TABLE 8.5A Will sample by rank

	1430–59	1460–89	1490–1519	1520–49	1550–79	Totals
	n	n	n	n	n	n
Gentry	3	19	7	11	11	51
HST	16	37	33	16	18	120
IST	5	29	30	19	14	97
Yeomen	14	33	22	29	47	145
LST	12	46	46	23	28	155
Husbandman	16	28	17	27	36	124
Labourers	0	0	0	7	9	16
Females	22	62	51	42	24	201
Unknown	61	233	155	82	76	607
Total	149	487	361	256	263	1516
	%	%	%	%	%	%
Gentry	2.0	3.9	2.0	4.3	4.2	3.4
HST	10.8	7.6	9.1	6.3	6.8	7.9
IST	3.4	5.9	8.3	7.4	5.3	6.4
Yeomen	9.4	6.8	6.1	11.3	17.9	9.6
LST	8.0	9.4	12.7	9.0	10.7	10.2
Husbandmen	10.7	5.8	4.7	10.6	13.7	8.2
Labourers	0	0	0	2.7	3.4	1.0
Females	14.8	12.8	14.2	16.4	9.1	13.3
Unknown	40.9	47.8	42.9	32.0	28.9	40.0
Total	100	100	100	100	100	100

transcribed and published, together with a significant number that have been specifically transcribed for this study.[176] Care has been taken to ensure that those used include examples proved at each of the three levels of church court in an attempt to include evidence of consumption by as wide a strata of society as can be represented by testamentary evidence and not just by the social elite.

The trends indicated by these numbers are not inconsistent with the breakdown of the social rank for the inventory sample (Table 8.5b), with the exception of the figure for testators whose occupation/social status was unknown which is much higher than that for inventories. A range of factors have generally led to lower figures than those for the inventory sample. Firstly, wills were less likely to include the status designation or occupation of their subject than inventories so that the number of identified occupations was considerably lower. Secondly, will-making was far more commonplace amongst men with high status so that a significantly higher proportion of these men made wills. Men with low status made wills only infrequently so that although more wills of men with low status have been used for this study than of men with high status, they are likely to represent a much smaller proportion of their status group. Finally, as has been noted, the landholding status designations of 'yeoman' and 'husbandman' were in a state of some fluidity during this period so that some of the men who referred to themselves as 'husbandman' held land in excess of 40 acres and would have subsequently been termed yeoman. It has been noted that the use of the term 'husbandman' was in decline in the early modern period and it seems reasonable to conclude that this process had begun by the very end of the medieval period.

Table 8.5b shows the inventory sample broken down by social rank which, again, used the categories developed by Weatherill and is based on Brodsky Elliott's study of mobility and marriage in pre-industrial England. About a quarter of inventories in the sample had no designated occupation but in the second half of the eighteenth century, the percentage of those recorded as of unknown rank was falling in most counties. Breakdown by sex showed that most inventories (86 per cent) were for males and 14 per cent for females, mainly widows.

Although the period covered by the inventory sample was much longer than that covered by Weatherill, the breakdown by social rank was very similar for gentry and the three tradesmen groups. Gentry represented 4 per cent of inventories, the same percentage as Weatherill's sample of 2,902 inventories. Professionals of 'high status' were also the same percentage as Weatherill's at 5 per cent. Tradesmen (intermediate and low status) inventories were 26 per cent of the sample compared to Weatherill's 27 per cent. Weatherill had a much higher percentage of yeomen (33 per cent compared to 17 per cent) and husbandmen (11 per cent compared to 5 per cent), but considerably fewer labourers (only 28 in total). Weatherill's yeomen were a particularly high percentage compared with other inventory samples; for example, Overton *et al.* had 19 per cent yeomen inventories in Cornwall and 14 per cent in Kent. The use of the term 'husbandman' and hence husbandmen inventories declined over time and Huntingdonshire was deliberately selected for the present study because of the large number of labourers' inventories, particularly

TABLE 8.5B Inventory sample by rank

	1551–1600	1601–29	1630–59	1660–89	1690–1719	1720–49	1750–1800	Totals
	n	n	n	n	n	n	n	n
Gentry	10	21	20	74	69	43	32	269
HST	54	24	31	74	81	47	61	372
IST	26	48	30	105	158	145	151	662
Yeomen	74	57	71	203	312	268	274	1,259
LST	93	109	77	276	284	265	186	1,290
Husbandmen	78	66	41	63	64	68	27	407
Labourers	14	63	43	95	68	55	15	353
Females	63	99	78	214	262	210	150	1,076
Unknown	174	123	116	293	401	440	205	1,752
Total	586	610	507	1,396	1,699	1,541	1,101	7,440
	%	%	%	%	%	%	%	%
Gentry	2	4	4	5	4	3	3	4
HST	9	4	6	5	5	3	5	5
IST	4	8	6	7	9	9	14	9
Yeomen	13	9	14	15	18	17	25	17
LST	16	18	15	20	17	17	17	17
Husbandmen	13	11	8	5	4	4	2	5
Labourers	2	10	8	7	4	4	1	5
Females	11	16	16	15	15	14	14	14
Unknown	30	20	23	21	24	29	19	24
Total	100	100	100	100	100	100	100	100

in the seventeenth century. Weatherill had considerably fewer female inventories (7 per cent compared to 14 per cent) and far fewer inventories for those recorded as of unknown status (11 per cent compared to 24 per cent).

There is no doubt that inventories were biased towards the upper end of the social spectrum and were not representative of the whole population but the extent of this is difficult to ascertain. An innovative method for measuring bias is to use Anglican baptism registers which record the occupation of fathers. Recording a father's occupation was not a statutory requirement until Rose's Act of 1813. Before this date recording depended on the initiative of incumbents, which meant that information was not usually consistently recorded over a sufficient period to create sequences of robust data. This source also excludes most nonconformists, Catholics and Jews. However, Nigel Yates suggested that in 1720 nonconformists represented only about 6 per cent of the population and James Bradley found no significant difference between social structures of Anglicans and dissenters.[177]

Two Huntingdonshire market towns included in the selected sample of inventories give at least some indication of bias in probate inventories compared with the whole population of these towns. Table 8.6 sets out a relatively rare run of 11 consecutive years of recorded occupational data from the early seventeenth century in Ramsey, and a period almost a century later in St Ives. Results of the comparison of parish register and inventory data show that the percentage of inventories relating to tradesmen such as butchers, bakers and cordwainers was more than half of the total but fairly representative of the population as a whole. Huntingdonshire had a relatively high survival rate of labourers' inventories, particularly in the seventeenth century, and results for labourers are unlikely to be replicated more generally. But they did suggest that, at least in some small market towns, labourers may be a somewhat lesser percentage of the population than is sometimes assumed.

Examination of baptismal occupational data from Calverley and Sandal Magna showed that parishes within Pontefract Deanery in Yorkshire could have very different occupational structures (Table 8.7). Calverley is in the north of the deanery adjacent to Bradford, and Sandal Magna is in the south next to Wakefield. In Calverley, 88 per cent of baptisms between 1721 and 1760 identified the status or occupation of the father and in Sandal Magna it was 92 per cent between 1776 and 1793. In Calverley, 59 per cent of fathers were clothiers or clothworkers (more than twice the percentage in West Riding) and only 15 per cent designated labourers. By contrast, in Sandal Magna, only 1 per cent of fathers were clothiers or clothworkers and 45 per cent labourers. In both Calverley and Sandal Magna, only 9 per cent of fathers were designated either 'farmers', yeomen or husbandmen. The parish register in Sandal Magna invariably used the term 'farmer' and did not attempt to distinguish between yeomen and husbandmen. The differences

TABLE 8.6 Social bias of probate inventories

	Ramsey				St Ives			
	Baptism registers 1617–27		17th-century inventories		Baptism registers 1706–15		Inventories 1651–1750	
	no.	%	no.	%	no.	%	no.	%
Gentry	9	2	3	3	9	2	4	6
Professions	3	1	1	1	9	2	4	6
Yeomen	15	4	20	22	4	1	5	7
Tradesmen	202	53	43	46	282	65	54	75
Husbandmen	2	1	10	11	0	0	0	0
Labourers	147	39	16	17	128	30	4	6
Sub-total	**378**	**100**	**93**	**100**	**432**	**100**	**71**	**100**
Females			26				32	
Status Unknown	56		33		86		31	

TABLE 8.7 Social bias of probate inventories: Yorkshire

	Yorkshire inventories 1710–95		West Riding inventories 1710–95		Calverley baptism registers 1721–60		Sandal Magna baptism registers 1776–93	
	No.	%	No.	%	No.	%	No.	%
Gentry	34	4	21	4	4	0	8	1
Yeomen	264	34	153	30	56	2	75)	9
Husbandmen	62	8	15	3	203	7	)	
Labourers	17	2	10	2	402	15	384	45
Tanners	4	1	3	1	21	1	22	3
Apothecaries/Doctors	1	0	0	0	3	0	1	0
Shopkeepers, etc.	19	2	11	2	1	0	1	0
Clergy	3	1	3	1	4	0	4	1
Glovers	3	1	1	0	0	0	0	0
Innkeepers, etc.	25	3	21	4	33	1	11	1
Bakers	3	1	1	0	0	0	3	0
Clothiers/Clothworkers	124	16	136	27	1,634	59	7	1
Blacksmiths	15	2	9	2	53	2	14	2
Cordwainers/Shoemakers	19	2	14	3	53	2	51	6
Carpenters/Joiners	16	2	11	2	66	2	29	3
Mariners	0	0	0	0	0	0	0	0
Masons	11	2	8	2	48	2	20	2
Weavers	21	2	16	3	14	1	76	9
Butchers	11	2	9	2	28	1	14	2
Tailors	8	1	6	1	61	2	29	3
Bricklayers	1	0	0	0	5	0	12	1
Other tradesmen	112	14	56	11	86	3	89	11
Total	**773**	**100**	**504**	**100**	**2775**	**100**	**850**	**100**

between Calverley and Sandal Magna were far greater than the comparison of these parishes with the inventoried populations of both West Riding and Yorkshire taken as a whole. Calverley had more than twice the percentage of clothiers than inventoried clothiers in industrialising West Riding.

The Occupational Structure Project of CAMPOP at the University of Cambridge is carrying out a major project to examine occupational structure using Anglican baptism registers. This has shown the extent to which the percentage of males employed in the agricultural sector continued to fall whilst males employed in the secondary and tertiary sector rose. There was considerable variation in occupational structure between regions of the country.[178] Whilst employment in agriculture was shrinking, the composition of the agricultural sector was changing in that labourers comprised a greater proportion of the agricultural sector leading to greater social polarisation.[179]

It is instructive to compare inventory values for certain occupational and status groups calculated for this study with data produced by Weatherill. The period covered by Weatherill was 1675–1725 and for this period our inventory sample is similar in size; 2,981 inventories compared with Weatherill's 2,902. The data produced similar results. Overall mean values were £124 compared to Weatherill's £128 (Table 8.8a). In the status groups, the traditional order prevailed, with median values of gentry £243, yeomen £114, husbandmen £66 and labourers £18. Despite the historiographical arguments, there was little difference between the inventory values of widows and spinsters.

The rank order of occupational groups, i.e. from mercers to tailors, in Table 8.8a was based on median inventory values. The median is a more effective measure of central tendency because the mean can be unduly influenced by extreme values. Mercers and drapers had the highest median inventory values, slightly higher even than gentry. Shopkeepers' and chandlers' values were the second highest of those in occupational groups at £153, significantly lower than mercers and drapers. Tanners had the third highest median values. Unfortunately, Weatherill did not report the more meaningful median results for individual occupations but her mean values were also high for tanners, supporting their claim to be classified as higher in status than most tradesmen. However, a substantial proportion of their inventory values were, like shopkeepers, invested in stock which might have been purchased with borrowed money. If sufficient data from probate accounts were available, they might well show that their net wealth might not be so impressive. Nevertheless, the ability to borrow substantial sums was, in itself, a reflection of status and good standing in the community. Clergy, apothecaries, doctors of physick and surgeons also had high values.

It is important to consider an additional method, the standard deviation, to describe the amount of dispersion of the data around the mean. The coefficient of variation enabled the degree to which variables differed from their respective means to be compared.[181] Blacksmiths (CV=100) had the least and widows (CV=204) the greatest degree of variation (Table 8.8b). It was not surprising that widows had the highest coefficient of variation as their deceased husbands represented a wide range of occupational and status groups.

The social mix of the inventories showed significant changes over time. Table 8.9 excluded inventories which did not record occupations. Dorset was omitted because its inventories had a substantially higher percentage of non-recorded occupations, rendering analysis of social structure for this county largely meaningless. More than three quarters of Bristol inventories were for professionals and tradesmen and this increased to 92 per cent in the second half of the seventeenth century. All the other counties showed an increasing percentage of tradesmen's

TABLE 8.8A Inventory values by status and occupation, 1675–1725

	Weatherill			Sneath & Sear		
	Sample size	Median	Mean	Sample size	Median	Mean
STATUS GROUPS	No.	£	£	No.	£	£
Gentry	122	154	320	101	243	425
Yeomen	952	104	165	519	114	185
Husbandmen	332	30	32	135	66	104
Labourers	26	13	16	143	18	29
Spinsters	30	}30	56	38	35	67
Widows	187	}	86	411	32	76
Sub Total	1,649			1,347		
OCCUPATIONAL GROUPS						
Mercers and Drapers	21		303	21	247	397
Shopkeepers/Chandlers	95		121	38	153	243
Tanners	12		146	16	147	252
Apothecary etc.[180]	14		189	15	128	198
Clerk/clergy	24		217	24	125	183
Innkeepers	24		138	43	97	205
Victuallers	77		155	22	62	84
Bakers	10		147	16	56	100
Blacksmiths	49		56	48	39	51
Weavers	48		88	29	38	83
Mariners	40		85	32	37	126
Joiners	4		48	13	34	63
Butchers	37		129	24	30	102
Carpenters	32		70	44	29	61
Tailors	32		56	41	22	46
ALL INVENTORIES	**2,902**		**128**	**2981**	**53**	**124**

inventories over the period, with all counties being close to or above 40 per cent of the total by the mid-eighteenth century. There was a further significant rise in the percentage of tradesmen by the end of the century.

Inventory values and ownership of household goods were related to social rank and therefore analysing the social mix of inventories in any sample is crucial when comparisons are made between localities and over time. Gregory Clark argued that the consumer revolution was a statistical artefact for the average testator was at a much higher level in the distribution of wealth within society than the average testator of 1600.[182] There was a changing composition of the population with probate documents over time with considerably more tradesmen but it cannot be assumed that this change reflected actual changes in the occupational structure of the population as a whole. Clark further argued that there was no gain either in

TABLE 8.8B Inventory values by status and occupation, 1675–1725

	Sample size	Lowest	Median	Highest	Mean	Standard deviation	Coefficient of variation
STATUS GROUPS	No.	£	£	£	£	£	%
Gentry	101	5	243	3,158	425	645	152
Yeomen	519	2	114	3,369	185	261	141
Husbandmen	135	3	66	766	104	105	101
Labourers	143	2	18	233	29	37	128
Spinsters	38	4	35	500	67	103	154
Widows	411	1	32	2,509	76	155	204
Sub Total	1,347						
OCCUPATION GROUPS							
Innkeepers/ Victuallers	65	3	90	1,163	164	225	137
Blacksmiths	48	1	39	228	51	51	100
Weavers	29	4	38	531	83	116	140
Butchers	24	5	30	627	102	163	160
Cordwainers/ Shoemakers	43	1	30	387	56	76	136
Carpenters	44	5	29	353	62	80	129
Tailors	41	2	22	459	46	73	159
ALL INVENTORIES	**2,981**						

wages or real incomes between 1500 and 1800.[183] Further research is required but Broadberry *et al.* suggested that output per head grew five-fold and output per head doubled between 1450 and 1700 and was increasing again towards the end of the eighteenth century. The occupational structure of the whole population and not just the inventoried population was changing rapidly from agriculture towards industry and services.[184]

Conclusion

Contemporaries viewed the structure of society in the late medieval and early modern periods in various ways and used a variety of terms to describe the different social ranks. However, contemporary descriptions of the lower orders tended to group them together without distinguishing between the different social strata. Despite this, members of these poorer groups comprised the vast majority of the population in the late medieval and early modern periods. Historians have used various models to represent the structure of society. For this study, society has been structured according to the stratification theory and has been presented as a series of gradations with status defined in terms of lifestyle and prestige as viewed by other members of that society.[185]

TABLE 8.9 Social structure change over time

	Gentry	Yeomen	Husbandmen	Labs	Spinsters	Widows	Sub total	Trades men
			CORNWALL					
1600–49	9.4	24.5	19.8	1.8	2.1	19.6	77.2	22.8
1650–99	9.2	30.4	8.7	0.5	4.6	20.2	73.6	26.4
1700–49	5.4	31.9	5.3	1.4	2.9	13.9	60.8	39.2
			KENT					
1600–49	5.2	23.8	12.1	2.8	2.3	23.5	69.7	30.3
1650–99	8.2	25.2	9.2	1.5	2.1	17.6	63.8	36.2
1700–49	3.2	23.8	7.8	0.9	1.3	15.2	52.2	47.8
			HUNTINGDONSHIRE					
1600–49	6.3	11.8	6.9	18.1	1.4	23.6	68.1	31.9
1650–99	4.4	16.4	6.3	9.4	1.3	21.7	59.5	40.5
1700–49	4.1	18.9	5.4	8.1	1.1	19.2	56.8	43.2
1750–1800	2.2	29.0	2.2	0.7	1.4	10.9	46.4	53.6
			YORKSHIRE					
1600–49	N/A	N/A	N/A	N/A	N/A	N/A	N/A	N/A
1650–99	6.3	27.5	11.6	2.6	2.1	11.1	61.2	38.8
1700–49	3.8	30.2	8.3	2.0	2.8	11.1	58.2	41.8
1750–1800	3.0	29.3	2.5	1.5	1.0	12.9	50.2	49.8
			GLOUCESTERSHIRE					
1600–49	2.0	24.3	25.0	4.1	2.0	16.2	73.6	26.4
1650–99	4.9	33.9	7.4	2.1	2.9	24.5	75.7	24.3
1700–49	2.5	33.3	1.5	2.0	2.5	18.9	60.7	39.3
1750–1800	4.5	22.7	4.5	4.5	0.0	9.1	45.3	54.7
			BRISTOL					
1600–49	3.0	0.0	0.0	2.0	1.0	10.2	16.2	83.8
1650–99	0.9	0.0	0.0	0.0	1.7	5.2	7.8	92.2
1700–49	1.7	1.7	0.0	0.0	0.0	8.3	11.7	88.3
1750–1800	0.0	0.0	0.0	0.0	7.1	14.2	21.3	78.7
			SHROPSHIRE					
1600–49	N/A	N/A	N/A	N/A	N/A	N/A	N/A	N/A
1650–99	5.5	18.6	2.8	3.4	0.0	15.9	46.2	53.8
1700–49	7.9	21.3	0.5	3.0	1.0	9.9	43.6	56.4
1750–1800	5.0	0.0	0.0	0.0	0.0	15.0	20.0	80.0

However, while these representations of society are a means by which changes in consumption patterns can be identified and tracked over time, it is important to remember that the social structure was not a rigid hierarchy. The social status of an occupation could vary over time and between different practitioners. Social groups were not homogenous but represented a wide range of people. Dual occupations or 'by-employment' were also commonly practised so that many tradesmen at all levels of the social hierarchy also engaged in agriculture.

Wills and inventories were infrequently made by the lower tiers of late medieval and early modern society. Only a very few wills made by labourers have been included in this study and although rather more probate inventories have been used (5 per cent of the inventory sample), this social status category is still substantially underrepresented. Very few probate records appear to exist made by cottagers and paupers whose status was below that of labourers and none of the probate records that have been used for this study can be identified as being made by members of these lowest tiers of society. This is almost certainly a reflection of the fact that wills or inventories were rarely made for these groups, except for perhaps 'pauper inventories'.[186] Women are also underrepresented as married women did not generally make wills or inventories, so that the probate records made by women and used for this study were almost always those made by widows and single women. Around 14 per cent of the probate records used for this study were those of females. However, even though the overall percentages of probate records relating to both labourers and women remain small, as so many wills and inventories have been used for this study, these include a significant number of records relating to these groups. As a result, valid observations can be made about the consumption patterns of both women and labourers. In the following chapter, we now examine who benefited from the consumer revolution.

Notes

1 L. Weatherill, *Consumer Behaviour and Material Culture in Britain 1660–1760* (London: Routledge, 1996), pp.209–12.
2 S. Rigby, *English Society in the Later Middle Ages: Class, Status and Gender* (Basingstoke: Macmillan, 1995), p.191.
3 M. Swanton (ed. and trans.), 'Wulfstan: The institutes of polity' in M. Swanton (ed. and trans.), *Anglo-Saxon Prose* (London: J.M. Dent & Sons Ltd, 1993), p.189.
4 G. Edelen (ed.), *The Description of England: The Classic Contemporary Account of Tudor Social Life by William Harrison* (London: Constable Company, Ltd, 1994), p.94; Sir Thomas Smith, *De Republica Anglorum: The Maner of Governement or Policie of the Realme of England* (Amsterdam and New York: Scolar Press Ltd, 1970), pp.20–33 cited in P. Laslett, *The World We Have Lost* (London: Methuen, 1971), p.31.
5 J. Taylor (ed.), *British Empiricism and Early Political Economy: Gregory King's 1696 Estimates of National Wealth and Population* (Westport: Praeger, 2005).
6 G. Macaulay (ed.), *The Complete Works of John Gower* (Oxford: Clarendon Press, 1902), p.3; A. Schmidt (ed.), *William Langland, Piers Plowman: A Parallel-Text Edition of the A, B, C and Z Versions, Volume 1. Text* (London: Longman, 1995), p.325.
7 D. Palliser, 'Urban society' in R. Horrox (ed.), *Fifteenth-Century Attitudes: Perceptions of Society in Late Medieval England* (Cambridge: Cambridge University Press, 1994), p.140.
8 For example, 'The procession of the Crafts on Corpus Christi Day, c.1449' in W. Hudson and J. Tingey (eds), *The Records of the City of Norwich, Vol. II* (Norwich: Jarrold & Sons, 1910), p.230; W. Bird (ed.), *The Black Book of Winchester* (Winchester: Warren & Son Ltd, 1925) pp.27–30; E. Weissengruber, 'The Corpus Christi procession in medieval York: a symbolic struggle in a public space', *Theatre Survey*, 38 (1997), pp.117–38.
9 See also Palliser, 'Urban society', p.140.
10 Bird (ed.), *Black Book of Winchester*, pp.27–30.

11 See, for example, E. Lipson, *The Economic History of England, Vol. 1: The Middle Ages* (London: A & C Black, 1959); R. Hilton, *Class Conflict and the Crisis of Feudalism: Essays in Medieval Social History* (London: Hambledon Press, 1985); M. Keen, *English Society in the Later Middle Ages, 1348–1500* (Harmondsworth: Penguin Books, 1990); C. Dyer, *Standards of Living in the Later Middle Ages: Social Change in England, c.1200–1520* (Cambridge: Cambridge University Press, 1989); Rigby, *English Society in the Later Middle Ages*.

12 Rigby, *English Society in the Later Middle Ages*, p.1.

13 See, for example, Hilton, *Class Conflict*; Z. Razi, 'The Toronto School's reconstitution of medieval peasant society: a critical view', *Past and Present*, 85 (1979), pp.141–58, cited in S. Rigby, 'Introduction: social structure and economic change in late medieval England', in R. Horrox and M. Ormrod (eds), *A Social History of England: 1200–1500* (Cambridge: Cambridge University Press, 2006), p.2.

14 Rigby, *English Society in the Later Middle Ages*, p.3; D. Robertson, *Chaucer's London* (New York: John Wiley & Sons, 1968), p.4.

15 Rigby, *English Society in the Later Middle Ages*, p.6.

16 E. Britton, *The Community of the Vill: A Study in the History of the Family and Village Life in Fourteenth-Century England* (Toronto: Macmillan of Canada, 1977), p.168.

17 Britton, *Community of the Vill*, pp.12–15, 167.

18 See, for example, M. Bailey, *The Decline of Serfdom in Late Medieval England: From Bondage to Freedom* (Woodbridge: Boydell Press, 2014); M. Bailey, 'Rural society', in Horrox (ed.), *Fifteenth-Century Attitudes*, pp.150–68.

19 Bailey, *Decline of Serfdom*, p.3; Bailey, 'Rural society', pp.150–1.

20 *Ibid.*

21 P. Coss, 'An age of deference', in Horrox and Ormrod (eds), *Social History of England*, p.69; Bailey, 'Rural society', p.151.

22 Bailey, *Decline of Serfdom*, p.333.

23 K. Lilley, *Urban Life in the Middle Ages* (Basingstoke: Macmillan, 2002), p.200.

24 *Ibid.*, p.200.

25 Rigby, *English Society in the Later Middle Ages*.

26 Rigby, 'Introduction', p.1.

27 M. James, 'Ritual, drama and social body in the late medieval English town', *Past and Present*, 98 (1983), pp.4, 18–19.

28 The term 'gentleman' was formally recognised by the Statute of Additions in 1413; Coss, 'An age of deference', p.42.

29 G. Harriss, 'The king and his subjects', in Horrox (ed.), *Fifteenth-Century Attitudes*, p.15.

30 C. Muldrew, 'Class and credit: social identity, wealth and the life course in early modern England', in H. French and J. Barry (eds), *Identity and Agency in England, 1500–1800* (Basingstoke: Palgrave Macmillan, 2004), p.149; N. Rogers, 'The middling sort in eighteenth-century politics' in J. Barry and C. Brooks (eds), *The Middling Sort of People: Culture, Society and Politics in England, 1550–1800* (Basingstoke: Macmillan, 1994), p.159.

31 K. Wrightson, 'Sorts of people in Tudor and Stuart England' in Barry and Brooks (eds), *Middling Sort*, p.50.

32 H. French, 'Social status, localism and the middle sort of people in England, 1620-1750', *Past and Present*, 166 (2000), pp.66–99.

33 H. French and J. Barry, 'Introduction', in French and Barry (eds), *Identity and Agency*, pp.22–23.

34 C. Muldrew, *The Economy of Obligation: The Culture of Credit and Social Relations in Early Modern England* (Basingstoke: Palgrave, 1998), pp.95–119.

35 Muldrew, 'Class and credit: social identity', p.149.

36 S. Hindle, *The State and Social Change in Early Modern England, 1550–1640* (Basingstoke: Palgrave, 2002), p.49.

37 G. Nair, *Highley: The Development of a Community, 1500–1880* (Oxford: Basil Black-well, 2009), p.129.

38 P. Earle, *The Making of the English Middle Class: Business, Society and Family Life in London, 1660–1730* (London: Methuen, 1989), p.3.

39 M.R. Hunt, *The Middling Sort: Commerce, Gender and the Family in England 1680–1780* (Berkeley: University of California Press, 1996), p.15.

40 J. Barry, 'Introduction', in Barry and Brooks (eds), *Middling Sort*, p.12.

41 M. Berg, *Luxury and Pleasure in Eighteenth-Century Britain* (Oxford: Oxford University Press, 2005), p.208.

42 S. D'Cruze, 'The middling sort in eighteenth-century Colchester: independence, social relations and the community broker' in Barry and Brooks (eds), *Middling Sort*, p.207.

43 J. Smail, *The Origins of Middle Class Culture: Halifax Yorkshire 1660–1780* (Ithaca: Cornell University Press, 1994), p.222.

44 Nair, *Highley*, p.161.

45 *Ibid.*, pp.246–47, 253–54.

46 A. Shepard, *Accounting for Oneself: Worth, Status and the Social Order in Early Modern England* (Oxford: Oxford University Press, 2015), pp.1–14, 40-41, 82ff.

47 *Ibid.*, pp.37–38.

48 *Ibid.*, p.68ff.

49 M. Overton, *Agricultural Revolution in England: The Transformation of the Agrarian Economy, 1500–1850* (Cambridge: Cambridge University Press, 1996), p.38.

50 A. Fletcher and J. Stevenson (eds), *Order and Disorder in Early Modern England* (Cambridge: Cambridge University Press, 1985), p.1.

51 K. Wrightson, 'Estates, degrees and sorts in Tudor and Stuart England', *History Today*, 37 (1987), p.20.

52 R. Hall, 'Profiling the Yorkshire county elector of the early eighteenth century: new material and methods', *Historical Research*, 74 (2001), p.188.

53 Muldrew, 'Class and credit: social identity', pp.150–56.

54 V. Brodsky Elliott, 'Mobility and marriage in pre-industrial England', (unpublished PhD thesis, University of Cambridge, 1978), pp.1–149.

55 Weatherill, *Consumer Behaviour*, pp.209–12; V. Brodsky Elliott, 'Mobility and marriage in pre-industrial England' (unpublished PhD thesis, University of Cambridge, 1979).

56 Weatherill, *Consumer Behaviour*, p.3.

57 This change in perceived status of barbers and barber-surgeons was possibly related to the close association between barbers and surgery which was confirmed in London in 1540 when the Fellowship of Surgeons merged with the Company of Barbers, a London livery company, to form the Company of Barbers and Surgeons – The Worshipful Company of Barbers http://barberscompany.org/history-of-the-company/[last accessed 7 March 2017].

58 D. Edwards, M. Forrest, J. Minchinton, M. Shaw, B. Tyndall and P. Wallis (trans. and ed.), *Early Northampton Wills Preserved in Northamptonshire Record Office: Northamptonshire Record Society Vol. XLII* (Northampton: Northamptonshire Record Society, 2005), pp.161–62.

59 NRO NCC Attmere 74 (Ballys); E179/150/209.

60 R. Almond and A. Pollard, 'The yeomanry of Robin Hood and social terminology in fifteenth-century England', *Past & Present*, 170 (2001), p.59; NRO ANW Bakon 332 (Bott).

61 See Weatherill, *Consumer Behaviour*, pp.101, 177.

62 A distinction was often made in the Corpus Christi procession instructions between different types of weavers so that, for example, a division was made in Winchester between coverlet-weavers and weavers, and in Norwich between 'bedweavers', 'woollenweavers' and 'worstedweavers'; Bird (ed.), *Black Book of Winchester*, pp.27–30; Hudson and Tingey (eds), *Records of the City of Norwich*, p.230; Weatherill, *Consumer Behaviour*, p.211.

63 TNA PCC PROB 11/33/98 (Benyngton).
64 TNA PCC PROB 11/5/285 (Bernham).
65 Weatherill, *Consumer Behaviour*, p.168.
66 A.M. Froide, 'Marital status as a category of difference', in J.M. Bennett and A.M. Froide (eds), *Singlewomen in the European Past, 1250–1800* (Philadelphia: University of Pennsylvania Press, 1999), pp.236–37.
67 Weatherill, *Consumer Behaviour*, pp.104–5.
68 M.H. Long, 'A study of occupations in Yorkshire parish registers in the eighteenth and early nineteenth centuries', *Local Population Studies*, 71 (2003), p.16.
69 Edwards *et al.* (trans. and ed.), *Early Northampton Wills*, p.101.
70 The coefficient of variation enabled the degree to which variables differed from their respective means to be compared, R. Floud, *An Introduction to Quantitative Methods for Historians* (London: Methuen, 1973), pp.75–76, 82.
71 Weatherill, *Consumer Behaviour*, pp.209–10.
72 *Ibid.*, pp.209–10; Donald Woodward argued that there was a 'disputed no-man's land' between the work of carpenters and joiners that proved difficult to police and cited the case of carpenters employed by the council in Hull in 1671 to make beds and doors which was strictly the work of joiners. Woodward also found a detailed bill of work for Hull Council for the year 1713 relating to 11 master carpenters and two joiners in which both groups were paid the same rate of pay, D. Woodward, *Men at Work: Labourers and Building Craftsmen in the Towns of Northern England, 1450–1750* (Cambridge: Cambridge University Press, 2002), p.18.
73 C. Carpenter, *Locality and Polity: A Study of Warwickshire Landed Society, 1401–1499* (Cambridge: Cambridge University Press, 1992), pp.44–45.
74 Harriss, 'The king and his subjects', p.20.
75 F. Heal and C. Holmes, *The Gentry in England and Wales, 1500–1700* (Basingstoke: Macmillan Press, 1994), pp.7–9.
76 T. Adams, *An Exposition on the Second Epistle General of St Peter* (London: Henry Bohn, 1848), p.172.
77 B.G. Blackwood, *The Lancashire Gentry and the Great Rebellion* (Manchester: Manchester University Press for the Chetham Society, 1978), p.11; K. Wrightson, *English Society, 1580–1680* (London: Routledge, 2003), p.31.
78 P. Coss, *The Origins of the English Gentry* (Cambridge: Cambridge University Press, 2003), p.6.
79 *Ibid.*, p.6.
80 J. Bedells, 'The gentry of Huntingdonshire', in *Local Population Studies*, 44 (1990), pp.35–36.
81 Wrightson, *English Society*, p.31.
82 Edelen (ed.), *Description of England*, p.114; E. Rimbault (ed.), *The Miscellaneous Works in Prose and Verse of Sir Thomas Overbury* (London: John Russell Smith, 1856), p.149.
83 TNA PCC PROB 11/9/261 (Gaysley); NRO, ANW Randes 308 (Bassyngtwyte).
84 TNA PCC PROB 11/33/379 (Porter); NRO ANW Randes 308 (Bassyngtwyte).
85 Bailey, 'Rural society', p.151.
86 E. Miller, 'Introduction: Land and People', in E. Miller (ed.), *The Agrarian History of England and Wales: Vol. III, 1348–1500* (Cambridge: Cambridge University Press, 1991), p.16; Coss, 'An age of deference', p.65.
87 Bailey, 'Rural society', p.151.
88 Almond and Pollard, 'The yeomanry of Robin Hood', p.59; NRO ANW Bakon 332 (Bott).
89 Almond and Pollard, 'The yeomanry of Robin Hood', pp.52–53.

90 L. Shaw-Taylor, 'The development of agrarian capitalism and the decline of family farming in England 1500–1851', Department of Geography Seminar, University of Cambridge, Michaelmas term, 2004.

91 Wrightson, *English Society*, pp.39–40.

92 K. Wrightson and D. Levine, *Poverty and Piety in an English Village: Terling, 1525–1700* (Oxford: Clarendon Press, 1995), pp.25–26.

93 M. Spufford, *Contrasting Communities: English Villages in the Sixteenth and Seventeenth Centuries* (Cambridge: Cambridge University Press, 1974), pp.66–70, 100.

94 G.E. Mingay, *Enclosure and the Small Farmer in the Age of the Industrial Revolution* (London: Macmillan Press, 1968), pp.14–15.

95 Edelen (ed.), *Description of England*, p.117; M. Campbell, *The English Yeoman under Elizabeth and the Early Stuarts* (London: Merlin Press, 1942), pp.23–25.

96 P. Laslett, *The World We Have Lost: Further Explored* (London: Methuen, 1983), p.43.

97 Weatherill, *Consumer Behaviour*, p.171.

98 TNA PROB 11/22/486 (Smyth); SROB Baldwyne 585 (Hovell).

99 Shepard, *Accounting for Oneself*, p.69ff.

100 *Ibid.*, p.92.

101 M. Overton, J. Whittle, D. Dean and A. Hann, *Production and Consumption in English Households 1600–1750* (Abingdon: Routledge, 2004), p.26.

102 Shepard, *Accounting for Oneself*, p.92.

103 J. Sharpe, *Early Modern England: A Social History, 1550–1760* (London: Arnold, 1997), pp.206–7.

104 K. Wrightson and D. Levine, *The Making of an Industrial Society: Whickham 1560–1765* (Oxford: Clarendon Press, 1991), p.234.

105 Weatherill, *Consumer Behaviour*, pp.171–72.

106 Sharpe, *Early Modern England*, p.207; F. Steer, *Farm and Cottage Inventories of Mid-Essex 1635–1749* (Chichester: Phillimore, 1969); P. Ripley, 'Village and town: occupations and wealth in the hinterland of Gloucester, 1660–1700', *Agricultural History Review*, 32 (1984), pp.170–79.

107 Other Gloucestershire parishes were: Stoke Gifford, Frampton Cotterell, Iron Acton, Westerleigh and Winterbourne.

108 In 1609 Pendean, was sold to a yeoman, Richard Clare, son of John Clare, who held a neighbouring farm called Hurstlands. The property consisted of 40 acres of land, a barn and herbage and pasture for 100 sheep and 14 bullocks on the common land of Woolavington manor, www.wealddown.co.uk/buildings/pendean-farm house/[last accessed 19 October 2017].

109 Laslett, *The World We Have Lost: Further Explored*, p.44.

110 G. Markham, *The English Husbandman* (London [publisher not identified], 1613), p.a3.

111 Bailey, 'Rural society', p.151.

112 *Ibid.*, p.151.

113 Sharpe, *Early Modern England*, p.208.

114 TNA PROB 11/11/169 (Bavise).

115 K. Wrightson, *Earthly Necessities: Economic Lives in Early Modern Britain, 1470–1750* (New Haven: Yale University Press, 2000), p.34.

116 B. Coward, *Social Change and Continuity: England 1550–1750* (Harlow: Longman, 1997), p.3.

117 Wrightson, *English Society*, pp.142–44.

118 NRO NCC Puntyng 43 (Draper).

119 B. Trinder, 'The wooden horse in the cellar: words and contexts in Shropshire probate inventories', in T. Arkell, N. Evans, and N. Goose (eds), *When Death Do Us Part: Understanding and Interpreting the Probate Records of Early Modern England* (Oxford: Leopard's Head Press, 2000), pp.269, 272.

120 Weatherill, *Consumer Behaviour*, p.209.

121 Shepard, *Accounting for Oneself*, p.69.

122 L. Shaw-Taylor, 'The rise of agrarian capitalism', *Economic History Review*, 65 (2012), pp.54–55.
123 Spufford, *Contrasting Communities*, pp.37–38.
124 A. Everitt, 'Farm labourers', in C. Clay, *Rural Society: Landowners, Peasants and Labourers 1500–1750* (Cambridge: Cambridge University Press, 1990), p.162.
125 L. Shaw-Taylor and E.A. Wrigley, 'Occupational structure and population change' in R. Floud, J. Humphries and P. Johnson (eds), *The Cambridge Economic History of Modern Britain: Vol. I: Industrialisation, 1700–1870* (Cambridge: Cambridge University Press, 2014), p.60.
126 E. Miller, 'Introduction: land and people' in Miller (ed.), *Agrarian History of England and Wales: Vol. III*, p.9; C. Fenwick (ed.), *The Poll Taxes of 1377, 1379 and 1381: Part Two, Lincolnshire – Westmorland* (Oxford: Oxford University Press, 2001), pp.516–18.
127 S. Broadberry, B. Campbell, A. Klein, M. Overton and B. van Leeuwen, *British Economic Growth, 1270–1870* (Cambridge: Cambridge University Press, 2015), p.321.
128 *Ibid.*, p.321.
129 SROB Brydone 128 (Crupens).
130 Coward, *Social Change and Continuity*, p.56.
131 Wrightson, *Earthly Necessities*, p.307.
132 Laslett, *The World We Have Lost: Further Explored*, p.32.
133 J.A. Raftis, *Early Tudor Godmanchester: Survivals and New Arrivals* (Toronto: Pontifical Institute for Medieval Studies, 1990), p.130.
134 Sharpe, *Early Modern England*, p.213.
135 Everitt, 'Farm labourers', p.161.
136 Overton *et al.*, *Production and Consumption*, p.170.
137 B. Coward, *The Stuart Age: England 1603–1714* (London: Routledge, 2003), p.55.
138 C. Muldrew, *Food, Energy and the Creation of Industriousness* (Cambridge: Cambridge University Press, 2011), pp.172–73.
139 Wrightson, *English Society*, p.41.
140 *Ibid.*, p.42; Wrightson, *Earthly Necessities*, p.312.
141 *Ibid.*, pp.308–11.
142 D. Woodward, 'Wage rates and living standards in pre-industrial England', *Past and Present*, 91 (1981), p.29.
143 M. de Moor, L. Shaw-Taylor and P. Warde (eds), *The Management of Common Land in North West Europe, c.1500–1850* (Turnhout: Brepols, 2002); Wrightson, *Earthly Necessities*, p.314.
144 Poplar Cottage was probably built in the mid-seventeenth century, or possibly a little earlier. It occupied a small plot of land on the southern edge of the common at Washington, near Steyning. Cottages like Poplar were the homes of landless or near-landless husbandmen, labourers and craftsmen, for whom the commons were an important resource, if only to pasture a cow or gather fuel, www.wealddown.co.uk/buildings/poplar-cottage/[last accessed 19 October 2017].
145 This was according to the instructions for the Corpus Christi processions; for example, Hudson and Tingey (eds), *Records of the City of Norwich*, p.230; Bird (ed.), *Black Book of Winchester*, pp.27–30.
146 K. Wood-Legh, *A Small Household of the Fifteenth Century: Being the Account Book of Munden's Chantry, Bridport* (Manchester: Manchester University Press, 1956).
147 *Ibid.*, p.21.
148 Broadberry *et al.*, *British Economic Growth*, p.321.
149 TNA PROB 11/22/568 (Parsey); NRO NCC Cobald 7 (Iskyn).
150 Laslett, *The World We Have Lost: Further Explored*, pp.32–33.
151 Sharpe, *Early Modern England*, pp.191–92.
152 A. Macfarlane, *The Family Life of Ralph Josselin, a Seventeenth-Century Clergyman: An Essay in Historical Anthropology* (New York: Norton, 1976), p.34.
153 Macfarlane, *Family Life of Ralph Josselin*, p.36.

154 A. Hughes (ed.), *Sussex Clergy Inventories 1600–1750* (Lewes: Sussex Record Society, 2009), pp.xxxviii–xlii; five of the 183 listed inventories had no valuation.
155 Weatherill, *Consumer Behaviour*, pp.209–11.
156 H.C. Mui and L.H. Mui, *Shops and Shopkeeping in Eighteenth-Century England* (London: Routledge, 1989), p.6.
157 Hudson and Tingey (eds), *Records of the City of Norwich*, pp.230, 312–13; see, for example, SROB Baldwyne 255 (Taylour alias Wyllyamsone), NRO ANW Aleyn 46 (Hadley) and TNA PCC PROB 11/11/573 (Michell).
158 *Ibid.*
159 A.J. Kershen, *Uniting the Tailors: Trade Unionism Amongst the Tailors of London and Leeds, 1870–1939* (London: Cass, 1995), p.8.
160 *A New Way to Secure a Majority*, printed engraving 1784 British Museum London BM Sat 6572; J. Styles, *The Dress of the People: Everyday Fashion in Eighteenth-Century England* (New Haven: Yale University Press, 2007), pp.73–74.
161 M. Smith (ed.), *Human Biology and History* (London: Taylor & Francis, 2002), p.49.
162 Hudson and Tingey (eds), *Records of the City of Norwich*, pp.230, 312–13.
163 S. Flood (ed.), *St Albans Wills, 1471–1500: Hertfordshire Record Publications Vol. IX* (Hertfordshire: Hertfordshire Record Publications, 1993), p.112.
164 A.L. Erickson, *Women and Property in Early Modern England* (London: Routledge, 1993), pp.24, 237; A.L. Erickson, 'Coverture and capitalism', *History Workshop Journal*, 59 (2005), p.3.
165 J. Bailey, 'Favoured or oppressed? Married women, property and coverture in England', *Continuity and Change*, 17 (2002), p.351.
166 K. Grannum and N. Taylor, *Wills and Other Probate Records: A Practical Guide to Researching your Ancestors' Last Documents* (Kew: National Archives, 2004), p.80.
167 A.M. Froide, 'Hidden women: rediscovering the singlewomen of early modern England', *Local Population Studies*, 68 (2002), pp.26, 38.
168 A.M. Froide, *Never Married: Singlewomen in Early Modern England* (Oxford: Oxford University Press, 2005), p.19.
169 B. Hill, *Women Alone: Spinsters in England 1660–1850* (New Haven: Yale University Press, 2001), pp.68, 177.
170 A. Cowan, 'Widowhood in medieval and early modern Europe' www.history.ac.uk/reviews/paper/cowanAlex.html [last accessed 29 February 2008].
171 Hill, *Women Alone*, p.5.
172 N. McKendrick, J. Brewer and J. Plumb, *The Birth of a Consumer Society: The Commercialization of Eighteenth-Century England* (London: Hutchinson, 1982), p.23.
173 M. Berg, 'Consumption in Britain', in Floud *et al.* (eds), *Cambridge Economic History of Modern Britain: Vol. I*, p.380.
174 M. Finn, 'Men's things: masculine possession in the consumer revolution', *Social History*, 25(2) (2000), p.142.
175 Shepard, *Accounting for Oneself*, p.70.
176 For example, P. Northeast (ed.), *Wills of the Archdeaconry of Sudbury, 1439–1474: Wills from the Register 'Baldwyne', Part I: 1439–1474* (Woodbridge: Boydell Press, 2001); Flood (ed.), *St Albans Wills*.
177 N. Yates, *Eighteenth-Century Britain: Religion and Politics* (Harlow: Pearson Longman, 2008), pp.38, 56; J. E. Bradley, *Religion, Revolution and English Radicalism* (Cambridge: Cambridge University Press, 1990), pp.63–9.
178 Shaw-Taylor and Wrigley, 'Occupational structure and population change', pp.59, 65.
179 Muldrew, *Food, Energy and the Creation of Industriousness*, pp.26–28.
180 Apothecaries, surgeons and doctors of physick.
181 Floud, *Quantitative Methods*, pp.75–76, 82.
182 G. Clark, 'The consumer revolution: turning point in human history or a statistical artefact?' University of California, Davis Working Paper, 4 July 2010, p.15.

183 G. Clark, 'The macroeconomic aggregates for England, 1209–1869', *Research in Economic History*, 27 (2010), pp.51–140.
184 Broadberry *et al.*, *British Economic Growth*, p.182ff.
185 Rigby, *English Society in the Later Middle Ages*, p.6.
186 Peter King analysed a sample of 51 paupers' inventories from Essex. These inventories were compiled for those who became chargeable to a parish and thus relinquished ownership of movable possessions in return for out-relief. King warned that these inventories need to be properly contextualised as they included those who were formerly relatively prosperous artisans who spent their final days on poor relief and formerly more affluent widows who were unable to support children following the death of their husband, P. King, 'Pauper inventories and the material lives of the poor in the eighteenth and early nineteenth centuries', in T. Hitchcock, P. King and P. Sharpe (eds), *The Voices and Strategies of the English Poor, 1640–1840* (Basingstoke: Macmillan, 1997). King's work has been taken further by Adrian Green and Joseph Harley in A. Green, 'Heartless and unhomely? Dwellings of the poor in East Anglia and north-east England', in J. McEwan and P. Sharpe (eds), *Accommodating Poverty: The Housing and Living Arrangements of the English Poor, c.1600–1850* (Basingstoke: Palgrave Macmillan, 2011), pp.69–101, and J. Harley, 'Material lives of the English poor and their strategic use of the workhouse during the final decades of the English old poor law', *Continuity and Change*, 30 (1) (2015), pp.71–103. Harley's study was based on 350 fully contextualised pauper inventories from Dorset, Kent and Norfolk and showed that the material lives of those of the lowest tiers of society substantially improved during the eighteenth century, particularly for those living in the Home Counties and urban areas.

9

WHO BENEFITED FROM REVOLUTION?

The previous chapters discussed the goods which were the focus of the consumer revolution and which included both domestically produced items, such as brass pots and clocks which were supplied in ever increasing numbers, and imports of often novelty goods which people progressively wanted to own, like fine cloth and porcelain. Chapter 8 explored the various social groups that comprised the probate population; this chapter addresses the key questions about which of these social groups benefited from the consumer revolution and to what extent. How far down the social scale did ownership of consumer goods extend? How great were the differences in consumption patterns between the various social groups? Who were the first groups to own new and novel goods and when did they start to own them?

The post-Black Death period

In the introduction to this study it was observed that calculating real incomes for the late Middle Ages is somewhat controversial.[1] It was further noted that it is difficult to apply wage rates to the late medieval period for various reasons but particularly because the main focus for most households was on their own production rather than on working outside the domestic unit for work-related earnings, so that calculations of household income should not be based simply on the waged labour of the head of the household, but should include receipts from the sale of agricultural produce and artisanal items.[2] When a more inclusive approach is adopted, it is evident that the greatest beneficiaries of the economic and demographic changes that occurred in the late Middle Ages were the very poorest sections of society: the rural landless, who were able to acquire some land, to earn more, to produce some of their food and to buy the rest more cheaply; and the urban labourers, who also benefited from higher wages, more employment opportunities and lower food prices.[3] The next tier of society also experienced major improvements: in the countryside, smallholders could obtain more land, access higher wages and more work and pay less rent; and in towns, artisans were paid more for their work, as can be seen by higher prices for manufactured goods and services in the post-Black Death period. However, the economic fortunes of those higher up the social scale were rather more mixed. Peasant farmers of larger landholdings could also acquire more land and pay lower rents, but they had to contend with lower prices for their produce and were forced to pay higher wages to the workers they employed to work their land. At the highest end of the social spectrum, the gentry and the nobility suffered overall constraints on their income as receipts from rents and the sale of agricultural produce declined and at the same time the wages they had to pay increased. These richer households still managed to enjoy strong levels of disposable incomes and indulge in the consumption of luxury and better-quality items, but their overall level of expenditure was somewhat constrained in comparison to the pre-Black Death period.

These revised income levels are reflected in the social tables produced by Stephen Broadberry, Bruce Campbell, Alexander Klein, Mark Overton and Bas van Leeuwen which show that the most significant changes to household incomes in the post-Black Death period were occurring at the lowest end of the social strata. According to the findings of these authors, the percentage of the total number of households which fell below the poverty line declined from 41 per cent in 1290 to 22 per cent in 1381, whilst over the same period the mean yearly income for these poorest households increased from £1.73 to £3.0. For the social tiers just above these households, ranging from those which were just above the poverty line to those that were comfortably off, the mean annual income initially appears to have decreased, albeit very marginally, from £4.3 to £4.2. However, whereas this category included 43.9 per cent of total households in 1290, by 1381 this figure had risen to 58.1 per cent of total households. As this increase was predominantly caused by the number of households who had improved their social status and moved from below to above the poverty line, this meant, in effect, that for many the mean annual income had risen from £1.73 to £4.2.[4]

Most consumption decisions are based on choices which are heavily influenced by the income of the consumer. Consequently, it is inevitable that these revised income patterns were the main determinant of the changed consumption patterns that occurred in this period and that, therefore, the sections of the population which saw the largest revisions were those which comprised these poorest sections of society. As has been noted in Chapter 3, the impact of the population pressure on land use and frequent famines had combined to ensure that the diet of most people in the pre-Black Death period had been highly restrictive in terms of its quantity, quality and variety.

After the Black Death, people benefited from rising household incomes and a wider availability of land which, together, led to dietary improvements for most of the late medieval population in the form of more wheat (for bread), barley (for ale) and animal protein. Whilst these changes were relatively limited, they are likely to have had a significant impact on the lives of the lower classes in terms of both the quantity and quality of the diet and changes to the calorific composition. The most significant changes to consumption in the late medieval period can therefore be summarised as being a larger *per capita* demand for predominantly basic foodstuffs and a moderate rise in the range and variety of foods that were commonly eaten, whilst the main beneficiaries were the poorer classes who benefited from increases in the quantity and quality of the food that they consumed.

Other consumption changes were also taking place which were affecting both the poorer classes and other groups within society. As has been shown by Broadberry *et al.* in their tables comparing the contents, prices and costs of bare-bones and respectability consumption baskets for 1290 and 1381, although the largest proportion by far of a household's income continued to be spent on food items in the post-Black Death period, the actual share of expenditure on these goods declined (see Table 9.1).[5] Although this was the most significant for households consuming the bare-bones basket, where the share of expenditure on food-related items dropped by 6.4 per cent, households consuming the respectability basket were also affected. As these households spent less on food, they could increasingly afford to spend more on other items such as household commodities.

Figures 9.1 and 9.2 are an analysis of certain items bequeathed by will-makers which highlight testamentary evidence for ownership of three items identified as being emblematic of the category of luxury goods: silver, featherbeds and books; and three which have been chosen as examples of better-quality goods: brass pots, pewter and bedding. It is worth highlighting the fact that whilst reference to an item in a will confirms ownership, the absence of a reference does not prove lack of ownership so that the data given in the figures can only be taken to suggest patterns of ownership and not to prove ownership or otherwise of these goods.

TABLE 9.1 Consumption baskets – share of expenditure on food-related items

	1290	1381	
	%	%	% change
Bare-bones basket	63.6	57.2	−6.4
Respectability basket	72.8	69	−3.8

Source: Percentages derived from Broadberry *et al.*, pp.333–34.

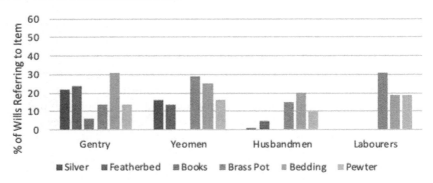

FIGURE 9.1 Testamentary evidence for ownership of consumer goods by rank, 1430–1579 (agricultural ranks)

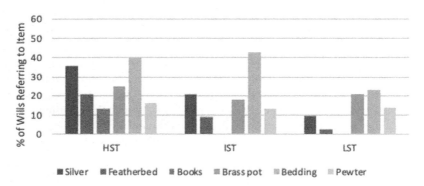

FIGURE 9.2 Testamentary evidence for ownership of consumer goods by occupational groups, 1430–1579 (tradesman/craftsmen)

The figures suggest that members of the lower-status groups of husbandmen and labourers (in the rural setting) and low-status tradesmen (in the urban and semi-rural settings) were significantly less likely to indicate ownership of the luxury items of silver, featherbeds and books than men from higher-status groups (gentry or high-status tradesmen) or intermediate-status groups (yeomen or intermediate-status tradesmen). Men from the rural low-status groups rarely indicated ownership of these items, whilst ownership amongst low-status trades-men would have been similarly low but for an unusual pattern of behaviour by a group of Northampton craftsmen. Bequests such as this are highly untypical of this social status group and out of all the wills used for this study, only one low-status tradesman other than these Northampton craftsmen bequeathed any silver items. Silver ownership was higher for the high-status groups of gentry and high-status tradesmen than for the intermediate groups of yeomen and inter-mediate-status tradesmen although these groups did record levels of ownership, whilst members of the rural gentry and yeomen classes owned marginally more featherbeds than their counterparts from urban or semi-rural locations. The only references to the ownership of books was in wills made by men from the high-status groups of gentry or high-status tradesmen.

By contrast, men from the lower-status groups did indicate ownership of some of the better-quality consumption items (brass pots, bedding or pewter) which suggests that these items were increasingly to be found in the households of a wide strata of late medieval society. The indicated ownership of brass pots ranged from 14 per cent (gentry) through to 31 per cent (labourers) with the other groups recording between these two figures. This high figure for labourers may reflect the fact that, for these men, a brass pot may have been the most valuable item within the household and therefore worth recording in a will whereas, by contrast, for members of the gentry it may have held a low value in relation to other household goods and was less likely to have been recorded. The 'middling' group of yeomen also demonstrated a strong level of ownership with 29 per cent of wills referring to a brass pot.

Men from the lower-status groups indicated broadly similar levels of owner-ship of better-quality bedding (sheets, pillow or coverlets) which was referred to in around 20 per cent of the wills made by members of these groups. This was generally lower than the ownership levels shown by men from the other agricul-tural ranks with 31 per cent of gentry wills and 25 per cent of yeomen wills recording bedding, and significantly lower than the other tradesmen groups with 40 per cent of high-status tradesmen and 43 per cent of intermediate-status tradesmen indicating ownership of better-quality bedding.

Indicated ownership of pewter, a rather more exclusive household item, was generally lower than that of brass pots or bedding but was broadly consistent across all of the groups. Surprisingly, the highest incidence was recorded by labourers (19 per cent) whilst the groups that might have been considered the most likely to own pewter (gentry, yeomen and high-status tradesmen) recorded slightly lower ownership levels of 14 per cent (gentry) and 16 per cent (yeomen and high-status tradesmen). Once again, these lower levels may reflect that pewter items were becoming more commonplace within these households and less likely to be recorded in a will.

Perhaps surprisingly, indicated ownership amongst members of the gentry for the three items identified as better-quality goods was generally broadly compar-able or lower than that for the 'middling' groups. Whilst the gentry did suffer overall constraints to their income levels during this period, they still managed to enjoy strong levels of disposable income and it seems likely that they did own these goods, but were more concerned with ensuring that their lands and prop-erty were effectively bequeathed rather than what were, for them, less significant household goods.

Figures 9.3 and 9.4 set out ownership of goods by selected occupations. The tradesmen in Table 9.3 are those which have been designated as high-status trades (HST), namely drapers/mercers and clergy; and of intermediate-status

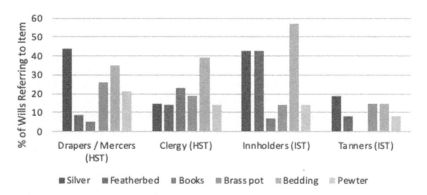

FIGURE 9.3 Ownership of consumer goods by selected HST/IST occupations, 1430–1579

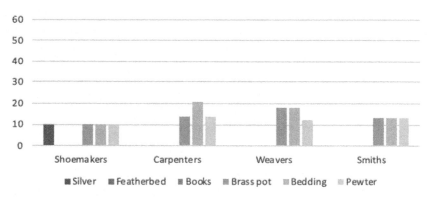

FIGURE 9.4 Ownership of consumer goods by selected LST occupations, 1430–1479

trades (IST), innholders and tanners. The tradesmen in Table 9.4 include examples of lower-status trades (LST).[6] The trades chosen are those which are commonly represented amongst the testators whose wills have been used for this study. In addition, the category of clergy gives an insight into the collective behaviour of a group who were clearly significant consumers prior to the Reformation.

Drapers/mercers and innholders were much more likely to own silver items than either tanners or members of the clergy, whilst innholders frequently owned featherbeds and did so more frequently than men from any of the other occupations, which reflects the nature of their occupation with featherbeds being offered to customers of their inns. Indeed, Robert Depyng of Hertford stated that his four featherbeds were in specified chambers within his hospice called 'the Ston Hall or the Signe of the Sarsyns Hede'.[7] The ownership of books by drapers/mercers and innholders was low, or even negligible in the case of tanners, but, as has been noted in Chapter 5, these were often bequeathed by members of the clergy. Almost all of the books identified by their titles were liturgical texts so that, again, these bequests reflected the occupation of their owners. By contrast, bequests of all three of the luxury items by men with the designated low-status trades (LST) were almost negligible.

Men with the designated low-status trades also had a general lower ownership of the goods designated as better-quality items than men with the specified high- or intermediate-status occupations. Men with the high-status occupations of draper/mercer or clergyman had higher indicated ownership of these goods than men with intermediate-status trades with the exception of bedding where, as with featherbeds, innholders had a high level of indicated ownership.

Table 9.2 shows the percentage of indicated ownership of these luxury and better-quality consumer goods over a period of 150 years. The complete set of the wills has been included in the analysis and the table therefore reflects findings from all seven of the counties used for this study.

It is recognised that the data contains some anomalies and inconsistencies; however, some broad suppositions can be made. The data suggests that the ownership of the luxury items of silver and featherbeds was very low at the beginning of the period but was increasing over the period for members of some of the status groups. The possession of silver items appears to have been rising amongst men from the higher classes of gentry and high-status tradesmen and by the intermediate classes of yeomen and intermediate-status tradesmen. However, ownership by the lower-status group of husbandmen was almost negligible, whilst ownership by low-status tradesmen was generally limited. The raised figures for the periods 1460 to 1489 and 1490 to 1519 were specifically caused by the high level of ownership by low-status tradesmen in Northampton referred to earlier. The ownership of featherbeds also seems to have risen over the period. Only one will from the period 1430 to 1459 contained a reference to a featherbed: that made in 1459 by Margery Harleston of Bardwell, the widow of the affluent and well-connected Suffolk landowner John Harleston, esquire, in which she bequeathed three separate featherbeds together with a range of other luxury and more basic household items.[8] Indicated ownership of featherbeds increased on an incremental basis from this time and the data suggests that this adoption was initially by the high-status groups of gentry and high-status occupations, and then spread to the intermediate-status groups. Indicated ownership amongst the lower-status groups of husbandmen and low-status tradesmen was meagre and did not emerge until much later than the high-status groups. The indicated ownership of books was generally very low across the whole of the time period but appears to have declined from the time period 1520–49. As has been discussed earlier, most of the books referred to in wills were bequeathed by members of the clergy and this apparent decline probably reflects the fact that the number of clergymen fell following the Reformation so that clergy wills formed a lower proportion of the will sample from this time onwards.

TABLE 9.2 Indicated ownership of consumer goods over time and by rank, 1430–1579

	1430–59	1460–89	1490–1519	1520–49	1550–79
SILVER	%	%	%	%	%
Gentry	0	26	29	18	18
Yeomen	7	9	18	17	21
Husbandmen	0	0	0	0	3
Labourers	N/A	N/A	N/A	0	0
HST	19	35	30	50	50
IST	0	28	27	21	0
LST	0	11	22	0	0
Females	14	32	39	12	21
Unknown	3	7	8	0	13
Mean	6	14	18	9	14
FEATHERBED	%	%	%	%	%
Gentry	0	16	29	27	36
Yeomen	0	0	5	28	23
Husbandmen	0	0	0	4	14
Labourers	N/A	N/A	N/A	0	0
HST	0	3	30	50	33
IST	0	3	10	21	7
LST	0	0	4	0	7
Females	5	6	8	24	17
Unknown	0	4	8	12	11
Mean	1	4	10	17	16
BOOKS	%	%	%	%	%
Gentry	0	10	0	9	0
Yeomen	0	0	0	0	0
Husbandmen	0	0	0	0	0
Labourers	N/A	N/A	N/A	0	0
HST	13	16	18	6	6
IST	0	0	0	0	0
LST	0	0	0	0	0
Females	0	2	2	0	0
Unknown	0	2	2	0	1
Mean	1	3	3	1	1
BRASS POTS	%	%	%	%	%
Gentry	0	11	0	18	27
Yeomen	21	27	36	41	21
Husbandmen	13	7	18	22	14
Labourers	N/A	N/A	N/A	29	33
HST	6	27	33	25	22
IST	0	17	13	26	21
LST	25	17	33	4	21
Females	32	40	39	36	42
Unknown	10	13	8	15	26

(*Continued*)

TABLE 9.2 (Cont.)

	1430–59	1460–89	1490–1519	1520–49	1550–79
Mean	15	19	20	23	24
BEDDING	%	%	%	%	%
Gentry	0	21	71	27	36
Yeomen	29	21	18	41	19
Husbandmen	31	7	0	15	39
Labourers	N/A	N/A	N/A	14	22
HST	13	27	48	56	61
IST	40	28	50	53	50
LST	17	17	33	13	25
Females	32	42	33	60	67
Unknown	10	7	13	11	11
Mean	19	17	25	30	30
PEWTER	%	%	%	%	%
Gentry	0	5	29	18	18
Yeomen	0	12	0	52	9
Husbandmen	0	7	0	15	17
Labourers	N/A	N/A	N/A	14	22
HST	6	5	24	25	22
IST	0	7	13	37	0
LST	0	4	24	13	18
Females	5	21	12	43	50
Unknown	0	1	1	15	18
Mean	1	6	9	26	19

In contrast with the findings for luxury items, the data suggests that owner-ship of the better-quality items of brass pots and bedding was much wider by the mid-fifteenth century. Broadly, ownership of these items appears to have risen from the mid-fifteenth to the mid-sixteenth centuries, albeit marginally. This is not typical of all groups; for example, indicated ownership by men from some of the status groups, particularly yeomen, rose to the beginning of the sixteenth century and then declined. These figures may reflect a growing perception that these were basic household commodities rather than items with special status or value so that they were less inclined to be bequeathed. This may also explain the low indicated ownership of brass pots by members of the gentry.

The ownership of pewter appears to have been negligible in the period from 1430 to 1459, but to have risen strongly from the mid-fifteenth to mid-sixteenth centuries at which point ownership seems to have declined. Unfortu-nately, the data for the indicated ownership of pewter is somewhat inconsistent which makes it impossible to draw any firm conclusions about the changes in the ownership of pewter by rank.

Conclusion

In conclusion, it appears that the ownership of household goods was increasing from the late medieval period but that whilst demand for better-quality items such as brass pots and bedding came from all social groups, demand for luxury items was more restricted to the higher social groups. However, by the end of the sixteenth century, even men from the poorer groups were indicating ownership of items such as pewter and featherbeds. Two of the three items which William Harrison suggested had been 'marvelously altered in England' within the 'sound remembrance' of the old men in his village were improvements in bedding and 'the exchange of vessel, as of treen [wooden] platters into pewter, and wooden spoons into silver or tin' (the third being an increase in the number of chimneys).[9] The testamentary data used for this study indicates that these were two significant changes which were increasingly being adopted by broader swathes of late medieval and early modern society and reflect an increased adoption of household items which were slowly changing the lifestyles of the population.

Inventory evidence from 1550–1800

When Sara Horrell summarised increased consumption over the eighteenth century and beyond, she wrote:

> Britons added the new commodities of tea, coffee and sugar to their diets, they drank the beverages from china cups, they wore printed cotton clothes, improved the beds and bed linen they slept in, drew window curtains while they did so and used a clock to tell the time when they woke up...[10]

Who were these Britons?

There is broad agreement that the main beneficiaries of increased consumption from the end of the sixteenth century were the 'middling sort', better-off members of English society. Broadberry *et al.* suggested that (based on Overton's data from five counties) median inventory values of household effects at constant prices increased by two-and-a-half-fold between the 1630s and the 1740s.[11] This was a considerably higher rate than real income per head or real wage rates. They concluded that *from the 1640s*, economic growth was delivering steadily improving living standards to *better off members of society*.[12] The better off were for Broadberry *et al.* the inventoried population, with the poorest 40 per cent of the population excluded. For Joel Mokyr, countries where the vast bulk of the population lived close to the margin of subsistence would not be places where consumer goods such as clocks and pottery were purchased by many people. What set Britain apart from other countries was the large group of merchants, professionals, well-to-do farmers and artisans who would vaguely fall into the modern notion of a 'middle class'. These were the main purchasers of consumer durables and other middle-class goods.[13]

Table 9.3 sets out ownership of 15 selected goods by rank over a period of 250 years. The complete set of the inventory sample (7,296 inventories) has been included in the analysis, except for Buckinghamshire.[14] The dataset therefore reflected findings from 15 locations. Broadberry *et al.* claimed evidence for steadily rising living standards from as early as the 1640s.[15] Rising living standards is of course a much wider concept than ownership of consumer goods, but it is clear that reference was being made to household goods in probate inventories. As Chapter 7 showed, ownership of many consumer goods was very limited in many parts of the country until much later than the mid-seventeenth century. This chapter shows that it was mainly the gentry who tended to own new consumer goods first, as much as a generation earlier or two generations in the case of clocks and looking glasses. For new goods such as clocks, knives and forks, and items associated with hot drinks, the substantial increase in incidence of ownership across the middling sort did not really happen until the second half of the eighteenth century. Significant increases in ownership of new consumer goods in the seventeenth century were largely confined to the gentry and some high-status groups (Overton *et al.*'s service occupations and Lorna Weatherill's HST occupational group) and not the middling sort as a whole.

Turning to each item in turn, the first three items (clocks, knives and forks and items associated with the new hot drinks) all showed that gentry tended to own them before other social groups. By the second half of the eighteenth century, most other ranks had largely caught up with the gentry so that by then yeomen, middling and lower-status tradesmen had a higher incidence of owning clocks than gentry. Nearly all social groups, including inventoried labourers, were not far behind. For knives and forks and goods associated with hot drinks, gentry had the highest levels of ownership but, except for husbandmen and labourers, the gentry's lead over other social groups in owning these goods was relatively small.

Looking glasses, pictures and window curtains showed a different pattern of ownership. Whilst gentry had the highest levels of ownership in the first third of the period (1550–1629), incidence of ownership of pictures and window curtains by gentry did not increase thereafter. Ownership of looking glasses by gentry increased sharply after the Restoration rather than in the eighteenth century. However, once again incidence of ownership by other social groups had largely caught up by the second half of the eighteenth century. The high-status group of professionals and tradesmen such as clergy, merchants, mercers and drapers (HST) had a higher incidence of owning looking glasses, pictures and window curtains than gentry by the end of the eighteenth century.

TABLE 9.3 Ownership of consumer goods over time and by rank

	1551–99	1600–29	1630–59	1660–89	1690–1719	1720–49	1750–1800
CLOCKS	%	%	%	%	%	%	%
Gentry	0	0	5	26	56	44	50
Yeomen	0	0	1	8	24	36	62
Husbandmen	0	0	0	2	5	25	41
Labourers	0	0	0	0	3	4	40
HST	0	0	0	13	14	23	39
IST	0	2	0	6	18	38	54
LST	0	1	0	5	10	28	60
Females	0	1	0	1	7	13	45
KNIVES and FORKS	%	%	%	%	%	%	%
Gentry	0	0	0	5	7	21	28
Yeomen	0	0	0	0	0	3	13
Husbandmen	0	0	0	0	0	0	4
Labourers	0	0	0	0	0	0	7
HST	0	0	0	2	5	11	25
IST	0	0	0	3	3	3	23
LST	0	0	0	0	1	4	14
Females	0	0	0	1	2	1	25
HOT DRINKS	%	%	%	%	%	%	%
Gentry	0	0	0	5	10	35	47
Yeomen	0	0	0	0	0	3	39
Husbandmen	0	0	0	0	0	2	22
Labourers	0	0	0	0	0	2	7
HST	0	0	0	0	4	17	57
IST	0	0	0	1	3	4	29
LST	0	0	0	0	1	8	41
Females	0	0	0	1	2	6	42
LOOKING GLASSES	%	%	%	%	%	%	%
Gentry	20	14	5	50	63	61	41
Yeomen	0	2	1	8	19	23	31
Husbandmen	0	2	0	5	6	9	30
Labourers	0	0	0	1	6	13	20
HST	13	8	16	38	54	45	54
IST	0	10	27	26	30	36	32
LST	3	7	3	18	27	33	43
Females	3	7	6	12	22	22	42
PICTURES	%	%	%	%	%	%	%
Gentry	30	38	15	17	17	33	22
Yeomen	0	2	0	1	2	7	13
Husbandmen	1	0	0	2	0	2	7

(*Continued*)

TABLE 9.3 (Cont.)

	1551–99	1600–29	1630–59	1660–89	1690–1719	1720–49	1750–1800
Labourers	0	0	0	0	0	4	7
HST	7	13	26	33	31	32	46
IST	0	8	7	6	11	24	24
LST	0	2	4	5	5	20	19
Females	3	1	1	3	5	8	17
WINDOW CURTAINS	%	%	%	%	%	%	%
Gentry	40	10	20	24	20	30	22
Yeomen	1	0	1	3	5	5	11
Husbandmen	0	0	2	0	2	0	11
Labourers	0	0	0	0	4	0	0
HST	20	8	16	8	34	26	33
IST	15	6	23	15	20	15	18
LST	7	3	1	3	4	13	20
Females	0	6	1	3	8	6	19
PEWTER	%	%	%	%	%	%	%
Gentry	70	95	85	88	90	83	77
Yeomen	84	90	91	89	90	85	80
Husbandmen	86	81	82	80	79	92	47
Labourers	50	77	72	82	72	63	63
HST	78	83	83	90	84	75	63
IST	81	88	97	85	83	83	81
LST	86	76	87	90	86	82	81
Females	80	71	79	84	83	85	84
BOOKS	%	%	%	%	%	%	%
Gentry	50	62	75	60	54	42	41
Yeomen	7	12	44	17	16	12	11
Husbandmen	0	8	5	11	8	0	4
Labourers	0	2	0	2	3	2	7
HST	32	58	77	55	55	28	25
IST	4	40	43	22	16	17	12
LST	5	22	23	21	14	16	15
Females	5	13	13	14	17	9	17
WARMING PANS	%	%	%	%	%	%	%
Gentry	10	24	35	42	58	46	80
Yeomen	3	9	19	33	33	46	52
Husbandmen	3	3	13	26	21	33	N/A
Labourers	0	4	0	36	35	19	38
HST	7	21	20	40	51	42	25
IST	4	23	43	44	42	48	58
LST	3	11	19	35	37	43	54
Females	8	5	21	35	41	50	52

(*Continued*)

TABLE 9.3 (Cont.)

	1551–99	1600–29	1630–59	1660–89	1690–1719	1720–49	1750–1800
BED CURTAINS	%	%	%	%	%	%	%
Gentry	70	62	50	64	54	58	22
Yeomen	12	11	24	31	27	24	17
Husbandmen	5	5	7	16	13	18	7
Labourers	0	2	2	14	15	16	7
HST	65	33	58	60	53	28	26
IST	27	31	63	53	40	28	12
LST	26	17	18	36	38	35	24
Females	23	14	27	33	30	17	21
FEATHERBEDS	%	%	%	%	%	%	%
Gentry	90	71	40	68	63	58	60
Yeomen	53	49	51	47	50	50	42
Husbandmen	33	28	33	39	36	33	N/A
Labourers	21	11	11	32	21	19	25
HST	83	54	63	67	57	33	33
IST	58	63	77	61	51	48	50
LST	61	47	46	51	42	40	48
Females	55	38	58	52	49	39	54
SILVER	%	%	%	%	%	%	%
Gentry	50	67	70	62	61	61	53
Yeomen	4	40	31	22	18	13	23
Husbandmen	3	3	5	5	0	2	19
Labourers	0	3	0	0	0	4	0
HST	52	46	61	52	53	38	41
IST	19	27	33	30	29	21	27
LST	11	12	12	18	17	17	26
Females	22	28	26	20	30	18	33
STOOLS	%	%	%	%	%	%	%
Gentry	60	81	90	71	68	40	10
Yeomen	61	74	73	65	53	35	18
Husbandmen	45	52	42	52	34	16	0
Labourers	21	40	21	32	29	27	13
HST	76	83	77	77	58	21	7
IST	50	75	90	65	64	46	31
LST	57	65	62	64	46	32	26
Females	34	46	56	60	45	27	27
CHAIRS	%	%	%	%	%	%	%
Gentry	60	91	85	86	88	86	50
Yeomen	66	72	70	73	82	75	58
Husbandmen	47	61	54	67	72	60	36
Labourers	21	48	49	68	66	71	60
HST	83	71	87	92	81	68	55

(Continued)

TABLE 9.3 (Cont.)

	1551–99	1600–29	1630–59	1660–89	1690–1719	1720–49	1750–1800
IST	65	67	87	83	86	83	71
LST	66	60	66	77	78	78	76
Females	47	53	57	73	64	62	63
FORMS	%	%	%	%	%	%	%
Gentry	70	86	75	43	36	21	0
Yeomen	80	68	72	52	46	33	8
Husbandmen	74	83	61	56	31	22	7
Labourers	43	64	47	36	22	9	0
HST	61	50	42	32	15	13	3
IST	77	60	63	49	29	26	5
LST	72	55	52	39	24	16	5
Females	42	48	45	38	25	19	8

Pewter was owned by most of the middling sort throughout the period whereas books were recorded more frequently in inventories of the gentry and high-status groups, including, unsurprisingly, the clergy. Comfortable sleeping arrangements were clearly important to the gentry who had the highest incidence of owning warming pans and featherbeds throughout almost the entire period under consideration. Whilst only 10 per cent of gentry owned warming pans in the second half of the sixteenth century, 80 per cent of the gentry owned them two hundred years later. Starting from very low levels of ownership of warming pans by yeomen, tradesmen and widows in the second half of the sixteenth century, more than half had a warming pan by the end of the eighteenth century. Warming pans were also attractive to labourers, for more than a third owned a warming pan in three of the four periods after the Restoration. Featherbeds were more frequently recorded in the second half of the sixteenth than the second half of the eighteenth centuries. In the earlier period, more than half of the inventoried population owned them, with the exception of husbandmen and labourers.

Ownership of silver goods was related to rank. More than half of gentry inventories recorded silver throughout the period and high-status occupations and tradesmen (HST) were not far behind. Husbandmen and labourers rarely owned silver. The nature of seating changed during the period. Whereas more than 60 per cent of most social groups except labourers and females owned forms at the beginning of the period, very few were recorded by the end of the eighteenth century. There was a tendency for chairs to be less frequently recorded in the second half of the eighteenth century, but very high levels of ownership were recorded before then. Labourers were three times more likely to own them at the end of the period.

Comparison with Weatherill's data

Weatherill only collected probate inventory data for a 50-year time frame (1675–1725). The number of inventories and the distribution of inventories by value between the two samples for the same 50-year period was similar to our dataset (Table 9.4).

The pattern and incidence of ownership of nine selected consumer goods by agricultural ranks was similar to Weatherill's findings (Table 9.5a) One particular weakness of Weatherill's dataset was the lack of inventoried labourers in her sample, just 26. Our dataset had a more robust 143 for this 50-year period but the substantial increase in the sample made very little difference to the results for labourers. Apart from pewter, both labourers and husbandmen owned very few consumer goods during this 50-year period.

In Table 9.5b, ownership of selected consumer goods by Weatherill's three professional and tradesmen groups can be compared with that of gentry. Weatherill claimed that in spite of the gentry's superior wealth and social standing, many expressive decorative goods such as pictures, looking glasses, pewter and a few other items were less frequently recorded in gentry inventories.[16] The only goods for which her IST and LST occupations had higher percentages of ownership were pewter (marginally higher and an item which generally had very high levels of ownership) and window curtains and hot drinks for IST occupations. It was only Weatherill's HST occupations which had similar levels of ownership of goods to gentry. Jane Whittle confirmed Weatherill's findings in the Overton *et al.* dataset for mirrors, utensils for hot drinks and even books.[17] Again it was their 'services' group of occupations (a related group of occupations to Weatherill's HST occupations) that had similar ownership levels to gentry.[18]

The additional data collected by the present authors (Sear and Sneath) were also included in Table 9.5b. The same time period (1675–1725) was used for all

TABLE 9.4 Comparison of datasets, 1675–1725

Inventory value	Weatherill		Sear & Sneath	
£	No.	%	No.	%
No valuation	0		6	
1–5	84	3	160	5
6–10	150	5	205	7
11–25	500	17	588	20
26–50	552	19	507	17
51–100	628	22	561	19
101–250	627	22	587	20
251–500	234	8	242	8
Over 500	127	4	125	4
Total	2,902	100	2,981	100

TABLE 9.5A Ownership of consumer goods by rank

	Weatherill 1675–1725	Sneath & Sear 1675–1725	Weatherill 1675–1725	Sneath & Sear 1675–1725
	Gentry		Yeomen	
	N=122	N=101	N=952	N=519
	%	%	%	%
Pewter	93	93	95	88
Books	39	53	18	16
Clocks	51	46	19	22
Pictures	33	18	4	3
Looking glasses	62	62	20	17
Window curtains	26	23	5	5
Knives and forks	11	8	1	0
Hot drinks	7	10	1	0
Silver	61	64	13	18
	Husbandmen		Labourers	
	N=332	N=135	N=28	N=143
	%	%	%	%
Pewter	89	83	89	79
Books	4	7	4	3
Clocks	4	8	0	2
Pictures	0	2	4	0
Looking glasses	9	5	4	4
Window curtains	2	1	4	2
Knives and forks	0	0	0	0
Hot drinks	1	0	0	0
Silver	2	2	0	0

data. This data was collected from 11 counties and approaching two thirds of the total inventories from Yorkshire, Huntingdonshire and Dorset. These results showed that the three trade occupational groups (HST, IST, LST) tended to have lower ownership levels for goods such as clocks, looking glasses and pictures than Weatherill's groups. This was consistent with the findings in Chapter 7 that ownership of many of these goods, such as clocks, knives and forks and hot drink utensils, rose rapidly after the end of Weatherill's 50-year period and a generation after Kent and London.

Tables 9.5c and 9.5d set out ownership of goods by selected occupations for which Weatherill provided data. The tradesmen were mainly those designated by Weatherill as low-status trades (LST) but drapers and mercers were an example of high-status trades (HST) and innkeepers and victuallers and

TABLE 9.5B Ownership of consumer goods by occupational groups

Item	Weather-ill	Sear & Sneath	Weather-ill	Sear & Sneath	Weather-ill	Sear & Sneath
	HST		IST		LST	
	N=152	N=137	N=344	N=274	N=435	N=519
	%	%	%	%	%	%
Pewter	95	81	94	84	96	88
Books	45	50	24	18	17	17
Clocks	34	14	25	19	18	10
Pictures	35	29	29	12	15	8
Looking glasses	62	49	56	32	37	26
Window curtains	21	25	29	18	12	5
Knives and forks	7	4	11	3	3	1
Hot drinks	7	5	10	3	4	2
Silver	51	52	38	29	23	19

shopkeepers were two intermediate trades (IST). The six LST occupations represent over half (56 per cent) of inventories in the LST group. The results of Weatherill's data had many similarities with ours. However, Weatherill's blacksmiths and butchers had higher percentages of clock ownership, carpenters and blacksmiths were more likely to own window curtains and her blacksmiths, tailors and shoemakers were more likely to own looking glasses. Weatherill's HST and IST groups all had higher ownership of clocks and looking glasses.

Labourers

Tim Hitchcock bemoaned the fact that for 'much of the last twenty to twenty-five years' academic historians had largely abandoned the poor to focus on the middling sort. Hitchcock argued that the poor have been excluded from studies of consumption because of their limited ability to buy.[20] A crucial element of the present study was to examine the extent to which ownership of consumer goods descended down the social scale and this included lower orders as well as high- and intermediate-status groups. In the case of labourers this was challenging since they only infrequently left probate records so that, for example, the wills used for this study included only 16 (1 per cent) which had been made by men referred to as 'labourer'. Weatherill had just 26 (less than 1 per cent) in her sample of 2,902 inventories, whilst Overton et al. also had a very low percentage of labourers in their sample and as a result they received very little attention in their study.[21] The sample of inventories used for this study included a large number of labourers' inventories (351 or 5 per cent) for the period from

TABLE 9.5C Ownership of consumer goods by selected LST occupations

	Weatherill 1675–1725	Sneath & Sear 1675–1725	Weatherill 1675–1725	Sneath & Sear 1675–1725
	Shoemakers		Tailors	
	N=45	N=42	N=32	N=41
	%	%	%	%
Pewter	93	81	100	88
Books	16	14	22	22
Clocks	8	10	16	5
Pictures	8	2	16	5
Looking glasses	38	17	34	20
Window curtains	2	2	6	2
Knives and forks	2	0	0	0
Hot drinks	2	0	13	2
Silver	16	21	17	15
	Carpenters[19]		Weavers	
	N=32	N=44	N=48	N=29
	%	%	%	%
Pewter	97	95	96	83
Books	9	16	15	31
Clocks	16	9	17	14
Pictures	3	7	2	14
Looking glasses	22	25	27	21
Window curtains	13	0	4	10
Knives and forks	0	0	0	0
Hot drinks	0	2	2	0
Silver	19	9	8	17
	Blacksmiths (LST)		Butchers (LST)	
	N=49	N=48	N=37	N=24
	%	%	%	%
Pewter	90	86	97	81
Books	10	15	16	17
Clocks	22	10	19	4
Pictures	8	0	19	17
Looking glasses	33	17	46	38
Window curtains	12	2	11	8
Knives and forks	0	0	0	0
Hot drinks	0	0	3	4
Silver	8	6	43	17

TABLE 9.5D Ownership of consumer goods by selected HST and IST occupations

	Innkeepers/Victuallers (IST)		Drapers and Mercers (HST)	
	Weatherill 1675–1725	Sneath & Sear 1675–1725	Weatherill 1675–1725	Sneath & Sear 1675–1725
	N=101	N=65	N=21	N=21
	%	%	%	%
Pewter	98	89	95	86
Books	19	12	43	43
Clocks	30	22	24	10
Pictures	39	15	43	33
Looking glasses	70	46	67	57
Window curtains	40	29	24	43
Knives and forks	21	6	5	14
Hot drinks	17	5	10	5
Silver	46	32	43	52

	Shopkeepers (IST)	
	Weatherill 1675–1725	Sneath & Sear 1675–1725
	N=87	N=27
	%	%
Pewter	95	84
Books	37	22
Clocks	25	11
Pictures	34	26
Looking glasses	67	48
Window curtains	40	22
Knives and forks	15	4
Hot drinks	11	0
Silver	45	41

1550–1799. By examining inventoried labourers, the present study moves a little further down the social scale, but it must be recognised that labourers with inventories were among the more affluent labourers and were likely to own more material wealth than labourers as a whole.

Craig Muldrew recently completed a major study of labourers based on almost a thousand inventories.[22] Analysed together with labourer's inventories from the present study doubled the available sample for the crucial period after 1750, as the two sets of data relate to different locations. Nevertheless, the sample size for 1750–99 was still a relatively meagre 30 inventories.

A comparison of the incidence of ownership of selected consumer goods with Muldrew's data is given in Table 9.6.

Now that we have data for labourers from more than 1,300 inventories, how well do assertions about the extent to which labourers owned consumer goods stand up? Keith Thomas suggested that by the late eighteenth century, 'cotton and linen, pewter, pottery, tea sets, and decorative household items would reach even labourers' cottages.'[23] The data suggests that pewter had been reaching over two thirds of inventoried labourers' cottages for nearly two centuries. On the other hand, inventoried labourers rarely owned items that were specifically described as *coffee* cups, *tea* cups, *tea* kettles, etc. It may be that that if tea-drinking was widespread by the end of the eighteenth century, it was drunk in labourers' households in more mundane crockery that

TABLE 9.6 Ownership of selected goods: labourers

Muldrew

	1550–99	1600–49	1650–99	1700–99	1750–99
	N=119	N=201	N=445	N=207	N=15
	%	%	%	%	%
Clocks	3	1	1	6	40
Looking glasses	0	1	5	14	33
Pewter	43	78	76	71	N/A
Bed curtains	25	31	37	41	N/A
Window curtains	2	3	19	20	20
Featherbeds	29	35	40	34	N/A
Chairs	41	61	66	71	N/A
Stools	41	50	37	33	N/A

Sear and Sneath

	1550–99	1600–49	1650–99	1700–99	1750–99
	N=14	N=103	N=117	N=117	N=15
	%	%	%	%	%
Clocks	0	0	1	8	40
Looking glasses	0	0	1	12	20
Pewter	50	74	83	65	63
Bed curtains	0	2	14	15	7
Window curtains	0	0	1	2	0
Featherbeds	21	5	31	20	25
Chairs	21	48	68	68	60
Stools	21	31	35	24	13
Hot Drinks	0	0	0	2	7

appraisers did not consider worthy of describing as tea cups. Whilst Table 9.3 reveals that only a few inventoried labourers (7 per cent) owned goods associated with the new hot drinks, 41 per cent of the rank above, low-status tradesmen, did so. Amanda Vickery found supporting evidence in criminal records when in 1784 a Kendal weaver accused two men of stealing his wife's green teapot.[24]

E.P. Thompson maintained that *no* labourer could have afforded a clock in the mid-eighteenth century and Norman Pounds suggested that clocks did not penetrate lower than petty burgesses until much later.[25] However, the new data showed that 40 per cent of inventoried labourers owned a clock so that Maxine Berg was correct to assert that clocks were not so expensive that only elites could afford them.[26] However, it must also be recognised that, as Sara Pennell pointed out, aggregating different types of clock using quantitative analysis obscures the differences between them, including their age and quality.[27] Unfortunately, probate sources only rarely specified this information.

The overall picture provided by the data was that in the late sixteenth century, none of the selected consumer goods were owned by the majority of labourers. Moving into the seventeenth century, most labourers owned pewter and at least one chair. By the second half of the eighteenth century, 40 per cent of labourers owned clocks and around a quarter owned mirrors and featherbeds. Contrary to Thompson's view, the benefits of the industrial revolution to the working man were more than just 'more potatoes and a few articles of cotton clothing'.[28] The consumer revolution was at last beginning to penetrate into the bottom half of society.

The evidence also shed light on Jan de Vries' conundrum about the difficulty of reconciling low levels of real wages with increased ownership of consumer goods. Jan de Vries' solution was an 'industrious revolution' beginning in the mid-seventeenth century.[29] Inventory data demonstrated that until well into the eighteenth century, labourers, and to a large extent husbandmen, still owned few consumer goods (Table 9.5a). There was therefore no conundrum at this point in time! Change largely began to take place during the second half of the eighteenth century when, despite the rapidly rising population, real wages were rising rather than falling as the economy broke free from the Malthusian model.[30]

Consumption and inventoried wealth

Ownership of selected goods by quartile inventory values for the last half century of the seventeenth and eighteenth centuries is shown in Tables 9.7a and 9.7b. The first quartile represents those with the lowest values and the fourth quartile the highest. All ranks and occupations from all locations in the period sampled were included. The results revealed a clear positive correlation between inventoried wealth and ownership of goods.

The second period included the third quarter of the eighteenth century, the period that Neil McKendrick claimed saw an explosion in the ownership of

TABLE 9.7A Ownership of selected goods by quartile: 1650–99

	1st Quartile	2nd Quartile	3rd Quartile	4th Quartile
	%	%	%	%
Clocks	1	3	6	16
Looking glasses	7	12	16	31
Knives and forks	0	0	0	2
Pictures	2	4	4	11
Hot drinks	0	0	0	1
Warming pans	27	31	40	40
Silver	4	11	23	45
Book	12	15	20	32
Pewter	74	86	91	90
Bed curtains	22	28	39	48
Window curtains	0	3	6	13
Featherbeds	38	48	60	60
Chairs	64	75	78	84
Stools	43	54	61	72
Forms	32	43	47	45

consumer goods. The comparison with ownership patterns a century earlier showed that for many goods a substantial consumer change had indeed taken place. Again, in the great majority of cases, ownership levels increased over time for each quartile. For several goods, ownership increased markedly by the second quartile of wealth.

TABLE 9.7B Ownership of selected goods by quartile: 1750–1800

	1st Quartile	2nd Quartile	3rd Quartile	4th Quartile
	%	%	%	%
Clocks	38	52	58	65
Looking glasses	20	34	42	44
Knives and forks	5	17	20	26
Pictures	10	17	20	23
Hot drinks	19	30	38	56
Warming pans	41	49	55	57
Silver	11	22	28	39
Book	7	12	14	22
Pewter	66	79	77	81
Bed curtains	12	18	16	24
Window curtains	3	12	17	26
Featherbeds	29	47	47	48
Chairs	70	64	63	58
Stools	20	21	31	20
Forms	4	7	8	8

Females

To what extent did gender shape taste and material culture? This is not easy to answer from inventory evidence. Weatherill found little difference between goods recorded in male and female inventories.[31] One exception was ownership of silver and gold and particularly by widows. Weatherill concluded that silver and gold resources were accumulated as assets for use during widowhood.[32] Overton *et al.* had between 15 (Kent) and 17 (Cornwall) per cent of female inventories in their sample.[33] This was a similar percentage to the present sample (14 per cent).

Both rank and location were more important influences upon ownership of goods in probate evidence than gender. For example, gentry were much more likely and labourers much less likely to own silver than females (Table 9.3). Most female inventories related to widows and some died not long after their husbands, so that the contents of their inventories were similar. In Kent, 23 per cent of widows owned a clock in the period 1700–49, whereas none were recorded in Cornwall.[34]

Olwen Hufton deplored the neglect of spinsters in historical analysis which she claimed was 'almost total', despite spinsters representing a significant proportion of the population.[35] Comparison of ownership patterns between widows and spinsters was hampered by the relative paucity of spinster inventories. However, the limited comparisons revealed that overall there was not a great difference between widows' and spinsters' ownership of goods. Widows were more likely to own clocks and looking glasses; on the other hand, incidence of ownership of silver and items associated with hot drinks was slightly higher amongst spinsters. The 30 spinster inventories in Huntingdonshire and Yorkshire for the years 1690–1800 recorded just two clocks (7 per cent) whereas 42 clocks (18 per cent) were recorded in the 235 widows' inventories in this period for these two counties.

Conclusion

By extending the present study both backwards and forwards chronologically, significant changes missed by Weatherill's concentration on a 50-year period were revealed. Data relating to the second half of the eighteenth century and for labourers also filled an important gap in our knowledge of consumption that was missing from the studies by Weatherill and Overton *et al.*

The evidence showed that in the early modern period, between 1550 and 1800, those who benefited from increasing ownership of consumer goods were the middling sort, but the benefits were not universally shared within this group. The gentry tended to be the first social group to own most goods. Clocks were a good example. A quarter of gentry inventories recorded clocks after the Restoration in 1660, double the incidence of ownership by high-status occupations (HST) and treble that of yeomen. By the end of the century, ownership of clocks by gentry had more than doubled to 56 per cent, way ahead of other ranks. However, towards the end of the eighteenth century, other ranks caught up and, in some cases, even exceeded the incidence of ownership by gentry. There was a clear positive correlation between inventoried wealth and ownership of the great majority of consumer goods in the second half of the eighteenth century.

Inventoried labourers were the lowest in social status of any group considered by this study. Analysis of probate inventory evidence showed that by the second half of the eighteenth century significant consumer change had spread throughout the middling sort and beyond. By then, 40 per cent of labourers owned a clock, nearly two thirds owned at least one chair and around a quarter owned mirrors and featherbeds.

Notes

1 See pp.18–19.
2 J. Hatcher, 'Unreal wages: long-run living standards and the "Golden Age" of the fifteenth century', in B. Dodds and C. Liddy (eds), *Commercial Activity: Markets and Entrepreneurs in the Middle Ages: Essays in Honour of Richard Britnell* (Woodbridge: Boydell Press, 2011), pp.6–7.
3 S. Broadberry, B. Campbell, A. Klein, M. Overton and B. van Leeuwen, *British Economic Growth, 1270–1870* (Cambridge: Cambridge University Press, 2015), pp.317–18, 321.
4 *Ibid.*
5 *Ibid.*, p.334.
6 Whilst the occupation of 'clergy' cannot strictly be considered to have been a trade, it has been considered as such for the purposes of this study to bring the terminology used for this study in line with that used by Lorna Weatherill.
7 S. Flood (ed.), *St Albans Wills, 1471–1500: Hertfordshire Record Publications Vol. IX* (Hertfordshire: Hertfordshire Record Publications, 1993), p.144.
8 NRO NCC Brosyard 168 (Harleston).
9 G. Edelen (ed.), *The Description of England: The Classic Contemporary Account of Tudor Social Life by William Harrison* (London: Constable Company Ltd, 1994), pp.200–1.
10 S, Horrell, J. Humphries and K. Sneath, 'Consumption conundrums unravelled', *Economic History Review*, 68 (2015), p.257.
11 The five counties were Cornwall, Hertfordshire, Kent, Lincolnshire and Worcestershire.
12 Broadberry *et al.*, *British Economic Growth*, pp.296–306.
13 J. Mokyr, *The Enlightened Economy: An Economic History of Britain, 1700–1850* (New Haven: Yale University Press, 2009), p.116.
14 7,183 inventories (Table 2.4) less Buckinghamshire (144) plus the later (1750–99) Kent inventories (257).
15 Broadberry *et al.*, *British Economic Growth*, pp.296–306.
16 L. Weatherill, *Consumer Behaviour and Material Culture in Britain 1660–1760* (London: Routledge, 1996), p.169.
17 J. Whittle, 'The gentry as consumers in early 17th-century England' in J. Stobart and A. Hann (eds), *The Country House: Material Culture and Consumption* (Swindon: Historic England Publishing, 2015), p.24.
18 Barbers, apothecaries, surgeons, lawyers, clerics, scriveners and schoolmasters; M. Overton, J. Whittle, D. Dean and A. Hann, *Production and Consumption in English Households 1600–1750* (Abingdon: Routledge, 2004), p.183.
19 No joiners are included in order to make the two sets of data comparable.

20 T. Hitchcock, *Down and Out in Eighteenth-Century London* (London: Hambledon and London, 2004), p.239.

21 Weatherill, *Consumer Behaviour*, p.210; Overton *et al.*, *Production and Consumption*, p.22.

22 C. Muldrew, *Food, Energy and the Creation of Industriousness* (Cambridge: Cambridge University Press, 2011), p.194.

23 K. Thomas, *The Ends of Life: Roads to Fulfilment in Early Modern England* (Oxford: Oxford University Press, 2009), p.122ff.

24 A. Vickery, *Behind Closed Doors: At Home in Georgian England* (New Haven: Yale University Press, 2009), p.272.

25 E.P. Thompson, 'Time, work-discipline and industrial capitalism', *Past and Present*, 38 (1967), p.76; N.J.G. Pounds, *Hearth and Home: A History of Material Culture* (Bloomington: Indiana University Press, 1989), p.201.

26 M. Berg, *Luxury and Pleasure in Eighteenth Century Britain* (Oxford: Oxford University Press, 2005), p.227.

27 S. Pennell, 'Mundane materiality, or, should small things still be forgotten? Material culture, micro-histories and the problem of scale', in K. Harvey (ed.), *History and Material Culture: A Student's Guide to Approaching Alternative Sources* (London: Routledge, 2009), p.224.

28 E.P. Thompson, *The Making of the English Working Class* (London: Victor Gollancz, 1963), p.318.

29 J. de Vries, 'The industrial revolution and the industrious revolution', *Journal of Economic History*, 54 (1994), p.254.

30 E.A. Wrigley, 'European marriage patterns and their implications', in C. Briggs, P. Kitson and S. Thomson (eds), *Population, Welfare and Economic Change in Britain 1290–1834* (Woodbridge: Boydell Press, 2014), p.32.

31 L. Weatherill, 'A possession of one's own: women and consumer behaviour in England 1660–1740', *Journal of British Studies*, 25 (2) (1986), pp.131–56.

32 Weatherill, 'A possession of one's own', p.142.

33 Overton *et al.*, *Production and Consumption*, p.23.

34 *Ibid.*, p.191.

35 O. Hufton, 'Women without men: widows and spinsters in Britain and France in the eighteenth century', *Journal of Family History*, 9 (1984), p.357.

10
CONCLUSIONS

Much of this study was initially inspired by the much-quoted work on consumption published by Lorna Weatherill in 1988, and subsequently by that of Mark Overton, Jane Whittle, Darron Dean and Andrew Hann which first appeared in 2004.[1] Despite its title, Weatherill's pioneering *Consumer Behaviour and Material Culture in Britain 1660–1760* focussed on a 50-year period between 1675–1725 whilst that produced by Overton *et al.*, *Production and Consumption in English Households 1600–1750*, extended Weatherill's time period. Whilst this extension was valuable, it still did not capture the third quarter of the eighteenth century, the very period which Neil McKendrick originally claimed for a 'consumer revolution'.[2] Both studies recognised that consumption patterns were affected by location and deliberately chose to encompass a range of places so as to explore the differences between them. Weatherill chose eight separate regions spread around the country but only analysed up to 390 inventories for each of these.[3] Whilst Overton *et al.* used many more inventories, they focussed on just two counties, Kent and Cornwall, which were at opposite ends of the wealth spectrum. As with the present study, the reliance placed by these two studies on probate records was such that it was difficult to include the lower classes within the scope of the work done since these groups rarely made wills or inventories. Indeed, Weatherill acknowledged that her work was on 'the middling sorts' and whilst Overton *et al.* tried to extend their work to incorporate these groups, they candidly admitted that neither their study, nor that of Weatherill, had much to say about labourers.[4]

As the literature review in Chapter 1 demonstrates, there have been a significant number of consumption studies since 2004. Authors including Karen Harvey, Giorgio Riello, Roberta Gilchrist, Sarah Pennell, Tara Hamling and Catherine

Richardson and others have focussed on a range of topics including the goods themselves, the personal experience of material goods and even the impact of the environment upon the material life of households.[5]

Nevertheless, gaps remain in our present knowledge and this new research has attempted to fill some of these. It has extended the chronological period backwards to the later Middle Ages to explore the origins of a gradually growing consumerism, and forwards to the period after 1750. It has tried to enhance the geographical focus, in particular by complementing the large amount of data obtained by Overton *et al.* from affluent Kent and poor Cornwall with more evidence from 'middle England' so as to provide a more complete picture of England as a whole. It has also attempted to consider a wider range of consumption goods and to acknowledge that whilst households spent most of their income on essentials such as food and clothing, other purchased items could include fuel, things associated with leisure and goods and services associated with religion which could absorb sizeable sums of money. Finally, it has extended the study of consumerism a little further down the social scale by including the inventories of a large number of labourers in an attempt to gain an insight into how the lower groups of society were being affected by the rise in the consumption of material goods.

The evidence contained within this study contains little to suggest that a dramatic 'consumer revolution' occurred at any specific point in the late medieval or early modern periods despite the claims made by various historians for specific dates, since at no stage was there a comprehensive rise in the consumption of goods and services which significantly affected all social groups. However, what is evident is that this period saw a gradual restructuring of demand and supply so that on a piecemeal basis, more goods were becoming available, and to a wider proportion of the population. The evidence contained within this study suggests that the origins of this rise in consumption were in the period after the Black Death. At this time, economic and demographic changes led to higher wages, more employment opportunities and lower food prices and these in turn led to revised income patterns which were the determinant of slowly changing consumption patterns.

The findings of this study that consumption changes took the form of a slow and steady evolution which happened over a prolonged period of time, rather than that of a dramatic consumer revolution occurring within a limited time period, complements the recent work on historic wage levels initiated by John Hatcher and later endorsed and developed by Jane Humphries and Jacob Weisdorf.[6] As Chapter 1 has shown, much of the earlier historiography which made claims for significant and demarcated increases in consumption was based on real wage data which suggested complementary periods of high real wage increases. The revised income series devised by Humphries and Weisdorf indicates that these real wage peaks happened at a much lower level and that real earnings rose much more gradually than indicated by this earlier wage data and over a much longer period of time.[7] If this is the case, this supports our assertion that living standards improved from the late fourteenth century onwards, and that these changes were gradual rather than abrupt.

What?

This book has considered food, clothing, household goods and religious consumption. Evidence from the late medieval period revealed that significant changes in food consumption were taking place as lower population levels, increased availability of land and higher wages combined to make food more plentiful and accessible. Diets gradually included a higher proportion of wheat (for bread) and barley (for ale) and more milk, cheese and meat were consumed. Grocery goods started to become more popular and, for the more affluent, spices. These changes ensured that diets generally became more varied and of a higher nutritional quality. By the end of the Middle Ages, a rise in the use of material goods associated with methods of cooking other than boiling and stewing showed that more affluent households were increasingly eating meat and that this was of a better quality. As foodstuffs became more refined, so did the wares associated with eating; pewter vessels became the tableware of choice and, in the early modern period, plates slowly took over from platters. The most dramatic change to drinking habits was the appearance in England of the new hot drinks of tea, coffee and chocolate in the seventeenth century and their gradual spread down the social scale.

Throughout the period, clothing fashions altered and, generally, shorter closer-fitting clothes were worn by both sexes. People owned more garments and replaced them more frequently. For men, coats, waistcoats and breeches replaced doublets and hose and subsequently breeches were replaced by trousers. For women, gowns replaced kirtles. Clothing was not just for keeping the body warm but could also be used as a means of expressing social rank and an adherence to fashion. Whilst members of the aristocracy and nobility had been using clothing as a signifier for some time, during this period the practice spread beyond the social elite to the middling class and even to some members of lower-status groups. Better-quality fabrics such as double worsted, premium broadcloths, scarlet, velvet and damask became increasingly popular and a range of darker colours were considered desirable. During the early modern period, cotton textiles were increasingly imported from India by the East India Company. These cotton fabrics were considered superior to wool in that their colour fastness enabled them to be regularly washed and their resistance to light meant that they did not fade. Cotton was used for women's clothing and certain items worn by men, such as waistcoats. Towards the end of the period, home-produced goods were substituted for imports. Whereas in the late medieval period, only a few items of clothing could be purchased made up, a ready-made market gradually emerged in the early modern period. In particular, shoes were a commodity increasingly purchased 'off-the-peg' and cordwainers' inventories revealed large stocks of ready-made shoes.

Household goods changed in several ways. An expansion of domestic space and the increased adoption of individual living spaces rather than communal rooms encouraged people to furnish their living spaces with items which made these areas more personal and comfortable. Sleeping arrangements were subject to significant improvements; featherbeds were exclusive, luxury items in the medieval period but by the early modern period, they were widely owned and households owned greater numbers of sheets. New goods such as clocks and items associated with hot drinks appeared, were initially owned by very few but were found in the majority of inventoried households in several counties by the second half of the eighteenth century. Certain items of household furniture were supplanted by others; stools and forms were replaced by chairs and chests of drawers superseded chests. The number of goods that people owned increased markedly; for example, chairs per household increased five-fold.

Religious expenditure showed that consumption had a broader meaning than just material goods and could involve significant sums. In the late medieval period, money was spent on prayers, masses, pilgrimages and gild membership as well as tangible, material items associated with religion. Although the Reformation brought major changes, as the rituals and practices of Roman Catholicism were largely abandoned, increasing amounts were spent on funeral arrangements so that most people were buried in wooden coffins, often with a headstone, while the assets of affluent deceased persons were frequently spent on mourning clothes and appropriate hospitality for those attending the funeral.

When and where?

The piecemeal development of the 'consumer revolution' meant that different areas of the country embraced new consumer goods at varying rates. Overton *et al.*'s study charted the development of the *early modern* consumer revolution. In the first third of the seventeenth century, very few of the selected consumer goods were to be found even in Kent. By the period 1660–89, 18 per cent of inventoried persons owned clocks and looking glasses in Kent. By choosing Kent and Cornwall, Overton *et al.* revealed the opposite ends of the consumption spectrum in England. Kent was in the vanguard of the new 'consumer society' which was largely absent from Cornwall. J.M. Ellis was therefore correct in suggesting that the term 'consumer revolution' was inappropriate for the years between 1660 and 1688 since not all of the population were consumers of a wide range of goods.[8] Towards the end of the seventeenth century, wider ownership of certain goods began to take place, and this is captured by the period of Weatherill's study which commences in 1675.

In terms of ownership of consumer goods, Huntingdonshire, Yorkshire and Dorset were not such contrasting counties as Kent and Cornwall. The 'take off' in ownership of goods like clocks, knives and forks and goods associated with hot drinks did not occur in Huntingdonshire, Dorset and Yorkshire until the second half of the eighteenth century, during the period of McKendricks' 'consumer revolution'. Middle England was fast catching up with counties like Kent which were in the forefront of consumer change. By the second half of the eighteenth century, Huntingdonshire and Dorset had very similar levels of clock ownership to those recorded in Kent a generation before. Kent continued to forge ahead as ownership of clocks continued to rise, reaching more than three quarters of the inventoried population by the end of the century, whilst ownership of utensils for hot drinks also increased.

The results of this study have endorsed the findings of historians such as Jeremy Goldberg and Carl Estabrook who claimed that urban areas were associated with higher levels of consumption.[9] Urban areas, from a large city, Bristol, to a coaching town, Marlborough, had markedly higher levels of ownership of consumer goods than more rural locations. They also led the way in acquiring goods. In the 30-year period, 1720–49, both Bristol and Marlborough had higher levels of ownership of knives and forks, hot drinks utensils, looking glasses, pictures, window curtains, books, warming pans, bed curtains and silver than the three major comparative counties: Huntingdonshire, Yorkshire and Dorset. Bristol also had higher ownership levels of clocks.

Who?

In the same way in which increased consumption of goods developed at varying stages depending on the area of the country, the evidence suggests that ownership of consumer goods was also affected by social status, so that ownership of more desirable items, particularly goods newly introduced into England, were initially adopted by the social elite and gradually permeated down the social scale.

As has been noted, in the late medieval period, the most significant consumption change was a larger *per capita* demand for predominantly basic foodstuffs together with a modest increase in the range and variety of foods that were commonly eaten. Whilst these changes were adopted by most levels of society, higher-status households were increasingly able to supplement the acquisition of subsistence items with purchases of non-essential material goods. In particular, there was an increased emphasis on improving the comfort of the domestic environment so that the articles commonly acquired included items of bedding, wall hangings, rudimentary furniture, metalware for cooking, serving and eating food, and textile items such as towels, tablecloths and napkins. This pattern of increased ownership of consumer goods by the 'middling sort' continued throughout the whole of the period of this study to the extent that they can be identified as being the key beneficiaries of the 'consumer revolution'. For the early modern period, there was a clear positive correlation between inventoried wealth and ownership of the great majority of consumer goods. Contrary to Weatherill's view, the gentry tended to be the first social group to own most goods, but by the second half of the eighteenth century, ownership of consumer goods was extending further down the social scale.

Whilst rising ownership by the middle tiers of society was fundamental to changes that were taking place, an important element of the present study is the insight it provides into consumption by the more affluent inventoried labourers, although it is important to reiterate that inventoried labourers represented a minority of the labouring population, since most members of this group had too few moveable goods to be covered by probate inventories. Overton *et al.* suggested that a rough estimate of the total population without inventories was about 40 per cent but, as they recognised, this proportion varied in different parts of the country.[10]

Very few inventoried labourers owned many of the selected goods such as knives and forks, utensils for hot drinks, window curtains, pictures, books and silver. However, the take off in ownership of clocks and looking glasses was reaching ever further down the social scale as the eighteenth century progressed. Whilst less than 5 per cent of labourers' inventories recorded clocks before 1750, 40 per cent did so in the second half of the eighteenth century. Hardly any inventoried labourers owned looking glasses in the seventeenth century, but in the eighteenth century between a fifth and a third did so. This indicates that consumption goods were acquired by at least better-off workers, earlier than suggested by Peter Gurney.[11]

Good or bad?

Was this consumer revolution for good or ill? Has advertising created false needs for ephemeral goods or does an ever-widening choice of consumer goods make life more fulfilling for an increasing majority? Does the consumer society promote choice and liberty, or does it manufacture artificial wants and put individualism above the public good?[12]

Not all consumption goods are beneficial. Much household expenditure is on goods which bring both pleasure and detrimental effects on health. In England, the average household spent £613 on tobacco and alcohol in 2015/16, although spending on these goods was declining slightly.[13] Yet smoking and alcohol are two of the biggest lifestyle risk factors for disease and death.[14] Tobacco accounts for 7.2 million deaths in the world every year and alcohol accounts for a further 3.3 million deaths.[15] Overconsumption of food has led to an obesity epidemic in the United Kingdom, which now has the highest level in Western Europe. Nearly two thirds of British adults are overweight, and more than a quarter are obese.[16] In response to these and other health issues, public and private expenditure on healthcare continues to rise and now represents 9.6 per cent of GDP in the UK.[17] Health spending has doubled as a percentage of UK GDP since the early 1970s and more than quadrupled in real terms *per capita*.[18]

One of the highest categories of household spending is on transport. The number of cars on the road in the United Kingdom reached 31.7 million in 2016.[19] Despite consumers spending ever more on purchasing their motor cars and running them, Peter Dauvergne identifies the motor car as a consumption good which also has major ill effects on well-being. For Dauvergne, moves towards safer and cleaner cars still have a long way to go particularly in much of the third world.[20]

Many moralists, philosophers, religious figures and environmentalists have been strongly critical of the consumer society.[21] Plato suggested that desire for luxuries would lead to the destruction of the state and the biblical writer of the second letter to Timothy counselled against being a lover of pleasure rather than a lover of God. Whilst having little time for religion, the humanist Bertrand Russell agreed with the biblical writer about consumerism and argued, 'It is preoccupation with possessions, more than anything else, that prevents us from living freely and nobly'.[22] There is a huge literature on the environmental consequences of consumerism. It covers *inter alia* the impact of consumerism on climate change, levels of pollution, species loss and destruction of habitats.[23] The United Kingdom contributes to these adverse consequences and the National Footprint Accounts for 2016 suggested that the UK had a biocapacity deficit of minus 3.6 global hectares (GHA). Comparisons with other countries can be made by consulting the Global Footprint Network website.[24] Protest movements against climate change have spawned around the world, including most recently Extinction Rebellion. Their reported aim is to halt biodiversity loss and reduce greenhouse gas emissions to zero by 2025.[25] Whilst such ambitious targets will not be achieved, most governments are developing greenhouse gas mitigation policies and many individuals seek to respond by purchasing electric vehicles and installing solar panels on their homes.[26]

Despite these arguments, the experience of engaging with probate records in the early modern period is also shocking. Even more prosperous inventoried labourers in the seventeenth century typically owned little more than the clothes that they stood up in, their bed, a single sheet and a few pots and pans. How little then did the average labourer possess? Browsing through inventories from the late eighteenth century reveals a different world. People owned so many more goods, and items such as clocks were commonly recorded, even among inventoried labourers' possessions. It is not inappropriate to assert that a consumer revolution had finally taken place, albeit that it had taken some centuries for this to finally filter down to the lower tiers of society. The beginnings and development of a consumer society should therefore be seen positively as human material progress, a liberator from want.

In the nineteenth century, standards of living continued to rise modestly but from the late 1850s the average British worker enjoyed substantial and sustained advances in real wages.[27] One measure of a wider approach to the standard of living question is the Human Development Index (HDI) which includes life expectancy and literacy as well as *per capita* GDP. This showed that by 1870, Britain had the highest HDI in the world followed by the United States. This rise in living standards has continued into the twentieth century and beyond, but the question of inequality of consumption also has to be considered. Whilst consumption is not always easy to measure, use of the GINI (see Appendix) coefficient suggests that income inequality in the UK, which mirrors consumption inequality, is higher than it was in the 1960s and 1970s but has remained fairly constant in the last 25 years. Whilst the GINI coefficient has remained stable, the very highest earners (top 1 per cent) have continued to pull further ahead. Using another measure of inequality, share of income, reveals that the share of income received by the top 1 per cent has doubled since the beginning of the 1960s.[28] This has consequences for consumption and the demand for luxury goods.

The growth of consumerism shows little sign of slackening in the twenty-first century despite its many vociferous critics. However, the world will continue to face major economic changes. The millennial generation in the UK is the first for centuries not to see a significant improvement in their living standards compared to their parents. In 2016, the World Economic Forum debated a fourth industrial revolution in which the rise of new technologies such as artificial intelligence, 3D printing, machine learning and advanced robotics may result in major changes to employment patterns.[29] These economic changes will impact on consumption patterns in as yet unknown ways, but speculation about the future must be left to other disciplines better equipped than historians!

Whether consumerism is still beneficial or increases the sum of human happiness is now much more open to debate than in the eighteenth to the twentieth centuries. Perhaps Darma Mahadea helps to place the debate in perspective. He suggested that at the macroeconomic level, more happiness may come from a sustained growth in GDP that enables households to enjoy an improved quality of life, with rising income, consumption and employment opportunities. At the microeconomic or individual level, more income may also enable people to live happier and fuller lives relative to those who are poor. But he also suggested that this accounts for only a small contribution to happiness. Life circumstances, such as marital status, health, having children and the nature of the working environment, statistically make a greater contribution to happiness than income.[30]

Notes

1 L. Weatherill, *Consumer Behaviour and Material Culture in Britain 1660–1760* (London: Routledge, 1996); M. Overton, J. Whittle, D. Dean and A. Hann, *Production and Consumption in English Households 1600–1750* (Abingdon: Routledge, 2004).
2 N. McKendrick, J. Brewer and J. Plumb, *The Birth of a Consumer Society: The Commercialization of Eighteenth-Century England* (London: Hutchinson, 1982), p.9.
3 London area, north-east England, east Kent, Cambridgeshire, north-west England, Hampshire, north-west Midlands and Cumbria, Weatherill, *Consumer Behaviour*, p.44.
4 *Ibid.*, p.xix; Overton *et al.*, *Production and Consumption*, pp.22–23.
5 See, for example, K. Harvey (ed.), *History and Material Culture: A Student's Guide to Approaching Alternative Sources* (London: Routledge, 2009) which includes essays by Harvey, Riello and Pennell; R. Gilchrist, *Medieval Life: Archaeology and the Life*

Course (Woodbridge: Boydell Press, 2014); T. Hamling and C. Richardson (eds), *Everyday Objects: Medieval and Early Modern Material Culture and its Meanings* (Farnham: Ashgate, 2010).

6 J. Hatcher, 'Unreal wages: long-run living standards and the "Golden Age" of the fifteenth century', in B. Dodds and C. Liddy (eds), *Commercial Activity, Markets and Entrepreneurs in the Middle Ages: Essays in Honour of Richard Britnell* (Woodbridge: Boydell Press, 2011); J. Humphries and J. Weisdorf, 'Unreal wages? Real income and economic growth in England, 1260–1850', *Centre for Economic Policy Research*, Discussion Paper Series, Discussion Paper DP119999 (London, 2017); J. Hatcher and J.Z. Stephenson (eds), *Seven Centuries of Unreal Wages: The Unreliable Data, Sources and Methods that have been used for Measuring Standards of Living in the Past* (Cham, Switzerland: Palgrave Macmillan, 2019).

7 *Ibid.*

8 J.M. Ellis, 'Consumption and wealth', in L.K.J. Glassey (ed.), *The Reigns of Charles II and James VII and II* (Basingstoke: Macmillan, 1997), p.210.

9 P.J.P. Goldberg, 'The fashioning of bourgeois domesticity in later medieval England: a material culture perspective', in M. Kowaleski and P.J.P. Goldberg (eds), *Medieval Domesticity: Home, Housing and Household in Medieval England* (Cambridge: Cambridge University Press, 2011), pp.124–44; C. Estabrook, *Urbane and Rustic England: Cultural Ties and Social Spheres in the Provinces 1660–1780* (Manchester: Manchester University Press, 1998), p.154.

10 Overton *et al.*, *Production and Consumption*, p.26.

11 P. Gurney, *The Making of Consumer Culture in Modern Britain* (London: Bloomsbury Academic, 2017), pp.13, 19.

12 W.W. Rostow, *The Stages of Economic Growth: A Non-Communist Manifesto* (Cambridge: Cambridge University Press,1960); J.K. Galbraith, *The Affluent Society* (Harmondsworth: Penguin Books, 1989), pp.125–28.

13 D. Wainwright, 'Household spend rises to £531 a week', BBC www.investopedia. com/articles/markets/122415/worlds-top-10-retailers-wmt-cost.asp [last accessed 18 April 2017].

14 B. Milligan, 'ONS figures show UK spending less on alcohol and tobacco', BBC News www.bbc.co.uk/news/business-38991443 [last accessed 8 June 2019].

15 World Health Organization (WHO) www.who.int/mediacentre/factsheets/fs355/en/ [last accessed 16 April 2017].

16 NHS Choices www.nhs.uk/Livewell/loseweight/Pages/statistics-and-causes-of-the-obesity-epidemic-in-the-UK.aspx [last accessed 16 April 2017].

17 Total spending on healthcare www.ons.gov.uk/peoplepopulationandcommunity/ healthandsocialcare/healthcaresystem/bulletins/ukhealthaccounts/2017 [last accessed 6 June 2019].

18 G. Stoye, 'UK health spending', *Institute for Fiscal Studies Briefing Note 201* [last accessed 6 June 2019].

19 www.statista.com/statistics/299972/average-age-of-cars-on-the-road-in-the-united-king dom/[last accessed 16 April 2017].

20 P. Dauvergne, *The Shadows of Consumption: Consequences for the Global Environment* (Cambridge Massachusetts: MIT Press, 2008), p.91.

21 Gurney, *Making of Consumer Culture*, p.2.

22 Plato, *The Republic* (Harmondsworth: Penguin Books, 2007) p.188; 2 Timothy chapter 3 verse 4; BBC News '"Rampant consumerism" criticised', http://news.bbc.co.uk/1/hi/ uk/7436704.stm [last accessed 16 April 2017]; *Daily Telegraph* 15 January 2015; R. Bourne, 'Rampant consumerism: why the Archbishop of York is wrong', https://iea. org.uk/blog/rampant-consumerism-why-the-archbishop-of-york-is-wrong [last accessed 5 August 2019]; B. Russell, *Principles of Social Reconstruction* (London: G. Allen & Unwin Ltd, 1917), p.235.

23 Intergovernmental Panel on Climate Change (IPCC), *Climate Change 2014, Synthesis Report: Summary for Policy Makers* www.ipcc.ch/pdf/assessment-report/ar5/syr/AR5_SYR_FINAL_SPM.pdf [last accessed 24 April 2017]; World Wildlife Fund, wwf.panda.org/what_we_do/how_we_work/our_global_goals/markets/mti_solutions/[last accessed 24 April 2017]; E. Kolbert, *The Sixth Extinction: An Unnatural History* (New York: Picador, 2015).

24 Global Footprint Network, www.footprintnetwork.org/content/documents/ecological_footprint_nations/[last accessed 24 April 2017].

25 Z. Rahim, 'Climate change protest: Extinction Rebellion activists plan to disrupt London Tube Today', *The Independent*, 17 April 2019 [last accessed 10 June 2019].

26 K. Gillingham and J. Stock, 'The cost of reducing greenhouse gas emissions', *Journal of Economic Perspectives*, 32 (4), 2018, pp.53–72.

27 J. Mokyr, *The Enlightened Economy: An Economic History of Britain, 1700–1850* (New Haven: Yale University Press, 2009), p.452; C. Feinstein, 'Pessimism perpetrated: real wages and the standard of living in Britain during and after the Industrial Revolution', *Journal of Economic History*, 58 (3), 1998, pp.642–50.

28 F. McGuiness, 'Income inequality in the United Kingdom', House of Commons Briefing Paper 7484, (London, 2016).

29 www.weforum.org/reports/the-future-of-jobs [last accessed 27 April 2017]; www.economist.com/news/special-report/21700758-will-smarter-machines-cause-mass-unemployment-automation-and-anxiety [last accessed 27 April 2017]; www.brookings.edu/research/what-happens-if-robots-take-the-jobs-the-impact-of-emerging-technologies-on-employment-and-public-policy/[last accessed 27 April 2017].

30 D. Mahadea, 'On the economics of happiness: the influence of income and non-income factors on happiness', *The South African Journal of Economic and Management Sciences*, 16 (1) (2013), pp.39–51.

APPENDIX

Social status groups

Occupation or Status	Social Status Group
Apothecary	2
Attorney	2
Baker	5
Barber	5
Barker	3
Beekeeper	5
Blacksmith	5
Bladesmith	5
Bowyer	5
Brewer	3
Bricklayer	5
Butcher	3
Capper	5
Carpenter	5
Chandler	3
Chaplain	2
Chapman	3
Cheesewright	5
Clerk (clerical)	2
Clothier	2
Cook	5
Cooper	5
Cordwainer	5
Corvisor	5
Draper	2
Dyer	3

(Continued)

(Cont.)

Occupation or Status	Social Status Group
Dyster	3
Esquire	1
Farmer	6
Fisher	3
Fishmonger	3
Fletcher	5
Forester	4
Franklin	2
Freemason	5
Fuller	5
Furberer	5
Gentleman	1
Glover	5
Grazier	3
Haberdasher	3
Horner	5
Horsemaster	6
Husbandman	6
Innholder	3
Innkeeper	3
Labourer	7
Lawyer	2
Leapmaker	5
Leather–dealer	3
Limeburner	5
Linen draper	2
Linen weaver	5
Locksmith	5
Mason	5
Mercer	2
Merchant	2
Miller	5
Notary	2
Painter	5
Parish clerk	2
Parson	2
Pinner	5
Priest	2
Rector	2
Roper	5
Rough mason	5
Saddler	3
Salter	3

(Continued)

(Cont.)

Occupation or Status	Social Status Group
Schoolmaster	2
Scribe	2
Servant	7
Shearman	5
Sheepreeve	4
Shoemaker	5
Skepmaker	5
Skinner	3
Smith	5
Spicer	3
Surgeon	2
Tailor	3
Tallow chandler	3
Tanner	3
Tawyer	3
Thatcher	5
Turner	5
Vicar	2
Warrener	4
Weaver	5
Wheelwright	5
Wiredrawer	5
Woolman	2
Yeoman	4

GLOSSARY

Andirons   Horizontal bars in the hearth which support the roasting spit.

Chafing dish   A dish above a small brazier for heating food or keeping it hot.

Chantry   A chapel where masses were celebrated (literally sung) for the dead.

Chapbook   Cheaply produced popular books often sold by pedlars in the seventeenth century.

Coefficient of variation   Enables the degree to which variables differed from their respective means to be compared. CV = the standard deviation divided by the mean.

Coffer   Wooden box or chest used for storing clothes or valuable items.

Coverlet   Bed covering.

Customary rights   Rights which the individuals of a particular place acquire by custom rather than by prescription.

Damask   Reversible, patterned fabrics which could be made from a variety of fibres including silk, linen and wool.

Doom painting   A painting of the Last Judgement when in Christian belief souls are judged and sent to heaven or hell. Where doom paintings survive, they are usually found on the Chancel Arch.

Executor   Person appointed by the testator to carry out the intentions of the will.

Feodary survey   A survey of the obligations of tenants of the Crown.

Flaxen   Fabric made from flax.

Fustian   Heavy coarse cloth.

Gild or guild   An association of individuals with common goals. Medieval gilds existed for a variety of economic, social and religious purposes and included merchant gilds, craft gilds and religious gilds.

GDP   A measurement of output for the national economy based on the three constituent sectors: agriculture, industry and services. GDP per capita is a calculation of GDP divided by estimates of population.

GHA A global hectare is a biologically productive hectare with world average biological productivity for a given year.

Gini coefficient A measure of inequality in which 1 represents maximum inequality and 0 a perfectly egalitarian society.

Harden sheets Low-quality, cheaper sheets.

Hearth Tax A tax based on the number of hearths in a property. Introduced in 1662 and abolished after William III became King in 1689.

Hempteare sheets Made from hemp.

Heraldic visitations Tours of inspection throughout England to investigate the pedigrees of those who claimed the right to bear arms.

High-status Groups Lorna Weatherill developed a social hierarchy which categorised occupations of 'high status' such as clergy, apothecaries and doctors and placed them between gentry and yeomen.

Hogshead Cask for beer or foodstuffs such as sugar. It held 54 gallons of beer.

Holland sheets Made from fine, high-quality linen.

HDI The Human Development Index is a summary measure of average achievement in key dimensions of human development: a long and healthy life, being knowledgeable and a decent standard of living. The HDI is the geometric mean of normalised indices for each of the three dimensions.

Intermediate-status groups Lorna Weatherill developed a social hierarchy which categorised occupations of 'intermediate status' such as innkeepers, malsters and tanners and placed them between gentry and yeomen.

Jack Mechanism for turning a spit while roasting meat.

Joined furniture Generally higher-quality furniture made using mortice and tenon joints.

Kirtle A short gown or petticoat.

Lanthorn Lantern.

Latten Mixed metal similar in appearance to brass made from copper and zinc.

Lay subsidy A tax assessed against the laity (as opposed to clerics), and which was levied on movable property rather than land.

Looking glass Mirror.

Low-status groups Lorna Weatherill developed a social hierarchy which categorised occupations of 'low status' such as cordwainers and placed them between yeomen and husbandmen.

Manor An estate in land which was originally the nature of a feudal lordship given by the king to one of his vassals. The lord had domain over the manor and could exercise certain rights and privileges.

Mantle (from the Latin *matellum*, meaning cloak)A loose, cape-like garment worn over indoor clothing by both sexes in the same way as an overcoat.

Maslin (from the French *miscelin*, meaning mixture)A mixed crop of grains, grown together, which was commonly a mix of rye and wheat but which could include other corn combinations.

Maund A small basket with handles predominantly used for carrying.

Mortuary fee Customary payment to a priest upon the death of most parishioners.

Mullion window   Window divided by a vertical bar.

Nuncupative will   A will made by word of mouth before witnesses, and subsequently written out by a scribe.

Obits   (from the Latin *obitus*, meaning death)Late medieval commemorations for the souls of deceased persons which used the liturgy for the Office and Mass for the Dead. These were generally held on the day of death and on the yearly anniversary (although other days might also be commemorated with an obit) and could be both for an individual soul, or for the souls of a group of persons.

Posnet   Small cooking pot with a long handle and three legs for standing in the fire.

Posset   Hot milk drink.

Pricket   A spike on a candlestick which held the candle in place so that a pricket candlestick has a sharp point onto which candles are pushed to keep them upright.

Primer   Book of devotions used as a prayer-book by members of the laity from the thirteenth to the sixteenth centuries.

Rood   Large sculpture or painting of the crucifixion of Jesus Christ. In medieval churches these were placed above the panel which divided the chancel from the nave so that this was known as the rood screen.

Skep   A lidless basket predominantly used for storage.

Skillet   Another name for posnet.

Skimmer   Perforated ladle for skimming liquids such as milk.

Standard deviation   A measure of the extent to which variables are dispersed around the mean.

Tawyer   Dresser of leather using alum so as to produce a white-coloured leather.

Testator   The person making the will.

Transom window   A window set above a horizontal beam or bar known as a transom.

Trencher   A plate which originally took the form of a thick slice of bread upon which food was served, but which later became a flat piece of wood or metal.

Trental   An office of 30 masses said for the dead which were often performed on 30 consecutive days.

Truncated inventories   Inventories that were incomplete with goods omitted.

Trundle bed/truckle bed   Simple wooden frame bed which was stored beneath a standing bed during the day.

Worsted   Cloth made from worsted yarn which tended to be made from longer, thicker wool fibres. The resultant cloth was relatively lightweight and sturdier than woollen cloth and generally required less processing.

The reader is also directed to:

Joy Bristow, *The Local Historian's Glossary of Words and Terms* (Countryside Books, 2001).

Christopher Corèdon and Ann Williams, *A Dictionary of Medieval Terms and Phrases* (D.S. Brewer, 2013).

Rosemary Milward, *A Glossary of Household, Farming and Trade Terms from Probate Inventories* (Derbyshire Record Society, 1977).

INDEX

Cheshire 42, 54, **56**, 115, 118, 154, **207**, **209–214**, **216–224**, 248–249, **250**; Stockport 52–53, 149, 160; Wrenbury 54
Church of England 182, 192, 195, 258, 260
churchwardens accounts 148, 151, 186, 190, 234
Clark, G. 18, 262
clocks 2, 4, 10, 41, 155–158, 162, 183, 206, **207**, **226**, 228, 255, 273, 282–283, **284**, **289–290**, **291–292**, **293**, 294, **295**, 296, 302–303
cloth 10, 15, 45, 52–53, 79, 101–108, 112–113, 116, 122, 133, 135, 142, 145, 159, 183, 190, 196, 253–254, 273, 301; use of dyes 103–104; use of fur and leather 105–106
clothing 2, 3, 10–14, 16–17, 29, 37, 43, 56, 64, 92, 101–109, **110**, 111–123, 149, 183, 189, 191–192, 201, 253–254, 294, 300–301; aprons 109, **110**, 117; boots and shoes 101–102, 105, 112, 116–118, 123, 253, 301; breeches and trousers 102, 111, 113–114, 116–117, 119, 301; cloaks 41, 102, **110**, 112, 116; coats 102, 109, **110**, 111–114, 116, 301; doublets and hose 11, 101–102, 105, 108–109, **110**, 111, 114, 116–117, 301; girdles 102–103, 105, 108, **110**, 117, 148, 186; gloves 105, 117, 119, 121, 195, 253; gowns and kirtles 11, 15, 16, 102, 108–109, **110**, 111–112, 114, 117, 301; hats 102, 105, 109, **110**, 112, 116–117, 119–121; hoods 102, 109, **110**, 111, 119–120, 135; jackets 11, 109, **110**, 114; jerkins 11, **110**, 111; kerchers 11, 109, 119–120; petticoats 102, 109, **110**, 112, 114; ready-made clothing 104–105, 113, 118, 122–123, 301; shirts 105–106, 109, **110**, 111–112, 114, 116; smocks 109, **110**, 111–112; stays 117, 119; tunics 102, 109, **110**, 111; waistcoats 102, 112–114, 116, 301
Colman, G. 87
Colonial America 170; Virginia 10
consumption 1–21, 26, 35, 37–39, 42–43, 55–56, 64–67, 74, 80, 83–90, 92, 101, 106, 108, 113, 115, 142, 152, 162, 170–172, 182, 188, 191, 200, 204–206, 208, 227–228, 255, 257, 264–265, 273–275, 277, 282, 290, 296, 299–306; involuntary consumption 15; religious consumption 186, 188, 193

Cornwall 2, 9, 47, 55, **56**, 136, 147, 155, 205–206, **207**, 208, **209–214**, 215, **216–224**, 225, 257, **264**, 296, 300, 302; Madron 225; Saltash 155, 225; Tregony 225
Corpus Christi processions 189, 231–233, 236, 238–239, 253
Coryat, Thomas 77
Coss, P. 242
Cowan, A. 255
Cowan, B. 9, 83
Coward, B. 247
Cox, J. and N. 33
Cox N. 8
Cressy, D. 194–196
Culley George 47
Cumbria 9, 215, 225; Whitehaven and Workington 215

D'Cruze, S. 234
Dauteuille, K. 38, 163
Dauvergne, P. 305
Davenant, Charles 111
Davis, J. 14
Deanesley, M. 151
Defoe, Daniel 50, 90, 111, 144
Delano Smith, C. 146
De Vries, J. 7, 19, 170, 255, 294; industrious revolution 7, 19, 294
diaries 43; Carrington, John 14, 85; Evelyn, John 36, 83; Holland, William 12, 255; Hurst, Sarah 36, 43, 85, 117, 155; Josselin, Ralph 36, 41, 113, 252; Marchant, Thomas 36, 86, 198; Pepys, Samuel 36, 83, 85, 87, 113, 162, 253; Sharp, Robert 12, 255; Turner, Thomas 15, 33, 36, 86, 154–155; Wallington, Nehemiah 41, 135; Woodforde, James 12, 36, 131, 255
Dickens, Charles 200
disease 43, 304; plague 43, 52, 91; *see also* Black Death
Domesday Book 231
Doran, S. 153
Dorset 2, 9, 47, 50, **56**, 78, 90, 134, 158, 206, **207**, 208, **209–214**, **216–224**, 228, 245, **246**, 261, 289, 302, 303; Bridport 50; Cranborne 50; Dorchester 50, 186; Lyme Regis 50; Poole 50; Shaftesbury 50; Sherborne 50; Weymouth 50
Durham 250; Bishop of 252
Dutch East India Company 10